10/13

HANDBOOKS

W9-CFC-669

TUCSON

TIM HULL

Contents

Maps

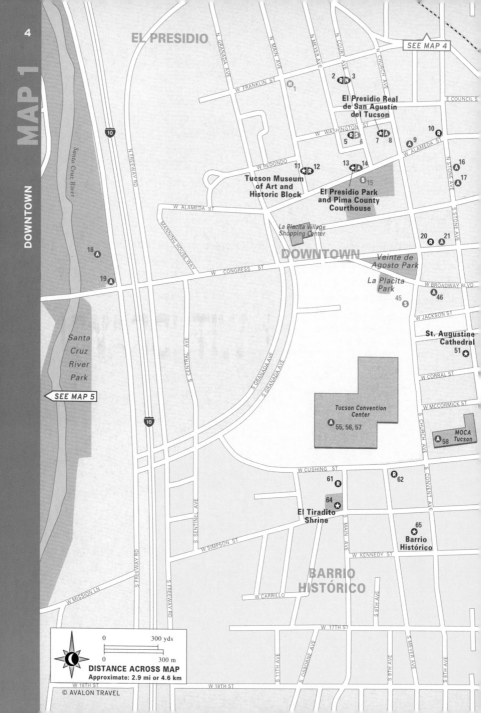

EL PRESIDIO

SEE MAP 4

El Presidio Real
de San Agustín
del Tucson

Tucson Museum
of Art and
Historic Block

El Presidio Park
and Pima County
Courthouse

La Placita Village
Shopping Center

DOWNTOWN

Veinte de
Agosto Park

La Placita
Park

St. Augustine
Cathedral

Santa
Cruz
River
Park

SEE MAP 5

Tucson Convention
Center

MOCA
Tucson

El Tiradito
Shrine

Barrio
Histórico

BARRIO
HISTÓRICO

Santa Cruz River

DISTANCE ACROSS MAP
Approximate: 2.9 mi or 4.6 km

0   300 yds
0   300 m

© AVALON TRAVEL

★ SIGHTS

7 EL PRESIDIO REAL DE SAN AGUSTÍN DEL TUCSON
11 TUCSON MUSEUM OF ART AND HISTORIC BLOCK
13 EL PRESIDIO PARK AND PIMA COUNTY COURTHOUSE
52 ST. AUGUSTINE CATHEDRAL
64 EL TIRADITO SHRINE
65 BARRIO HISTÓRICO
68 JARDÍN DE CÉSAR CHAVÉZ

🍴 RESTAURANTS

2 EL CHARRO CAFÉ
5 LA COCINA
10 THE LITTLE CAFE POCA COSA
12 CAFE A LA C'ART
20 CAFFÉ MILANO
22 REILLY CRAFT PIZZA AND DRINK
23 CAFE POCA COSA
24 47 SCOTT
26 ALEJANDRO'S CAFE
32 SPARKROOT
35 HUB RESTAURANT AND ICE CREAMERY
39 MAYNARDS MARKET & KITCHEN
40 THE CUP CAFE
47 JANOS DOWNTOWN KITCHEN AND COCKTAILS
61 EL MINUTO CAFE
62 CUSHING STREET BAR AND GRILL
63 CASA VICENTE
67 CAFÉ DESTA
69 BARRIO BREWING COMPANY

🌙 NIGHTLIFE

3 BAR TOMA
4 BORDERLANDS BREWING CO.
25 SCOTT & CO.
27 SAPPHIRE LOUNGE
28 ZEN ROCK
29 ELLIOTT'S ON CONGRESS
31 THE DISTRICT TAVERN
33 SHARKS
36 THE PLAYGROUND BAR & LOUNGE
41 CLUB CONGRESS
42 THE TAP ROOM

🎭 ARTS AND LEISURE

8 THE PRESIDIO TRAIL
9 LOHSE FAMILY YMCA
14 TUCSON MEET YOURSELF
16 ARIZONA HISTORICAL SOCIETY DOWNTOWN MUSEUM
17 DOWNTOWN FARMERS MARKET AND ARTS AND CRAFT MERCADO
18 SANTA CRUZ RIVER PARK
19 GARDEN OF GETHSEMANE/ FELIX LUCERO PARK
21 FOX TUCSON THEATRE
30 BEOWULF ALLEY THEATRE COMPANY
37 SOUTHERN ARIZONA TRANSPORTATION MUSEUM
38 OBSIDIAN GALLERY
44 THE RIALTO
46 BORDERLANDS THEATER
48 ETHERTON GALLERY
50 TUCSON YOGA
53 TUCSON CHILDREN'S MUSEUM
55 ARIZONA FRIENDS OF CHAMBER MUSIC
56 ARIZONA OPERA
57 TUCSON SYMPHONY ORCHESTRA
58 MOCA TUCSON
59 ARIZONA THEATRE COMPANY
60 TEMPLE OF MUSIC AND ART

🛍 SHOPS

6 OLD TOWN ARTISANS
15 EL PRESIDIO MERCADO
34 SACRED TIME MACHINE
45 LA PLACITA
49 TREEHOUSE THAI MASSAGE SPA
66 PHILABAUM GLASS STUDIO AND GALLERY
70 17TH STREET MARKET

🏨 HOTELS

1 EL PRESIDIO INN BED AND BREAKFAST
43 HOTEL CONGRESS
52 ROYAL ELIZABETH BED AND BREAKFAST INN
54 ROADRUNNER HOSTEL AND INN

Tucson Amtrak

SEE MAP 2

AVIATION BIKEWAY

Ironhorse Park

San Augustine Plaza Park

Military Plaza Park

SEE MAP 3

Jardín de César Chávez

SEE MAP 7

SEE MAP 2

E DRACHMAN ST

SEE MAP 4

E MABEL ST

E HELEN ST

De Anza
Park

W 1ST ST

Catalina
Park

E 1ST ST

W 2ND ST

E 2ND ST

3rd Street Bike Route

E UNIVERSITY BLVD

**WEST
UNIVERSITY**

W 4TH ST

SEE MAP 1

W 5TH ST

4th Avenue

E 5TH ST

DOWNTOWN

E 6TH ST

E 7TH ST

E COUNCIL ST

E 8TH ST

E STEVENS AVE

Tucson
Amtrak

E CADDIE ST

E 9TH ST

E FLORITA ST

E 10TH ST

Ironhorse
Park

E HUGHES ST

W BROADWAY BLVD

San Augustine
Plaza Park

**The
Diamondback
Bridge**

E 12TH ST

E 13TH ST

© AVALON TRAVEL

⊕ SIGHTS

4	THE UNIVERSITY OF ARIZONA MUSEUM OF ART	28	UNIVERSITY OF ARIZONA
26	ARIZONA STATE MUSEUM	34	4TH AVENUE
		66	THE DIAMONDBACK BRIDGE

⊕ RESTAURANTS

2	GARLAND BISTRO	32	THE B-LINE
7	1702	33	MAGPIE'S PIZZA
12	MISS SAIGON	38	DELECTABLES
19	EPIC CAFE	41	BROOKLYN PIZZA COMPANY
21	GENTLE BEN'S	43	ATHENS ON FOURTH
22	THE AULD DUBLINER	44	CHOCOLATE IGUANA ON 4TH
23	PASCO KITCHEN AND LOUNGE	47	MAYA QUETZAL
24	FROG & FIRKIN	50	CARUSO'S
25	FUKU SUSHI	59	BISON WITCHES
30	SOCIAL HOUSE KITCHEN & PUB	69	TOOLEY'S CAFE

The University
of Arizona Museum
of Art

E DRACHMAN ST

E MABEL ST

E HELEN ST

E SPEEDWAY BLVD

E 1ST ST

E 2ND ST

SEE MAP 3

E HAWTHORNE ST

SAM HUGHES

Arizona
State Museum

E UNIVERSITY BLVD

3rd Street Bike Route

E UNIVERSITY BLVD

E 3RD ST

E 4TH ST

University
of Arizona

E 4TH ST

E 4TH ST

ENKE DR

E LOWELL ST

N OLIVE RD

CHERRY AVE

N CAMPBELL AVE

N NORRIS AVE

N PARK AVE

N FREMONT AVE

N SANTA RITA AVE

N MOUNTAIN AVE

RINCON
HEIGHTS

E BROADWAY BLVD

E MILES ST   SEE MAP 7

0   300 yds
0   300 m

DISTANCE ACROSS MAP
Approximate: 2.0 mi or 3.2 km

E 13TH ST

NIGHTLIFE

8	DIRTBAGS	58	CHE'S LOUNGE
36	IBT'S	60	THE HUT
39	MR. HEAD'S ART GALLERY AND BAR	61	MALONEY'S
40	SKYBAR	62	O' MALLEY'S
45	PLUSH	64	THE SHANTY
51	SURLY WENCH	65	THE BUFFET

ARTS AND LEISURE

1	INVISIBLE THEATRE	17	3RD STREET BIKE ROUTE
3	CENTER FOR CREATIVE PHOTOGRAPHY	18	ROGUE THEATRE
5	JOSEPH GROSS GALLERY AT THE UA SCHOOL OF ART	29	UNIVERSITY OF ARIZONA SPORTS
		49	ORDINARY BIKE SHOP
6	ARIZONA REPERTORY THEATRE	55	CONRAD WILDE GALLERY
14	ARIZONA HISTORICAL SOCIETY MUSEUM	56	PLATFORM GALLERY

SHOPS

10	THE BUFFALO EXCHANGE	37	4TH AVENUE
11	MORNING STAR TRADERS	42	CREATIVE VENTURES CRAFT MALL
15	ARIZONA MERCANTILE: THE MUSEUM STORE AT THE ARIZONA HISTORICAL SOCIETY	46	DEL SOL
		48	ANTIGONE BOOKS
		52	POPCYCLE
		53	FOOD CONSPIRACY CO-OP
20	MAIN GATE SQUARE	54	ORIGINATE
27	NATIVE GOODS: THE ARIZONA STATE MUSEUM STORE	57	SANTA THERESA TILE WORKS
		63	THE BOOK STOP
35	DESERT VINTAGE AND COSTUME	67	MEXICAN TILE AND STONE CO.
		68	LOST BARRIO

HOTELS

9	ALOFT TUCSON UNIVERSITY	16	TUCSON MARRIOTT UNIVERSITY PARK
13	CATALINA PARK INN	31	SAM HUGHES INN BED AND BREAKFAST

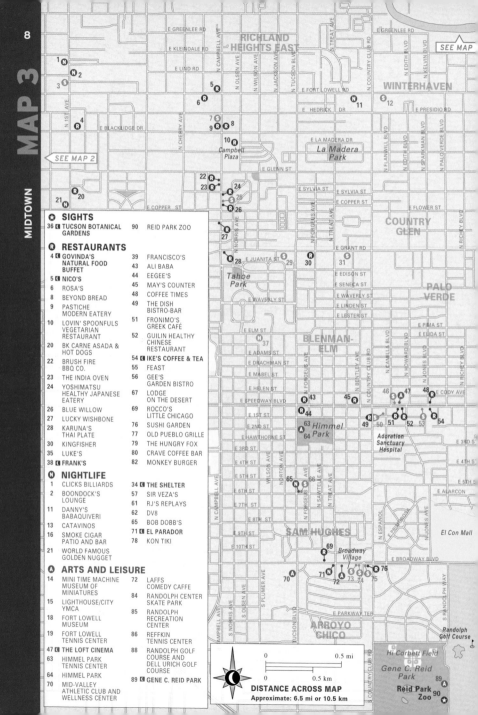

SEE MAP

SEE MAP 2

RICHLAND HEIGHTS EAST

WINTERHAVEN

COUNTRY GLEN

La Madera Park

Campbell Plaza

PALO VERDE

Tabbe Park

BLENMAN-ELM

Himmel Park

Adoration Sanctuary Hospital

SAM HUGHES

Broadway Village

El Con Mall

ARROYO CHICO

Randolph Golf Course

Hi Corbett Field

Gene C. Reid Park

Reid Park Zoo

✪ SIGHTS

- 36 ◖ TUCSON BOTANICAL GARDENS
- 90 REID PARK ZOO

ℝ RESTAURANTS

- 4 ◖ GOVINDA'S NATURAL FOOD BUFFET
- 5 ◖ NICO'S
- 6 ROSA'S
- 8 BEYOND BREAD
- 9 PASTICHE MODERN EATERY
- 10 LOVIN' SPOONFULS VEGETARIAN RESTAURANT
- 20 BK CARNE ASADA & HOT DOGS
- 22 BRUSH FIRE BBQ CO.
- 23 THE INDIA OVEN
- 24 YOSHIMATSU HEALTHY JAPANESE EATERY
- 26 BLUE WILLOW
- 27 LUCKY WISHBONE
- 28 KARUNA'S THAI PLATE
- 30 KINGFISHER
- 35 LUKE'S
- 38 ◖ FRANK'S
- 39 FRANCISCO'S
- 43 ALI BABA
- 44 EEGEE'S
- 45 MAY'S COUNTER
- 48 COFFEE TIMES
- 49 THE DISH BISTRO-BAR
- 51 FRONIMO'S GREEK CAFÉ
- 52 GUILIN HEALTHY CHINESE RESTAURANT
- 54 ◖ IKE'S COFFEE & TEA
- 55 FEAST
- 56 GEE'S GARDEN BISTRO
- 67 LODGE ON THE DESERT
- 69 ROCCO'S LITTLE CHICAGO
- 76 SUSHI GARDEN
- 77 OLD PUEBLO GRILLE
- 79 THE HUNGRY FOX
- 80 CRAVE COFFEE BAR
- 82 MONKEY BURGER

◐ NIGHTLIFE

- 1 CLICKS BILLIARDS
- 2 BOONDOCK'S LOUNGE
- 11 DANNY'S BABAQUIVERI
- 13 CATAVINOS
- 16 SMOKE CIGAR PATIO AND BAR
- 21 WORLD FAMOUS GOLDEN NUGGET
- 34 ◖ THE SHELTER
- 57 SIR VEZA'S
- 61 RJ'S REPLAYS
- 62 DV8
- 65 BOB DOBB'S
- 71 ◖ EL PARADOR
- 78 KON TIKI

◆ ARTS AND LEISURE

- 14 MINI TIME MACHINE MUSEUM OF MINIATURES
- 15 LIGHTHOUSE/CITY YMCA
- 18 FORT LOWELL MUSEUM
- 19 FORT LOWELL TENNIS CENTER
- 47 ◖ THE LOFT CINEMA
- 63 HIMMEL PARK TENNIS CENTER
- 64 HIMMEL PARK
- 70 MID-VALLEY ATHLETIC CLUB AND WELLNESS CENTER
- 72 LAFFS COMEDY CAFFE
- 84 RANDOLPH CENTER SKATE PARK
- 85 RANDOLPH RECREATION CENTER
- 86 REFFKIN TENNIS CENTER
- 88 RANDOLPH GOLF COURSE AND DELL URICH GOLF COURSE
- 89 ◖ GENE C. REID PARK

0   0.5 mi

0   0.5 km

DISTANCE ACROSS MAP
Approximate: 6.5 mi or 10.5 km

Tanque Verde Creek

Pantano Wash

OLD FORT LOWELL

E HARDY DR

E CAMP LOWELL 14 DR

13

15

McCormick Park

Plaza Palomino

16 17

E MONTE VISTA DR

E FORT LOWELL RD

Fort Lowell Park

18
19

VISTA DEL MONTE

E GLENN ST

E TOWNER ST

E COPPER ST

OAK FLOWER

34

33

E WATER ST

Crossroads Festival

Tucson Medical Center

E GRANT RD

32

35

ST CYRILS

SEE MAP 6

E NORTH ST

E WAVERLY ST

36

Tucson Botanical Gardens

E LINDEN ST

E LINDEN ST

38,39

MIDTOWN

41

E PIMA ST

40

42

E ELIDA ST

E LEE ST

E CAMDEN ST

E FAIRMOUNT ST

E MABEL ST

E BELLEVUE ST

55

56

57

58

59 60

E SPEEDWAY BLVD

61

62

E 1ST ST

DUFFY

E 1ST ST

E 2ND ST

PETER HOWELL

E 2ND ST

E 3RD ST

E 3RD ST

E ROSEWOOD ST

E 3RD ST

E 3RD ST

E 4TH ST

E BAKER ST

E BAKER ST

E 5TH ST

SEWELL

E 6TH ST

E 7TH ST

E 7TH ST

Highland Vista Park

E 8TH ST

67 68

E KILMER ST

E BURNS ST

E 9TH ST

E 10TH ST

77

E ELMWOOD ST

E WHITMAN ST

78 79

E 10TH ST

81

E BROADWAY BLVD

82

83

Park Place Mall

84,85,86

80

SAN CLEMENTE

E COOPER ST

E COOPER ST

E WHITTIER ST

E TIMROD ST

87

SAN GABRIEL

88

E 22ND ST

SHOPS

3 TUCSON'S MAP & FLAG CENTER

7 NATIVE SEEDS/SEARCH

12 CLUES UNLIMITED

17 PLAZA PALOMINO

25 PLAZA LIQUORS

28 MAC'S INDIAN JEWELRY

31 THE MEXICAN GARDEN

32 POTTERY BLOWOUT

33 GRANT ROAD ANTIQUES DISTRICT

40 CRIZMAC TUCSON MARKETPLACE

41 THE KID'S CENTER

42 TOM'S FINE FURNITURE AND COLLECTIBLES

46 GADABOUT SALON AND SPA

50 THE RUMRUNNER

53 ZIA RECORD EXCHANGE

58 SPEEDWAY ANTIQUES DISTRICT

59 SUMMIT HUT

60 COPPER COUNTRY ANTIQUES

66 RINCON MARKET

73 BROADWAY VILLAGE

74 PICANTE

75 BON BOUTIQUE

83 PARK PLACE MALL

HOTELS

37 ARIZONA INN

68 LODGE ON THE DESERT

81 EMBASSY SUITES

87 DOUBLETREE HOTEL AT REID PARK

SIGHTS

4 TOHONO CHUL PARK
26 DEGRAZIA GALLERY IN THE SUN
38 SABINO CANYON RECREATION AREA
42 ST. PHILIP'S IN THE HILLS EPISCOPAL CHURCH

RESTAURANTS

5 FROST
6 BLUEFIN SEAFOOD BISTRO
7 WILDFLOWER
11 THE LOOKOUT BAR AND GRILLE
14 MIGUEL'S AT LA POSADA
23 ACACIA
27 FLYING V BAR AND GRILL AT LOEWS VENTANA CANYON
34 THE GRILL AT HACIENDA DEL SOL
41 ZINBURGER
43 EL CORRAL RESTAURANT
44 UNION PUBLIC HOUSE
50 GHINI'S FRENCH CAFFE
57 MOTHER HUBBARDS CAFÉ
58 LA FUENTE

NIGHTLIFE

3 WORLD SPORTS GRILLE
15 ARMITAGE WINE LOUNGE AND CAFE
16 BLANCO TACOS + TEQUILA
28 CASCADE LOUNGE AT LOEWS VENTANA CANYON RESORT
31 AZUL LOUNGE AT THE WESTIN LA PALOMA
52 SKYBOX
54 WOODY'S

Canada del Oro
N LA CHOLLA BLVD
N SHANNON RD
N MONA LISA
W ALTERO DR
W SOLERO DR
N PASEO DEL NORTE
1
A
S
3
W INA RD
E SKYLINE DR
W MAGEE RD

Tohono Chul Park

4
11 12 13

5,6,7 8,9,10

N ORACLE RD
Pima Wash
W ORANGE GROVE RD
W ORANGE GROVE RD
E INA RD
E INA RD
E SKYLINE DR
N CAMPBELL AVE

20,21,22
17,18,19
A
15,16
23 24,25

31 32 33

W RUDASILL RD

14

W RIVER RD
N LA CANADA DR
N ORACLE RD
N 1ST AVE
N CAMPBELL AVE
N HACIENDA DEL SOL RD

Rillito Park Bike Route
Rillito Creek
W RUTHRAUFF RD
N STONE AVE
W RIVER RD
E RIVER RD

St. Philip's in the Hills Episcopal Church

41 42
43
39
40
44 48
45 46,47
49

W WETMORE RD

10
SEE MAP 5

W ROGER RD
E ROGER RD
N CACTUS BLVD
N COUNTRY CLUB RD

FLOWING WELLS RD
N CAMPBELL AVE
E ALLEN RD

54
50

E PRINCE RD

Santa Cruz River
N SILVERBELL RD
E FORT LOWELL RD
N 1ST AVE

W MIRACLE MILE

55

57

W GRANT RD
E GRANT RD

10
56
N ORACLE RD
N 6TH AVE
N EUCLID AVE
SEE MAP 3
58

SEE MAP 2

© AVALON TRAVEL

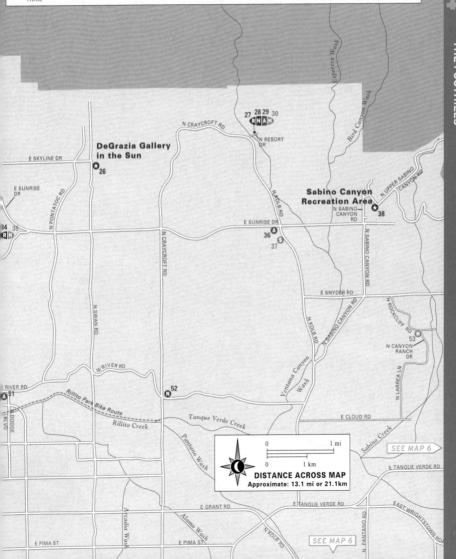

Ⓐ ARTS AND LEISURE

1 NORTHWEST YMCA
20 GALLERY WEST FINE AMERICAN INDIAN ART
21 SANDERS GALLERIES
22 SETTLERS WEST GALLERY
24 GALLERY ROW AT EL CORTIJO
25 MADARAS GALLERY
29 VENTANA CANYON TRAIL
36 Ⓒ MARK SUBLETTE MEDICINE MAN GALLERY
39 RILLITO PARK BIKE ROUTE
49 TUCSON RACQUET & FITNESS CLUB
51 BRANDI FENTON MEMORIAL PARK
56 SOUTHERN ARIZONA BALLOON EXCURSIONS

Ⓢ SHOPS

2 THE FOOTHILLS MALL
8 CASAS ADOBES PLAZA
9 J. GILBERT FOOTWEAR
10 MAYA PALACE
12 SONORAN SPA
17 Ⓒ LA ENCANTADA
18 AJ'S FINE FOODS
19 MILDRED AND DILDRED TOY STORE
32 ELIZABETH ARDEN RED DOOR SALON
37 VENTANA PLAZA
40 TUCSON MALL
45 Ⓒ BAHTI INDIAN ARTS
46 GREY DOG TRADING COMPANY
47 ST. PHILIP'S SATURDAY FARMERS MARKET
55 MONTEREY COURT

Ⓗ HOTELS

13 WESTWARD LOOK RESORT
30 LOEWS VENTANA CANYON RESORT
33 THE WESTIN LA PALOMA RESORT & SPA
35 Ⓒ HACIENDA DEL SOL GUEST RANCH RESORT
48 WINDMILL INN
53 CANYON RANCH

SIGHTS
1 SAGUARO NATIONAL PARK WEST
6 ARIZONA-SONORA DESERT MUSEUM
8 OLD TUCSON STUDIOS

RESTAURANTS
7 OCOTILLO CAFÉ
12 TERESA'S MOSAIC CAFÉ
13 LI'L ABNER'S STEAKHOUSE
14 MARISCOS CHIHUAHUA
15 PAT'S DRIVE-IN
16 ST. MARY'S MEXICAN FOOD
18 AGUSTÍN BRASSERIE
25 COYOTE PAUSE CAFÉ

19 TUCSON MOUNTAIN PARK AND GATES PASS SCENIC OVERLOOK
20 TUMAMOC HILL
21 SENTINEL PEAK

NIGHTLIFE
4 RIVER'S EDGE LOUNGE

ARTS AND LEISURE
2 SAGUARO NATIONAL PARK WEST
3 GADSDEN-PACIFIC DIVISION TOY TRAINS OPERATING MUSEUM
10 TUCSON MOUNTAIN PARK
11 INTERNATIONAL WILDLIFE MUSEUM
17 TUMAMOC HILL TRAIL
24 STARR PASS BIKE TRAIL

SHOPS
19 SANTA CRUZ RIVER FARMERS MARKET
22 HASHANI SPA
26 CAT MOUNTAIN STATION

HOTELS
5 CASA TIERRA ADOBE BED AND BREAKFAST INN
23 JW MARRIOTT STARR PASS RESORT & SPA
27 CAT MOUNTAIN LODGE

Saguaro

National

Park

1 2
Saguaro National
Park West

To
5 Casa Tierra Adobe
Bed and Breakfast Inn

6 7
Arizona-Sonora
Desert Museum

8
Old Tucson
Studios

W TRAILS END RD

Tucson Mountain

County Park

W GATES PASS RD

N KINNEY RD

W GATES PASS RD

9 10
Tucson Mountain
Park and Gates Pass
Scenic Overlook

11

TUCSON
MOUNTAINS

HAL GRAS RD

S PORTON
EL DORADO

W TUCSON ESTATES PKWY

W LONE STAR DR

Tucson Estates Country Club

W FLYING CIRCLE ST

S KINNEY RD

W NAOMI RD

25 27
26

S JAMIE AVE
S CAROL AVE
S SHEILA AVE

0   0.5 mi
0   0.5 km

DISTANCE ACROSS MAP
Approximate: 8.9 mi or 14.3 km

© AVALON TRAVEL

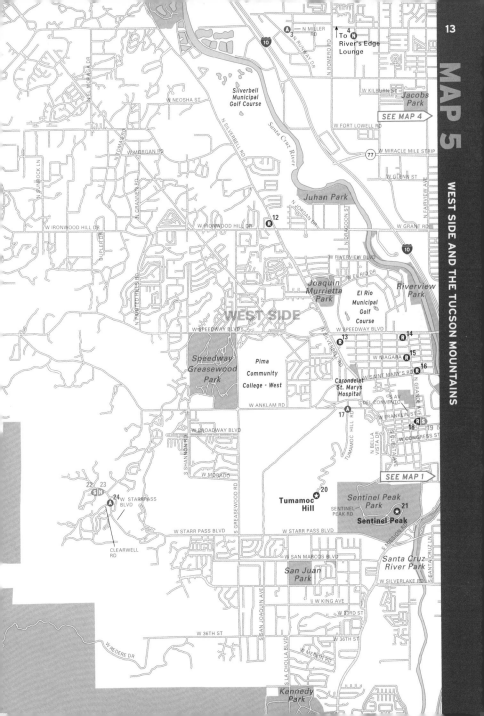

MAP 6   EAST SIDE AND THE RINCON VALLEY

Tucson Country Club

SEE MAP 4

SEE MAP 3

Tanque Verde River Park

E TANQUE VERDE RD

Pantano Wash

E GRANT RD

N SABINO CANYON RD

N INDIAN RUINS RD

E TANQUE VERDE RD

E WRIGHTSTOWN RD

0   500 yds
0   500 m

DISTANCE ACROSS MAP
Approximate: 2.8 mi or 4.5 km

Trail Dust Town

Morris K. Udall Regional Park

N PANTANO RD

RINCON VALLEY

E PIMA ST

Dorado Golf Course

N KOLB RD

N WILMOT RD

E SPEEDWAY BLVD

EAST SIDE

Carondelet St. Joseph Hospital

●	**SIGHTS**	●	**ARTS AND LEISURE**
6	TRAIL DUST TOWN	3	MORRIS K. UDALL PARK
●	**RESTAURANTS**	4	MORRIS K. UDALL RECREATION CENTER
1	ECLECTIC CAFE	5	VISTA DEL RIO CULTURAL RESOURCE PARK
7	PINNACLE PEAK STEAK HOUSE	16	GASLIGHT DINNER THEATRE
9	MILLIE'S PANCAKE HAUS	18	DAN YERSAVICH MEMORIAL BIKEWAY
12	CASA MOLINA	19	BROADWAY BICYCLES
14	NEW DELHI PALACE	●	**SHOPS**
15	LITTLE ANTHONY'S DINER	2	SANTA FE SQUARE
●	**NIGHTLIFE**	10	LA PLAZA SHOPPES
8	THE MAVERICK	13	BOOKMANS
11	COW PONY BAR AND GRILL	●	**HOTELS**
20	PEARSON'S PUB	17	HILTON TUCSON EAST
21	MUSIC BOX LOUNGE		
22	WHISKEY TANGO		
23	HIDEOUT BAR & GRILL		

E BROADWAY BLVD

Dan Yersavich Memorial Bikeway

Dan Yersavich Memorial Bikeway

E KORALEE DR

Palo Verde Park

Jesse Owens Park

S WILMOT RD

S MELVILLE AVE

S KOLB RD

S PANTANO RD

S SARNOFF DR

E ARTURO

E KENYON DR

E FLO DR

E 18TH ST

S PRUDENCE RD

Oxford Plaza

Eastpoint Marketplace

E 22ND ST

S REGULO

S LEIGH CH DR

S SHERWOOD VILLAGE DR

E BEVERLY ST

© AVALON TRAVEL

SEE MAP 1

SEE MAP 5

Santa Rita Park

Randolph Park

Randolph Park Golf Course

Randolph Plaza

Quincie Douglas Park

Tucson Veterans

Administration Hospital

Diablos Sports Bar & Grill

Davis-Monthan Air Force Base

Kino Veterans Memorial Sports Arena

SOUTH SIDE

Tucson Rodeo Grounds

Pima County Rodeo Park

Sunnyside Park

Mission Park

Pima Air and Space Museum

Tucson International Airport

SIGHTS
11 PIMA AIR AND SPACE MUSEUM

RESTAURANTS
1 LA CAVE'S BAKERY
2 MI NIDITO
3 TAQUERIA PICO DE GALLO
10 EL GUERO CANELO

NIGHTLIFE
4 WOODEN NICKEL TAVERN
5 DIABLOS SPORTS BAR & GRILL
7 NIMBUS BREWING COMPANY

ARTS AND LEISURE
8 FC TUCSON
9 TUCSON RODEO PARADE MUSEUM

SHOPS
6 COMMUNITY FOOD BANK FARMERS MARKET

HOTELS
12 HOLIDAY INN EXPRESS
13 DESERT DIAMOND HOTEL AND CASINO

© AVALON TRAVEL

0   750 yds
0   750 m

DISTANCE ACROSS MAP
Approximate: 4.5 mi or 7.2 km

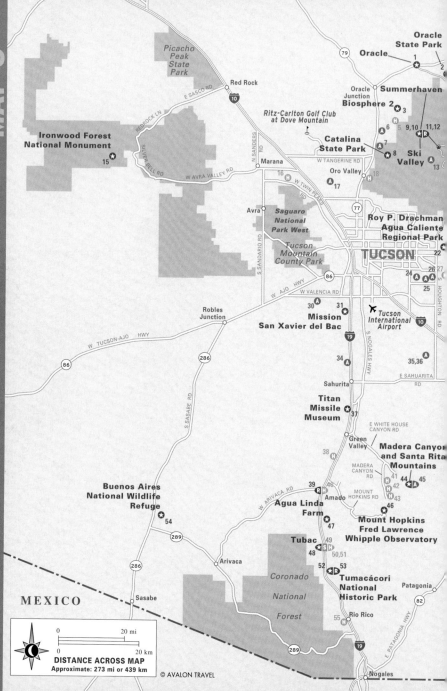

Picacho Peak State Park

Red Rock

79 Oracle

Oracle State Park
1
2

E SASCO RD

10

Oracle Junction

Summerhaven

Biosphere 2 3

Ritz-Carlton Golf Club at Dove Mountain

6 5 9,10 11,12
A R

Ironwood Forest National Monument
15

PEDROCK LN

SILVER BELL RD

N SANDERS RD

Catalina State Park
7 8
Marana

8 **Ski Valley**
13

W AVRA VALLEY RD

W TANGERINE RD

Oro Valley 18

16 W TWIN PEAKS RD H
17

Avra

77

Saguaro National Park West

Roy P. Drachman Agua Caliente Regional Park

S SANDARIO RD

Tucson Mountain County Park

TUCSON

22

26 27
24 A A
25

S HOUGHTON RD

86

W AJO HWY

W VALENCIA RD

Robles Junction

30 A 31
Mission San Xavier del Bac

✈ **Tucson International Airport**

10

W TUCSON-AJO HWY

86

286

S SASABE RD

34 A

19

S NOGALES HWY

35,36

E SAHUARITA RD

Sahurita

Titan Missile Museum 37

E WHITE HOUSE CANYON RD

Green Valley

38 H

Madera Canyon and Santa Rita Mountains

MADERA CANYON RD

Buenos Aires National Wildlife Refuge

41 44 45
H A A
42 A
43

MOUNT HOPKINS RD

54

39 R
40 H
Agua Linda Farm
Amado

46

289

47

286

Arivaca

Tubac
49
48 A
50,51

52 53
R

Mount Hopkins Fred Lawrence Whipple Observatory

Sasabe

MEXICO

Coronado National Forest

Tumacácori National Historic Park

Patagonia

82

55 H Rio Rico

E PATAGONIA HWY

289

Nogales

0   20 mi

0   20 km

DISTANCE ACROSS MAP
Approximate: 273 mi or 439 km

© AVALON TRAVEL

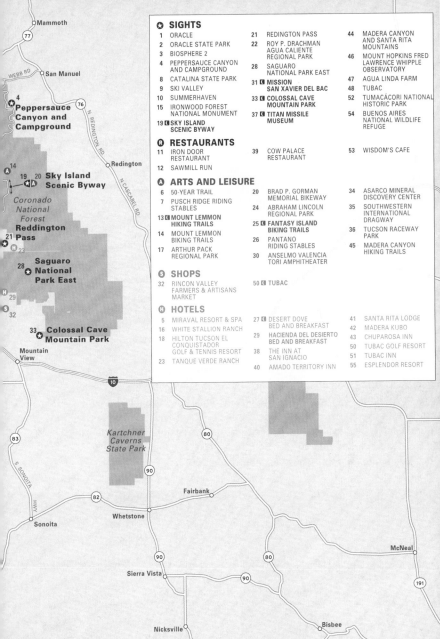

Map Labels

Mammoth
San Manuel
WEBB RD
N REDINGTON RD
Peppersauce Canyon and Campground
Redington
N CASCABEL RD
Sky Island Scenic Byway
Coronado National Forest
Reddington Pass
Saguaro National Park East
Colossal Cave Mountain Park
Mountain View
Kartchner Caverns State Park
Fairbank
Whetstone
Sonoita
S SONOITA HWY
Sierra Vista
McNeal
Nicksville
Bisbee

SIGHTS

1 ORACLE
2 ORACLE STATE PARK
3 BIOSPHERE 2
4 PEPPERSAUCE CANYON AND CAMPGROUND
8 CATALINA STATE PARK
9 SKI VALLEY
10 SUMMERHAVEN
15 IRONWOOD FOREST NATIONAL MONUMENT
19 SKY ISLAND SCENIC BYWAY
21 REDINGTON PASS
22 ROY P. DRACHMAN AGUA CALIENTE REGIONAL PARK
28 SAGUARO NATIONAL PARK EAST
31 MISSION SAN XAVIER DEL BAC
33 COLOSSAL CAVE MOUNTAIN PARK
37 TITAN MISSILE MUSEUM
44 MADERA CANYON AND SANTA RITA MOUNTAINS
46 MOUNT HOPKINS FRED LAWRENCE WHIPPLE OBSERVATORY
47 AGUA LINDA FARM
48 TUBAC
52 TUMACÁCORI NATIONAL HISTORIC PARK
54 BUENOS AIRES NATIONAL WILDLIFE REFUGE

RESTAURANTS

11 IRON DOOR RESTAURANT
12 SAWMILL RUN
39 COW PALACE RESTAURANT
53 WISDOM'S CAFE

ARTS AND LEISURE

6 50-YEAR TRAIL
7 PUSCH RIDGE RIDING STABLES
13 MOUNT LEMMON HIKING TRAILS
14 MOUNT LEMMON BIKING TRAILS
17 ARTHUR PACK REGIONAL PARK
20 BRAD P. GORMAN MEMORIAL BIKEWAY
24 ABRAHAM LINCOLN REGIONAL PARK
25 FANTASY ISLAND BIKING TRAILS
26 PANTANO RIDING STABLES
30 ANSELMO VALENCIA TORI AMPHITHEATER
34 ASARCO MINERAL DISCOVERY CENTER
35 SOUTHWESTERN INTERNATIONAL DRAGWAY
36 TUCSON RACEWAY PARK
45 MADERA CANYON HIKING TRAILS

SHOPS

32 RINCON VALLEY FARMERS & ARTISANS MARKET
50 TUBAC

HOTELS

5 MIRAVAL RESORT & SPA
16 WHITE STALLION RANCH
18 HILTON TUCSON EL CONQUISTADOR GOLF & TENNIS RESORT
23 TANQUE VERDE RANCH
27 DESERT DOVE BED AND BREAKFAST
29 HACIENDA DEL DESIERTO BED AND BREAKFAST
38 THE INN AT SAN IGNACIO
40 AMADO TERRITORY INN
41 SANTA RITA LODGE
42 MADERA KUBO
43 CHUPAROSA INN
50 TUBAC GOLF RESORT
51 TUBAC INN
55 ESPLENDOR RESORT

Discover Tucson

Over the past two centuries, Tucson has grown from an adobe-hut village on the far edge of the Spanish frontier into a major Sunbelt city, and yet through all that time and change the Old Pueblo has held on to the disparate cultural ingredients that have made it one of North America's most unique destinations.

In Tucson, visitors will find the true Southwestern experience, one that is neither encased under glass nor petrified through architectural uniformity; the Southwestern lifestyle is lived, not merely marketed. And what is this lifestyle? It involves a dedication to cultural mixing and a concentration on an active life lived outdoors on the saguaro-lined trails of the desert. This lifestyle is casual and laid-back, with flip-flops and shorts sufficing for dinner-wear, and a friendly margarita-and-sunshine-inspired smile sufficing for a general greeting.

If you're looking for extreme pampering, holistic poolside navel-gazing, brisk hikes into the cactus foothills, and horseback rides along ancient trails, there are numerous world-famous resorts at which to stay and play. If you're longing for physical proof of the myths of the Old West, you'll find it in many of the city's museums and historic buildings. If you want to experience the Sonoran Desert, one of the continent's most exotic natural landscapes, you'll find it within a short drive of your hotel. This Old Pueblo is bustling with life, the Southwestern life—one lived just a bit off center, a bit slower, with a mild sunburn and a big happy smile.

Planning Your Trip

▶ WHERE TO GO

DeGrazia Gallery in the Sun

Downtown

The downtown area is where Tucson began and where its heart still beats today—although downtown usually becomes a bit deserted after 5 P.M. on Friday. History is everywhere here, and it's the only truly pedestrian-friendly section of the city.

University District

The University District has 4th Avenue—the city's bohemian-chic enclave—sometimes called a smaller version of Telegraph Avenue in Berkeley, California. It's busy here most hours of the day with a mix of University of Arizona students and hipsters.

Midtown

Tucson's midtown neighborhood is where most of the Old Pueblo's real-life living takes place. The Fort Lowell Museum in the northern part of this district preserves the artifacts of the military's role in Tucson, and the Tucson Botanical Gardens are the best place to learn about the unique local flora that thrives on aridity. The small but prestigious Reid Park Zoo is a must for families.

The Foothills

The foothills area features artist Ted DeGrazia's romantic DeGrazia Gallery in the Sun and renowned architect Josias Joesler's imprint on Tucson. And at Sabino Canyon Recreation Area, the desert meets the mountains and a cool-water creek rushes down from the peaks to create one of the state's most beautiful and popular desert riparian areas.

West Side and the Tucson Mountains

This rugged desert land, west of central Tucson, is where you'll find Tucson's premier attraction, the world-renowned Arizona-Sonora Desert Museum. Here you'll see mountain lions and black bears lounging on warm rocks, and watch baby bighorn sheep

boulders on Mount Lemmon

and the very best place to learn about and witness the desert's fauna and flora. Head east from the park to tour Colossal Cave Mountain Park, where Old West outlaws used to hide out.

South Side

The South Side holds one of Tucson's top sights, San Xavier del Bac (the "white dove of the desert"), one of the nation's finest remaining examples of mission architecture. Lovers of Mexican food in all its varieties will want to return to the small incorporated city of South Tucson again and again, for it is here that you'll find the region's best enchiladas, tamales, and carne asada.

Greater Tucson

Greater Tucson includes the forested heights of the Santa Catalina range, whose highest peak, Mount Lemmon, reaches above 9,000 feet and holds the nation's southernmost ski run. The mountains feature such a different ecosystem that the trip along the twisting Sky Island Scenic Byway is like driving from Mexico to Canada in about an hour. To the south is the lush Santa Cruz Valley, where you can learn all about the nuclear missiles that once ringed the city.

negotiating the man-made cliff sides. But before you even reach the museum, you'll rise and descend over spectacular Gates Pass, looking down across a sweeping saguaro-dotted landscape.

East Side and the Rincon Valley

The top draw here is Saguaro National Park East, the park's largest and oldest section. You can walk, bike, or drive through a thick saguaro forest, one of the best and most accessible portions of the Sonoran Desert

▶ WHEN TO GO

The Tucson calendar can be divided into just three seasons: spring, summer, and second spring. In January, the average high is about 64°F. February is the Old Pueblo's so-called "golden month," with an average daily high of 70°F. At least three major events—the Gem, Mineral, and Fossil Showcase, the Fiesta de los Vaqueros, and the Accenture Match Play golf tournament—have the hotels booked solid during this time. Unless you're coming to town for one of these popular events, I'd recommend staying away from town in February, despite the near-perfect weather.

In March, the average high is about 73°F, and in April, Tucson and Southern Arizona

is a paradise, with an average daily high of 81°F.

The high season, during which prices are highest and tourists are everywhere, runs from February to the end of April. This is the first spring, and it is the most popular time of the year. You need to plan ahead and get a reservation if you're coming to town during this time. The spring months also feature the multicolored bloom of all the desert's cacti, trees, and wildflowers.

It's very hot in the desert in the summer (often over 105°F), but it's perfect in the mountains, and in July and August Tusconans can usually count on near-daily late-afternoon thunderstorms.

Explore Tucson

▶ THE THREE-DAY BEST OF THE OLD PUEBLO

The following suggested itinerary is meant to guide you to the city's very best—the essential Old Pueblo experience. You'll need your own car, a camera, a hat, and a comfortable pair of walking shoes.

Day 1

▶ Try to get an early start for sightseeing, especially during the hot months, when you only have a few hours before the weather gets unbearable. If you're an early riser, I'd suggest heading downtown to the St. Augustine Cathedral before 7 A.M. You can stand across the street and watch as the rising sun lights up the Spanish revival cathedral, and the tall, skinny imported palm trees cast their shaggy shadows against the glowing building. It's a perfect Southwestern scene.

▶ Head downtown to the Hotel Congress, have a big breakfast at The Cup Café, and take a look around the historic old hotel.

▶ Hop in the car and head west from downtown into Tucson Mountain Park, stopping to enjoy the view of the desert below at Gates Pass.

▶ Spend a few hours exploring the Arizona-Sonora Desert Museum, just down the hill.

▶ Next, head back over the Tucson Mountains to downtown and stroll, shop, and eat a late lunch or early dinner on 4th Avenue and nearby Main Gate Square.

▶ If you have it in you, barhop around Congress Street, 4th Avenue, and Main Gate Square, taking in a few bands at The Hut, The Playground, and Plush along the way.

Day 2

▶ Drive to midtown for a filling greasy-spoon breakfast at Frank's.

▶ On your way back downtown, stop by the

St. Augustine Cathedral in early morning light

Tucson Museum of Art, downtown

Arizona Inn and have a look around the lush grounds.

▶ Then drive to the El Presidio district downtown and explore the Tucson Museum of Art and Historic Block and El Presidio Real de San Agustín del Tucson for a few hours.

▶ For lunch, go to El Charro, right near the museum, or to Little Cafe Poca Cosa, a short walk away, then take a short drive south on I-19 and check out San Xavier del Bac.

▶ In the late afternoon, drive into the foothills to Sabino Canyon Recreation Area and take a tram ride up into the canyon or hike one of the trails.

▶ As the sun dips behind the Santa Catalina Mountains, head on over to Hacienda del

SONORAN DESERT ADVENTURES

There are myriad ways to experience the Sonoran Desert's unique landscape. At the top of the list should be a visit to the **Arizona-Sonora Desert Museum.** On your way to the museum you'll drive through **Tucson Mountain Park,** where some of the largest saguaro stands in the world are protected.

Both sections of **Saguaro National Park** have some of the oldest and largest saguaros in the desert. Consider hiking the many desert trails around the park, or visit one of Tucson's many stables, where you can hire a horse to do the work for you.

To see how just a small but steady amount of water can change the desert into a relatively verdant Eden, make sure to visit **Sabino Canyon Recreation Area.**

To learn about the various ways the indigenous peoples of Southern Arizona have adapted to life in the desert, check out the **Arizona State Museum;** and to learn how other cultures have learned (or failed to learn) to live in this harsh land, check out the **Arizona Historical Society Museum.**

For gifts, souvenirs, food, and other items related to the desert, make sure to visit **Native Seeds/SEARCH.**

Sol for drinks and appetizers (or dinner) on the patio overlooking the city.

▶ Hit El Parador (assuming it's a Friday or Saturday night) for salsa dancing, or knock back a few drinks at The Tap Room and dance, or watch a band at Club Congress.

Day 3

▶ Depending on your personal inclinations, you should either tour Kartchner Caverns State Park near Benson, or head north up the Sky Island Scenic Byway into the Santa Catalina Mountains. Both trips are scenic and fun and take about two hours of driving time round-trip; it just depends on whether you prefer sweeping mountain views or otherworldly underground sights.

▶ If you're headed up to the mountains, stop at the Rincon Market on your way out of town and pick up a picnic lunch. If you take a trip to the caverns, stop afterwards at the Horseshoe Café in Benson for lunch. Either way you go, you'll likely get back to town in the late afternoon if you get an early start.

▶ Once back downtown, head to Old Town Artisans to have a few drinks in the lush courtyard and check out the shops.

▶ For your final dinner in Tucson, go to Mi Nidito or La Fuente, where you'll be sent home with the brassy sounds of mariachi ringing in your sunburned ears.

▶ MIDTOWN BIKE RIDE

Tucson is a biker's paradise, what with the nearly constant beautiful weather, the many dedicated bike routes, and that perfect mixture of flatland breezeways and steep mountain roads. This ride through Midtown's residential neighborhoods stays on the flats.

▶ Pick up the 3rd Street Bike Route at the far eastern edge of Midtown at Wilmot Road and Rosewood Street. Follow the signs along the quiet residential streets, checking out all the little desertland bungalows along the way.

▶ After about five miles of easy pedaling, you'll pass Himmel Park, where you can pause for a dip in the public pool, or a quick set of tennis at the Himmel Park Tennis Center.

▶ Cruise through the beautiful tree-lined Sam Hughes neighborhood. Cross Campbell Avenue and you're on the campus of the University of Arizona.

▶ Ride to the west side of campus on the bike lanes, then take a rest and have some lunch

at one of the many restaurants and bars at Main Gate Square.

▶ From there you can continue your ride along the same route through the West University neighborhood, to 4th Avenue and the many attractions downtown.

University of Arizona campus

SOUTHWEST STYLE

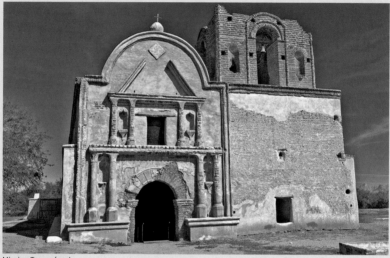

Mission Tumacácori

There are many Southwest art and architectural styles in Tucson, from Spanish realism to Spanish revival, pueblo chic to adobe row house, mission revival to railroad hacienda, to dryland art nouveau:

- The top draw, of course, is the "white dove of the desert," **San Xavier del Bac,** a mission that dates back to the 1600s. A bit south of San Xavier, the half-ruin **Mission Tumacácori** awaits at **Tumacácori National Historical Park.**

- Take a look around the elegant old hotels from the golden age of Southwestern tourism, such as the **Arizona Inn** and **Hacienda del Sol.**

- Two churches warrant a look: **St. Augustine Cathedral,** a Spanish revival church that puts on a mariachi mass every Sunday; and the Josias Joesler-designed, Mexican-influenced **St. Philip's in the Hills Episcopal Church.**

- Several buildings on the **University of Arizona** campus reflect both revival and territorial styles.

To really get an idea about the various styles that influence Tucson, visit the **Tucson Museum of Art and Historic Block.**

- Lovers of Western art should visit the **galleries in the foothills,** around the intersection of Campbell and Skyline.

Great examples of Western art can be found in the galleries in the foothills.

SIGHTS

Many of Tucson's attractions are meant to provide easy access to, and to put a human-made frame around, the exotic natural beauty of the Sonoran Desert, one of the rarest and strangest landscapes in North America. Even the Old Pueblo's most urban sights—art museums and galleries, historic neighborhoods, the ruins of lost civilizations—must be seen and judged within the context of how their creators, residents, and builders adapted and responded to the area's unique, often harsh environment.

Sightseeing in and around Tucson, you'll discover not only the arid beauty of a mythic landscape, but also a kind of living timeline of a region that has been home to many different, often contradictory cultures going back at least 12,000 years.

You'll see the left-behind evidence of the Hohokam, desertland farmers who lived here long before the Spanish came to the New World. You'll learn the lifeways of the Tohono O'odham, and the Apache, who fought the Spanish, the Mexicans, the Americans, and each other for the right to make a life in this forbidding land. You'll see the remains of the Spanish, who were building whitewashed missions and ranching the region's fertile river valleys back when Jamestown was just somebody's crazy idea. Everywhere you go you'll feel and see the influence of Mexico, just an hour or so south of the city: The language, the culture, and the food of that dynamic nation infuse Tucson and its environs quite thoroughly. And you'll also see evidence of

SIGHTS

HIGHLIGHTS

LOOK FOR ◖ TO FIND RECOMMENDED SIGHTS.

◖ **Best Museum:** See the art and artifacts left behind by the many cultures who have called this desert home at the **Tucson Museum of Art and Historic Block** (page 29).

◖ **Best In-Town Walk:** At the **Tucson Botanical Gardens,** you can stroll through the varied gardens that are cool and quiet, yet right in the heart of town (page 34).

◖ **Best Artist-Built Gallery:** Even if you aren't a fan of famous artist Ted DeGrazia's impressionistic work, you must visit the **DeGrazia Gallery in the Sun** to see the romantic home he built in the desert (page 35).

◖ **Best Place to See Water in the Desert: Sabino Canyon Recreation Area** is a popular riparian area that will change your idea about aridity (page 36).

◖ **Best Place to Learn about the Desert:** The world-famous **Arizona-Sonora Desert Museum** is both a museum and zoo, where you can learn about the general structure and the minute details of the surrounding desert and see live native animals in a tame environment (page 37).

◖ **Best Place to See the Desert:** At **Saguaro National Park West** you can really get to know the saguaro and its desert compatriots; also check out the eastern section of the park (page 39).

◖ **Best Adventure with Kids:** At **Colossal Cave Mountain Park** you can tour an old cave (once a hideout for Old West bandits), ride horses, say hello to ancient tortoises, and much more (page 43).

◖ **Best Historical Site: Mission San Xavier del Bac,** called the "white dove of the desert," is the foremost example of mission architecture remaining in the United States (page 45).

◖ **Best Place to Outrun the Heat:** On the **Sky Island Scenic Byway,** an hour-long scenic drive takes you from the desert into a cooler ecosystem akin to Canada's (page 49).

◖ **Best Reminder of the Cold War:** Learn about Tucson's past as a nuclear missile hot spot at the **Titan Missile Museum** (page 50).

© TIM HULL

DeGrazia Gallery in the Sun

the American pioneers, who began moving into the valley about 150 years ago, and their generations-long efforts to create a pretty typical American city in a decidedly atypical environment. Most of all, though, you will see the land. Its secrets may seep into your soul, and you may find yourself irrevocably changed because of it.

Downtown
Map 1

BARRIO HISTÓRICO
Bordered by S. Stone Ave., I-10, W. Cushing St., and W. 18th St.

The photogenic Sonoran-style row houses in the Barrio Histórico district on the southwest edge of downtown are well adapted to the desert environment. Their front entrances hug the property line (unlike their Anglo counterparts with large front and back yards) to make space for central courtyards hidden from the street, which provide a shaded outdoor living space within the home. Many of the adobes here have been lovingly and colorfully restored and now serve as offices, working galleries, and private residences. Sometimes called Barrio Viejo (the Old Neighborhood), the barrio has been on the National Register of Historic Places since the 1970s. It dates from the mid-1850s and, as its dominant architecture suggests, has traditionally been a Mexican enclave. Many similar neighborhoods once sprawled out to the edge of the El Presidio district, a large quarter referred to as Barrio Libre (Free Neighborhood), due either to the anything-goes atmosphere in some corners or because the Mexican population was mostly left alone to follow its own rules and culture. Much of the quarter was razed in the late 1960s to make way for the "urban renewal" program that built the Tucson Convention Center. The best examples of the adobe row houses can be found along Myer, Main, and Cushing. Along Myer look for the old Teatro Carmen, a now-empty Spanish-language theater that opened in 1915. The adobe building, which over the years would become a movie house, a boxing arena, and an Elks Lodge, still retains the charm and historic interest that once pervaded this district.

EL PRESIDIO PARK AND PIMA COUNTY COURTHOUSE
160 W. Alameda St.

HOURS: El Presidio Park daily 6 A.M.-10:30 P.M.; Pima County Courthouse Mon.-Fri. 8:30 A.M.-noon and 1-5 P.M.

COST: Free

The 80-year-old Pima County Courthouse has a sea-green tiled dome that is a landmark of the Old Pueblo's modest skyline, and it's worth a walk around the grounds of the city's government beehive to take in the Spanish colonial revival touches and, on weekdays, to see downtown at its most industrious. On the weekends, especially in the summer, you'll likely find the area mostly deserted but still inviting. Walk across the front courtyard through a few arches and you'll be in El Presidio Park, with its fountains and memorial to the Mormon Battalion, which occupied the presidio briefly in late 1846. There are also memorials and statues in this large, urban government-center park honoring World War II veterans, John F. Kennedy, and various pioneers of the Old West. There's usually a hot-dog cart on the plaza on weekdays, and plenty of opportunities for people-watching and shade.

EL PRESIDIO REAL DE SAN AGUSTÍN DEL TUCSON
Corner of Washington St. and Church Ave., 520/884-4214, www.tucsonpresidiotrust.org

HOURS: Oct.-May Mon.-Sun. 10 A.M.-4 P.M.; June-Sept. Thurs.-Sun. 10 A.M.-3 P.M.

COST: Free

Experts on the history, lifeways, and architecture of the original Spanish settlers of the Tucson valley have re-created a portion of the

© TIM HULL

El Presidio Real de San Agustín del Tucson

old Presidio de San Agustín del Tucson at the downtown corner of Washington Street and Church Avenue. Within the newly raised adobe walls there's a large, realistic mural depicting daily life in and around the fort; the details are all historically accurate, and there are a few dark, cool adobe rooms set up in period style to show visitors what life was like on the far, lonely northern edge of the Spanish Empire circa 1776, when an Irishman working for the crown rode north to Tucson from Tubac to establish the fort in an effort to outrun Apache predations. During the week parking is available in a nearby parking garage on Alameda Street; metered parking is also available on nearby streets. On weekends, street parking is free.

EL TIRADITO SHRINE

221 S. Main Ave.
HOURS: Daily 24 hours
COST: Free

Roadside shrines are common in Southern Arizona even in the most out-of-the-way places, but only one is dedicated to a folk saint who was, by the Catholic Church's standards, an unredeemed sinner. El Tiradito (The Castaway) dates to the 1870s, when Juan Oliveras, a young shepherd, fell in love with his mother-in-law and the two gave in to an illicit passion. They were discovered by her ax-wielding husband, who killed Oliveras and tossed his dead body away on the land that now holds the shrine (such is the legend, anyway). The church wouldn't allow the doomed lover to be buried on consecrated land, so the people of the barrio interred him where he was "cast away" and erected a shrine. Some say that if you make a wish at the shrine by night and leave a lit candle, and you find it still burning in the morning, your wish will come true—this is why it's sometimes called the Wishing Shrine. Next door to the shrine is La Pilita, an old adobe house that now holds a small museum and store selling handmade items by local schoolchildren, with a few exhibits on local history created by neighborhood kids. There's an excellent mural on the south wall that tells the story of Tucson's Mexican American community.

© TIM HULL

El Tiradito shrine

JARDÍN DE CÉSAR CHÁVEZ

S. 6th Ave. and W. 18th St.

HOURS: Sunrise-sunset

COST: Free

This tiny park on the edge of South Tucson is dedicated to the Mexican American labor organizer and human-rights activist (a native of Yuma, Arizona), and is worth seeing for its brilliant mural depicting ancient Aztec gods lounging around and seemingly passing stern judgment on all who pass. Artist Melchor Ramirez, known for painting the heroes and legends of the Aztec and Maya, painted the mural in vibrant yet earthy colors, and the names and dates of well-known human-rights advocates—Tolstoy, Ghandi, etc.—are scrawled alongside the oversized figures. There isn't a parking lot here, but you can park along a small road on the west side of the park. As you drive south on Stone Avenue, look to your right as you approach 6th Avenue. There are several benches perfect for sitting and contemplating the fascinating paintings as the traffic zips by.

ST. AUGUSTINE CATHEDRAL

192 S. Stone Ave., 520/623-6351,
www.augustinecathedral.org

HOURS: Mass Mon.-Fri. 7 A.M. and noon, Sat. 7 A.M. (Spanish), 5:30 P.M., Sun. 6:30 A.M., 8 A.M. (Spanish, mariachi), 10 A.M., noon, 5:30 P.M. (Spanish); office hours Mon.-Fri. 9 A.M.-5 P.M.

COST: Free

Facing Stone Avenue on the eastern edge of Barrio Histórico in downtown, this cathedral dedicated to Tucson's patron saint was built in 1896 and remodeled several times over the years. The facade has stone-carved yucca, saguaro, and horned-toad flourishes, and there are statues of the Virgin Mary and the titular saint near the big heavy-wood entrance. Catholics or anyone interested in regional variations on the Mass may want to attend the lively mariachi mass at 8 A.M. every Sunday. Inside, one of the bells formerly used in the Spanish-era cathedral is preserved in the vestibule.

◖ TUCSON MUSEUM OF ART AND HISTORIC BLOCK

140 N. Main Ave., 520/624-2333,
www.tucsonmuseumofart.org

HOURS: Wed. and Fri.-Sat. 10 A.M.-5 P.M., Thurs. 10 A.M.-8 P.M., Sun. noon-4 P.M.

COST: $10 adult, $8 senior, $5 student

The Tucson Museum of Art's permanent collection is heavy with mysterious artifacts of the Americas prior to Columbus's arrival in the New World, the art of the American West, and contemporary art with a Latin flavor. This is a good place to introduce yourself to that tri-cultural mixing that makes Southern Arizona unique. Together known as the "historic block," five historic homes built in the last half of the 19th century survive next to the museum. Just beyond the museum's wide Main Avenue entrance is the oldest of the historic block's buildings (and probably the oldest building in Tucson), La Casa Cordova, its two west rooms built several years before the Gadsden Purchase made Tucson part of the United States in 1854. The home is a perfect example of the style of Mexican townhouse that once lined the city's

© TIM HULL

St. Augustine Cathedral

core, with its central courtyard and entrance right on the street. A shady courtyard behind the museum's main building, the Plaza of Pioneers has a wall honoring Tucson pioneers from the Spanish, Mexican, and American periods.

University District   Map 2

ARIZONA STATE MUSEUM
1013 E. University Blvd., 520/621-6302,
www.statemuseum.arizona.edu
HOURS: Mon.-Sat. 10 A.M.-5 P.M.
COST: $5 per person suggested donation

Established in 1893 the Arizona State Museum is the oldest anthropology museum in the Southwest. Here you'll find several rooms of fascinating displays on the state's various Native American tribes, and the world's largest collection of Southwest Indian pottery, including many contemporary pieces that prove pottery-making is certainly not a lost art. Every year in February the museum's grassy grounds play host to the Southwest Indian Art Fair, one of the more important and well attended of such events in the Southwest. A permanent exhibition inside the stately old building explains the origins and histories of 10 of Arizona's Native American groups, including the Hohokam, the O'odham, and the Apache, all of whom ruled Southern Arizona at one time or another.

THE DIAMONDBACK BRIDGE
Spanning Broadway Blvd. near Euclid Ave.
COST: Free

Artist Simon Donovan completed this rather literal work of public art in 2002 to be a kind of memorable entrance to downtown. The Diamondback Bridge, spanning Broadway Boulevard just as the busy street dips into the central city, has since become a popular local landmark, winning the prestigious American

Public Works Project of the Year in 2003. The pedestrian bridge, which looks like a monster-sized rattlesnake taking it easy (albeit with his jaw perpetually stretched open), is 300 feet long and cost about $2.7 million to build. There's a small, pleasant park on either end of the snake. The easiest way to see it is to pull over at Euclid and Broadway, park, and walk across. Just after the snake bridge, as you enter downtown, you'll see huge black-and-white photographs on the sides of the underpass. These are actual photos from the 1940s and 1950s of Tucsonans walking, shopping, and generally bustling about downtown, back when it used to be a place where people did such things.

4TH AVENUE
4th Ave., 520/624-5004, www.fourthavenue.org

Lined with chic thrift stores, exotic clothing boutiques, smoke shops, ethnic food restaurants, and cocktail lounges, this is an ideal place to people-watch, and there are some really good places to eat and many treasures to be found in the quirky shops. Beware the young men and women of the bohemian persuasion who spend their days panhandling along the street. Twice a year, in spring and fall, the area closes to vehicle traffic for a street fair featuring artisan booths, concerts, and greasy food galore. Located between downtown and the university district, 4th Avenue is just a short walk from campus, and on Friday and Saturday nights you can expect hordes of college kids out looking for inebriation. It's best to avoid driving in this area on weekend nights altogether.

UNIVERSITY OF ARIZONA
Campbell Ave. and 3rd St. (eastern entrance), Park Ave. and University Blvd. (western entrance), 520/621-2211, www.arizona.edu

Since it was founded in 1885 as the first institution of higher learning in the Arizona Territory, the University of Arizona's fate and that of its host pueblo have been inextricably linked. It's difficult to imagine what Tucson would be without the shady central campus. A land-grant school that has educated countless Arizona leaders and citizens, UA has nearly 37,000

THE MODERN STREETCAR

The **Sun Link Modern Streetcar** (tucsonstreetcar.com), a sleek rail system being constructed across several neighborhoods downtown, is expected to transform the Old Pueblo's downtown and entertainment districts—only it won't be complete until sometime in late 2013. If you happen to experience ripped-up streets and the dust-up of construction before then, just concentrate on the future, which will likely be grand.

The project will put seven brand-new railcars on the streets of downtown, 4th Avenue, Main Gate Square near the University of Arizona, and the so far mostly undeveloped Mercado district west of I-10—connecting all the neighborhoods to each other. All told the route will comprise about four miles. The streetcars, each with a 180-passenger capacity, will run the route every 10 minutes during the day and every 20 minutes in the evening, making 17 stops along the way.

© TIM HULL

New tracks await the arrival of the Modern Streetcar.

SIGHTS

© TIM HULL

Arizona State Museum

students (more than the number of residents of most Arizona towns). Not surprisingly, the school is world-renowned for its arid land research, and it has an allopathic medical school founded by best-selling healer-doctor Andrew Weil. It's also the place where anthropology, archaeology, and many other disciplines were revolutionized through the discovery of tree-ring dating. For more information on the campus, or to book a tour, stop by the state-of-the-art **UA Visitor Center** (811 N. Euclid Ave., 520/621-5130, Mon.–Fri. 9 A.M.–5 P.M.).

The university is also becoming known for contributing to the U.S. space program (particularly the exploration of Mars) in a big way. Check out the displays on the HiRISE Mars Camera, the Phoenix Mars Lander, and the Cassini mission to Saturn at the **Sonett Visitor Center** (northwest corner of University Blvd. and Cherry St., 520/626-7432, Mon.–Fri. 9 A.M.–5 P.M.).

Kids will enjoy the hands-on exhibits, laser shows, and sky-watching at **Flandrau: The UA Science Center** (1601 E. University Blvd., 520/621-7827, www.flandrau.org, Mon.–Thurs. 10 A.M.–3 P.M., Fri. 10 A.M.–3 P.M. and 6–9 P.M., Sat. 10 A.M.–9 P.M., Sun. 1–4 P.M.). Downstairs at Flandrau, you'll find the **UA Mineral Museum** (520/621-4227, www.ua-mineralmuseum.org, Thurs. 9 A.M.–3 P.M., Fri. 9 A.M.–3 P.M. and 6–9 P.M., Sat. noon–9 P.M., Sun. noon–4 P.M.), which has on display a wondrous collection of rocks from Arizona and beyond.

On campus you'll find a number of other museums and galleries, and the entire campus itself is an arboretum. Indeed, the green central campus claims to be the "oldest continually maintained green space in Arizona." Flora enthusiasts can stroll around the campus and take in a cactus garden, a collection of rare tropical trees, and various arid land species that have been brought to UA from all over the world. If you want to learn more about the campus's natural wonders, go by the **Campus Arboretum** at Herring Hall (520/621-7074, http://arboretum.arizona.edu, Mon.–Fri. 9 A.M.–5 P.M.). Don't miss the Joseph Wood Krutch Cactus Garden in the center of the campus's long, grassy mall.

There are also numerous public art installations on campus. One that should not be missed is the hulking border commentary called **Border Dynamics,** created by artists Alberto Morackis and Guadalupe Serrano.

It's not always easy to find parking on campus, and it's impossible during sporting events. Visitors can pay to park at the Park Avenue Garage at the corner of Park and Helen Street, and at the Main Gate Parking Garage at Euclid Avenue and East 2nd Street.

THE UNIVERSITY OF ARIZONA MUSEUM OF ART

University of Arizona campus, 1031 N. Olive Rd., 520/621-7567, www.artmuseum.arizona.edu
HOURS: Tues.-Fri. 9 A.M.-5 P.M., Sat.-Sun. noon-4 P.M.
COST: $5 adult, kids free

This worthwhile museum's permanent collection has mostly minor works by Tintoretto, Piazzetta, Goya, Bruegel, Rodin, Picasso, Hopper, Pollock, Rothko, O'Keeffe, and many more. Asian and Latin American traditions are also well represented. Special shows often feature the work of well-known local artists and artists from Mexico. The museum has an impressive collection of Spanish medieval art, the signature piece of which is the 26-panel *Retablo of Ciudad Rodrigo,* an altarpiece depicting the sweep of biblical events from Genesis, through the life of Jesus Christ, to the Last Judgment.

© TIM HULL

University of Arizona

SIGHTS

Midtown Map 3

REID PARK ZOO
1100 S. Randolph Way, 520/791-4022,
www.tucsonzoo.org
HOURS: Daily 9 A.M.-4 P.M.
COST: $9 adult, $7 senior, $5 child 2-14

Take Broadway Boulevard east to Randolph Way at Reid Park to Tucson's small but prestigious zoo. The zoo specializes in anteater research, and there are several of these strange beasts to look at here. Make sure to take the kids to the giraffe habitat, where for $1 they can buy some treats to feed the long-necked residents, who stick out their long, purple tongues, dripping with saliva, to capture the treat—much to the squealing delight of the feeders. A gift shop sells all kinds of zoo-related stuffed animals, shirts, and books, and a fast food–style eatery serves hamburgers, corn dogs, and the like. If you get there early enough you might catch a glimpse of the sleek black jaguars, sisters born at a wildlife park outside of Phoenix, lounging in the cool of the morning. The zoo is small enough that little kids aren't likely to get too tired out. Plan about three hours, less if you don't have kids.

◖ TUCSON BOTANICAL GARDENS
2150 N. Alvernon Way, 520/326-9686,
www.tucsonbotanical.org
HOURS: Daily 8:30 A.M.-4:30 P.M.
COST: $13 adult, $7.50 child 4-12

Gardeners and anybody who appreciates beauty should stop at this midtown oasis for a few hours. Flat walking trails wind around the nearly six-acre property, which feels secluded and hidden away even though it's right in the path of busy midtown. There are benches throughout on which to sit and contemplate the various gardens—16 in all, each one showcasing a different gardening tradition. Especially lovely is the Mexican-influenced garden,

Nuestro Jardín (Our Garden), with its shrine of the Virgin of Guadalupe and found items. A cactus and succulent garden has examples of cacti not just from the nearby deserts but also from around the world, and the xeriscape garden demonstrates how you can grow desert-adapted plants without using a lot of water. If you go between October and March you'll get to see Butterfly Magic, a live tropical butterfly exhibit. Call ahead for times and availability.

Included in the price of admission is your choice of one of several tours of the gardens. Different tours are offered throughout the month, and not every tour is offered every day, so it's best to call ahead or check the website. The Garden Gallery has rotating art shows that can be viewed daily 8:30 A.M.–4:30 P.M.

© TIM HULL

Tucson Botanical Gardens

The Foothills

Map 4

◖ DEGRAZIA GALLERY IN THE SUN

6300 N. Swan Rd., 520/299-9191,
www.degrazia.org

HOURS: Daily 10 A.M.-4 P.M.

COST: Free

Images of Ettore "Ted" DeGrazia's sad-eyed native children are ubiquitous here, on mugs and Christmas ornaments and other such objects. A visit to DeGrazia's amazing foothills home and gallery, which he largely built himself, may help you better appreciate the artist. When you see the home he built, and get a close-up look at the more serious paintings that hang throughout the gallery—epic cycles about the Mexican Revolution, the "founding" of the Southwest by Cabeza de Vaca and his doomed companions, and the lives and traditions of the Tohono O'odham, to name just a few—you may conclude that DeGrazia actually created some of the most enduring impressionistic visions in the Southwest. A native of Southern Arizona, DeGrazia attended the UA and published his first work in *Arizona Highways* magazine. He went on to study in Mexico with muralists Diego Rivera and Jose Clemente Orozco. He died in 1982 at the age of 73, but the DeGrazia Foundation carries on his memory at the Gallery in the Sun, DeGrazia's first studio and gallery in Tucson, built in honor of Padre Kino and dedicated to Our Lady of Guadalupe. A mission on the grounds features DeGrazia murals, with a roof open to the sky. The gallery has a gift shop stocked with DeGrazia reproductions for sale. Even if you can't muster an appreciation of this admittedly overexposed artist's work, go for the native architecture and design to be found at his Gallery in the Sun, which may, after all, be DeGrazia's greatest work of art.

© TIM HULL

The chapel at DeGrazia Gallery in the Sun is dedicated to Our Lady of Guadalupe.

SHUTTLE YOUR WAY THROUGH SABINO CANYON

If you don't feel like walking to the many popular trailheads in the Sabino Canyon Recreation Area, or if you don't want to walk up the paved road to see the upper reaches of the gorgeous riparian canyon, consider a ride on the **Sabino Canyon Shuttle** (520/749-2861, www.sabinocanyon.com, July-mid-Dec. Mon.-Fri. 9 A.M.-4 P.M., Sat.-Sun. 9 A.M.-4:30 P.M., mid-Dec.-June daily 9 A.M.-4:30 P.M., $8 adult, $4 child 3-12, free under 2). The shuttle runs 45-minute narrated trips into the canyon all day, pausing at nine stops along the way to pick up or drop off hikers at various trailheads. At the last tram stop, 3.8 miles into the canyon, hikers can get off and take an easy stroll down the road, crossing the creek at nearly every turn, or try the Phoneline Trail, which winds along the canyon slopes overlooking the riparian beauty below. Perhaps the most popular trail in the entire Tucson valley is the hike through nearby Bear Canyon to Seven Falls, a wonderful series of waterfalls and collecting pools. You can access the Bear Canyon Trail from just outside the visitors center, or take the shuttle to a trailhead 1.5 miles on. From the trailhead to the falls it's a total of 3.8 miles one-way, and worth every step. The Bear Canyon shuttle leaves the visitors center every hour on the hour (daily 9 A.M.-4:30 P.M., $3 adult, $1 child 3-12).

C SABINO CANYON RECREATION AREA
5700 N. Sabino Canyon Rd., 520/749-8700,
www.fs.usda.gov/coronado
HOURS: Recreation area daily sunrise-sunset;
visitors center and bookstore Mon.-Fri. 8 A.M.-4:30 P.M.,
Sat. 8:30 A.M.-4:30 P.M.
COST: $5 per car for one day, $10 for a week,
$20 for annual pass

Though in the range's foothills, Sabino Canyon is inextricably linked to the Santa Catalinas because without the mountains there would be very little water to fill up Sabino Creek, and without Sabino Creek this Edenic desert canyon would be just another rugged notch dominated by saguaro. As it is, though, Sabino Creek starts as springs high up in the mountains, gathering snowmelt and runoff as it descends into the foothills, where it rushes through Sabino Canyon with sometimes-deadly vigor, creating a riparian oasis of cottonwoods, willow, walnut, sycamore, and ash, while saguaro, barrel cactus, prickly pear, and cholla dominate the rocky canyon slopes away from the creek's influence. It is a truly spectacular place that should not be missed. Sabino Canyon Recreation Area, about 13 miles northeast of downtown Tucson, is easily accessible, user-friendly in the extreme, and heavily used—best estimates say 1.25 million people visit every year. Many locals use the canyon's trail system for daily exercise, and hikers, picnickers, and sightseers usually pack the canyon on any given day in any given season. A paved road, closed to cars since 1978, rises nearly four miles up into the canyon, crossing the nearly always-running creek in several places. During Southern Arizona's summer and winter rainy seasons, it is nearly impossible to cross the small overflowing bridges without getting your feet wet. It's a relatively easy walk along the road to the top of the canyon and access to trails that go far into the Santa Catalinas. The Sabino Canyon Visitors Center and Bookstore has trail guides and sells gifts and books. There are bathrooms, drinking fountains, and dozens of tucked-away picnic areas throughout the canyon, and many of the trails link up with one another, so it is easy to cobble together a loop hike that will take you through all of the various life zones. Bikes are allowed in the canyon only before 9 A.M. and after 5 P.M., never on Wednesday and Saturday, and never on trails that lead into the Pusch Ridge Wilderness. Consider a ride on the **Sabino Canyon Shuttle** (520/749-2861, www.sabinocanyon.com, $8 adult, $4 child 3–12, free under 2).

ST. PHILIP'S IN THE HILLS EPISCOPAL CHURCH

4440 N. Campbell Ave., 520/299-6421,
www.stphilipstucson.org

HOURS: Mass Tues. 10 A.M. and 6 P.M., Thurs. 11 A.M.,
Sun. 7:45 A.M., 9 A.M., 11:15 A.M., 4 P.M., and 5:30 P.M.

COST: Free

This church was originally designed in 1936 by Josias Joesler, a Swiss-born architect who designed the majority of the tony foothills structures and is responsible for the amalgam of native and revival architecture sometimes known as the Tucson Style. Joesler's structures can be counted on to mimic Mexican, Spanish, and Moorish styles with upscale flourishes, many of them stylish desertland haciendas on the bajada of the Catalinas, an area long reserved for the region's wealthy. A longtime Tucson architect once told me that Tucson, at least when it came to architecture, divorced itself from Mexico (and thereby Spain and its Moorish traditions) too quickly; these styles, with their courtyards and native materials and passive solar heating, are ideal for living in the hot, dry Sonoran Desert, certainly much better than the cheaply built tract homes that proliferate in the valley these days. Very few Tucsonans build homes in the Joesler style anymore (to do so, or to live in one that's already extant, is out of the financial question for most of us), and that's too bad, because Joesler, like the originals he was inspired by, had it right. St. Philip's, my favorite of all Joesler's structures in Tucson, is along the busy River Road corridor and yet retains a peaceful atmosphere with gardens and fountains and thick, silent walls. The building and grounds have been added to and changed over the years, but always with respect to the original vision. Church officials welcome visitors and students of architecture and anybody else who wants to look around. It's best not to go on a Sunday if you're just looking, and best to go before 4 P.M. weekdays if you want to talk to someone about the church and its history.

TOHONO CHUL PARK

7366 N. Paseo del Norte, 520/742-6455,
www.tohonochulpark.org

HOURS: Daily 8 A.M.-5 P.M.

COST: $8 adult, $6 senior, $4 student, $2 child 5-12

This 49-acre desert preserve is worth the short drive north on Oracle Road out into Tucson's sprawl. Turn left on Ina Road, and then right on Paseo del Norte, and you'll find native-plant gardens with easy trails punctuated by interpretive signs. The Ethnobotanical Garden, with rows of maize and other crops once planted by the O'odham and the Spanish settlers, demonstrates the different methods used by each group to coax subsistence out of the dry ground. Kids will love floating little boats shaped like fish on the miniature stream in the Garden for Children, where they can also see some old desert tortoises lolling about. If you stay quiet and sit by one of the many fountains or other water features on the grounds, you might get a glimpse of the many bobcats or javelina that call the preserve home.

One night a year, in June or July, the garden's night-blooming cereus comes to life, an event so rare and spectacular that there's a hotline (520/575-8468) for visitors to keep up-to-date on the expected bloom. There are gift shops and galleries on the property, and exhibits generally feature Native American and Mexican folk and fine arts.

West Side and the Tucson Mountains   Map 5

◗ ARIZONA-SONORA DESERT MUSEUM

2021 N. Kinney Rd., 520/883-2702,
www.desertmuseum.org

HOURS: Mar.-May and Sept.-Feb. daily 7:30 A.M.-5 P.M.,
June-Aug. Sun.-Fri. 7:30 A.M.-5 P.M., Sat. 7:30 A.M.-10 P.M.

COST: $14.50 adult, $5 child 6-12

A big part of the fun of a visit to the Arizona-Sonora Desert Museum is the getting there. Driving west out of Tucson over dramatic Gates Pass, you'll see thousands of sentinel-like saguaros standing tall on the hot, rocky ground below, surrounded by pipe cleaner–like ocotillo

© FLORENCE MCGINN/123RF.COM

a bobcat at the Arizona-Sonora Desert Museum

and fuzzy cholla, creosote, and prickly pear. But the saguaro forests of Tucson Mountain Park and Saguaro National Park West, both of which surround the Desert Museum, are only one of several distinctive desert life zones you'll see and learn about at this world-famous museum and zoo, where native mammals, birds, reptiles, amphibians, fish, and arthropods live in displays mimicking their open-desert habitats. This is the best place to learn about both the general structure and the minute details of the surrounding desert, and probably your only realistic chance to see all of the unique creatures that call it home. Easy trails wind through the beautiful 21-acre preserve, passing exhibits on semidesert grasslands and mountain woodlands similar to those surrounding and growing on the Sonoran Desert's high mountain ranges. The Desert Loop Trail leads through a lowland scrub and cactus landscape with javelina and coyote. In Cat Canyon, a bespeckled ocelot sleeps in the shade and a bobcat lounges on the rocks. A mountain lion can be seen close up through a viewing window, and a black bear strolls along a man-made stream and sleeps on a rock promontory. There are also

rare Mexican wolves, white-tailed deer, bighorn sheep, and adorable prairie dogs with which to commune. A riparian habitat has beavers and otters, water lovers that were once abundant in the Southwest. There's a desert garden exhibit, a cactus and succulent garden, and a butterfly and wildflower display. There are also displays on desert fish, dunes, and a walk-in aviary that holds dozens of native birds. Docents are scattered throughout the complex to help with questions and give presentations on special topics. All this, plus a restaurant, snack bars, and a gift shop that sells excellent Pueblo and Tohono O'odham crafts make the Desert Museum Tucson's very best attraction. If you're planning on doing any exploring in the desert, do so after a trip to the Desert Museum, where you'll get a comprehensive mini-course in desert ecology.

OLD TUCSON STUDIOS

201 S. Kinney Rd., 520/883-0100, www.oldtucson.com
HOURS: Oct.-May daily 10 A.M.-5 P.M.
COST: $16.95 adult, $10.95 child 4-11
Since 1939 Old Tucson has been the setting for more than 400 film productions, the majority of them Westerns. It was originally constructed

to make the film *Arizona,* starring Jean Arthur and William Holden, which tells the story of Tucson's early days before and after the Civil War. In the 1950s, impresario Bob Shelton bought the disused property and rebuilt its circa-1860s town, again drawing productions west from Hollywood, several starring Shelton's friend John Wayne. It remained popular as a movie set as long as Westerns were popular at the box office, and so went through boom and bust periods along with the genre. Shelton added gunfight shows and other family-oriented tourist attractions to ride out the lean times. Today a rebuilt Old Tucson (the town burned to the ground in the 1990s) concentrates on re-creating a movie-house version of the Old West for tourists. Make sure to check out the collection of vintage posters from the films produced at the studio. Tours talk about the history of the studio and the stars who walked its dusty streets, and musical acts and vaudeville-style revues go on all day. There are several restaurants on-site, including Big Jake's, which serves up good barbecue and beans, and El Vaquero, offering Southwestern-style entrées and a wide variety of specialty drinks. Unless you're a Western-film buff, Old Tucson is a little stale. If you're into the genre you'll find the film-related aspects worth a look. Kids might enjoy it, but the entry price is rather expensive for what you get.

◖ SAGUARO NATIONAL PARK WEST

2700 N. Kinney Rd., 520/733-5158, www.nps.gov/sagu
HOURS: Daily 7 A.M.-sunset; visitors center daily 9 A.M.-5 P.M.
COST: $10 per vehicle, valid at both sections

This is where the icon of arid America holds court. The split Saguaro National Park has a western section at the base of the Tucson Mountains and a larger eastern section at the base of the Rincon Mountains. Both are worth visiting, but if you have time only for one go to the eastern section, which is older and larger. Together they protect about 91,300 acres of magnificent Sonoran Desert landscape, including large and crowded saguaro forests surrounded by a thick underbrush of ocotillo,

prickly pear, cholla, mesquite, and palo verde. If you want to see an accessible and wondrous example of the Sonoran Desert at its best, there are few better places to go. The place to start your tour of the western park is the **Red Hills Visitor Center,** where you can learn about the ancient symbiotic friendship between the Tohono O'odham and the saguaro. Here you'll find a guide to the park's 40 miles of trails, and you can also book a tour with a naturalist and peruse the bookstore stocked with titles on local history and nature. A good way to see the park, especially in the heat of summer, is to drive the six-mile Bajada Loop through a thick saguaro forest. The route is graded dirt and it can get dusty; you can also walk or bike the loop. Or you can drive the loop and stop at the Valley View Overlook Trail, an easy one-mile round-trip trail off the loop road that rises to an expansive view of the Avra Valley, the saguaro-lined desert, and the skulking rock mountains. A half-mile round-trip walk to the Signal Hill Picnic Area offers a look at ancient petroglyphs. Both trails can be accessed off the Bajada Loop drive and are well marked. There are also a few very short, paved walks around the visitors center featuring interpretive signs about the saguaro and other desert fauna.

SENTINEL PEAK AND TUMAMOC HILL

Sentinel Peak: 1000 S. Sentinel Peak Rd.,
Tumamoc Hill: Tumamoc Hill Rd.
HOURS: Mon.-Sat. 8 A.M.-8 P.M., Sun. 8 A.M.-6 P.M.
COST: Free

Also called "A" Mountain for the large "A" repainted on its face every year by University of Arizona students (a tradition that began in 1915), Sentinel Peak served the early populations of the Tucson valley with spring water and black basalt. When Father Kino first rode into the valley in the 1690s, he found the native population living in the small peak's shadow, and it was surely an important landmark in the basin for eons before that. During the presidio days it earned its name as a promontory from which soldiers would scan the desert for Apaches. Now there's a park on the peak, reached by a paved, winding road to the top: Take Congress Street west under I-10 and follow the signs. There are a few short trails around the park, a little rock shelter to sit under, charcoal barbecues, and some great views of the valley. The hill just to the north of Sentinel Peak is called Tumamoc (horned-lizard) Hill, and is home to a living-desert laboratory founded in 1903. For thousands of years indigenous residents of the Tucson valley farmed on and around Tumamoc Hill, as evidenced by numerous archaeological sites found there. Among the legends of the Tohono O'odham is the story of a giant horned lizard that threatened to devour the tribe had not the god I'itoi, in response to prayers, turned the great reptile into a hill—hence the name Tumamoc Hill.

TUCSON MOUNTAIN PARK AND GATES PASS SCENIC OVERLOOK

Gates Pass to Kinney Rd.
HOURS: Daily sunrise-sunset
COST: Free

Robert Gates was a typical Southwestern frontier entrepreneur: He did a little mining, a little ranching, a bit of saloon keeping, some homesteading. In 1883, in order to connect his Avra Valley mine with his other interests in Tucson, he set about building a precipitous route over the Tucson Mountains, and in the process set the stage for local officials, about 50 years later, to establish one of the largest public parks of its kind in the nation. Thus we have the 37-square-mile Sonoran Desert preserve called Tucson Mountain Park. The 20,000 acres of wild desert features one of the largest saguaro forests in the world, and has something like 62 miles of trails for hiking and mountain biking. The park has a rifle and pistol range, and three large picnic areas with grills, ramadas, and picnic tables; also within park boundaries is the world-renowned

Sentinel Peak, also known as "A" Mountain

Arizona-Sonora Desert Museum. If all these activities seem a bit sweaty and active for your taste, at least make it to the top of the road named for the man who conquered the comparatively short Tucson Mountains at Gates Pass. You can drive to the pass and park at a large lot with bathrooms and a ramada and two little stacked-rock huts decorated inside with eons of graffiti. There are short trails out to a promontory from which you can see the whole sweeping expanse of the desert below. It's one of the best views in Arizona—a state that has no shortage of sweeping views. If you want to stay the night at the park, the **Gilbert Ray Campground** (8451 W. McCain Loop, off Kinney Rd., 520/883-4200, $10–20) has sites with RV hookups and picnic tables, plus restrooms and a dumping station.

East Side and the Rincon Valley   Map 6

TRAIL DUST TOWN

6541 E. Tanque Verde Rd., 520/296-4551,
www.traildusttown.com
HOURS: Daily 5-8 P.M.
COST: $2-3 for each attraction

The best way to visit Trail Dust Town, an Old West–themed family attraction on the east side, is to wrap it up with a cowboy steak-and-beans dinner at Pinnacle Peak Steak House. But if you don't have kids, rethink the entire

© TIM HULL

Trail Dust Town

venture. I'm not saying that there's nothing for the adult at Trail Dust Town; anyone interested in the more popularized notions of Old West culture might get a kick or two here—there's some movie set–style buildings, a miniature train that circles the property, a few on-cue gunfights in the dusty streets, and various shops and displays featuring touristy gifts and frontier artifacts. There's also a gold-panning game, a shootout gallery, and a lot of other commotion. If you have young or even youngish children, though, you and the spouse can sit in the saloon and wait for your table while the kids explore the attractions.

South Side
Map 7

PIMA AIR AND SPACE MUSEUM
6000 E. Valencia Rd., 520/574-0462,
www.pimaair.org
HOURS: Daily 9 A.M.–5 P.M.
COST: $15.50 adult, $12.75 senior and military,
$9 child 7-12

One of the largest museums of its kind in the West, the Pima Air and Space Museum has interesting exhibits and an impressive number of decommissioned aircraft that tell the story of our fascination with defying gravity. Nearly 300 rare airplanes, many of them military—among them Kennedy's Air Force One and the Blackbird spy plane—rest on the grounds and in six different hangars. The Air and Space Museum is operated by the same group that operates the Titan Missile Museum near Green Valley, and for one price you can see both attractions. Warplane enthusiasts will have to take the hour-long bus tour to the Aerospace Maintenance and Regeneration Center (AMARC) to see the hundreds of dust-gathering planes ending their days in this "boneyard."

Greater Tucson
Map 8

AGUA LINDA FARM

2643 E. Frontage Rd., Amado, 520/398-3218,
www.agualindafarm.net
HOURS: By reservation only
COST: Free except during festivals

A local leader in the Community Supported Agriculture movement, this small riverside farm in the lush Santa Cruz Valley south of Tucson sells fresh seasonal crops from a farm store open on weekends. The family-owned farm also puts on several festivals throughout the year, including one in fall involving pumpkin patches and hayrides. There isn't always something going on at Agua Linda, and often the farm is used for private events like weddings. If you're interested in looking around and touring the farm, picking your own vegetables, and generally communing with the fertile land, check the farm's website to make sure there's something happening.

BIOSPHERE 2

32540 S. Biosphere Rd., Oracle, 520/838-6200,
www.b2science.org
HOURS: Daily 9 A.M.–4 P.M.
COST: $20 adult, $13 child 6-12

In the early 1990s eight scientists took up residence in this 3.14-acre simulation of the earth in hopes of lasting two years and gaining important knowledge about how humans will survive in the future. They weren't able to remain self-contained owing to problems with the food supply, but two members of the team fell in love at least.

The unique laboratory may yet save the world, however, as the UA is now running experiments under the dome and researching ways to combat climate change. While the science is fascinating—there are actually small savannas, rainforests, deserts, and even an ocean under the glass—many who take the tour seem more intrigued by the doomed experiments

Biosphere 2

© TIM HULL

in togetherness. The tour takes you into the "Biospherians'" apartments and kitchen, and guides field more questions on this part of the tour than all the others. The tour lasts about 45 minutes and is not wheelchair-accessible. The Biosphere is in a beautiful 35-acre desert setting about 30 minutes north of Tucson near the small town of Oracle.

BUENOS AIRES NATIONAL WILDLIFE REFUGE

Hwy. 286, milepost 7.5, Sasabe, 520/823-4251, ext. 116, www.fws.gov/refuge/Buenos_Aires

HOURS: Refuge: daily 24 hours; visitors center: June 1-Aug. 15 Mon.-Fri. 7:30 A.M.-4 P.M., Aug. 16-May 31 daily 7:30 A.M.-4 P.M.

COST: Free

This remote 118,000-acre refuge preserves large swaths of endangered semidesert grassland, home to the pronghorn. The refuge's flagship program was once the reintroduction of the rare masked bobwhite quail to the grasslands, but the program was transferred to a private organization in 2007. Its proximity to the U.S.-Mexico border has caused some trouble on the refuge, and portions are indefinitely closed to the public because of smuggling activity. One of the most accessible portions of the refuge is the Arivaca Cienega, a swamplike desert wetland just outside the tiny village of Arivaca. The easy two-mile loop trail includes boardwalks over the wetter portions, and birds, frogs, and snakes abound. Take Arivaca Road about 20 miles from I-19 exit 48 until you see the sign for the Cienega, just east of Arivaca. At the western end of town, turn at the Y and drive 2.5 miles to Arivaca Creek, also managed by the refuge, where there's easy creekside hiking among cottonwoods and mesquite. Keep on Arivaca Road to Highway 286 and turn left at milepost 7.5 to get to refuge headquarters. Far off to the northwest in the Baboquivari Mountains is Brown Canyon, a riparian area accessible only with a guide and by appointment.

CATALINA STATE PARK

11570 N. Oracle Rd., Oro Valley, 520/628-5798, www.azstateparks.com

HOURS: Daily 5 A.M.-10 P.M.

COST: $7 per vehicle

This popular desert preserve just north of Tucson (about 14.5 miles from midtown) in the saguaro-dotted north-side foothills of the Santa Catalinas is heavily used, especially on weekends—hikers shouldn't be surprised to pass large families carrying coolers and bags of chips up the trail. The 5,500-acre park has eight trails—most of them range in difficulty from easy to moderate—picnic areas, charcoal grills, and a small gift shop. It's an easily accessible place to see the desert, lush here thanks to the runoff and snowmelt that barrels down from the mountains through boulder-strewn washes. In the early spring and late summer there are many natural pools that fill up with runoff, some of them deep enough to be called swimming holes. The seven-mile Romero Canyon Trail will take you to an array of natural pools—and you don't have to hike the whole trail to get there. If you want to get off the beaten track a little, veer right about a mile into the trail near a bench and pick your way down into the wash, then head up the wash following a footpath that leads to some out-of-the-way, less-used pools. For an easy walk, take the 0.5-mile round-trip Romero Ruin Interpretive Trail to an ancient Hohokam site. The ranger station/gift shop has a guide to all of the park's trails, some of which link to other trails going all the way up into the mountains.

🅒 COLOSSAL CAVE MOUNTAIN PARK

16721 E. Old Spanish Trail, Tucson, 520/647-7275, www.colossalcave.com

HOURS: Mar. 16-Sept. 15 daily 8 A.M.-5 P.M., Sept. 16-Mar. 15 daily 9 A.M.-5 P.M.

COST: Park entry $5 per vehicle; cave tours $13 adult, $6.50 child 6-12

Sure it's a "dead cave," and certainly in recent years it has become but a poor country cousin to the living underground wonderland that is Kartchner Caverns State Park just a few dozen miles to the southeast, but Colossal Cave Mountain Park near Vail, about a half-hour drive through the desert east of Tucson proper, has many charms nonetheless. The cave has been used as a shelter, an altar, a hideout, and a tourist attraction by various bands of natives and colonists for the last 1,000 years or so, according to prehistoric artifacts and historical local newspaper accounts. In the 1930s the Civilian Conservation Corps built a few structures near the cave's entrance in that inimitable stacked native-stone style, and installed lights and railings through about a half mile of the sprawling grotto. The typical tour follows this route, while the guide narrates a general natural history of the cave with a bit of human history (including a tale of outlaws) peppered in. It's all very basic, but interesting and really fun, especially with kids. Those looking for a more adventurous route should check out the Saturday-night **Ladder Tour** (5:15–9 P.M., $45 with dinner, must be at least 12 years old and fit, reservations required), on which you'll shimmy and squeeze through passageways far off the tourist path in a helmet and headlamp. After the cave tour, there's a gift shop and a café and long views of the desert. A few miles down the road but still within the park, the 130-year-old La Posta Quemada Ranch offers more activities, particularly for children. In addition to trail rides and a gift shop, the ranch features a large sundial, displays on the cave and the CCC's work in the park, and a habitat for two old desert tortoises, Henry and Big Nasty. It's unlikely you'll see either tort unless you arrive in the morning, especially during the hotter months. There are plenty of shady and peaceful places to picnic here, and you can even camp if you make a reservation.

IRONWOOD FOREST NATIONAL MONUMENT

Avra Valley Rd., Marana, 520/258-7200, www.blm.gov
HOURS: Daily 24 hours
COST: Free

The long-lived tree that lends its name to this 129,000-acre Sonoran Desert preserve about an hour's drive northwest of Tucson is likely to appear a bit underwhelming to the uninitiated. The gray-green monotony of the surface-level desert tends to blur the vision, and one bushy little tree tends to look a lot like another. As it usually is, however, the truth is in the details. The ironwood, which can live 800 years or more, is an anchor for a deceptively busy desert ecosystem, providing shade and succor for a whole host of flora and fauna unique to the region. Like most of Arizona's BLM-monitored national monuments, Ironwood Forest is a vast and empty place, inviting to hikers and hunters and campers and other outdoor types. There's no visitors center, no campgrounds, no rangers. It is a perfect place for a long daytime drive through the desert on its dirt roads, which are mostly smooth and accepting of regular cars, although an SUV is best. More so than even Saguaro National Park, Ironwood is a place where the wild desert is there for you to discover—unvarnished, uncultivated, and unforgiving. It's not a good idea to venture out here in the summer. If you want to head out to this wilderness, the easiest way to see it is to drive slowly along the dirt roads that traverse part of the monument, stopping here and there to look into the details. The best way to do this is to take I-10 north to Avra Valley Road, then continue southwest on Avra Valley Road until it turns to dirt around the waste-pile remainders of the Silverbell Mine. Just follow the road through the monument, passing the mine, the Silverbell Mountains, Ragged Top Mountain, and Wolcott Peak. Take Silverbell Road out of the monument and back to the interstate. The whole trip could take all day if you stop often to look around. Archaeologists say that people have been living out here for about 5,000 years, though these days there's usually only campers and hunters hanging around this glorious desert outback.

MADERA CANYON AND SANTA RITA MOUNTAINS

Madera Canyon Rd., east of Green Valley
HOURS: Daily 6 A.M.-10 P.M.
COST: $5 per vehicle

Black bears, mountain lions, ring-tailed cats, deer, and too many birds to count call this sky island range home, where mining and logging once were legitimate pursuits but now outdoor recreation rules. The range's highest peak is

9,453-foot Mount Wrightson. Most visitors to the Santa Ritas head to Madera Canyon and its trails to the peak's summit. A classic example of the kind of pine-oak woodland that grows in the sky island regions, Madera Canyon is the part-time home to many subtropical bird species that stop off on their migrations north to mate along a cool mountain creek in conditions not dissimilar from more tropical climes to the south. Consequently the canyon is a kind of mecca for serious bird-watchers fulfilling their life lists. It is one of a very few places in North America that one can see the fat green-and-red elegant trogan, a relative of the quetzal and the source of much thrill and consternation for birders visiting from points far away. The great variety of hummingbird species flitting about the canyon also draws visitors from far and wide. A paved two-lane leads from the desert floor up to about 6,000 feet, where well-used and relatively steep trails climb the slopes of Mount Wrightson all the way to its bare and rocky peak. During the summer rainy season, the usually small Madera

Creek becomes a torrent. The average summertime temperature in the canyon is about 85°F, about 15 to 20 degrees cooler on any given summer day than it is down in the valley. It gets cold in the high country October–April, and it regularly snows up there in deep winter. Madera Canyon is an extremely popular day-use area and hiking destination for Tucson and Santa Cruz Valley residents, so expect to see quite a few people on the trails and using the three developed picnic areas, all of which have tables, charcoal grills, and bathrooms. You can pick up a trail map at any of the lodges in the canyon, or you can get one at the welcome station at the canyon's entrance, but it is staffed irregularly.

◀ MISSION SAN XAVIER DEL BAC

1950 W. San Xavier Rd., Tucson, 520/294-2624, www.sanxaviermission.org

HOURS: Daily 7 A.M.–5 P.M.

COST: Free; donations encouraged

Founded in 1692 by Father Eusebio Francisco Kino and then built slowly over decades by

© TIM HULL

Mission San Xavier del Bac, the "white dove of the desert"

other priests, missionaries, and natives, the mission sits pure white against the perpetually blue sky about nine miles south of Tucson on the Tohono O'odham's San Xavier Indian Reservation. It is considered by many to be the foremost example of mission architecture remaining in the United States, blending elements of Moorish, Byzantine, and late Mexican Renaissance architecture. Few Arizona landmarks have received as much worldwide attention as the "white dove of the desert," which has also been called America's answer to the Sistine Chapel. Mass is still celebrated daily in the church (check website for times), but non-Catholic visitors are encouraged and welcomed. Most days there are tables and booths set up in the mission's plaza selling burritos, fry bread, and other delicious eats, and across the wide plaza to the south is San Xavier Plaza, with a snack bar and several shops selling Native American crafts. Statues and paintings of St. Francis Xavier and the Virgin of Guadalupe decorate the cool, dark interior of the domed church. A continuous videotape about the mission runs throughout the day as a self-guided tour, and there's a gift shop on-site that sells religious items and books about the history of the mission and the region. A small museum presents the history of the area's native inhabitants and the construction and ongoing rehabilitation of the mission. The mission is continually being worked on, but the seemingly ever-present scaffolding doesn't detract too much from its grandeur. In late 2008 the front of the mission was finally revealed again after years of being covered with scaffolding.

MOUNT HOPKINS FRED LAWRENCE WHIPPLE OBSERVATORY

Mount Hopkins Rd., Amado, 520/670-5707, www.sao.arizona.edu/FLWO/whipple.html
HOURS: Mon.-Fri 8:30 A.M.-4:30 P.M.
COST: $7 adult, $2.50 child 6-12

The Smithsonian Institution operates this observatory atop 8,550-foot Mount Hopkins, where astronomers take advantage of the dark Southern Arizona sky to scan space for very faint objects. The MMT, the largest

single-mirror telescope in North America, is one of four you can see up close during a six-hour tour of the facility (mid-Mar.–Nov. Mon., Wed., and Fri.). It's a good idea to call far in advance for reservations. The visitors center near Amado has displays about the work being done on the mountain and the history of the telescope. No kids under six.

ORACLE

Hwy. 77 (Oracle Rd.) to the northeastern slopes of the Santa Catalina Mountains

This small historic town about 30 miles north of Tucson has a few historic buildings and a proliferation of high desert–dwelling artists. The **Acadia Ranch Museum** (825 Mount Lemmon Rd., 520/896-9609, Thurs. 4–6 P.M., Sat. 1–5 P.M., free) tells the colorful history of the ranch—once a sheep ranch and later a sanatorium for suffers of TB and other ailments—and the town, which today has about 3,500 people, many of them artists and other desert runaways. The **Oracle Union Church** (705 E. American Ave., oracleunionchurch.org) is on the National Register of Historic Places and is worth a look, as is nearby Oracle State Park. There are several restaurants, including a historic steak house, and even a few little bed-and-breakfasts if you'd rather stay out here in the relative cool of 4,000 feet.

ORACLE STATE PARK

3820 Wildlife Dr., Oracle, 520/896-2425, www.azstateparks.com
HOURS: Thurs.-Mon. 7 A.M.-5 P.M.
COST: $7 per vehicle

This small state park about 40 miles north of Tucson preserves about 4,000 acres of oak woodlands and rare semidesert grasslands. This is a great place to see the high desert, with a picnic and a hike on some of the 15 miles of trails within the park. The whole area was once a ranch, and the historic, architecturally thrilling Mediterranean-style **Kannally Ranch House** is preserved in the park and open for tours (Sat.–Sun. 10 A.M.–2 P.M.). There's probably not enough here to inspire a trip just to the park, but it should definitely be wrapped into a car trip north into Pinal County and the northeast foothills—a trip best taken in the summer, when the higher elevations here provide a welcome respite from the sweating lowlands.

PEPPERSAUCE CANYON AND CAMPGROUND

Six miles southeast of Oracle on Forest Rd. 38, 520/749-8700

HOURS: Daily 24 hours

COST: $10 per vehicle

If you're up for yet another dirt-road drive into the mysterious desert landscape, consider the easy and smooth—albeit dusty—drive six miles southeast of Oracle (about 40 miles northeast of Tucson proper) to Peppersauce Canyon and Campground. This beautiful riparian area, with shady cottonwood and walnut trees guarding an intermittent stream, has 18 camping spaces and is a good place for picnics and general creek-side rambling. If you go during the rainy seasons you might even see the creek rushing. The lushness of the riverine environment in the canyon is quite shocking

THE LEMMON ROCK LOOKOUT

Arizona still has 72 active or semi-active fire lookouts, meaning they are staffed at least intermittently, especially during fire season or times of high risk and emergency.

Only Oregon, with 106, and Florida, with 130, have more active fire lookouts than Arizona, according to the Forest Fire Lookout Association, a group that advocates for the preservation of lookouts and their traditions. What's more, Arizona has a higher ratio of active to standing lookouts than most states—72 active or semi-active out of 83 still standing. Contrast that with California, where 198 lookouts still stand but just 50 of those are active.

Only a small handful of lookouts classified as active are still staffed full-time for the entire fire season—roughly April 1 to September 1—and one of these rare huts happens to be lashed to a rock overhang in the Santa Catalinas above Tucson, overlooking the Wilderness of Rocks and beyond that the unfurled basin and range territory as far as the urban haze will allow. The Lemmon Rock Lookout, at 8,820 feet, has been occupied for about five months a year for going on 70 years. On the face of the 14-foot-by-14-foot lookout shack, the side that stares down on the vast pine and boulder land below, someone stenciled long ago the words No Diving, as if aware of the risks of so much war with oneself.

Fire lookouts like Lemmon Rock have been around, in one form or another, for a very long time, but they really started to proliferate in the 1930s with the advent of the Civilian Conservation Corps (CCC) and the U.S. Forest Service's all-or-nothing suppression policy.

Responding to several huge, unprecedented backcountry forest fires that plagued the nation during the first third of the 20th century, government foresters enacted the 10 A.M. policy, decreeing that every fire on public lands must be quelled by 10 A.M. the morning after its initial spark. The fire lookout was an integral component of that policy. There is still some debate about the scientific efficacy of suppression, and we are, in many ways, paying for it now with overgrown, drought-ridden forests just waiting for a slash of dry lightning or a tossed cigarette to molt and be reborn, in the process ripping through the million-dollar homes we build in the forest hoping old Smokey the Bear will keep us safe from nature's cycles. Around the same time as the lookout was first constructed, the stock market crashed and so too the job market, hence the birth of the New Deal and the CCC, which put thousands of out-of-work Americans in the national forests building trails, fire breaks, and, in some of the most remote areas in the country, fire lookouts. Lemmon Rock was built by a CCC crew in the early 1930s, replacing a more primitive lookout on Mount Lemmon that had stood since 1913.

You can take a look at the Lemmon Rock Lookout for yourself, and, during the summer months, even sit down and have a high-altitude chat with the friendly current occupant of the little hut. To get there, drive up the Sky Island Scenic Byway to Ski Valley and park at the trailhead parking lot at the top of Mount Lemmon (keep going past the ski slopes and take the dirt road after the pavement ends). Once you park, pick up the short Lemmon Rock Trail.

compared to the aridity of the oak scrublands around it, making the bustling green life of the creek and canyon all the more inviting. There are a few trails around here as well, and if you're into mounting a larger expedition, you can drive to Peppersauce from high in the Catalinas along four-wheel-drive-friendly routes. Otherwise, coming from Oracle, you can reach the canyon in a regular old sedan. From Tucson take Oracle Road for 27 miles to Highway 77, then turn right and go 10 miles to the town of Oracle. Take the first Oracle exit and drive 4 miles through the tiny town to Forest Road 38, then on to Peppersauce Canyon.

REDINGTON PASS

Tanque Verde Rd. (at Wilmot and Grant Rds.) to Redington Rd.

Take Tanque Verde Road, which eventually turns into Redington Road, as far as it will go—until it turns to dirt—and you'll be in the pass between the Santa Catalinas and the Rincons, a wild saguaro-crowded desert with some dramatic views. Unless you're a hiker or a desert rat, there's not a lot to do out here, but it's a great place to look back on the city, especially at night with all the lights in the valley twinkling. One of the huge mansions you'll see right before the road turns to dirt (you can guess which one it is; it's fairly obvious) belongs to Sir Paul McCartney, and is where Linda McCartney died on April 17, 1998, with Paul and her children by her side.

ROY P. DRACHMAN AGUA CALIENTE REGIONAL PARK

12325 E. Roger Rd., Tucson, 520/749-3718
HOURS: Park daily 7 A.M.–sunset; visitors center and art gallery Nov.–Apr. Wed.–Fri. 1–4 P.M., Sat.–Sun. 8 A.M.–4 P.M.
COST: Free

Approaching the shock of wet greenery among the otherwise gray-green of the foothills, it's easy to see why this spring-fed oasis has been a popular spot for humans for the last 5,000 years or more. Now a 100-acre public park with a visitors center, gallery, nature shop,

and wildlife-attracting springwater ponds, the site has over the millennia been a stopover for hunter-gatherers and the farming Hohokam culture, as well as a ranch and a resort built to exploit the supposedly curative powers of the springs. Much of the vegetation here, as well as the fish and the log-lounging turtles you'll see everywhere, are decidedly nonnative. The shaggy palms, encircling the ponds like at some Spice Road camp, were planted long ago, but the 200-year-old mesquite tree next to the former ranch house, a tree that hosts a whole eco-system of its own, is native to the area and one of the oldest mesquites in the valley. This is a contemplative, peaceful spot, a good place for a walk, a picnic, or a long talk by the 87°F ponds, with the lazy turtles listening in.

SAGUARO NATIONAL PARK EAST

3693 S. Old Spanish Trail, Tucson, 520/733-5153
HOURS: Daily 7 A.M.–sunset; visitors center daily 9 A.M.–sunset
COST: $10 per vehicle, valid at both sections

The eastern portion of Saguaro National Park is backed by the 8,600-foot Rincon Mountains. At the visitors center are a bookstore and exhibits about the desert. The easiest way to see this section is to stroll, bike, or drive very slowly along the paved Cactus Forest Drive, an eight-mile one-way road that begins at the visitors center and winds up and across the bajada. The desert here is gorgeous, especially after a rainstorm or early in the morning during the bloom months (Mar.–May and July–Aug.). There are more than 100 miles of trails here, including one that goes to Rincon Peak above 8,000 feet. The park's newspaper guide has a full description of the major trails.

SKI VALLEY

10300 Ski Run Rd., Mount Lemmon, 520/576-1321, snow report 520/576-1400, www.skithelemmon.com
HOURS: Daily 9 A.M.–4 P.M.
COST: $11-32

Just up a bit from Summerhaven and near the peak of Mount Lemmon, the highest in the Santa Catalina range, are the 22 runs of Ski Valley, the nation's southernmost ski hill.

FIRE ON FROG MOUNTAIN

The Coronado National Forest barred campfires and smoking in mid-June 2003, saying it would take just one careless spark to send flames surging through the brush-choked, bone-dry Santa Catalina Mountains.

But the precautions weren't enough to keep the worst from happening. On June 17, 2003, a hiker dropped a cigarette on the Aspen Loop Trail in the range's Pusch Ridge Wilderness. A month later 84,750 acres had turned black, and 333 structures, including much of the mountain village Summerhaven, had turned to ash. It cost $16.3 million to put the fire out; it was finally "contained" (stopped from spreading to new ground) on July 15.

At the fire's peak, some 1,270 firefighters and support workers battled the blaze, and half a dozen air tankers rumbled through great plumes of black smoke to drop their dark red fire retardant on the forest. The smoke, and at night the flames, were visible across Southern Arizona, especially in Tucson, where residents sat outside on hot nights to watch their mountains burn.

President George Bush declared the fire a federal disaster on July 14, and a month later he visited the Santa Catalina Mountains. By August 2, when the public was allowed back on Mount Lemmon to survey the damage for the first time, Summerhaven's residents had already started to rebuild, and later came a prom-ise of funding help from Pima County. Crews began mulching and reseeding the burned areas from the air before the fire was even out, and that rehabilitation would continue until the spring of 2004.

A decade later the mountain is alive with new growth, though it looks much different than it did before the fire. Especially on Mount Lemmon's upper reaches, trails lead through large stands of burned-out husks, and you can't help but get black smudges on your arms and hands if you lean on one for balance. Summerhaven promised to come back better than ever, though now the village, born in the 1940s, has a just-built look, where it used to seem like an inevitable part of the mountain environment. As everything in nature runs in cycles, Summerhaven may be just starting to look snug and lived-in again in another 60 years or so—just about in time for another historic conflagration.

A few months after life got back to normal in Tucson, a young college student was charged with making false statements to law enforcement. Police had questioned the young man about allegations that he'd been smoking in the area where investigators believed the fire had started, on the day it started. He originally denied the accusation, but then later pled guilty to lying to police. He was sentenced to six months of probation and 200 hours of community service.

The ski season runs, roughly, mid-December–early April in a very good year. But if you happen to arrive in "winter" and are expecting to get a few runs in, don't make too many set-in-stone plans. While the ski run does open from time to time and provides some acceptable skiing and snowboarding, it's not to be counted on. In late 2008, for example, it snowed up on the mountain, and the TV newscasters and everybody else in the valley headed up to play in the white stuff. About a month later it was 91°F on the valley floor, and there was not a patch of dirty snow left. My advice is to get your skiing in elsewhere; the chairlift, however, operates year-round, and a cool, refreshing, and scenic ride up to nearly 10,000 feet in August, while everybody else sweats or breathes in the packaged air in their office buildings, is one of the best rides to be had in Southern Arizona.

◖ SKY ISLAND SCENIC BYWAY

E. Catalina Hwy. to Summerhaven

HOURS: Daily 8:30 A.M.–4:40 P.M.

COST: $5 per vehicle

About 50 miles—an hour or so up a twisty, paved two-lane road—from the desert floor northeast of midtown, you're at nearly

10,000 feet. This two-lane road is known as the Sky Island Scenic Byway, a nod to the fact that the 10,000-foot forested peaks look like lonely islands in an endless dried-up sea. The trip, it is often said, is like traveling from Mexico to Canada in one short, scenic drive. Until the 1930s Tucsonans couldn't reach the cool heights in great numbers. But then former U.S. Postmaster General Frank Hitchcock called in some federal favors and secured money and convict labor to begin building a road into the mountains; the indomitable Civilian Conservation Corps eventually finished the job. There are dozens of trails on the range, and there are several public bathrooms, campgrounds, and lookout points. It's a good idea to stop at the **Palisade Visitor Center** (milepost 19.6, 520/749-8700), at 7,200 feet, which has trail maps, a bookstore, and displays about the mountain's ecology. To begin your drive, take either Broadway Boulevard or Speedway Boulevard east to Wilmot Road, which becomes Tanque Verde Road. Head northeast on Tanque Verde Road for about 10 miles and then turn left at East Catalina Highway, which rises into the Santa Catalina Mountains. At various points, East Catalina Highway becomes the General Hitchcock Highway and the Mount Lemmon Highway (the name most locals use for the route). The road ends at the tiny village of Summerhaven.

SUMMERHAVEN
End of the Sky Island Scenic Byway

People began building and buying cabins in this mountain village at 7,840 feet in the 1940s, and by the early 2000s Summerhaven had a wonderful sort of lived-in look that made it especially romantic to desert dwellers. It burned down in the summer of 2003 after a careless hiker left a cigarette burning. That which burned was soon rebuilt bigger and better and newer; the oversized "cabins" on slopes cleared by wildfire don't provide the same aesthetic pleasures that the funky pre-fire cabins once did, but it's still a fun place to spend a few

hours looking around the gift shops and grabbing a bowl of chili or a hamburger.

◖ TITAN MISSILE MUSEUM
1580 W. Duval Mine Rd., Sahuarita, 520/625-7736, www.pimaair.org
HOURS: Daily 9 A.M.–5 P.M.
COST: $8.50 adult, $5 child 7-12

This deactivated missile site, one of several missile facilities that were staffed with underground-dwelling Cold Warriors in what was once referred to as the Titan Valley, had its Titan II aimed squarely at the USSR from 1963 to 1982. The site was decommissioned in 1986 and became a National Historic Landmark in 1994. The one-hour tour takes you deep underground, where volunteer guides, some of them former crew members, explain what daily life was like working at the silo. The highlight of the tour for many is seeing an actual Titan II waiting there in the launch duct. Guides also simulate the launch sequence that crewmembers hoped they would never have to complete. The visitors center provides context with a Cold War timeline and artifacts from the era, and a gift shop sells souvenirs and books.

TUBAC
Tubac exit off I-19

This small village along the Santa Cruz River is steeped in the history of the Spanish adventurers in Pimería Alta. Padre Kino established the mission at nearby Tumacácori in 1691, and Tubac, an Akmiel O'odham village, became a mission farm and ranch. By the 1730s Spanish colonists had arrived from the south to farm and ranch the fertile river valley. In 1751 the violent Piman revolt convinced the Spanish crown to establish the Presidio San Ignacio de Tubac, which was founded the next year. The famous Basque Juan Bautista de Anza II was the second commander of the presidio, and in 1776 he led the first of two overland journeys to establish a fort at San Francisco, California, taking along about 60 colonists from Tubac. In 1860 silver strikes nearby briefly made Tubac the largest town in the Arizona Territory. It eventually fell into obscurity but was discovered again as an artists' colony during the second half of the 20th century, and today its many galleries and shops are a draw for tourists and locals alike. Crowds flock to Tubac during the weeklong Tubac Festival of the Arts in February, during which artisans and artists from around the country set up booths and music and the smell of greasy, delicious food fills the village. **Tubac Presidio State Historic Park** (520/398-2252, www.pr.state.az.us, daily 8 A.M.–5 P.M., $3 adult, $1 child 7–13), Arizona's first state park, founded in 1959, preserves the history and foundations of the Presidio San Ignacio de Tubac. You can see the fort's original foundation and peruse a museum that explains what life was like for the natives, settlers, and soldiers. Guided tours and hands-on interpretation programs are available on request. The park's annual Anza Days celebration, around the third week of October, honors the fort's most famous commander with historical re-creations, music, and food. The Tubaquenos, a historical reenactment society, put on living-history demonstrations at the park (Oct.–Mar. Sun. 1–4 P.M.).

A good place to start your Tubac visit is the **Tubac–Santa Cruz Visitor Center** (4 Plaza Rd., 520/398-0007, www.toursantacruz.com, Mon.–Fri. 9 A.M.–4 P.M., Sat.–Sun. 10 A.M.–4 P.M.), just to the left as you enter the village by the big Tubac sign.

TUMACÁCORI NATIONAL HISTORIC PARK

Three miles south of Tubac, E. Frontage Rd., 520/398-2341, www.nps.gov/tuma

HOURS: Daily 9 A.M.–5 P.M.

COST: $3 adult, free for children under 16

Padre Kino founded the Mission San Jose de Tumacácori in 1691, and much of it stills stands today on this 310-acre national park. You can explore the mission and its grounds, which include an old graveyard, an orchard, and a re-created Piman shelter. A museum tells the history of the mission and Pimería Alta,

© JAMES MATTIL/123RF.COM

the graveyard at Mission San Jose de Tumacácori

and most days you can buy tortillas and refried beans made right before your eyes in the traditional fashion. A gift shop sells a wide assortment of books on local history. The mission at Tumacácori still holds masses on holidays, but the two other missions protected by the park are mostly in ruins. The ruins of **Mission San Cayetano de Calabazas,** normally closed to the public, can be visited on monthly guided tours ($10 pp); reservations are required.

MISSION TUMACÁCORI

When the Jesuit missionary Eusebio Francisco Kino visited the Akimel O'odham village of Tumacácori in January 1691, he did little more than say mass and promise the natives immediate and lasting salvation. But since he arrived there a day before he did the same in nearby Guevavi, technically the Mission Tumacácori is the oldest, though not the most famous nor most visited, Spanish colonial mission in Arizona.

In 2007 some 45,000 visitors walked the shady grounds of Mission Tumacácori. That's a far cry from the approximately 200,000 that flocked to San Xavier del Bac, its more famous and prettier sister to the north. But the experience at Tumacácori is very different from the still-living traditions available at San Xavier. It's as much about experiencing a long-lost landscape as it is about seeing a crumbling church ruin.

For many years the church was an adobe hovel on the east side of the Santa Cruz River, which back in those days flowed seasonally and gave the O'odham their lives. While the same river today flows north from Mexico past the same land, now it has surface water year-round; it's a few inches deep with reclaimed wastewater and high levels of E. coli and coliform bacteria, so much so that you wouldn't want to dip your feet in it.

It wasn't until after the coming of the Franciscans that construction on the church we can all visit today got under way on the west side of the river, in about 1800. Then the narrow adobe church with the fired-brick bell tower was renamed in honor of St. Joseph, Jesus of Nazareth's step-dad. In 1908 Teddy Roosevelt, who more than any other president saved Arizona from Arizonans, established Tumacácori National Historic Park.

To celebrate its momentous hundredth birthday, in early 2009 the park opened a new $400,000 museum. Eight years in the making, the museum is a long leap forward from the somewhat dusty early-1970s exhibits that used to tell the mission's history. One of the most striking elements of the new museum is a huge photo of the bajada stretching west from the Santa Rita Mountains; it has been digitally cleaned of the many homes that now dot the area, showing visitors what the valley looked like when Kino first saw it. There are also large digitally illustrated panels featuring photo-realistic scenes of native life along the Santa Cruz circa 1690; they reportedly took the artist two years to complete. The new museum is organized around three intricate wax-figure dioramas made in the 1930s that were part of the old museum but now seem fresh in their sleek new surroundings. And for the first time since 1840 a striking statue of Jesus is on display. In late 2008 the statue was returned to Tumacácori from San Xavier del Bac, where it had been kept for more than 150 years.

© TIM HULL

Mission Tumacácori

RESTAURANTS

The Old Pueblo's culinary scene is famously dominated by the ranchland comfort food available at the dozens of Mexican eateries in town, most of them serving classic variations of a cuisine formed in Mexico's arid northern states and on the hot, dry coastlines of the nearby Sea of Cortez. While such home-style Mexican food represents one of the most popular cuisines in America, in Tucson it has a kind of authenticity and diversity of taste that's available nowhere else—except perhaps just across the border, about an hour's drive from the city.

While you could spend a lifetime here eating carne asada, chiles rellenos, and enchiladas exclusively, you'd not only join the ranks of the obese but you'd miss out on sampling the work of some of the most creative, adventurous chefs and restaurateurs in the Southwest. The amorphous hodge-podge that is New American cuisine thrives in Tucson through an impressive array of mid- to high-end locally owned "Tucson originals," many of which combine spices, flavors, ingredients, and crops common to the borderlands with American, French, and other culinary traditions to create a new hybrid that goes by the inexact term Southwestern.

To be totally honest, though, when you've got year-round outdoor patio dining—with gentle heaters when it's chilly, and cold water–spitting "misters" when it's hot—and the sky above that patio is ever blue and clear, and the views from that patio are of looming high mountains and sweeping desert valleys, the

© TIM HULL

HIGHLIGHTS

LOOK FOR  TO FIND RECOMMENDED RESTAURANTS.

© TIM HULL

Hub Restaurant and Ice Creamery

Best Gourmet Mexican Food: Don't miss the creative and adventurous food at **Cafe Poca Cosa,** one of Tucson's top eateries, which is often featured in gourmet and lifestyle magazines (page 57).

Best Lunch with a Hug: At **The Little Cafe Poca Cosa** the music is loud, the servers kiss and hug their customers, and a bit of attitude comes along with some of the best chiles rellenos in town (page 58).

Best Creative Comfort Food: The **Hub Restaurant and Ice Creamery** downtown serves decadent fries smothered in prime rib and cheese sauce, shrimp and grits, chicken pot pie, and homemade ice cream (page 59).

Best Breakfast: Frank's, the Old Pueblo's best greasy spoon, has tasty and filling American and Mexican breakfasts that will definitely fuel you up for a day of fun (page 68).

Best Coffeehouse: Ike's Coffee & Tea serves a great cup of joe and offers free wireless Internet, delicious baked goods, and a perfect central location (page 70).

Best Late-Night Fast Food: Beans, meat, cheese, salsa, and tortillas–is there any better late-night menu? There's a **Nico's** on nearly every corner, and they're always open to serve the best Mexican fast food in town (page 71).

Best Vegetarian Food: Enjoy a tasty, expertly prepared, and inexpensive all-you-can-eat vegetarian and vegan buffet at **Govinda's Natural Food Buffet** (page 75).

Best Cowboy Steak and Beans: If you're hankering for a nice piece of mesquite-grilled meat, a big bowl of beans, and a festive, tourist-friendly atmosphere, there's no better place than **Pinnacle Peak Steak House,** a popular ranch-style family eatery (page 84).

Best Sonoran Hot Dog: Find out what all the fuss is about at **El Guero Canelo,** where they know just how to make northern Mexico's outrageously delicious variation on the great American street food (page 84).

Best Mexican Food: There's a reason why there is always a line to get into **Mi Nidito,** where you'll find classic Sonoran food cooked to perfection and colorful decor (page 85).

PRICE KEY

⑤ Entrées under $10
⑤⑤ Entrées $10-20
⑤⑤⑤ Entrées over $20

quality of the food in front of you often becomes a secondary issue. Whenever you can, barring something unlikely like rain or cold, ask to sit on the patio or in the Spanish-style courtyard—scores of restaurants here have them, and al fresco dining in, say, February is one of the great joys of desert living.

Downtown   Map 1

RESTAURANTS

You'll find breakfast, lunch, and dinner choices from all over the globe in the Old Pueblo's downtown and university district. Some of the restaurants downtown exist primarily to serve the lunch crowd in the business and government districts, but most of the best places keep the same hours as restaurants in other neighborhoods. If none of the suggestions given here appeal, stroll up and down 4th Avenue or head over to Main Gate Square; both areas have dozens of restaurants, one of which is sure to whet your appetite. I can't think of a single place in this neighborhood where the "Tucson Casual" dress code (shorts or jeans and whatever shoes you desire, including sandals—basically an emphasis on staying cool and comfortable and on active, outdoor living), or lack thereof, wouldn't be acceptable.

BAR AND GRILL
BARRIO BREWING COMPANY ⑤
800 E. 16th St., 520/791-2739,
www.barriobrewing.com
HOURS: Mon.-Wed. 11 A.M.-10 P.M.,
Thurs.-Sat. 11 A.M.-midnight, Sun. 11 A.M.-9 P.M.
The same folks that own Gentle Ben's brewery also operate this cavernous bar and grill and brewery in an old warehouse district just off downtown. It's worth a visit just to see the

building, an ancient Quonset hut–style warehouse. Barrio Brewing serves the same style of bar food and microbrews as Gentle Ben's, but the crowd is a bit older.

COFFEE AND TEA
SPARKROOT ⑤
245 E. Congress St., 520/272-8949,
http://sparkroot.com
HOURS: Mon.-Sat. 7 A.M.-10 P.M., Sun. 8 A.M.-9 P.M.
Sparkroot, a sleek multilevel cafe with an eco-hip sensibility and a burnished-metal aesthetic, is the only cafe in Arizona that serves organic, fair trade Blue Bottle Coffee. They also offer light, generally healthy fare, such as granola and yogurt, oatmeal, and pressed ciabatta sandwiches, all of them vegetarian. Stop here in the morning for a warm nut-butter and jam sandwich on a ciabatta and you're almost guaranteed to have a great day.

ITALIAN
CAFFÉ MILANO ⑤⑤
46 W. Congress St., 520/628-1601,
www.caffemilano.com
HOURS: Mon.-Wed. 8:30 A.M.-3:30 P.M.,
Thurs.-Sat. 8:30 A.M.-3:30 P.M. and 5:30-9:30 P.M.
Located on Congress not far from the Pima County Courthouse, this elegant and bustling

© TIM HULL

Sparkroot

Italian café serves breakfast, lunch, and dinner, offering pastries and coffee, omelets, pizza, salads, panini, bruschetta, and dinners like veal scaloppine and *pollo al marsala*. All of it is excellent and creatively prepared, and there are a few tables on the sidewalk out front.

REILLY CRAFT PIZZA AND DRINK ❸❸

101 E. Pennington St., 520/882-5550,
www.reillypizza.com

HOURS: Mon.-Sun. 11 A.M.-11 P.M.

Some of the most toothsome pizza in town is served out of this tastefully refurbished, 100-year-old building that once housed a former funeral home downtown. The restaurant kept the funeral home's name and sign but little else. With an urban-cool interior and sophisticated menu, Reilly is a standout in the ever-expanding downtown culinary scene. The "craft pizzas" have a thick-but-light, toasted crust and come with a variety of toppings far removed from the usual slice-on-the-corner variety (fennel pollen, truffle cheese, eggplant, fontina).

Reilly also serves extraordinary salads—the one with watermelon and goat cheese is truly something special—and pasta dishes.

MEXICAN AND LATIN AMERICAN
ALEJANDRO'S CAFÉ ❸

31 N. Scott Ave., 520/623-3277

HOURS: Mon.-Fri. 7 A.M.-3 P.M.

This ultra-casual Mexican eatery downtown claims to have the best burritos and chimichangas in town, and they may have a point. The deep-fried, enchilada sauce–drenched burritos are big and delicious here, available with various fillings (I prefer simple bean and cheese, but there's chicken, beef, green chile, red chile, etc.), and not as pricey as most other places (the most expensive chimi on the menu is $5.25). This is a popular lunch spot during the week for downtown workers and isn't open on the weekends. If you're in the mood for Sonoran-style Mexican food and you're downtown, this is a quick and inexpensive place to satisfy your cravings.

© TIM HULL

Alejandro's Café

CAFE POCA COSA $$$

110 E. Pennington St., 520/622-6400,
www.cafepocacosatucson.com

HOURS: Tues.-Thurs. 11 A.M.-9 P.M.,
Fri.-Sat. 11 A.M.-10 P.M.

Featured far and wide in gourmet and lifestyle magazines, Cafe Poca Cosa is one of the Old Pueblo's top two or three eateries. Reservations are basically required, and the menu changes twice daily. The day's specials are printed in English and Spanish on a chalkboard that servers take around to each table. The food is usually an adventurous, learned, and creative hybrid—a kind of gourmet Mexican food, created by Chef Suzanna Davila, a native of Guaymas, Sonora, Mexico, on the Sea of Cortez, that you won't find anywhere else in Southern Arizona. If you're looking for the usual enchiladas and burritos, this isn't the place. But if you want something on the far creative edge of Mexican cuisine—a much more varied style than most Americans are led to believe exists—then you must eat here. The interior is done up in a smooth, cool modernism with contemporary Latino art, including a print by the great Daniel Martin Diaz, peppered throughout.

EL CHARRO CAFÉ $$

311 N. Court Ave., 520/622-1922,
www.elcharrocafe.com

HOURS: Sun.-Thurs. 10 A.M.-9 P.M.,
Fri.-Sat. 10 A.M.-10 P.M.

El Charro serves what is probably the city's most beloved Mexican food, or at least it's always a contender. The food is excellent, especially the huge, filling chimichangas, a dish El Charro is often credited with inventing. The margaritas here may be the city's best. At least half the attraction is the little house the restaurant is squeezed into—spilling out onto a cool, verdant patio—which was once lived in by Jules Flin, a French stonemason who came to Tucson to work on the cathedral. The restaurant has a bar, ¡Toma!, with half-price drinks and appetizers (delicious Mexican favorites like cheese crisps and quesadillas) daily 3–6 P.M.

EL MINUTO CAFE ❸

354 S. Main Ave., 520/882-4145,
www.elminutocafe.com
HOURS: Sun.-Thurs. 11 A.M.-10 P.M., Fri.-Sat. 11 A.M.-11 P.M.

This small Sonoran-style café in the Barrio Histórico has been serving up home-style Mexican favorites since 1939. The food is top-notch and recognizable: enchiladas, chiles rellenos, carne seca, and the like—all of it expertly prepared. On the weekends there's often a mariachi group playing, and a lush patio out front is a perfect place for a long springtime lunch, with tequila perhaps. If you were going to check out the El Tiradito Shrine anyway, you might consider combining it with lunch here—it's right next door.

🄲 THE LITTLE CAFE POCA COSA ❸

S. Stone Ave. at W. Alameda St., no phone,
www.littlepocacosa.com
HOURS: Mon.-Fri. 7:30 A.M.-2:30 P.M.

Do you like loud music while you eat, waitresses who kiss and hug their customers, and a bit of attitude with your chiles rellenos? I would have said no to all of the above until I had lunch at this tiny café on Stone Avenue right in the heart of downtown. The food is so spectacular that I'd be willing to put up with just about anything to get the simple Mexican and Latin American fare at this beloved lunch spot. The food is unassailable, and the hugs and even the cheek-kisses are all right with a belly full of goodness. Make sure to tip big; a large percentage of everything made in this place goes to causes. They only take cash, no exceptions.

NEW AMERICAN AND SOUTHWESTERN

CAFÉ A LA C'ART ❸❸

150 N. Main Ave., 520/628-8533,
www.cafealacarttucson.com
HOURS: Mon.-Wed. 7 A.M.-2 P.M., Thurs.-Fri. 7 A.M.-2 P.M. and 5-9 P.M., Sat.-Sun. 8 A.M.-2 P.M.

A little French-inspired café at the Tucson Museum of Art, Café a la C'art is housed in a historic building with patio dining and serves the perfect fare for an art-and-lunch outing.

The best items on the menu are under the "Artistry with Bread" heading—a grilled eggplant sandwich with caramelized onions or a salmon club with chipotle aioli, both on fresh-baked focaccia bread. An inspired selection of salads is also on the menu, and the freshly made lemonade is worth the trip in itself.

THE CUP CAFÉ ❸❸

311 E. Congress St., 520/798-1618,
www.hotelcongress.com
HOURS: Sun.-Thurs. 7 A.M.-10 P.M., Fri.-Sat. 7 A.M.-11 P.M.

Inside the Hotel Congress downtown, The Cup is a popular weekend breakfast destination, as well as a perfect choice for lunch or dinner anytime. They serve an eclectic blend of American food with a dash of several ethnic traditions, jumping from hummus to nachos, with entrées like *borracho* (drunk) pork tenderloin, marinated in tequila and chipotles and served with a sweet-potato gratin, country green beans, and a red-onion marmalade.

CUSHING STREET BAR AND GRILL ❸❸

198 W. Cushing St., 520/622-7984,
www.cushingstreet.com
HOURS: Winter Tues.-Sat. 4 P.M.-close, summer Thurs.-Sat. 5 P.M.-close

On the edge of the Barrio Histórico, this family-owned place has been operating out of its circa-1860s historic building since 1972. It's a charming space, with garden patio dining available when the weather permits (which is most of the time). Cushing Street Bar and Grill is known for its carefully made mojito ($8), concocted with loads of fresh mint. Many of the entrées have a Southwestern flair—try the gulf tacos, with fish fresh from the Sea of Cortez, just a few hundred miles south. Reservations are recommended.

47 SCOTT ❸❸

47 N. Scott Ave., 520/624-4747, www.47scott.com
HOURS: Mon.-Fri. 4 P.M.-close, Sat.-Sun., 10 A.M.-close

Hidden away behind a nondescript storefront on downtown's Scott Avenue, this small bistro has a romantic, brick-walled patio that's lit subtly after dark. The menu is seasonally adjusted, but they generally serve a familiar but no less appetizing take on New American comfort food. To know what's going on here you need only order the phyllo-wrapped chicken—a juicy breast cased in toasted phyllo dough, stuffed with goat cheese and spinach, drizzled with a rich and hearty chicken jus, flanked by smashed potato cakes and sage carrots. It's a wonderful kind of deconstructed chicken pot pie. The charming patio is even better during the daily happy hour (4–6 P.M.), when you can relax at a small table in the cool of the afternoon (as long as it's Oct.–Apr.) and enjoy discounted orders of grilled bread and olive oil, house-made mozzarella, and distinctive cocktails like the Vagabond—a delicious and refreshing blend of tequila, agave nectar, lime, and orange bitters.

HUB RESTAURANT AND ICE CREAMERY $$

266 E. Congress St., 520/207-8201,
www.hubdowntown.com

HOURS: Sun.-Wed. 11 A.M.-close,
Thurs.-Sat. 11 A.M.-2 A.M.

This downtown favorite has a hipster style and the soul of a great American diner. The food

is certainly a few cuts above the usual countertop fare: fries smothered in prime rib and cheese sauce, shrimp and grits, chicken pot pie, warm lobster roll...So is the decor: white faux-leather booths, thick ropes like vines on the redbrick walls, upside-down house lamps hanging from the exposed rafters. There's a small bar off the long dining room, where scarfed and jerseyed soccer fans have been known to gather on occasion. Offering about 20 draft beers, with frequent emendations, and a rather long and encouraging cocktail menu, the Hub appears to support the glorious Southwestern tradition of daytime drinking with a daylong happy hour (11 A.M.–5 P.M.). And then there's the house-made ice cream, in all its varieties. I suspect there are many frequent patrons who have no idea that the Hub serves anything else.

JANOS DOWNTOWN KITCHEN AND COCKTAILS $$

135 S. 6th Ave., 520/623-7700,
http://downtownkitchen.com

HOURS: Mon.-Fri. 11 A.M.-2 P.M., Sat.-Sun. 11 A.M.-2 P.M. and 5-10 P.M.

Chef Janos Wilder was among the first local

Hub Restaurant and Ice Creamery

chefs to focus on reforming and repurposing regional ingredients and styles in the 1980s. He's credited with reimagining Southwestern cuisine, infusing it with French mechanisms and a New American ethos. His influence can be seen in restaurants all over the Old Pueblo. These days, Janos, who is something of a local celebrity, serves a creative, seasonal menu heavy with local and regional ingredients and strong links to the various flavors of Mexico, Italy, and Asia. The stylish street-side patio and open, modernist interior make this restaurant and bar one of downtown's best places to kick back, sample unique dishes, and toss back a few expertly made cocktails. The inexpensive happy hour (4–6 P.M.) menu has much to offer, including the JDawg, Janos' take on the Sonoran hot dog, with smoked poblano crema and pickled nopalitos; the fish tacos with cilantro cabbage slaw; and the Oaxacan fries, with roast pork, a distinctive Oaxacan cheese, and scallions. If you're lucky enough to be visiting on a Sunday when Janos offers his fried chicken special, you shouldn't pass it up. The crunchy pieces come stacked on top of a heap of rich mac and cheese with chunks of sausage.

LA COCINA ❸❸

201 N. Court Ave., 520/622-0351,
www.lacocinatucson.com
HOURS: Mon. 11 A.M.-3 P.M., Tues. 11 A.M.-10 P.M., Wed.-Fri. 11 A.M.-2 A.M., Sat. 9 A.M.-2 A.M., Sun. 9 A.M.-3 P.M.

A shady, secluded, and convivial little grotto in the Old Town Artisans block downtown, La Cocina offers outdoor dining and drinking at its best. Sit back in the enclosed, leafy courtyard and order up a plate of hummus, fish tacos, or a caprese salad and maybe one of the many specialty cocktails or revolving selection of draft beers from Arizona. (Recommendation: the Bloody Maria—a bloody Mary with jalapeno-infused tequila and homegrown vegetables). Most evenings local bands play in the courtyard, mostly in laid-back, acoustic style. The kitchen closes at 10 P.M., but they offer a late-night menu (Wed.–Sat. 10 P.M.–2 A.M.). Prices drop during happy hour (Tues.–Fri. 4–7 P.M. and Wed.–Sat. 10 P.M.–midnight).

MAYNARDS MARKET & KITCHEN ❸❸

400 N. Toole Ave., 520/545-0577,
www.maynardsmarkettucson.com
HOURS: Sun.-Wed. 11 A.M.-10 P.M.,
Thurs.-Sat. 11 A.M.-midnight; market, pastry,
and coffee service daily 10 A.M.-7 P.M.

This café, bar, and market in the refurbished old Southern Pacific train depot downtown serves some excellent sandwiches—the Cuban pork with garlic mayo, cilantro, caramelized onions, and grilled jalapeños captures the pan-American chic of the place perfectly. If you're a vegetarian, try the roasted eggplant sandwich with an olive tapenade—it'll change your relationship with the eggplant. The four-cheese mac and cheese is filling and tasty, and their

TUCSON'S FOOD TRUCK SCENE

The Old Pueblo's culinary pioneers—and there are many of them—have embraced the food truck revolution wholeheartedly. They are everywhere these days, and they often serve the best food around. There's **Animal Farm,** serving gourmet eats made with local and sustainable ingredients, or **Serial Grillers,** who sling drop-dead delicious meat dishes with murderous intent. Also, don't miss **Planet of Crepes** or **Trucking Good Cupcakes**—there seems to be an ever-expanding roster of these often cleverly named mobile kitchens. They are so varied that it's difficult to choose, especially when they are crowded together at some event. Why not get one of everything?

Check out www.tucsonfoodtrucks.com and www.tucsonfoodtruckroundup.com for updates on events and locations. The former has links to the Facebook pages of many of the best trucks in town, so you can find out where they're serving at any given moment.

© TIM HULL

La Cocina

creative pizzas are good anytime. The bar is cool and stylish and looks out on the railroad tracks. They serve their menu late into the night on the weekends.

SPANISH

CASA VICENTE $$

375 S. Stone Ave., 520/884-5253,
www.casavicente.com
HOURS: Tues.-Thurs. 4:30-10:30 P.M.,
Fri.-Sat. 4:30-11 P.M.

Though it was once owned by the Spanish Crown, the Old Pueblo these days clings to its Mexican roots more than its Spanish when it comes to culinary traditions; there aren't many places in town to sample the latest and greatest of the cuisine of Spain. Luckily Casa Vicente is here, offering a seemingly unending parade of tapas and other delights, with flamenco dancing, guitarists, and other entertainment all week. They also have an excellent wine list.

VEGETARIAN

CAFÉ DESTA $$

758 S. Stone Ave., 520/370-7000,
http://cafedesta.com
HOURS: Mon.-Sun. 11 A.M.-9 P.M.

This bright cafe on the southern edge of downtown serves exceptional Ethiopian cuisine, much of it vegan, and has a full coffee bar. Bring your own bottle of wine and a few friends and try the "vegan signature plate" ($30, serves up to three people), a sampling of several spicy and exotic vegan dishes featuring mushrooms, lentils, cabbage, onions, collard greens, spinach, and more, served with rice and the spongy Ethiopian flatbread, Injera (which is also vegan). If you have carnivores in tow, Desta also has flavorful dishes with beef, lamb, and fish.

TUCSON ORIGINALS

This big city that still thinks it's a small town has been, for at least the last 25 years, a regional leader in developing locally owned and locally focused restaurants.

And while the worldwide economic slowdown of 2008 sunk a few beloved local eateries (including one, Terra Cotta, which many considered to be a major local pioneer of the New American, Mexican, and French hybrid called Southwestern), there are still dozens of Tucson-owned eateries doing their part to make the Mexican food capital of the nation into an even more diverse and exciting place to fill up your stomach. Many of these locally owned eateries have gathered together in a group called Tucson Originals (www.tucsonoriginals.com), marketing themselves as the "authentic flavors of Tucson."

Just over a decade old, Tucson Originals now boasts something like 40 different restaurant members—eateries from the world-renowned, upscale **Janos Downtown Kitchen and Cocktails** to the decidedly, and proudly, downscale **Frank's/Francisco's.** There are typically Tucson Mexican joints among the membership, like **El Charro,** as well as restaurants serving cuisines developed far, far away from the desert, like **Ghini's French Caffe.** And, of course, the membership swells

with cutting-edge New American joints, where these days just about anything goes—Old Pueblo favorites like **The Cup Café, Barrio,** and **Acacia.**

Every year, since 2003, Tucson Originals has put on the exciting and flavorful **Tucson Culinary Festival** (www.tucsonculinaryfestival.com), a charity event that includes all kinds of tastings and competitions, including the Margarita Challenge to see who can make the best version of the Old Pueblo's signature cocktail. The final-night Grand Tasting ($85 pp) at the Loews Ventana Canyon Resort features food from all 40 or so members of Tucson Originals. The festival typically takes place over four days in early October, but you can sample the very rich and diverse Tucson culinary scene any time you're in town by patronizing one or more of the Tucson Originals.

Quite a few member restaurants are listed in this book; if you want to try others, check the Tucson Originals website or pick up one of their brochures—which has a map pinpointing the location of each member restaurant—at the **Tucson Visitor Center** at La Placita Village downtown (110 S. Church Ave., 520/624-1817, Mon.-Fri. 9 A.M.-5 P.M., Sat.-Sun. 9 A.M.-4 P.M.), or at most hotels and attractions around town.

University District   Map 2

BAR AND GRILL
THE AULD DUBLINER ❸❸

800 E. University Blvd., 520/206-0323,
www.aulddublinerpubs.com
HOURS: Daily 11 A.M.-2 A.M.

Corporate-bred Irish pubs have been popping up all over the Southwest over the last few years, and many of them have a pre-fab look that is somewhat insulting, like some kind of Irish World at Disneyland. For the patron who's looking for a bit of authentic atmosphere and a good pint of Guinness in Tucson, however, there's The Auld Dubliner at Main Gate Square. While it is indeed part of the recent

pub trend, it stands above the others with a deceptively worn-in and comfortable atmosphere (the wood interior was handcrafted in Ireland) and top-notch eats like fish-and-chips, bangers and mash, and curry fries. They've got the usual Irish pub beers on tap, including the always refreshing Boddingtons and the hard-to-find Magners Irish Cider. There's also a happy hour (Mon.–Fri. 3–6 P.M.). This is a perfect place to spend a day chatting and drinking, and on most Sunday nights there's a pick-up Irish music jam in a back room. The menu has a lot more to offer than pub fare, by the way, and this is a good place for a nice dinner as well.

© TIM HULL

The Auld Dubliner

FROG & FIRKIN ❺
874 E. University Blvd., 520/623-7507,
www.frogandfirkin.com
HOURS: Sun.-Thurs. 11 A.M.-1 A.M., Fri.-Sat. 11 A.M.-2 A.M.
This British-influenced pub has a front patio that's very popular with the college crowd at Main Gate Square. There's usually an acoustic set going down outside on the weekends, and the tables seem to always be full and festive. Come here for the beer—it has one of the most complete selections in town, with brews from all over the world, including the rare Belgian Lindeman's Framboise, and several hard ciders as well. Most of the beers are offered in bottles, but there's a wide selection of drafts here too. They have a full bar, plus pub food, pizzas, and burgers.

GENTLE BEN'S ❺
865 E. University Blvd., 520/624-4177,
www.gentlebens.com
HOURS: Mon.-Wed. 11 A.M.-10 P.M.,
Thurs.-Sat. 11 A.M.-2 A.M., Sun. noon-10 P.M.
Serving pub eats, burgers, sandwiches, and the obligatory Southwestern-inspired dishes, Gentle Ben's at Main Gate Square has been a favorite student and former-student hangout since the 1970s. While the food is more than edible, the real attractions here are the eight craft brews made on-site. The top three, from my seat, are the Red Cat Amber, the Tucson Blonde, and MacBlane's Oatmeal Stout, but all are excellent. On weekend nights when school's in session, both floors of Gentle Ben's are likely to be crowded with frat boys and other UA types.

BREAKFAST, BRUNCH, AND LUNCH
GARLAND BISTRO ❺❺
119 E. Speedway Blvd., 520/882-3999,
www.garlandtucson.com
HOURS: Wed.-Sun. 8 A.M.-3 P.M.; summer hours vary, call ahead
This small house on Speedway serves a wide range of mostly vegetarian ethnic dishes, but there's plenty here for carnivores to enjoy as well. The Garland is particularly popular as a

breakfast spot, and they make their own bread. I'd say they make the best Greek salad in town. The decor is eclectic garage-sale chic, and the waitstaff is hippie-friendly.

COFFEE AND TEA
CHOCOLATE IGUANA ON 4TH $

500 N. 4th Ave., 520/798-1211, www.chocolateiguanaon4th.com
HOURS: Mon.-Thurs. 7 A.M.-8 P.M., Fri. 7 A.M.-10 P.M., Sat. 8 A.M.-10 P.M., Sun. 9 A.M.-6 P.M.

A charming café, sweet shop, and gift shop on busy 4th Avenue, the Chocolate Iguana serves excellent coffee drinks and light gourmet sandwiches and salads (turkey pesto, black-bean salad, etc.) They also sell adorable, one-of-a-kind gifts and offer homemade candy and other treats in a relaxing and casual patio setting.

EPIC CAFÉ $

745 N. 4th Ave., 520/624-6844, www.epic-cafe.com
HOURS: Sun.-Wed. 6 A.M.-midnight, Thurs.-Sat. 24 hours

The best coffeehouse on 4th Avenue serves all the usual coffee drinks, chai, ice cream floats, and juices, plus homemade pie and other desserts, including many that are vegan-approved. There's an omelet bar on the weekends (8 A.M.–1 P.M.), and there's always a changing selection of soups, sandwiches, salads, bagels, and hummus plates. The café has free Internet and all kinds of comfortable couches and coffee tables, plus a few outdoor sidewalk tables. The crowd is a typically Tucson mix of the young, the hip, and the college crowd, with old hippies, assorted downtown artists, writers, musicians, and desert rats.

DELI
BISON WITCHES $

326 N. 4th Ave., 520/740-1541, www.bisonwitches.com
HOURS: Daily 11 A.M.-midnight, bar open daily 11 A.M.-2 A.M.

This small deli-bar on 4th Avenue has over-stuffed sandwiches, soup in bread bowls, and good beers on tap. It gets a little crowded around lunchtime and on the weekends, but is

worth the wait. There's a patio outside in the back that's pleasant on a temperate day. The waitresses here are usually hot-girl college students, and the service can be a bit indifferent, even condescending if it's really busy. Still, the food is great, and filling. If you're not a championship eater, consider ordering the half-sandwich-and-soup combo—that's plenty here for even the biggest belly.

GREEK
ATHENS ON FOURTH $$

500 N. 4th Ave., 520/624-6886, www.athenson4th.com
HOURS: Mon.-Sat. 4-10 P.M.

The best place in Tucson to find sweetbreads, spiced lamb, tzatziki sauce, stuffed grape leaves, baklava, and other delectable Greek offerings is Athens on Fourth, a longtime favorite temple for those of us who never met an olive-and-cheese plate we didn't love.

ITALIAN
BROOKLYN PIZZA COMPANY $$

534 N. 4th Ave., 520/622-6868, www.brooklynpizzacompany.com
HOURS: Mon.-Sat. 11 A.M.-11 P.M., Sun. noon-10 P.M.; slices served Fri.-Sat. 11 P.M.-2:30 A.M.

There's nothing better than a greasy slice of authentic New York–style pizza after a night of hitting the bars, and this 4th Avenue joint serves them late into the night (or rather, morning) on the weekends (Fri.–Sat. 11 P.M.–2:30 A.M.). The pizza here rivals anything you can find back East, and the meatball subs, calzones, and gelato are the best in town. If you're staying downtown, they'll deliver—even beer and cigarettes, not a common occurrence in Tucson. What's more, the little pizza place has recently gone solar-powered.

CARUSO'S $$

434 N. 4th Ave., 520/624-5765, www.carusositalian.com
HOURS: Tues.-Sun. 11:30 A.M.-10 P.M., Fri.-Sat. 11:30 A.M.-11 P.M.

The Zagona clan has been serving delicious

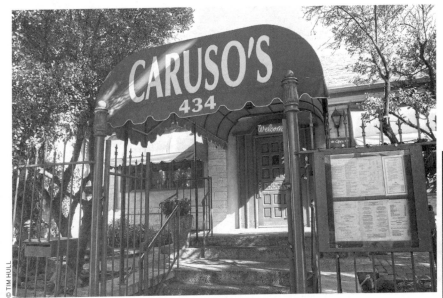
© TIM HULL

Caruso's

Italian favorites on and around 4th Avenue since 1938 (the original Caruso's was a block away from the current place). Shaded patio dining next to trickling fountains is the perfect way to enjoy the lasagna, pasta, and pizzas created here. It's nothing fancy—just well-prepared Italian favorites in a laid-back atmosphere with, of course, checkered tablecloths and fat bottles of chianti. There's often a wait to be seated on weekend nights, and you can expect to be eating alongside a lot of families.

MAGPIE'S PIZZA ❸❸
605 N. 4th Ave., 520/628-1661,
www.magpiespizza.com
HOURS: Sun.-Thurs. 11 A.M.-10 P.M., Fri.-Sat. 11 A.M.-11 P.M.

Magpie's has four other locations around Tucson, but in my opinion the 4th Avenue shop is the best. The pizza, thick and creative and cheesy—nearly to a fault—is a sure bet, having won the *Tucson Weekly*'s Best of Tucson poll every year since 1989. It's not cheap, but pizza lovers should not miss sampling this local legend.

1702 ❸❸
1702 E. Speedway Blvd., 520/325-1702,
www.1702az.com
HOURS: Mon.-Fri. 11 A.M.-11 P.M., Sat. noon-11 P.M., Sun. 11 A.M.-9 P.M.

This pizza joint on the western edge of the University of Arizona campus draws a mixed crowd of college kids, grad students hanging with their profs, and various lovers of beer in its natural state—that is, unbottled. The slices are huge and eminently satisfying here, and the wings are spicy and flavorful, but the real draw is the 46 ever-changing draft beers on tap at all times, many of them microbrews from California, Arizona, Colorado, and other western states. The service can get a bit harried, and it's often quite loud in the small space, what with all the good times that generally occur in the presence of outstanding food and beer.

MEXICAN AND LATIN AMERICAN
MAYA QUETZAL ⊙
429 N. 4th Ave., 520/622-8207

HOURS: Mon.-Thurs. 11:30 A.M.-2 P.M. and 5-8 P.M., Fri.-Sat. noon-9 P.M.

With so much Mexican food to choose from in the Old Pueblo, restaurants serving other Latin American cuisines tend to get forgotten, but not Maya Quetzal. This colorful eatery on 4th Avenue has been serving delicious Guatemalan food for more than 16 years. The small place opens up onto a shaded back patio with small fountains, and there's a mystic mural on one wall inside that conjures up the romance of Central America. The dishes typically offer a mixture of rice, black beans, beef and chicken, corn tortillas, and vegetables from the exotic to the recognizable. There are several vegetarian dishes, and sauces here tend to be creamier and less spicy than their Mexican counterparts. Make sure to try the cheesy "specialty rice"—a favorite of the house that you won't soon forget.

The B-Line

© TIM HULL

TOOLEY'S CAFE ⊙
299 S. Park Ave., 520/203-8970, www.tooleyscafe.com

HOURS: Mon.-Fri. 7 A.M.-4 P.M., Sat.-Sun. 7 A.M.-3 P.M.

Located in the Lost Barrio since 1989, Tooley's is a charming, laid-back, family-run place that serves up some of the best Mexican-style breakfasts in town, like corn pancakes with spiced black beans and jalepeño syrup and chipotle pork hash. For lunch or an early dinner, they've got their own versions of burros, tacos, and quesadillas, and a tortilla soup that will delight fans of the genre.

NEW AMERICAN
THE B-LINE ⊙
621 N. 4th Ave., 520/882-7575, www.blinerestaurant.com

HOURS: Sun.-Thurs. 7 A.M.-9 P.M., Fri.-Sat. 7 A.M.-10 P.M.

This café on 4th Avenue has huge breakfast burritos, a full coffee bar, and free wireless Internet. For lunch and dinner they offer soups, salads, and sandwiches, along with creative Southwestern-style burritos, quesadillas, and tacos, and some interesting pasta dishes. Everything is delicious, and the fresh ingredients are given center stage. Make sure to check out the art on the walls. The bar seating along the front window is a perfect place to kick back, watch the people pass by, and have a plate of fresh guacamole and one or more of the dozen or so craft brews on offer from California, Colorado, and Mexico.

DELECTABLES ⊙⊙
533 N. 4th Ave., 520/884-9289, www.delectables.com

HOURS: Sun.-Thurs. 9 A.M.-9 P.M., Fri.-Sat. 9 A.M.-2 P.M.

This bistro is a 4th Avenue institution, serving light, fresh lunches and dinners in the gourmet mode. My favorite sandwich is the jalapeño BLT on freshly made French bread. There are vegetarian dishes like the awesome asparagus crepes, and bistro plates with all kinds of top-shelf meats and cheeses and fresh fruit. After 5 P.M. they serve hearty dinners like rib eye, wild Pacific salmon, and chicken picatta, and they have a wide range of pasta dishes. They serve a good selection of craft brews and wine, and there's usually some fascinating, or at least intriguing, art on the walls, most of it by local artists.

PASCO KITCHEN AND LOUNGE 😊😊

820 E. University Blvd., 520/882-8013,
http://pascokitchen.com

HOURS: Mon.-Wed. 11 A.M.-10 P.M., Thurs. 11 A.M.-11 P.M., Fri.-Sun. 7:30 A.M.-midnight

Occupying a tastefully remodeled old building on shady Geronimo Plaza, along University Boulevard's Main Gate Square block, this charming New American restaurant and bar serves "Urban Farm Fare." That means designer comfort food with an ever-present Southwestern attitude, made from ingredients supplied mostly by farms, ranches, and food-artisans in Arizona. Try the amazing sloppy Joe sliders, spiced with various chiles and served with beans. They offer a separate vegetarian menu with excellent salads, pasta dishes, and panini. One could easily waste a warm fall afternoon sitting on Pasco's patio, sampling the extensive cocktail menu and

watching the college kids slouching to and fro. It's cheapest to do so during happy hour (3–6 P.M. weekdays).

SOCIAL HOUSE KITCHEN & PUB 😊😊

446 N. Campbell Ave., 520/747-5223,
www.soho-az.com

HOURS: Daily 11 A.M.-close

It seems a risk, mixing a foodist menu with a laid-back collegiate party vibe, but it works well here. Social House takes full advantage of its location right across Campbell Avenue from the University of Arizona's east entrance, but still manages to retain a certain elegance, if not peace. While you might be startled by a cheering crowd while biting into your local grass-fed beef, your pork belly and eggs, or your fish tacos, the bite will be sublime nonetheless. The best time to sample the creative pub eats and cocktails here is during the two daily happy hours (3–7 P.M. and 10 P.M.–close), when prices drop precipitously on a small menu of filling and flavorful plates, including an obligatory variant of the Sonoran hot dog.

SUSHI
FUKU SUSHI 😊😊

940 E. University Blvd., 520/798-3858

HOURS: Daily 11 A.M.-11 P.M.

Open every day, and late at that, Fuku Sushi is popular with the college crowd around Main Gate Square. They serve fresh sushi and traditional Japanese fare as well as their own creative signature rolls. It's a perfect spot for a quick light lunch or a long fish-eating, sake-drinking marathon.

VIETNAMESE
MISS SAIGON 😊

1072 N. Campbell Ave., 520/320-9511,
www.misssaigon-tucson.com

HOURS: Mon.-Sat. 10:30 A.M.-9:30 P.M., Sun. 11:30 A.M.-9:30 P.M.

This popular Vietnamese eatery just east of the UA campus packs them in for the best *pho* in town. The traditional noodle soup is served with the freshest herbs and bean sprouts and jalapeños on the side, and the spring rolls are

Pasco Kitchen and Lounge

© TIM HULL

light and delicious when dipped liberally in Miss Saigon's awesome peanut sauce. Think about getting the small bowl of *pho*—it's big enough, believe me. They also serve rich and decadent slushes with either coconut-jelly or tapioca, and other exotic desserts and drinks.

Midtown   Map 3

The restaurant scene in midtown, the largest neighborhood covered in this guide, is extremely varied. You can get just about any kind of food you desire, from American to Middle Eastern, Thai to Greek, Mexican to French, and more. If none of the suggestions here excite your senses, explore Campbell Avenue between Grant and River Roads; there are dozens of eateries in this section of midtown. You'll also come across scores of eateries, mostly chains, while driving along Speedway Boulevard, Grant Road, and Broadway Boulevard within the borders of midtown (roughly Campbell Ave., Wilmot Rd., 22nd St., and River Rd.).

BARBECUE
BRUSH FIRE BBQ CO. $

2745 N. Campbell Ave., 520/624-3223, www.brushfirebbq.com
HOURS: Daily 11 A.M.–9 P.M.

If you're one those people who can't leave a town without sampling its take on ribs and brisket, then you really have to visit Brush Fire, a small barbecue joint on Campbell Avenue. It serves what is arguably the Old Pueblo's best barbecue, offering mouthwatering meats with a choice of six different house-made sauces, including a very hot chipotle variety. The sides are exceptional (mac and cheese, slaw, corn bread, green beans, baked beans), as are the fries and potatoes, which can be smothered or stuffed with meat, cheese, and chili.

BREAKFAST, BRUNCH, AND LUNCH
BEYOND BREAD $

3026 N. Campbell Ave., 520/322-9965, www.beyondbread.com
HOURS: Mon.-Fri. 6:30 A.M.–8 P.M., Sat. 7 A.M.–8 P.M.
The two locations of this Tucson original serve delicious omelets and breakfast sandwiches

every morning, perfect for a relatively quick bite. They also serve fresh-baked muffins, coffee cake, sweet rolls, and all kinds of other delectables on the sweeter side of breakfast. They offer an assortment of the usual coffee drinks too. Prepare to stand in line, especially on the weekends. This is a great place for a casual lunch as well, with all kinds of creative sandwiches on fresh-baked bread. There's a second location in midtown (6260 E. Speedway Blvd., 520/747-7477), and one on the north side of town (421 W. Ina Rd., 520/461-1111).

BLUE WILLOW $$

2616 N. Campbell Ave., 520/327-7577, www.bluewillowtucson.com
HOURS: Mon.-Fri. 7 A.M.–9 P.M., Sat.-Sun. 8 A.M.–9 P.M.
Huge and delicious omelets, salads, and sandwiches can be had at the Blue Willow, which has been serving out of a cute old house with a large covered patio in Campbell Avenue's busy commercial district since 1978. It's best for breakfast (the apple-smoked bacon may haunt your dreams), but after 5 P.M. they serve entrées like black angus meatloaf. The emphasis here is on fresh, homemade, all natural, and just-baked. A gift shop sells funny stickers, buttons, and knickknacks about politics and gender issues. It's likely to be busy here on weekend mornings.

◖ FRANK'S $

3843 E. Pima St., 520/881-2710, www.franksrestaurant.com
HOURS: Mon.-Fri. 6 A.M.–2 P.M., Sat. 7 A.M.–2 P.M., Sun. 8 A.M.–2 P.M.
Frank's is the best greasy spoon in Tucson, and perhaps the greasiest. Their motto, displayed proudly on a roadside sign out front, is "Elegant Dining Elsewhere." You can sit at a rickety table inside or on the patio, or belly up

to the bar and watch your hash browns cook on the grill. The breakfast menu has all you'd expect, with the addition of Mexican favorites, which are highly recommended—there's nothing like getting all spiced up early in the morning. This small place draws a big crowd on weekend mornings, so have patience.

THE HUNGRY FOX ●
4637 E. Broadway Blvd., 520/326-2835,
www.thehungryfox.com
HOURS: Mon.-Fri. 6 A.M.-2 P.M.,
Sat.-Sun. 6:30 A.M.-2 P.M.

If you need a big old-school breakfast to get your engine running in the morning, you won't find one more traditional than the double-yolk eggs and biscuits and gravy at this Broadway Boulevard home-style eatery. The Hungry Fox's dining room takes country kitsch to a level that teeters on parody, but once you taste the food you'll know that this is a very serious restaurant, despite the decor. You'll likely encounter a crowd of hungry churchgoers on Sunday mornings, but there's a little gift shop in the waiting area to keep you distracted.

BURGERS
MONKEY BURGER ●
5350 E. Broadway Blvd., 520/514-9797,
http://monkeyburgerrestaurant.com
HOURS: Mon.-Thurs. 11 A.M.-8 P.M., Fri.-Sat. 11 A.M.-9 P.M., Sun. noon-7 P.M.

High-piled gourmet burgers in a casual setting—it's a rather simple concept that seems like a stroke of genius when you're trying to bite into your towering, inventive Monkey Burger. They offer a dozen or so signature burgers and a few not-so-usual sides (fried pickles, sweet-potato fries, roasted corn-on-the-cob), plus draft beer and thick shakes. There's a Boca burger on the menu for your vegetarian friends, but I recommend Madness: a thick, juicy patty topped with pepper jack, jalapeño slices, fajita peppers, and a Tabasco scallion aioli. There is another location downtown (46 N. 6th Ave., 520/624-4416, Mon.–Wed. 10:30 A.M.–3:30 P.M., Thurs.–Fri. 10:30 A.M.–8 P.M., Sat. noon–9 P.M.).

CHINESE
GEE'S GARDEN BISTRO ●●
1145 N. Alvernon Way, 520/325-5353
HOURS: Mon.-Fri. 11 A.M.-9 P.M., Sat. 10 A.M.-10 P.M., Sun. 10 A.M.-9 P.M.

One of the few options in Tucson for authentic dim sum, Gee's has a kind of gaudy faux-temple look on the outside, and its interiors are just as confusing and delightful. The dining room is huge and high-ceilinged and packed with so many red-draped tables that it somehow always feels empty. Nevertheless, the usual favorites are more than acceptable here, if a bit overpriced. The weekend dim sum is excellent, full of exotic dumplings and other teahouse standards.

GUILIN HEALTHY CHINESE RESTAURANT ●
3250 E. Speedway Blvd., 520/320-7768
HOURS: Mon.-Thurs. 11 A.M.-9 P.M., Fri. 11 A.M.-10 P.M., Sat. 11:30 A.M.-9:30 P.M., Sun. 11:30 A.M.-9 P.M.

Tucsonans, especially those who have recently migrated from the right and left coasts, are wont to complain about the city's paucity of good Chinese restaurants. And while I can't disagree entirely, I've yet to be disappointed by the food at this midtown fixture. It always tastes fresh and is never too greasy, and the menu is heavy with vegetarian options. I always leave those industrial "Chinese" super-buffets around town feeling sick from grease, MSG, and guilt. Leaving Guilin all I feel is rightly and correctly full.

COFFEE AND TEA
COFFEE TIMES ●
3401 E. Speedway Blvd., 520/318-3698
HOURS: Mon.-Sat. 4:30 A.M.-7 P.M., Sun. 4:30 A.M.-5 P.M.

If you can't be bothered to get out of your car but think you still deserve an excellent latte, get in line at this tiny kiosk along Speedway Boulevard (just across the street from Ike's). Along with top-notch coffee drinks, the friendly staff (who will, after just a few return trips, invariably remember your usual) will make you a panini while you wait behind the wheel. During the morning rush on weekdays the line of cars here can be quite long, but the crack staff usually whittles it down in no time.

CRAVE COFFEE BAR ⑤
4530 E. Broadway Blvd., 520/445-6665,
http://cravecoffeebar.com
HOURS: Daily 6 A.M.–11 P.M.

A delightfully sleek and Euro-sophisticated little spot for rest and respite amid the busy comings and goings along Broadway Boulevard in midtown, Crave offers a quick and efficient drive-thru window as well. But, despite its inner stylishness, ample seating, and free Internet, it's Crave's deep, complex, and inspiring coffee drinks that make it worth a stop every time.

◖ IKE'S COFFEE & TEA ⑤
3400 E. Speedway Blvd., 520/323-7205
HOURS: Daily 6 A.M.–midnight

I've never seen Ike's Speedway Boulevard location empty—or even thinned out, for that matter. One can seemingly visit during any of the 18 hours this sleek, locally owned coffeehouse is open every day and hear the gentle tick-tick-tick of patrons at their laptops. It's a popular place for study sessions, business meetings, and general chit-chat, owing to its excellent free wireless network, its open, cool interior, its very good coffee drinks, and a host of delicious fare, mostly of the breakfast and lunch variety. The downtown location (100 N. Stone Ave., 520/792-1800, Mon.–Fri. 7 A.M.–5:30 P.M.) has truncated hours, as it exists primarily to serve downtown workers and their banker's hours.

FAST FOOD
EEGEE'S ⑤
2510 E. Speedway Blvd., www.eegees.com
HOURS: Sun.–Thurs. 9:30 A.M.–10:30 P.M., Fri.–Sat. 9:30 A.M.–11 P.M.

A homegrown enterprise, Eegee's has been a favorite among Tucsonans for more than 30 years. The most popular items on the menu are the frozen drinks—a Styrofoam cup full of flavored shaved ice that goes down very easy on a hot summer day in the desert. My favorite flavor is still the one they started with: lemon. They serve excellent deli-style sandwiches—many of them hot—and French fries and other, similar fare. The ranch fries, a heap of sliced and deep-fried potatoes smothered in ranch dressing and topped with bacon bits, are a delight if you can risk the coronary. There are 21 of these Tucson-only joints throughout the city.

LUCKY WISHBONE ⑤
2545 N. Campbell Ave., 520/323-9329,
www.luckywishbone.com
HOURS: Daily 11 A.M.–9 P.M.

Deep-fried food, nothing more and nothing less—that's what you'll find at this nostalgic Old Pueblo favorite. They serve deep-fried chicken, steak fingers, shrimp, gizzards, fish, onion rings, fries, and some of the best garlic toast in the world. It's not exactly healthy, and you're likely to feel a bit grease-spritzed afterwards, but a "family feast" from Lucky Wishbone is certainly one of the guilty pleasures to be had in Tucson. The local chain has six restaurants. The other midtown location is at 10 North Swan Road (520/327-5679).

© TIM HULL

Ike's Coffee & Tea

LUKE'S ❸
4444 E. Grant Rd., 520/321-9236,
www.chicagolukes.com

HOURS: Mon.-Sat. 10 A.M.–9 P.M., Sun. 11 A.M.–5 P.M.

Luke's serves the best hot dogs in town—as long as you're talking about Chicago-style dogs. In Tucson, the famous Sonoran-style hot dog gets all the press, but lovers of Polish sausage, bratwurst, all-beef dogs with the red-hot works, and posters of Chicago-area sports teams from the 1980s and 1990s should not miss lunch at this spot. These guys fancy themselves traditionalists. I once asked them to hold the onions on my Chicago dog and got a look like I had just spit in the mustard. There is a second Luke's location at 101 East Fort Lowell Road (520/888-8066).

◖ NICO'S ❸
1855 E. Fort Lowell Rd., 520/327-3190

HOURS: Daily 24 hours

It's three in the morning and you haven't had an enchilada in nearly 12 hours. You can't sleep, and when you do doze off your troubled, shallow dreams are filled with rice and beans, guacamole, carne asada burritos, and chiles rellenos. Don't panic. On nearly every corner in Tucson there's a Nico's taco shop (or some similar joint that is usually passable but not as good in my view), and they exist to fulfill late-night cravings. The food here is a bit on the greasy side, but it is so tasty and filling and satisfying that nobody cares. Not surprisingly, you'll usually find the drive-thru crowded shortly after the bars close down.

GREEK
FRONIMO'S GREEK CAFÉ ❸
3242 E. Speedway Blvd., 520/327-8321,
www.fronimos.com

HOURS: Daily 10 A.M.–9 P.M.

This casual eatery along Speedway serves excellent gyros, souvlaki, lamb shank, and all manner of other Greek and American delights (including burgers and other sandwiches). The Greek salad is always crisp and fresh, and the baklava is a treat. They also make really good onion rings for those of us who care nothing about our bulges. There's a decent selection of Greek wines and beers as well. A gyro with fries or onion rings, hummus, or Fronimo's special rice pilaf makes for a filling, tasty lunch.

INDIAN
THE INDIA OVEN ❸
2727 N. Campbell Ave., 520/326-8635

HOURS: Daily 11 A.M.–2:45 P.M. and 5-9:45 P.M.

There's nothing better than a well-stocked buffet when you're really craving the outlandishly delicious cuisine of the world's largest democracy. In Tucson you'll find the best Indian buffet in this small, nondescript eatery along Campbell Avenue. The dishes are always well made, and the buffet is generally kept fresh and full; try not to fill up on the perfect naan and crispy samosas before you get some saucy, spiced-up goodness from the buffet's various traditional Indian meat, lentil, and vegetable dishes. You can order off the menu if you don't want to pile up a multicolored, multiflavored plate.

ITALIAN
ROCCO'S LITTLE CHICAGO ❸❸
2707 E. Broadway Blvd., 520/321-1860,
www.roccoslittlechicago.com

HOURS: Mon.-Sat. 11 A.M.–10 P.M.

It's no secret that half the Rust Belt migrates to the Southwest come October. This explains the diversity of Midwestern-style restaurants in Arizona, and Tucson is no exception. Chicagoans missing their beloved pizza styles will find their homesickness cured in this seemingly always crowded little joint along Broadway Boulevard. They serve up thin- and thick-crust pies, calzones, cheesecake, pasta, and sandwiches—all so good and authentic that they've been known to convince a few snowbirds to finally put down roots in the Old Pueblo. After all, why go home if the pizza's this good out West?

JAPANESE
SUSHI GARDEN ❸❸
3048 E. Broadway Blvd., 520/326-4700,
www.sushigarden.com

HOURS: Mon.-Thurs. 11 A.M.–10 P.M.,
Fri.-Sat. 11 A.M.–11 P.M., Sun. noon-10 P.M.

Sushi Garden offers an all-you-can eat lunch

buffet, and the sushi here is always fresh and delicious. The midtown location, at Broadway Village, has a comfortable, stylish patio and is sleek, modern, and artful inside. It's a fun place to take a group for sake bombers and appetizers during happy hour (Sun.–Thurs. 4–7 P.M., Fri.–Sat. 10 P.M.–close). There is a second location in The Foothills Mall (7401 N. La Cholla, 520/877-8744, Mon.–Thurs. 11 A.M.–10 P.M., Fri. 11 A.M.–midnight, Sat. noon–midnight, Sun. noon–10 P.M.).

YOSHIMATSU HEALTHY JAPANESE EATERY ❸
2660 N. Campbell Ave., 520/320-1574, www.yoshimatsuaz.com
HOURS: Sun.-Thurs. 11:30 A.M.-2:30 P.M. and 5-9 P.M., Fri.-Sat. 11:30 A.M.-2:30 P.M. and 5-10 P.M.

The owners of Yoshimatsu, the best Japanese restaurant in Tucson, took a disused building along Campbell Avenue that was once a chain family dining joint and turned it into one of the most stylish and popular eateries in midtown. The interior of this casual place is all dark wood, framed Japanese pop-art images, and big, secluded booths for sake parties among friends. The staff is young and friendly, and the food—a variety of popular, traditional, and virtually unknown Japanese dishes unparalleled in Tucson—is fresh, light, and tasty. There's also a warm wood-floored little sushi bar off the main dining room that's a great scene for couples and romance over half-price happy-hour sake and a tempura-fried Jalapeño Seven roll. And yes, of course, they have karaoke.

MEXICAN

BK CARNE ASADA & HOT DOGS ❸
2680 N. 1st Ave., 520/207-2245, www.bktacos.com
HOURS: Sun.-Thurs. 9 A.M.-11 P.M., Fri.-Sat. 9 A.M.-midnight

A recognized leader among the Old Pueblo's many purveyors of the Sonoran hot dog, BK's cozy midtown location is the perfect place to have, say, 30 or so of the bacon-wrapped, bean-heaped dogs, and maybe a few dozen carne asada tacos, and an indeterminate number of cold beers. BK also serves awesome Caramelos. Apparently a local creation, they're a sort of grilled tortilla sandwich, usually overstuffed with meat, cheese, chiles, and other staples. There is also a location in South Side (5118 S. 12th Ave., 520/295-0105, Sun.–Thurs. 9 A.M.–midnight, Fri.–Sat. 9 A.M.–2:30 A.M.).

FRANCISCO'S ❸
3843 E. Pima St., 520/881-2710, www.franciscosintucson.com
HOURS: Sun.-Thurs. 5-10 P.M., Fri.-Sat. 5 P.M.-midnight

Everybody in midtown knows Frank's, the small breakfast and lunch joint at Pima and Alvernon that lets diners know from the start that they'll find "elegant dining elsewhere," but after the sun retires Frank's becomes Francisco's, serving family-style Mexican food from the state of Michoacán. The food here is on the spicier side, and you'll always get a *cebollita asada* (grilled onion) with your dinner. Big plates of carne asada, *birria*, and *pollo asada*—all alongside heaps of rice and beans—are served here, as well as many shrimp dishes and the usual enchiladas, burritos, tacos, and tostadas, but with regional twists (pig's-feet enchiladas, anyone?) that you won't find anywhere else in town.

ROSA'S ❸
1750 E. Fort Lowell Rd. No. 164, 520/325-0362, www.rosasmexicanfoodaz.com
HOURS: Daily 11 A.M.-10 P.M.

I have generally found that the great Willie Nelson provides a perfect model for the Western man. That's why I started going to Rosa's: The red-headed stranger's autographed photos are plastered all over this small strip-mall eatery at Fort Lowell and Campbell. It's Willie approved, and that's good enough for me. The Sonoran-style dishes here are always cheesy, sauce-slopped, and delicious. Even though the restaurant has expanded, it always seems to be hectic and even chaotic at Rosa's, and the service can be either horrendous or perfunctory depending on how busy it is. The food, however, is unassailable.

MIDDLE EASTERN
ALI BABA ❸

2545 E. Speedway Blvd., Ste. 125, 520/319-2559,
www.alibabatucson.com

HOURS: Mon.-Sat. 11 A.M.-8 P.M., Sun. noon-8 P.M.

From this ultra-casual storefront in one of Speedway Boulevard's ubiquitous commercial strips comes the best Middle Eastern (including Lebanese and Persian) food in Arizona other than Tempe's Haji Baba. The falafel is crunchy and wrapped together with a perfectly balanced sauce, and the baba ghanoush is the best I've ever had. The Persian dishes are less recognizable to the average American, but no less tasty. Try any of the Persian kabob plates served with rice and tomatoes—though you risk addiction if you do.

NEW AMERICAN
THE DISH BISTRO-BAR ❸❸

3131 E. 1st St. (inside The RumRunner), 520/326-1714,
www.dishbistro.com

HOURS: Tues.-Thurs. 5-9 P.M., Fri.-Sat. 5-10 P.M.

This warm bistro and wine bar inside The RumRunner, a popular local wine and spirits shop, is famous for its mussels—a big steaming bowl of them floating in saffron broth with diced tomatoes and oregano. The "big dishes" served in this very small bistro are all over $20 and include duck, salmon, and New York strip creations. The "small dishes," best enjoyed with a glass of wine or two from RumRunner's large inventory, run $8–15 and include lobster tails and warm goat cheese with grilled bread. Reservations are a good idea.

FEAST ❸❸

3719 E. Speedway Blvd., 520/326-9363 (reservations),
520/326-6500 (current menu preview),
www.eatatfeast.com

HOURS: Tues.-Sat. 11 A.M.-9 P.M., Sun. 10 A.M.-9 P.M.

A local favorite, this midtown bistro changes its menus every month to take advantage of the freshest local ingredients. The inimitable cuisine that results is generally bold and surprising: pasta with lamb meatballs, chicken soft tacos drizzled with pumpkin seed and chili sauce, a seared Halloumi and honey-roasted

RESTAURANTS

© TIM HULL

Feast

eggplant sandwich—to pick one month at random. The cocktails here are particularly creative; try the Beet Poetry: beet juice, vodka, and limoncello.

KINGFISHER ⓢⓢ

2564 E. Grant Rd., 520/323-7739,
www.kingfishertucson.com
HOURS: Mon.–Fri. 11 A.M.-10 P.M., Sat.–Sun. 5-10 P.M.

A local favorite for fresh and ingeniously prepared seafood, Kingfisher has a thick oyster menu with something like 15 different varieties. For lunch the pan-fried shrimp cakes are awesome, and the gulf shrimp is always fresh and sweet. For dinner there's a selection of fish, scallop, pasta, and meat dishes, including magnificent baby-back ribs smothered in prickly pear barbecue sauce. The bar usually stays open until 1 A.M. or so, and there's a late-night menu of small plates. Reservations are recommended, especially on the weekends. There's also a daily happy hour (Mon.–Fri. 4:30–6:30 P.M., Sat–Sun. 10 P.M.–midnight).

LODGE ON THE DESERT ⓢⓢ

306 N. Alvernon Way, 520/320-2000,
www.lodgeonthedesert.com
HOURS: Sun.-Thurs. 7-10:30 A.M., 11 A.M.-2 P.M., and 5-9 P.M., Fri.-Sat. 7-10:30 A.M., 11 A.M.-2 P.M., and 5-10 P.M.

With Executive Chef Ryan Clark, Tucson's reigning "Iron Chef," at the helm, the restaurant at Lodge on the Desert has become one of the city's most esteemed eateries. The midtown restaurant and bar, deep within the confines of the boutique hotel's property, exude a kind of Old West, high-walled coziness that pairs perfectly with Clark's regional take on New American cuisine (i.e., mussels with grilled prickly pear cactus and shredded pork belly). Grab a table on the patio, near the outdoor fireplace, and if you don't mind paying $12 for a drink, try the "World's Best Margarita" (Penasco Reposado Tequila, Grand Marnier, citrus syrup, pomegranate jam and vinegar). It was named so in 2012 by the group Tucson Originals after an annual citywide contest. Prices drop during the bar's daily happy hour (4–6 P.M.), providing an ideal excuse to try

several delicious, surprising dishes and cocktails at once.

PASTICHE MODERN EATERY ⓢⓢ

3025 N. Campbell Ave., 520/325-3333,
www.pasticheme.com
HOURS: Mon.-Fri. 11:30 A.M.-10 P.M., Sat.-Sun. 4:30-10 P.M.

The very definition of New American, Pastiche is an upscale eatery along Campbell Avenue that dips into culinary styles the world over and dribbles its findings on American-based dishes. The results are typically excellent, and the elegant atmosphere makes you want to stick around for a drink or two. If you're out on the town late, stop by between 10 P.M. and midnight any night, when Pastiche's myriad creative appetizers—fried avocado, coconut shrimp, pot stickers, and much more—are half price. If you're a Guinness drinker, you might want to make a special trip to try the Guinness Steak ($15): ground steak marinated in Guinness, with porter cheddar, pepper bacon, Guinness gravy, and a fried egg on grilled sourdough.

SOUL FOOD
MAY'S COUNTER ⓢⓢ

2945 E. Speedway Blvd., 520/327-2421,
www.mayscounter.com
HOURS: Mon.-Fri. 11 A.M.-10 P.M., Sat.-Sun. 8 A.M.-10 P.M.

Serving soul food with a pinch of Southwestern spice, this midtown favorite can lay claim to one of the best meals in the Old Pueblo, whether it be morning, noon, or late at night: A few juicy pieces of peerless fried chicken on top of a rich, crisp waffle, all smothered in syrup and washed down with a bacon bloody Mary (with bacon-infused vodka). May's also serves a huge, gravy-smothered slab of country fried steak, a superior shrimp po'boy, and all kinds of Southern-style sides, such as mac and cheese (with jalapeños mixed in), collard greens, grits, succotash, and sweet potatoes. The Totchos stand out among several inspired South-by-Southwest fusions on May's menu—a gooey, cheesy mess of nachos with tater tots where the corn chips should be.

© TIM HULL

Old Pueblo Grille

SOUTHWESTERN

OLD PUEBLO GRILLE $$

60 N. Alvernon Way, 520/326-6000, www.metrorestaurants.com

HOURS: Mon.-Thurs. 11 A.M.-9 P.M., Fri.-Sun. 11 A.M.-10 P.M.

Ask five people what Southwestern food is and you're likely to get at least three different answers. To many, it's Sonoran-style Mexican food all dressed up; to others it's about recovering the lost food knowledge of the desert peoples. To a late-century Arizona-reared fella like me, Southwestern food was whatever my mom put on the table—usually something fairly predictable and "American" (chicken, fish, or beef, plus potato and veggie), but with a little extra spice. That's exactly what they serve at the Old Pueblo Grille. Make sure to try the chipotle mashed potatoes and the green chile mac and cheese.

THAI

KARUNA'S THAI PLATE $

1917 E. Grant Rd., 520/325-4129

HOURS: Tues.-Thurs. noon-3 P.M. and 5-9 P.M., Fri.-Sat. noon-3 P.M. and 5-10 P.M., Sun. 5-10 P.M.

This tiny Thai restaurant on Grant, just across the street from Bookmans, is not much to look at (and the staff can be sullen and perfunctory and even grumpy at times), but it serves a reasonably priced and delicious buffet of Thai favorites, plus a full menu. The pad thai, curries, and spring rolls here are as tasty as they get, and everything is kept relatively fresh at the buffet. This is a perfect budget-minded or takeout lunch or dinner spot in midtown.

VEGETARIAN

GOVINDA'S NATURAL FOOD BUFFET $

711 E. Blacklidge Dr., 520/792-0630, www.govindasoftucson.com

HOURS: Tues. 5-9 P.M., Wed.-Sat. 11:30 A.M.-2:30 P.M. and 5-9 P.M.,, Sun. 11 A.M.-2:30 P.M.

Some of the best vegetarian eats in town can be found at Govinda's, where on Thursday night everything is vegan, and on Tuesday authentic Indian food is served. Sunday brunch

(11 A.M.–2:30 P.M.) features pancakes, home fries, and scrambled tofu. The restaurant is located at the Chaitanya Cultural Center, and its name refers to one of Krishna's many incarnations; you will be among Tucson's Hare Krishna community here, in a peaceful and always friendly atmosphere that may spark a meditative mood—post-buffet, of course.

LOVIN' SPOONFULS VEGETARIAN RESTAURANT §

2990 N. Campbell Ave., 520/325-7766,
www.lovinspoonfuls.com

HOURS: Mon.-Sat. 9:30 A.M.-9 P.M., Sun. 10 A.M.-3 P.M.

I know a few vegetarians in Tucson who'd like to eat all their meals at Lovin' Spoonfuls: For breakfast it'd be a Southwestern tofu scramble. For lunch, a portobello griller or maybe a soy burger. For dinner it'd be the lasagna with mock Italian sausage. The atmosphere here is calm and friendly and homegrown in the best possible sense, and if you go once you will likely return again and again.

The Foothills   Map 4

In the foothills of the Santa Catalina Mountains north of midtown, you'll find high-end, high-concept eateries that define the cutting edge of Tucson's culinary scene. Nearly all the upscale restaurants in this neighborhood offer patio dining with gorgeous views of the valley and the mountains. While still casual at heart, the scene in the foothills requires a bit more dressing up than it does elsewhere in the Old Pueblo. You can still wear jeans, but maybe replace those flip-flops with a pair of loafers.

BREAKFAST, BRUNCH, AND LUNCH
MOTHER HUBBARDS CAFÉ §

14 W. Grant Rd., 520/623-7976,
www.motherhubbardscafe.com
HOURS: Mon.-Sat. 6 A.M.-2 P.M., Sun. 7 A.M.-2 P.M.

Don't let the dodgy strip mall turn you off of this unique diner on the corner of Grant and Stone. It's not in the most scenic part of Tucson, but the adventurous "Nahuan cuisine" and Southwestern comfort food served here for breakfast and lunch—huevos rancheros, green corn waffles, and a host of less familiar Mexican-Native American hybrids—go far beyond the usual greasy-spoon fare. Don't worry if there's only one culinary adventurer in your party; Mother Hubbards also serves more "traditional" breakfasts as well.

DESSERT
FROST §

7131 N. Oracle Rd., 520/797-0188,
www.frostgelato.com
HOURS: Mon.-Thurs. 11 A.M.-10 P.M., Fri.-Sat. 11 A.M.-11 P.M., Sun. 11 A.M.-10 P.M.

Frost, a decadent, perhaps even sinful gelato shop, offers what has become a favorite after-dinner treat here in the almost year-round desert heat. The clean, bright, and sleek shops are generally packed just after the dinner hour with overheated residents and visitors seeking authentic Italian gelato in a dizzying array of flavors. It's simply the best dessert around, a fact attested to by the local chain's recent expansion to Phoenix, Albuquerque, and even Chicago. There are two other locations in Tucson (7301 E. Tanque Verde Rd., 520/886-0354; 2905 E. Skyline Dr., 520/299-0315).

FRENCH
GHINI'S FRENCH CAFFE §§

1803 E. Prince Rd., 520/326-9095,
www.ghiniscafe.com
HOURS: Tues.-Sat. 6:30 A.M.-3 P.M., Sun. 8 A.M.-2 P.M.

In a tucked-away space in a strip mall at Prince and Campbell, Ghini's French Caffe and La Baguette Bakery bring a bit of French taste to the desert city. Breakfast is the café's claim to fame, served all day on Saturday and Sunday. Ghini's Eggs Provençale, a fry-up of tomatoes and garlic and eggs on a crunchy baguette, is known far and wide, and their omelets are probably the best in town. The lunch menu includes a slew of unique Frenched-up sandwiches and salads, but my favorite is the simple, delicious *soupe a l'oignon.* Every Friday 3–7 P.M. the café stays open for an "aperitif hour," during which they serve little plates of escargots, mussels, and other French favorites, and offer discounts on glasses of wine from their smart collection. They also serve appetite-whetting pastis and various dark and decadent desserts from the bakery.

MEXICAN
LA FUENTE $$

1749 N. Oracle Rd., 520/623-8659, www.lafuenterestaurant.com

HOURS: Mon.-Thurs. 11 A.M.-9 P.M., Fri. 11 A.M.-10 P.M., Sat. noon-10 P.M., Sun. 11 A.M.-9 P.M.

The airy, tropical interiors at La Fuente, a popular Old Pueblo eatery since 1959, add to what always seems to be a busy, festive air in this popular Mexican restaurant on Oracle just north of downtown, but it's the loud and brassy mariachi band strolling among the tables (Thurs.–Sun.) that really brings in the crowds. The food here is excellent, if a bit pricey; the fresh guacamole, prepared before your eyes right at the table, is among the best in town—and the atmosphere can't be beat. There's a champagne brunch on Sunday (11 A.M.–2 P.M.).

MIGUEL'S AT LA POSADA $$

5900 N. Oracle Rd., 520/887-3777, www.miguelstucson.com

HOURS: Mon.-Thurs. 5-9 P.M., Fri.-Sat. 5-10 P.M.

Not your typical Tucson refried bean–slingers, the chefs at Miguel's at La Posada, on Oracle Road, serve a more varied and intricately prepared style of south-of-the-border cuisine than the comfort food offered at most Old Pueblo Mexican restaurants. New Latin American cuisine, one might call it. That's not to say you can't get an enchilada here, it's just that it will be filled with wild mushrooms. You can get beans and rice too, only they'll be black

beans and creamy Oaxacan rice. The chile relleno is filled with fresh seafood from the Sea of Cortez; the Guaymas prawns are wrapped in bacon and slathered with a horseradish and brown-sugar sauce. Get my drift? They also have something like a hundred different kinds of tequila in their cozy cantina (the margaritas here are among the best in town), where they serve a limited but delicious bar menu all day. Reservations are recommended.

NEW AMERICAN AND SOUTHWESTERN
ACACIA $$

3001 E. Skyline Dr., 520/232-0101, www.acaciatucson.com

HOURS: Daily 11 A.M.-9 P.M.

Perched in the Catalina Foothills and outfitted with big windows looking out over the sprawling desert city, Acacia offers some of the best view-accompanied dining in Tucson. The seasonal dinner menus generally combine French technique, locally sourced ingredients, and a few regional nods. In the bar there's a host of surprising cocktails, and the long menu of small plates (from 2 P.M.) reveals precisely what's going on in Acacia's kitchen for a bit less than you'd likely spend on dinner.

FLYING V BAR AND GRILL AT LOEWS VENTANA CANYON $$

7000 N. Resort Dr., 520/299-2020, www.loewshotels.com/en/restaurants/flying-v-bar-grill

HOURS: Mon.-Thurs. 5:30-9 P.M., Fri.-Sat. 5-10 P.M., Sun. 5-9 P.M.

An admirable restaurant in an incomparable setting, this bar and grill at the gorgeous Catalina Foothills destination resort combines all the best elements of Tucson's dining scene in one place: awesome views, a romantic terrace, table-side guacamole made to order by a "Guacamoliere," and inspired comfort food with a dollop of Southwestern flavor (grilled prickly pear chicken sandwich, lime and tequila shrimp, etc.). This is a particularly good choice for a Friday or Saturday night, when they serve thick, flavorful prime rib accompanied by live music.

© TIM HULL

Acacia

THE GRILL AT HACIENDA DEL SOL ⓢⓢ
5501 N. Hacienda del Sol Rd., 520/529-3500,
www.haciendadelsol.com
HOURS: Mon.-Thurs. 7 A.M.-10 A.M., 11 A.M.-4 P.M., and
5:30-10 P.M., Fri.-Sat. 7 A.M.-10 A.M. and 5:30-10 P.M.,
Sun. 9:30 A.M.-2:30 P.M. and 5:30-10 P.M.

Tucson, especially its foothills, is known
for its year-round patio dining and sweeping views of the city, with twinkling lights
from the valley like signal fires in the dark-
ness below. The best patio out of them all is
the Terraza del Sol bar, inside The Grill at
Hacienda del Sol, a charming historic resort in
the foothills. Terraza del Sol serves a relatively
low-priced bar menu ($7–26) of creative small
plates, and features live music Thursday–
Sunday. Inside at the Grill, dinner consists of
entrées on the order of pork osso buco with
a bing-cherry shallot confit, and Tasmanian
ocean trout with a roasted beer-and-potato
carpaccio. You know, the usual. Reservations
are strongly recommended.

THE LOOKOUT BAR AND GRILLE ⓢⓢ
245 E. Ina Rd., 520/297-1151, www.westwardlook.com/
Tucson-restaurant/lookout-bar-a-grill
HOURS: Mon.-Fri. 2-10 P.M., Sat.-Sun. 11 A.M.-10 P.M.

Go for the views, stay for the food: The
Lookout Bar and Grille literally looks out on
the sweeping desert and serves superior, if familiar, grille fare (burgers, sandwiches, salads,
steak and fish entrées, etc.) The resort setting
in the foothills is incomparable, and this, the
Westward Look's casual restaurant, provides
the 99 percent a chance to linger without taking out a loan. It's even more affordable during
happy hour (Mon.–Fri. 4–6 P.M.) On Friday
and Saturday nights they serve prime rib ($22)
while a band plays.

UNION PUBLIC HOUSE ⓢⓢ
4340 N. Campbell Ave., 520/329-8575,
www.uniontucson.com
HOURS: Daily 11 A.M.-close

An upscale pub on the edge of the foothills,

Union Public House has outstanding food and one of the best patios in town, looking out on St. Philip's Plaza, with its shady trees and trickling fountain. Order a jar of brined pickles and vegetables and a mess of pub chips with blue cheese and pork belly. Down a few Moscow mules, the pub's signature cocktail, a delicious blend of vodka and ginger beer served in a copper cup. For dinner there's creative variations on comfort classics—the pot pie, chicken and waffles, fish and chips, burgers, and flatbread pizzas. During the nightly reverse happy hour (10 P.M.–close), they even offer a dressed-up corn dog that is far superior to, but still pleasantly reminiscent of, the county fair classic. Prices drop late night and during the "social hour" (daily 4–7 P.M.). There's even a Sunday brunch (10 A.M.–2 P.M.).

WILDFLOWER ❶❷❸

7037 N. Oracle Rd., 520/219-4230, www.foxrc.com
HOURS: Mon.-Thurs. 11 A.M.-3 P.M. and 5-9 P.M.,
Fri.-Sat. 11 A.M.-3 P.M. and 5-10 P.M., Sun. 5-9 P.M.

This delightful, upscale New American eatery in Casas Adobes Plaza was the first in local success story Sam Fox's Southwestern restaurant empire (Scottsdale-based Fox Restaurant Concepts), an empire that now markets 11 different restaurant concepts (27 total restaurants) in Arizona, Texas, Colorado, and Kansas, including North, Sauce (next door to Wildflower), Zinburger, Blanco Tacos & Tequila, and many more. It all began with Wildflower at Casas Adobes in 1998, and it's still one of the better restaurants in town, with a charming patio and familiar but dressed-up lunches like roasted meatloaf and an excellent grilled chicken BLT with aged gouda and honey mustard. For dinner they offer steaks, seafood, duck, and even variations on pad thai and bok choy; my favorite dish is the brown sugar–braised short ribs—call it meat-candy. Reservations are recommended.

ZINBURGER ❶❷

1865 E. River Rd., 520/299-7799, www.foxrc.com
HOURS: Sun.-Thurs. 11 A.M.-10 P.M., Fri.-Sat. 1-11 P.M.

For those of us who could exist on beef alone and who believe that beef is best served ground, in patty form, and between two warm buns, there is Zinburger, Fox Restaurant Concepts' gourmet homage to the good old burger joint. Not surprisingly, the $14 Kobe Burger (with cheddar cheese and wild mushrooms) is quite popular, but I like the Samburger (with maple bacon, American cheese, and thousand island dressing)—a kind of dressed-up Big Mac. The sides are worth a visit alone: sweet-potato chips, zucchini fries, double truffle fries. Thick shakes, crème brûlée, and bananas Foster are among the perfectly paired desserts offered in this sleek and bright, young and hip, yet relatively affordable, upscale burger house. There's a happy hour (daily 4 P.M.); the bar closes an hour after the restaurant. Zinburger has a second location (6390 E. Grant Rd.).

RESTAURANTS

WHAT'S A WILLCOX TOMATO?

At several of the fine-dining establishments in the Foothills neighborhood (and at a few other eateries, grocery stores, and farmers markets in the Old Pueblo), you're likely to see some bragging on menus that this or that dish includes Willcox Tomatoes, or Heirloom Willcox Tomatoes.

Don't worry, it's not some newly engineered super-tomato or anything—quite the contrary, in fact. It simply means that the tomato was grown in the Sulphur Springs Valley near Willcox, about 80 miles east of Tucson. It turns out that the climatic conditions around Willcox are ideal for year-round agriculture, and the area is dotted with greenhouses and farms both large and boutique; **Sunzona** and **Eurofresh** are two of the most well known.

RESTAURANTS

SEAFOOD
BLUEFIN SEAFOOD BISTRO $$

7053 N. Oracle Rd., 520/531-8500,
www.bluefintucson.com
HOURS: Mon.-Thurs. 11:30 A.M.-9 P.M., Fri.-Sat.
11:30 A.M.-10 P.M., Sun. 11 A.M.-9 P.M.

There are at least half a dozen restaurants in and
around Casas Adobes Plaza, and each is a decent
place to spend your time and money. But if, like
most of us, your upscale or even midscale dining resources are rather limited, I'd recommend
handing them first to this charming seafood
bistro. Operated by the folks from midtown's
Kingfisher, Bluefin has a cozy open-air patio-bar
that looks out on a courtyard with a fountain.
They serve great fish-and-chips and clam chow-
der for lunch, and for dinner they bring out the
Alaskan king crab, Maine lobster, and all kinds
of creative seafood creations; I like their Sunday
brunch (11 A.M.–3 P.M.) and the poached lobster
Benedict the best. They've also got an oyster
bar, and serve a limited late-night menu until
midnight. Reservations are recommended, especially for dinner and brunch. Prices drop
for a nightly happy hour (4:30–6:30 P.M.).

STEAK HOUSE
EL CORRAL RESTAURANT $$

2201 E. River Rd., 520/299-6092,
www.elcorraltucson.com
HOURS: Mon.-Thurs. 5-10 P.M., Fri.-Sun. 4:30-10 P.M.

Maybe it's Southern Arizona's ranching heritage, but there's something about being
in Tucson that makes you crave beef. This
charming historic restaurant on the edge of
the foothills is the best place in town to get
prime rib, a thick steak, and a big bowl of cowboy beans. This restaurant, in a low-ceilinged
stone-and-wood-beam territorial ranch house
with flagstone floors, has been a Tucson institution for more than 60 years. The setting
is almost as inviting as the sizzling beef and
barbecue ribs, with Technicolor portraits of
movie-house cowboys on the walls and several
rooms that offer romantic fireside dining. It's
also a great place to take the kids, with an inexpensive children's menu and a friendly, helpful staff. The prices are reasonable, and you'll
likely agree as soon as you sink your teeth into
a perfectly prepared juicy hunk of the best beef
in town.

West Side and the Tucson Mountains   Map 5

The West Side, being a primarily wild desert
and residential area, doesn't have as diverse an
array of restaurants as other neighborhoods in
Tucson, but many of the eateries here are long-
established Old Pueblo institutions popular
with locals.

AMERICAN
COYOTE PAUSE CAFÉ $

2740 S. Kinney Rd., 520/883-7297,
www.coyotepausecafe.com
HOURS: Mon.-Thurs. and Sat.-Sun. 7:30 A.M.-2:30 P.M.,
Fri. 4-8 P.M.

This is the ideal place to refuel after exploring the desert in and around Tucson Mountain
Park, Saguaro National Park, and the Sonoran
Desert Museum. A casual diner-style eatery
serving classic American rib-stickers with a

few nods to the territory, it's in a refurbished
1950s-era desert outpost called Cat Mountain
Station and an easy drive from all the main
west-side attractions. The Coyote Burger, with
house-made prickly pear barbecue sauce (you
might want to take home several dozen bottles)
and thick, crunchy onion rings will restore any
energy that you left out on the saguaro-lined
trails nearby.

FAST FOOD
PAT'S DRIVE-IN $

1202 W. Niagara St., 520/624-0891
HOURS: Mon.-Thurs. 11 A.M.-9 P.M., Fri.-Sat. 11 A.M.-10 P.M.

Fans of the chili dog will want to try this
longtime local favorite, a throwback to the
early days of fast food in both style and sub-
stance. It's usually busy here at lunch time,

there isn't a lot of parking, and the staff can get overwhelmed on occasion, but it's worth the trouble if you like hot, flavorful chili over a hot dog with mustard and onions. The fries, onion rings, and burgers are pretty good too.

FRENCH
AGUSTÍN BRASSERIE ⑤⑤⑤

100 S. Avenida del Convento, Ste. 150,
www.agustinbrasserie.com

HOURS: Tues.-Fri. 11 A.M.-10 P.M., Sat. 5-10 P.M.,
Sun. 9 A.M.-3 P.M.

An elegant French restaurant at the west side's Mercado San Agustín, Agustín Brasserie serves eminently well-prepared dishes without trying to get all "southwestern" about it. The food is fresh, flavorful, and French. It's as simple as that. The trout meunière will haunt your memory for days. At lunch, try the soft-shell crab BLT and the French onion soup. Sunday brunch here is particularly good (though not inexpensive). The baked eggs with goat cheese will make your weekend.

MEXICAN
MARISCOS CHIHUAHUA ⑤⑤

1009 N. Grande Ave., 520/623-3563,
www.mariscoschihuahua.com

HOURS: Daily 9 A.M.-9 P.M.

Tucsonans like to get away to a little Sea of Cortez resort town called Puerto Penasco (Rocky Point) to play in the ocean, drink, and eat shrimp, among other activities. If you can't make the trip south, however, a visit to one of the four Mariscos Chihuahua locations around the Old Pueblo is the next best thing. Their shrimp cocktail is as good as anything served in a *palapa* bar on the beach, and they offer a host of other *mariscos* (shellfish) favorites in the Mexican style and all manner of other treasures from the gulf. Mariscos Chihuahua has seven locations in Tucson, with particularly good ones in Midtown (999 N. Swan Rd., 520/881-2372), South Side (2902 E. 22nd St., 520/326-1529), and the Foothills (356 E. Grant Rd., 520/884-3457). The ambience of the restaurant on Grande Avenue is the best, though. No credit cards are accepted.

RESTAURANTS

© TIM HULL

Agustín Brasserie

ST. MARY'S MEXICAN FOOD ❺
1030 W. Saint Marys Rd., 520/884-1629
HOURS: Mon.-Sat. 8 A.M.-6:30 P.M.

This tiny Mexican joint is a good place to stop for a quick burrito for lunch if you're in the neighborhood, but it's the tortillas that keep me coming back. They've been voted best in town by readers of the *Tucson Weekly* many times, which is quite an accomplishment considering the depth of the local competition. Order up a dozen, wait while they're prepared fresh, and then just try to get to your destination before you reach in and grab one. (It won't happen.)

TERESA'S MOSAIC CAFÉ ❺
2456 N. Silvermosaic Dr., 520/624-4512,
www.mosaiccafes.com
HOURS: Mon.-Sat. 7:30 A.M.-9 P.M., Sun. 7:30 A.M.-2 P.M.

This classic Sonoran-style restaurant on the west side serves up exactly what is expected of it—delicious northern Mexico favorites with a dash of individuality. The green-corn tamales are excellent here, and Alfonso's Plate—a heap of grilled beef and pork with an enchilada or one of their well-made chiles rellenos—will fill you up for at least a few days. The service here can be somewhat lackadaisical. It's not worth a drive to the West Side specifically to go here, but if you're on your way back from the desert preserves out this way and are hungry for a chimichanga, this is a fine place to stop.

SOUTHWESTERN
OCOTILLO CAFÉ ❺❺❺
2021 N. Kinney Rd., Arizona-Sonora Desert Museum, 520/885-5705, www.desertmuseum.org
HOURS: late Dec.-Apr. daily 11 A.M.-3 P.M., June-Aug. Sat. 5-9 P.M., closed May and Oct.-Dec.

The café at the Arizona-Sonora Desert Museum isn't always open, but when it is, it serves dishes like charred salmon with prickly pear wasabi glaze and Sonoran Niçoise salad (with a serrano pepper vinaigrette). The brand of Southwestern fusion served at Ocotillo Café is fresh and light and inventive, and of course you can't beat the setting. Their hours vary according to season; before you make the half-hour drive out to the desert, call to make sure they're serving.

STEAK HOUSE
LI'L ABNER'S STEAKHOUSE ❺❺
850 N. Silverbell Rd., 520/744-2800
HOURS: Sun.-Thurs. 5-10 P.M., Fri.-Sat. 5-11 P.M.

As you approach this Western-style steak house, you can see cord upon cord of mesquite stacked in the backyard, just waiting for the flame to turn it into flavor. The steaks and ribs and chickens here are cooked over a big open pit outside, and on the weekends there's often music and dancing. Many years of patron graffiti mark the walls inside, giving the place a friendly, casual air that could easily turn celebratory with the right mix of meat, music, and alcohol.

East Side and the Rincon Valley   Map 6

The sprawling east side has several excellent dining options, and the Eclectic Café offers patio dining with beautiful views of the mountains.

AMERICAN
LITTLE ANTHONY'S DINER ❺
7010 E. Broadway Blvd., 520/296-0456,
www.littleanthonysdiner.com
HOURS: Mon. 10 A.M.-9 P.M., Tues.-Thurs. 10 A.M.-10 P.M., Fri. 10 A.M.-11 P.M., Sat. 7:30 A.M.-11 P.M., Sun. 7:30 A.M.-9 P.M.

Located in the same east-side strip mall as the Gaslight Dinner Theatre, this 1950s-style diner plays the part perfectly. The servers all wear period getups, Elvis is ever on the radio, and there's a classic car show in the parking lot, featuring fins and chrome as far as the eye can see, at least twice a month (check website for dates). The food is just about perfect, as long as you like classic diner fare—and if you don't, you need to think about revising your opinions.

BREAKFAST AND LUNCH
MILLIE'S PANCAKE HAUS $

6530 E. Tanque Verde Rd., 520/298-4250

HOURS: Tues.-Sun. 6:30 A.M.-2 P.M.

If there's a wait at this country-style eatery at the east-side La Plaza Shoppes (as there often is for breakfast on weekends), you can always window shop around the few art galleries and boutiques nearby. Once you're inside, try the pancakes. I mean, you can get a good omelet here, and the bacon is excellent, but if you're at a place called the "pancake haus," why not try the pancakes? You won't be disappointed if you do, and they have all sorts of flavors and syrups.

INDIAN
NEW DELHI PALACE $

6751 E. Broadway Blvd., 520/296-8585,

www.newdelhipalacetucson.com

HOURS: Daily 11:30 A.M.-2:30 P.M. and 5-10 P.M.

The 18-item daily lunch buffet at this comfortable restaurant is outstanding, with all the favorites—curry, tandoori, vindaloo, tikka masala, samosas, etc. At dinner they serve big plates of traditional dishes from all over India, including dishes cooked in Karhai style. They stock a full bar with a great selection of bottled beer—there's nothing like a cold India pale ale alongside a spicy heap of Indian food.

NEW AMERICAN AND MEXICAN
CASA MOLINA $

6225 E. Speedway Blvd., 520/886-5468,

www.casamolina.com

HOURS: Daily 11 A.M.-10 P.M.

There are a few places in Tucson called Casa Molina, but this is the only one that matters. Since 1947, the Molina family has been serving up authentic Mexican favorites on the far eastern edge of midtown in a cool old adobe building with a life-size bull and matador battling each other outside. The building itself is an attraction: There's a lush outdoor patio and a perfectly round room (the Redondo Room) with a saguaro-rib ceiling; the handmade furniture, wall hangings, and murals will keep you entertained until your delicious high-piled plates

RESTAURANTS

© TIM HULL

Casa Molina

arrive. Attending the popular Sunday buffet (11 A.M.–3 P.M.) is a good way to sample a variety of Mexican dishes you might not otherwise order. There's a small, friendly cantina inside where they serve a mean margarita.

ECLECTIC CAFÉ ⑤⑤

7053 E. Tanque Verde Rd., 520/829-5039, www.eclecticcafetucson.com

HOURS: Mon.-Fri. 11 A.M.-9 P.M., Sat. 8 A.M.-9 P.M., Sun. 8 A.M.-8 P.M.

Part of the mini-empire of Tucson restaurants owned by the folks at Frank's/Francisco's in midtown, this casual east-side favorite serves a delicious, creative mixture of Mexican and New American dishes—everything from sugar-cured pit ham sandwiches to crab quesadillas to quiche Lorraine—in the Tanque Verde Shopping Center, on the northwest corner of Tanque Verde and Sabino Canyon. The tortilla soup here is excellent, as is the always freshly made guacamole; then again, so are the hamburgers and the chicken crepes. On Saturday (8 A.M.–noon) and Sunday (8 A.M.–1 P.M.) they

serve a diverse breakfast, and I can assure you that their green chile and cheddar omelet is a perfectly acceptable way to start the day.

STEAK HOUSE

◖ PINNACLE PEAK STEAK HOUSE ⑤⑤

6541 E. Tanque Verde Rd., 520/296-0911, www.traildusttown.com

HOURS: Mon.-Fri. 5-10 P.M., Sat.-Sun. 4:30-10 P.M.

Located in Trail Dust Town, the Old West theme park, Pinnacle Peak is a typical (and that means tasty, fun, and affordable) cowboy steak-and-beans hall that packs in families, tourists, and locals dining with out-of-town friends. It always seems like there's a celebratory atmosphere here. I guess that has something to do with the stage-dressing buildings and the loud cap-gun fights in the dusty streets out front. This is a fun place to bring kids—they can check out the harmless attractions while the adults have a few margaritas in the saloon before dinner. The steaks are well made and always fresh and hot, and the ranch beans go down easy on the side. There's also good prime rib and a low-priced kids' menu.

South Side   Map 7

The South Side is where the best Mexican restaurants are located, and a drive down South 6th Avenue or South 4th Avenue looks a bit like a drive through a similarly sized Mexican town. If none of the Sonoran-style places listed here sounds good, head down South 4th Avenue and you'll see several Mexican places along both sides of the road.

BAKERY

LA CAVE'S BAKERY ⑤

1219 S. 6th Ave., 520/624-2561

HOURS: Mon.-Fri. 7:30 A.M.-6 P.M., Sat. 7:30 A.M.-5 P.M., Sun. 7:30 A.M.-1 P.M.

This South 6th Avenue bakery is the best place in town to get Mexican wedding cookies and other South Tucson delicacies, but I keep coming back for the simple glazed doughnuts, the best in town hands-down. A variety of other freshly made pastries and breads are available

throughout the day at this longtime local favorite. If you're going in the early morning, remember that they don't serve coffee—just absolutely perfect doughnuts.

MEXICAN

◖ EL GUERO CANELO ⑤

5201 S. 12th Ave., 520/295-9005, www.elguerocanelo.com

HOURS: Sun.-Thurs. 10 A.M.-11 P.M., Fri.-Sat. 10 A.M.-midnight

The Arizona home of the Sonoran hot dog, El Guero Canelo has been serving authentic and fast Mexican street food in the Old Pueblo for two decades. The restaurant's three locations serve what many believe to be city's best Sonoran dogs—a grilled beef hot dog wrapped in bacon, nestled deep in a thick, rich bun, and smothered in beans, onions, mustard, mayo, and salsa. It's a decadent meal, especially because it's nearly impossible to have just one. Another must-try are the carne asada tacos, and don't forget to wash it all down with a bottle of soda from Mexico (these are much, much tastier than those north of the border). The South Side location has the look and feel of a Sonoran taco stand that grew out of proportion, and has a lively atmosphere at night. You'll swear you somehow crossed the border without noticing it. The two other locations are in the foothills (2480 N. Oracle Rd., 520/882-8977) and midtown (5802 E. 22nd St., 520/790-6000).

🄲 MI NIDITO 🌢

1813 S. 4th Ave., 520/622-5081, www.minidito.net
HOURS: Wed.-Thurs. 11 A.M.-10:30 P.M.,
Fri.-Sat. 11 A.M.-2 A.M., Sun. 11 A.M.-10:30 P.M.

If you only have the time or inclination to eat at one of Tucson's famous Sonoran-style Mexican restaurants, consider Mi Nidito ("my little nest"). Bill Clinton did. While on a short stopover in Tucson during his presidency, Clinton, known for his love of food (especially the comfort variety), stopped here and sampled pretty much one of everything. His order is still preserved as a special on the menu. It's difficult to say what it is about this bright South 4th Avenue restaurant, with its tropical decor

and friendly albeit always harried staff, that sets it apart from the dozens of other similar eateries in the Old Pueblo. It is the best; that's all there is to it. *Tucson Weekly* readers invariably name it the top (or at least among the top) Sonoran joints in town in that publication's annual Best of Tucson poll, and you shouldn't be surprised to see a line of people waiting to be seated at 10:45 A.M. on a Wednesday. On a weekend night, figure on at least an hour on the porch, waiting anxiously for your name to be called.

TAQUERIA PICO DE GALLO 🌢

2618 S. 6th Ave., 520/623-8775
HOURS: Mon.-Sat. 9 A.M.-9 P.M., Sun. 10 A.M.-5 P.M.

The distinctive fruit and chili concoction that gives this south-side taqueria its name is something to behold. In many places, *pico de gallo* ("beak of a rooster") is a chunky mixture of tomatoes, peppers, onions, and lime heaped on tacos; here it's a cup of fresh fruit cut in big chunks and doused with salty chili powder. The tortillas, made fresh for each order, are what set this place apart from other taquerias. This is a good place to get takeout; the dining room is serviceable but hardly comfortable.

Greater Tucson   Map 8

Outside of the Tucson metro area, the number of restaurant choices declines precipitously. There are a few that are definitely worth trying, however. While I wouldn't make a special trip to any of the places listed here, if you're nearby sightseeing, hiking, or shopping, all of them will more than do.

AMERICAN
COW PALACE RESTAURANT 🌢🌢

28802 S. Nogales Hwy., Amado, 520/398-8000,
www.cowpalacerestaurant.com
HOURS: Daily 7 A.M.-8 P.M.

Across the street from Longhorn Grill, a statue of a Hereford announces the locally beloved Cow Palace Restaurant, serving a wide variety

of favorites from chicken-fried steak to spaghetti. Despite its long history as a cowboy bar—and it's said that even John Wayne ate here back in the day—the Cow Palace has a family-friendly atmosphere with a ranch theme. On weekends there is often a crooner playing the piano during dinner hours.

IRON DOOR RESTAURANT 🌢

10300 E. Ski Run Rd., Mount Lemmon, 520/576-1321
HOURS: Mon. and Thurs.-Fri. 10 A.M.-4:30 P.M.,
Sat.-Sun. 9 A.M.-4 P.M.

Right across the road from the nation's southernmost ski run (and run by the same company), the Iron Door offers a menu of hearty fare for high altitudes. The selection here isn't that big, but the quality is typically high. They serve a bratwurst platter with a delicious applesauce that is the perfect accompaniment to the forested highland atmosphere. Service is patchy, and most likely you'll have to wait for a table, especially on weekends and on the rare occasions that there's snow on the mountain.

SAWMILL RUN ⊖⊖

12976 N. Sabino Canyon Pkwy., Mount Lemmon, 520/576-9147, www.sawmillrun.com
HOURS: Summer Mon.-Thurs. 11 A.M.-5 P.M., Fri. 11 A.M.-9 P.M., Sat. 9 A.M.-9 P.M., Sun. 9 A.M.-5 P.M.; winter Sun.-Fri. 11 A.M.-5 P.M., Sat. 11 A.M.-7 P.M.

Something happens to your body if you spend too much time hanging out in the mountain forest. It begins to crave meat and potatoes. When this inevitably occurs during your excursion up to Mount Lemmon, head straight to the Sawmill Run, where they serve a menu designed with the altitude in mind: smoked brisket dip, Reuben with creamy slaw, steak tacos, build-your-own burger. As one of just a few restaurants on the mountain, Sawmill Run can get very busy on summer weekends.

MEXICAN
WISDOM'S CAFÉ ⊖⊖

1931 E. Frontage Rd., Tumacácori, 520/398-2397 or 520/991-9652, www.wisdomscafe.com
HOURS: Mid-July-May Mon.-Thurs. 11 A.M.-3 P.M. and 5-8 P.M., Fri.-Sat. 11 A.M.-3 P.M. and 5-9 P.M.

Open since 1944 and still run by the same family, Wisdoms may be the best restaurant in the Santa Cruz Valley, serving Mexican food from passed-down family recipes. Don't miss the famous deep-fried fruit burrito for dessert. The chile relleno, encased in a thick cocoon of batter, is the best in the Tucson area as far as I'm concerned. To get there, head south on the frontage road from Tubac toward the Tumacácori Mission and look for the big chicken statue out front.

NIGHTLIFE

Tucson's nightlife and entertainment scene is casual and mixed, drawing drunken college kids, post-college slackers and go-getters, 30-something urban workers, hip parents who still haunt the alt-rock shows, and professors and professionals of indeterminate age. There's really something for everybody out there.

Tucson's youngest and sloppiest nightlife takes place on three blocks within easy walking, or stumbling, distance of each other: Congress Street downtown, 4th Avenue, and Main Gate Square near the UA. There are always plenty of cabs waiting around outside the bars in these neighborhoods, especially on the weekends. When school's in session these areas are fairly packed with college students. That doesn't mean that townies don't go out; in fact, some of the bars in these districts are just as busy during Spring Break and summer as they are when the students are in town. For more upscale watering holes, try the bars at the restaurants in the foothills.

Most of Tucson's nightlife is relatively low-tech, so to speak, meaning that, save for a few places, the bars in the Old Pueblo are mostly neighborhood joints where locals go to drink and socialize. There isn't a lot of importance put on the way you look and the way you dress. People here are friendly and laid-back, and they seem to be even more so once they've got a few margaritas in them.

There is no smoking in bars or restaurants in Tucson, but most have built outdoor patios to accommodate smokers. For a generation Arizona's bars closed at 1 A.M., but in 2007 the state legislature put off last call until 2 A.M.;

© TIM HULL

HIGHLIGHTS

LOOK FOR 🌙 TO FIND RECOMMENDED NIGHTLIFE.

© TIM HULL

Nimbus Brewing Company

NIGHTLIFE

🌙 **Best Dive Bar: The Buffet,** the oldest bar in town still in its original location, is the epitome of the great American shot-and-beer dive. It has been welcoming hard-core drinkers since the 1930s (page 89).

🌙 **Best Student Hangout: Dirtbags** is a longtime favorite student bar, just a few steps from campus, that is famous for its candy-like shot concoctions (page 89).

🌙 **Best Bar Decor:** The Kennedy pop-portraits, memorabilia of Cold War culture, and looping cult films make **The Shelter** a fun hideaway (page 90).

🌙 **Best Historic Watering Hole: The Tap Room,** a cramped little watering hole off the Hotel Congress lobby, has been serving drinks to thirsty desert travelers since 1919 (page 90).

🌙 **Best Neighborhood Pub: The Shanty** is the best place in town to become a regular. Its large patio lined with greenery and choice of a 100 different beers invites a mixed crowd of locals (page 92).

🌙 **Best Dance Club:** Salsa night at **El Parador** starts every Friday at 10:45 P.M., fea-

turing dance lessons for $5; then you can try out what you've learned in front of the powerful, brassy, fun-loving band Descarga (page 95).

🌙 **Best Place to See Local and National Bands:** The intimate space at **Club Congress** in the historic Hotel Congress packs in local music lovers with a constant stream of homegrown and national touring acts (page 97).

🌙 **Best Local Microbrew:** Whether purchased on tap at this local brewery's on-site bar or in six-pack form at the supermarket, the varied flavors of Tucson's finest craft beer will have you coming back to **Nimbus Brewing Company** for more (page 98).

🌙 **Best Margarita:** Fresh-squeezed lime juice, top-shelf tequila, and some ineffable skill make the refreshing margaritas at **Bar Toma** the best in town (page 99).

🌙 **Best Cocktail Menu:** At **Scott & Co.,** a tiny, elegant "speakeasy" downtown, they take their cocktails very seriously—everything is creatively constructed with fresh, house-made ingredients. The expert mixologists here will even make you a drink to fit your unique palate and personality (page 102).

however, many bars close much earlier than that on weekdays.

Once a month on Second Saturdays (www.2ndsaturdaysdowntown.com) the streets of Tucson come alive, as thousands of residents heat the Old Pueblo's traditional heart to meet and mingle. The event, which, as its name suggests, goes down on the second Saturday of every month (usually starting around 6 P.M.), features street vendors, performers, food, bands, art shows, and more, and all the downtown stores, bars, clubs, and restaurants are typically hopping with activity—it's downtown Tucson at its most active and interesting.

Bars

DIVE BARS
◖ THE BUFFET
538 E. 9th St., 520/623-6811, www.thebuffetbar.com
HOURS: Mon.-Sat. 6 A.M.-2 A.M., Sun. 11 A.M.-2 A.M.
COST: No cover
`Map 2`

The oldest bar in town still in its original location, the Buffet has been welcoming drinkers to the Iron Horse neighborhood since the 1930s. This is a shot-and-beer kind of place most of the day, the local professional drinkers' home bar. As such, it opens as early as 6 A.M., and there are numerous UA traditions that involve imbibing at The Buffet at that ungodly hour. This is a place where frat boys slum it with 80-year-old retired miners on oxygen, knocking back tequila. Settle in and order a cheap shot and a beer, and pretty soon you won't want to leave. There are no windows to speak of, and with that too-earnest Tucson sun blacked out and forgotten, the day just slips away on bar time. Make sure you're there around 6 P.M. for "Happy Minute," when the barkeep goes around and gives everybody one more of whatever they're having, on the house. At 11 P.M., refills are a mere dollar. The only food offered is cheap hot dogs cooked in Coors, which is the only beer offered on tap. They've got a few brews in the fridge that are more drinkable, but that's not really the point here, is it?

DANNY'S BABAQUIVERI
2910 E. Fort Lowell Rd., 520/795-3178,
www.dannyslounge.net
HOURS: Mon.-Sat. 2 P.M.-2 A.M., Sun. 6 P.M.-2 A.M.
COST: No cover
`Map 3`

Named for the mountains where the Tohono O'odham believe their creator dwells, this near-dive bar near Fort Lowell and Country Club is the perfect place to hide out from the heat, or anything else you might be running from. It's cool and cozy and dark, with a low ceiling and big cushy Naugahyde booths along the wall. The jukebox is excellent, the drinks are cheap, and there are a few pool tables in the back. It's one of the few bars in Tucson that hasn't added a semi-covered patio for smokers since a 2006 state law banned lighting up even at your favorite watering hole. Smokers at Danny's stand around outside under the front awning, watching traffic.

◖ DIRTBAGS
1800 E. Speedway Blvd., 520/326-2600,
www.dirtbagsbar.com
HOURS: Mon.-Sat. 11 A.M.-2 A.M.
COST: No cover
`Map 2`

The typical drinker at Dirtbags is a 20-something undergrad with, depending on gender, a skimpy summer outfit and bleached blonde hair or a baseball cap, cargo shorts, and flip-flops. This small, popular watering hole is on the corner of Speedway and Campbell, within easy stumbling distance of most University of Arizona dorms and frat houses. Dirtbags is famous for its shot concoctions, most of them mixed up to taste like cookies and candies. Consider the Sicilian Whore, a *pitcher* of pineapple-flavored shots made from eight different liquors that, according to the owners, "can only be served to a close group of friends."

RIVER'S EDGE LOUNGE

4635 N. Flowing Wells Rd., 520/887-9027

HOURS: Daily 10 A.M.-2 A.M.

COST: No cover

Map 5

This is a neighborhood tavern with a honky-tonk heart and rock-and-roll loins; it's a fun place to hang out and meet some locals on the rather shaggy northwest edge of midtown. Live bands rock the dive-ish joint on the weekends, and there's always some beer pong/karaoke/wet T-shirt event going on throughout the week. The drinks are relatively cheap here, the hot dogs go down easy, and the people are generally friendly and ready to have a raucous good time. Not a place for the prudish. Cash only.

WORLD FAMOUS GOLDEN NUGGET

2617 N. 1st Ave., 520/622-9202,

www.goldennuggettucson.com

HOURS: Daily 9 A.M.-2 A.M.; happy hour daily 11 A.M.-7 P.M.

COST: No cover

Map 3

You probably won't find a cheaper, stronger drink in town than here at the Golden Nugget, where all of Tucson's subcultures and classes mix it up for the sake of economy and value. There's nothing I can say to recommend the Nugget other than that it is a *real* bar in the classical sense, nothing more and nothing less. Everybody's friendly, and there are well-used pool tables and shuffleboard games and a good jukebox. They don't take credit cards, and they don't have a big selection of draft beer, but otherwise this is a great place to go at either the start or the sloppy end of an Old Pueblo night out. Be careful with the mixed drinks, though; they truly are stronger than any other place in town.

HISTORIC BARS

◖ THE SHELTER

4155 E. Grant Rd., 520/326-1345,

www.theshelfercocktaillounge.com

HOURS: Daily 3 P.M.-2 A.M.

COST: No cover

Map 3

The Tucson valley played a major role in the

Cold War: For years ICBMs ringed the city, locked and loaded beneath the desert and aimed directly at various targets in the USSR. While there's a museum south of town where you can learn all about the Old Pueblo's atomic-age bona fides, The Shelter is the best place to celebrate, so to speak, the era and its two coolest cold warriors. It's dark and cool like a shelter should be, and there's plenty of good booze and always a campy cult film playing out silently on a TV in the corner. The walls are covered with Jack and Bobby, and the pinball machines ding and flap. You could last out the nuclear winter in here, no problem. Check out happy hour, too (daily 3–7 P.M.).

◖ THE TAP ROOM

311 E. Congress St., 520/622-8848,

www.hotelcongress.com

HOURS: Daily 11 A.M.-2 A.M.

COST: No cover

Map 1

This cramped old bar (it has been around since 1919) still packs them in, especially when there's a band playing at Club Congress, to which The Tap Room serves as a kind of hideout from the crush and noise. But if you belly up here on an afternoon, or on a slow midweek night, you'll notice the details: the retro booths and stools, the scratchy juke in the corner, and especially the cowboy-life art of Pete Martinez, one of several lauded Western artists who once called Tucson home. Martinez, who lived in Tucson from 1935 until his death in 1971, was neighbor to the painter and illustrator Maynard Dixon and friend to Ted DeGrazia, and he reportedly spent a good deal of his time drinking at The Tap Room. Martinez's art can be seen on the bar's walls. People always used to say that he would from time to time trade his work for his drinks, and that's how they got there. But the management says that's just a rumor, and that the artist gifted the paintings to his favorite bar.

PUBS

BOB DOBB'S

2501 E. 6th St., 520/325-3767, www.bobdobbs.net

HOURS: Daily 10 A.M.–1 A.M.
COST: Generally no cover
Map 3

Despite its name, this popular Sam Hughes neighborhood bar and grill is not connected with the founder of the Church of the Subgenius, J. R. "Bob" Dobbs. It is, however, a casual, popular place that attracts aging jocks, UA sports fans, and college kids. It has a great patio looking out on 6th Street, and the food—burgers, dogs, and other pub fare—goes down easy. The walls are covered with several generations of graffiti, and it's easy to get sucked into reading all the drunken scrawls.

BORDERLANDS BREWING CO.

119 E. Toole Ave., 520/261-8773,
www.borderlandsbrewing.com
HOURS: Wed.-Fri. 4-7 P.M., Sat. noon-4 P.M.
COST: Generally no cover
Map 1

Though it's not open often, and offers rather spare accommodations when it is, Borderlands is the place to sample some of the best microbrews the Old Pueblo has to offer. The brewers here use local ingredients and follow in the footsteps of beer-loving Germans who settled in the Southwest in the 1800s. They serve several different beers in a tasting-room setting, including a citrus IPA, a prickly pear wheat and a rich vanilla porter. There's usually a food truck or two parked outside during the hours that the brewery is open for sampling, and there's often a band in residence. Borderlands has extended hours on Second Saturdays (noon–7 P.M.).

THE DISTRICT TAVERN

260 E. Congress St., 520/791-0081
HOURS: Mon.-Sun. 2 P.M.-2 A.M.
COST: Generally no cover
Map 1

A cool old-school drinker's bar on Congress, the District Tavern is a fine place to spend an hour or five drinking on the cheap and sitting back in cushy booths. They offer wine tasting (Fri. 5–7 P.M.), and the mixed drinks are always under $3. You can also always get a can of PBR for $1, and they've got what must be a

professional drinker's dream special: a bottle of Miller High Life and a shot for $3, all the time.

HIDEOUT BAR & GRILL

1110 S. Sherwood Village Dr., 520/751-2222
HOURS: Daily 10 A.M.-2 A.M.
COST: Generally no cover
Map 6

The Hideout is a fun, relaxing place to hang on the east side, with all you need to escape your daily routine for a few hours: cheap drinks, sports on the TVs, karaoke, live bands, delicious and filling burgers and other bar-style eats, pool, and typically friendly and welcoming local folks. Drinks are ridiculously cheap ($2.50 domestic beer and well) every day during happy hour (3–6 P.M.).

MALONEY'S

213 N. 4th Ave., 520/388-9355
HOURS: Daily 11 A.M.-2 A.M.
COST: Generally no cover
Map 2

A large, popular bar on 4th Avenue flanking the railroad tracks, Maloney's—part of a regional chain—draws a mostly college-age crowd for general drinking and eating revelry. They offer half-price drinks and appetizers (Mon.–Fri. 4–7 P.M.), and they have a good selection of beers. There are black-and-white still shots from famous movies and pictures of your favorite stars of yesterday and today throughout the place, and the lonely whistle of the passing train lends this rather typical college-town tavern a somewhat melancholy air. The food is edible—burgers and sandwiches and the usual beer-soaking bar food.

MR. HEAD'S ART GALLERY AND BAR

513 N. 4th Ave., 520/792-2710
HOURS: Mon.-Sun. noon-2 A.M.
COST: Generally no cover
Map 2

Mr. Head's draws a mixed 4th Avenue–style crowd of college kids and frolicking urbanites with live bands; curious, glorious, and strange artwork; and a large selection of Arizona microbrews. The patio here is particularly nice.

NIGHTLIFE

NIGHTLIFE

Drink and look at art at Mr. Head's Art Gallery and Bar.

The bands often rock and the people-watching is high-end, but it's too easy to get lost looking at the art. No matter what, you won't waste your time here.

O'MALLEY'S

247 N. 4th Ave., 520/623-8600
HOURS: Daily 11 A.M.–2 A.M.
COST: Generally no cover
Map 2

Just across the parking lot from Maloney's, O'Malley's is a laid-back bar popular with the college crowd, offering live cover bands several nights a week and a cozy enclosed patio for smoking. They serve food of the bar-menu variety; it's palatable, especially with a beer or two to wash it down. There are TVs playing sports events; the bartenders are friendly and efficient; and there are a few pool tables and video games scattered around the place.

THE SHANTY

401 E. 9th St., 520/623-2664
HOURS: Sun.–Wed. noon–1 A.M., Thurs.–Sat. noon–2 A.M.
COST: Generally no cover
Map 2

The Shanty is an old railroad bar turned Irish pub turned college-kid hangout. It's on the edge of the Iron Horse neighborhood (where the railroad workers used to live), just off 4th Avenue. It has a large patio lined with greenery and is usually crowded on the weekends with, as in most Tucson bars, a mixture of the young and the not-so-young, all drinking together. They've got between 80 and 100 different beers, with most of the exotic stuff in bottles; they certainly pour a good Guinness. Several pool tables get heavy use. There's no food other than free bar-top popcorn. Though it has moved once since it opened, the Shanty actually holds the oldest liquor license in Tucson.

SIR VEZA'S

4699 E. Speedway Blvd., 510/323-8226, www.sirvezas.com
HOURS: Daily 11 A.M.–2 A.M.
COST: Generally no cover
Map 3

© TIM HULL

© TIM HULL

The Shanty

With folks behind Tucson's icon restaurant El Charro in charge of the kitchen, Sir Veza's, a retro-motorhead "Taco Garage," is definitely a fine place to fill up; but it's even better if you combine dinner with an evening of sampling cocktails both classical and unique in the bar and watching a game on the TVs. The margaritas (try the CerVezarita: a margarita with a bottle of Pacifico mixed in) and mojitos here are as good as any in the city, and the specialty cocktails are ingenious: the Cartel Carbomb combines Guinness, Irish cream, and Jameson whiskey, while the Chico and the Man drops a scoop of ice cream into a mixture of Negra Modelo and coffee liqueur. Many items are half off during daily happy hours (3–6 P.M. and 9 P.M.–close). There's also a second location in the Foothills (220 W. Wetmore Rd., 520/888-8226, daily 11 A.M.–2 A.M.).

SURLY WENCH
424 N. 4th Ave., 520/882-0009,
www.surlywenchpub.com
HOURS: Mon.-Fri. 5 P.M.-2 A.M., Sat.-Sun. 2 P.M.-2 A.M.

COST: Generally no cover
Map 2

The Surly Wench is a cool 4th Avenue pub with a kind of punkabilly vibe. The holy trinity here is "booze, burlesque, and bands," but they also serve pretty good burgers, sandwiches, fried stuff, and a few Mexican dishes. This is the only place in town where you can see the tattooed and pulse-quickening bombshells that make up the Black Cherry Burlesque troupe (there's an up-to-date schedule of shows—and photos—on the website), and they are certainly something worth seeing.

WOODEN NICKEL TAVERN
1908 S. Country Club Rd., 520/323-8830,
www.woodennickeltucson.com
HOURS: Daily 11 A.M.-2 A.M.
COST: Generally no cover
Map 7

On the south end of Country Club below 22nd Street, this casual and fun tavern has cheap drinks and good food; every day at lunch you can get a burger and a pint for $6. On Friday and

Saturday nights they push the pool tables to the corners and a DJ spins dance music. Fridays it's Tejano music, popular with the city's Mexican and Latino population, and on Saturday it's hip-hop, which brings in a younger crowd. Outside there's a covered patio for smokers.

SPORTS BARS AND BILLIARDS

CLICKS BILLIARDS

3325 N. 1st Ave., 520/887-7312, www.clicks.com
HOURS: Daily 11 A.M.-2 A.M.
COST: Generally no cover
Map 3

Some of us need only a well-made cocktail and a view, but others require more distraction—like all those games pubgoers have always played to pass the time until the dreaded last call. This large, clean, and well-lit pool hall (part of a national chain) on 1st Avenue just south of Prince Road offers 20 pool tables, darts, foosball, eight televisions scattered throughout, and plenty of other distractions to go with the relatively low-priced beers and cocktails.

COW PONY BAR AND GRILL

6510 E. Tanque Verde Rd., 520/721-2781
HOURS: Daily 11 A.M.-2 A.M.
COST: Generally no cover
Map 6

This East Side joint is pure Tucson: a little bit country, a little bit rock and roll, and all casual, inexpensive, and fun. The name suggests a honky-tonk, but the Cow Pony has something for everybody—which is proven most weekend nights when the place is packed with a cross section of Tucson's drinking, partying crews. There are half a dozen or more TVs in the small place and comfortable half-moon booths perfect for a group of friends; pool tables and foosball fill up the back.

DIABLOS SPORTS BAR & GRILL

2545 S. Craycroft Rd., 520/514-9202
HOURS: Mon.-Sun. 11 A.M.-2 A.M.
COST: Generally no cover
Map 7

A laid-back sports bar near the Air Force base,

Diablos draws a mixed crowd of revelers with excellent burgers and wings; big, strong, and fairly priced drinks; and DJs spinning fun dance music every Friday and Saturday night. Diablos tends to pack them in during the long weekday happy hour (2–6 P.M.).

PEARSON'S PUB

1120 S. Wilmot Rd., 520/747-2181,
www.pearsonspub.com
HOURS: Mon.-Sat. 11 A.M.-2 A.M., Sun. 10 A.M.-2 A.M.
COST: Generally no cover
Map 6

A fun, friendly place on the east side, Pearson's is a typical neighborhood pub offering inexpensive drinks (a PBR here is just $1), bar games and all kinds of fun special events and parties. They have DJs and dancing, sports on the TVs, and karaoke and open mic every Wednesday at 9 P.M.. They also serve a daily buffet that is generally excellent. This is an easygoing place where you're likely to meet some interesting, if inebriated, locals.

RJ'S REPLAYS

5769 E. Speedway Blvd., 520/495-5136,
www.rjsreplays.com
HOURS: Mon.-Sat. 11 A.M.-2 A.M., Sun. 10 A.M.-2 A.M.
COST: Generally no cover
Map 3

A sports bar in the classical style, RJ's Replays is a commercial man-cave: 29 screens, some of them 3-D, pool tables and other distractions, a staff that, strangely, skews attractive and female, and dozens of varieties of beer and the foods that go with it. Appetizers and wings get downright cheap during happy hour (Mon.–Thurs. 3–6 P.M. and 10 P.M.–1 A.M.).

WORLD SPORTS GRILLE

2290 W. Ina Rd., 520/229-0011,
www.worldsportsgrille.com
HOURS: Daily 11 A.M.-2 A.M.;
must be 21 or older after 11 P.M.
COST: Generally no cover
Map 8

This huge high-concept restaurant, sports bar, and family gaming center at the Foothills Mall is a good place to take the kids, especially if you want them to leave you alone while you watch the game on a 103-inch flat-screen TV, choose from among scores of draft beers, and play a few games of pool. The video, old-school, and interactive games here are legion, which is not surprising given that the World Sports Grille model was developed by Sega—they've got more than 50 to choose from, including classic arcade and Japanese games.

Dance Clubs

DV8
5851 E. Speedway Blvd. #D, 520/885-3030
HOURS: Wed.-Thurs. 9 P.M.-2 A.M., Fri.-Sat. 8 P.M.-2 A.M.
COST: Women free before 10 P.M., otherwise cover varies
`Map 3`

This is a fun dance club for a mostly young college-age set, with a premium on dressing to impress, dancing wildly, and hooking up. Thursday nights get dangerous, with a $10 cover charge sufficient to get you penny drinks all night. Friday nights welcome the 18-and-over crowd with $1 mixed drinks all night for those 21 and older. DJs spin a mix of dance, hip-hop, top 40, and classic alternative dance beats. This is definitely a dress-up kind of place, but that means something different in Tucson than it does elsewhere. If you're clad in the fashions of the day, you're likely to pass muster.

◖ EL PARADOR
2744 E. Broadway Blvd., 520/881-2808,
www.elparadortucson.com
HOURS: Fri. and alternating Sat. 10 P.M.-2 A.M.
COST: $7
`Map 3`

With Tucson's deep Latino roots, it's no surprise that salsa dancing is all the rage, and the best place to learn the steps, find a partner, and cut a *caliente* rug is the colorful jungle-like atmosphere of El Parador. Every Friday starting at 10:45 P.M. a salsa master offers dance lessons for an extra $5; then you can try out what you've learned in front of the powerful, brassy, fun-loving band Descarga until the wee hours. This is a great place to commune with Tucson's Latino community; on many weekend nights, young men and women up from Ambos

Nogales crowd the dance floor, dressed to impress and swinging and kicking and sweating to the music. On alternating Saturdays the band Salsarengue plays a more traditional brand of salsa.

THE MAVERICK
6622 E. Tanque Verde Rd., 520/298-0430,
www.mavericktucson.com
HOURS: Tues.-Sat. 5 P.M.-2 A.M.
COST: $5 Thurs.-Sat.
`Map 6`

This east-side country-western nightclub has been calling in cowboys and cowgirls from all over Southern Arizona for nearly 50 years. A rotating lineup of three tight house bands plays country dance music Tuesday–Saturday. The sound system is excellent, and even if you can't two-step it's fun to watch those who can from the comfortable sidelines, which include a whiskey lounge. The kitchen serves burgers, sandwiches, fried foods, and appetizers until 11 P.M., but if you get to dancing you'll likely be on the floor long after that.

SAPPHIRE LOUNGE
61 E. Congress St., 520/624-9100 or 520/306-8116,
www.sapphiretucson.com
HOURS: Mon.-Sun. 6 P.M.-2 A.M.
COST: Generally no cover
`Map 1`

One of the pinnacles of Tucson's rather modest club scene, the Sapphire Lounge has all you'd expect from a high-end dance place (beautiful, dressed-up revelers, thumping beats, and top-notch cocktails) with the added attraction of the Sky Deck Lounge, a rooftop patio with views of the city. Call ahead for VIP service and details on the dress code.

NIGHTLIFE

SHARKS

256 E. Congress St., 520/791-9869
HOURS: Daily 5 P.M.-2 A.M.
COST: Cover varies
Map 1

Mexican rock bands have found fervent fans here in the borderlands for as long as there's been Mexican rock and roll, and it's been around nearly as long as the American kind—long before bands like Santana, Los Lobos, and Los Lonely Boys broke into the mainstream. At Sharks nightclub downtown the tradition continues every Friday night, when rock *en español* draws a crowd. Other nights the mostly youngish crowd hits the small, sweaty dance floor with the help of DJs playing a mix of rock, hip-hop, and dance music, and on Tuesday there's karaoke.

ZEN ROCK

121 E. Congress St., 520/306-8116, www.zenrocktucson.com
HOURS: Mon.-Sat. 6 P.M.-close
COST: Generally no cover
Map 1

One of just a few dance clubs in the Old Pueblo, downtown's Zen Rock is a semi-swanky place with the usual Vegas-style club pretensions and a mostly college-age crowd of regular weekend revelers. The music is loud and exciting, the DJs are deft and high-energy, and the crowd is generally sexy, slinky, scantily clad, and ready for fun. Call ahead for VIP service and dress codes.

Gay and Lesbian

IBT'S

616 N. 4th Ave., 520/882-3053, www.ibtstucson.com
HOURS: Daily noon-2 A.M.
COST: Generally no cover
Map 2

Tucson's most popular gay bar is a bit bigger inside than it looks to be from the outside, but not by much. Follow the revelers toward the back and you'll find a dance floor and a smoking patio. There's usually a fun mix of dudes and chicks here—college kids, young professionals, and older folks even, with everybody dancing to the beats. There are often live DJs, drag shows, and other revelry as announced, as well as karaoke on Sundays. IBT's is the perennial Best Gay Bar winner in the *Tucson Weekly*'s annual poll. It's not a fancy place by any means—the usual Tucson casual, or even less, will do.

WOODY'S

3710 N. Oracle Rd., 520/292-6702, www.mywoodysaz.com
HOURS: Daily 11 A.M.-2 A.M.
COST: Generally no cover
Map 4

Woody's has friendly servers and bartenders, a mixed clientele of various ages, and what is quite possibly the longest happy hour in town (daily 11 A.M.–8 P.M.). The patio bar opens most nights at 8 P.M., and amateur voices fill the air during the nightly karaoke sessions (9 P.M.–1 A.M.), with one of the better songbooks in town. There are usually DJs spinning, and they have a few pool tables and other games. On Sunday they serve brunch with a bloody Mary bar.

Live Music

BOONDOCK'S LOUNGE

3306 N. 1st Ave., 520/690-0991,
www.boondockslounge.com
HOURS: Mon. noon–2 A.M., Tues.–Sat. 10 A.M.–2 A.M.
COST: $5
Map 3

When you see the two-story bottle of chianti near 1st Avenue and Prince, you'll know you've found Boondock's Lounge, a friendly place with lots of pool tables and dartboards, a cast of regulars, and a stage that welcomes roots rock, reggae, and country bands throughout the week. The in-house Range Rider's Grille serves good burgers, sandwiches, and finger foods, and five nights a week there's a dinner special for a mere $5–6 a plate. It's an all-around fine place to spend your time.

☾ CLUB CONGRESS

311 E. Congress St., 520/622-8848,
www.hotelcongress.com

HOURS: Sun.–Mon. 9 P.M.–1 A.M., Tues.–Sat. 10 P.M.–1 A.M.
COST: Cover varies
Map 1

This small club inside the historic Hotel Congress is the city's premier spot for touring alternative rock and alt-country bands. Most nights, if there's not a band playing there's a DJ and dancing. Music geeks and college-town rock and rollers frequent the shows here, and it's a kind of headquarters for the thriving downtown music scene—the stage new local bands aspire to. If you're not in the mood for sweaty crowds, guitars, or break-beats, there's a somewhat quieter lounge in the lobby, but the music is the club's reason for being, and thank the gods for that. Check their website for the live music schedule and show times.

THE HUT

305 N. 4th Ave., 520/623-3200, www.huttucson.com
HOURS: Mon.–Fri. 4 P.M.–2 A.M., Sat.–Sun. noon–2 A.M.

NIGHTLIFE

© TIM HULL

This dude greets you as you stumble into The Hut.

COST: Cover varies
Map 2

This faux-tropical bar features roots rock, rock, blues, reggae, and even spoken-word performance art. It has a kind of slum-tiki vibe: laid-back and beach-bound with a lot of frozen drinks on the menu. A three-story cement tiki head saved from a beloved but defunct miniature golf course in east Tucson greets patrons as they enter, adding one more reason to visit this classic watering hole.

◖ NIMBUS BREWING COMPANY
3850 E. 44th St., No. 138, 520/745-9175,
www.nimbusbeer.com
HOURS: Mon.-Thurs. 11 A.M.-11 P.M., Fri.-Sat. 11 A.M.-1 A.M., Sun. 11 A.M.-9 P.M.
COST: $3-5
Map 7

The home of the best craft beer in the state also books local and touring rock, folk, blues, and country bands into the same ultra-casual brew-house setting from which they produce 22,500 barrels of delicious elixir every year. If you don't like beer, and you don't like to rock, you'll find there's not much to do here. But if you do like beer, especially European-style ales (Nimbus makes six different flavors), then you must go here. The bands are usually excellent and a lot of fun. They offer a small menu of tasty "munchies" to help soak up a few pints.

PLUSH
340 E. 6th St., 520/798-1298, www.plushtucson.com
HOURS: Mon.-Sat. 4 P.M.-2 A.M., Sun. 6 P.M.-2 A.M.
COST: Cover varies
Map 2

A well-appointed, comfortable club frequented by downtown artists and musicians, hipsters, and students, Plush is the place on 4th to experience Tucson's vibrant music scene, as well as nationally known alternative rock and alt-country acts. There are often acts playing in the front living-room area and on a stage in the back; there's also a patio for smoking.

SKYBOX
5605 E. River Rd., 520/529-7180,
www.skyboxrestaurant.com
HOURS: Sun.-Thur. 11 A.M.-1 A.M., Fri.-Sat. 11 A.M.-2 A.M.
COST: Generally no cover
Map 4

This midscale bar and restaurant in the Catalina Foothills has spectacular views of the city and sports on all the televisions. It generally attracts 30- and 40-somethings who are happy to be out of the house with a buzz on, and who aren't afraid to dance. Things reach a fever pitch on Friday nights around 9:30 P.M., when an afterwork crowd, well-lubricated in the aftermath of happy hour (Mon.–Fri. 4–7 P.M.), stays on to party with 80's and Gentleman, a 1980s pop cover band—featuring a spot-on retro Madonna singer—that gets the whole place hopping and cheering. It's a campy, memorable good time.

WHISKEY TANGO
1405 S. Kolb Rd., 520/344-8843
HOURS: Mon.-Fri. 11 A.M.-2 A.M., Sat.-Sun. 2 P.M.-2 A.M.
COST: Generally no cover
Map 6

Recently remodeled and repurposed, this eastside bar is worth a visit on Tuesday, Friday, and Saturday nights, when local bands rock the relatively small space and the crowd gets wild helped by the cheap drinks. This is a great non-downtown place to sample what the local music scene has to offer. You are almost guaranteed to have your socks entirely rocked off. Think about maybe wearing flip-flops.

Lounges

AZUL LOUNGE AT THE WESTIN LA PALOMA

3800 E. Sunrise Dr., 520/742-6000,
www.westinlapalomaresort.com
HOURS: Daily 2 P.M.-midnight
COST: Generally no cover
Map 4

Sipping a martini among stylish and stimulating surroundings while watching the desert city fade to black from high above the valley is just as much of a typical Tucson experience as scrambling up some rocky trail shadowed by saguaros. One of the best places to do the former is the Azul Lounge, a rather upscale but not forbidding lounge at the Westin La Paloma Resort in the Catalina Foothills. The lounge, decorated all in blue and washed by music that registers but doesn't get in the way, offers topnotch cocktails and delicious small plates, all complemented with a view that can't be beat. The least expensive time to go is during happy hour (Mon.–Fri. 5–7 P.M.).

☾ BAR TOMA

311 N. Court Ave., 520/622-1922,
www.elcharrocafe.com
HOURS: Mon.-Fri. 11 A.M.-9 P.M., Sat. 10:30 P.M.-2 A.M.
COST: Generally no cover
Map 1

El Charro, one of the Old Pueblo's oldest and best-loved restaurants, has several locations around town, each of them with a version of Bar Toma, from which the local chain serves some of the best margaritas available anywhere. During happy hour (Mon.–Fri. 3–6 P.M.), those margaritas are sold for half their usual price, as are the restaurant's distinctive Mexican appetizers. Bar Toma offers a long list of premium tequilas (all the *añejos, blancos,* and *reposados* you'll ever need) and, of course, all the usual beers and cocktails as well.

BLANCO TACOS + TEQUILA

2905 E. Skyline Dr., 520/232-1007, www.foxrc.com
HOURS: Sun.-Thurs. 11 A.M.-10 P.M., Fri.-Sat. 11 A.M.-11 P.M.

NIGHTLIFE

© TIM HULL

Blanco Tacos + Tequila

COST: Generally no cover
Map 4

A sleek, high-style Mexican place in the urban mode, with a delightful patio looking over the valley from a foothills perch at high-end La Encantada, Blanco Tacos + Tequila usually attracts a youngish and necessarily moneyed crowd; even a few drinks and appetizers on the patio is going to cost you $50 at least. They serve some delicious signature margaritas and cocktails, the best of which are the white peach and hibiscus margarita ($9); their Sangria Rojo, made with red wine, raspberries, strawberries, plums, and currants ($8); and the distinctive black-and-blue mojito, with fresh blackberries

and raspberries mixed in ($10). A daily happy hour (4–6 P.M.) puts the excellent drinks here somewhat within the normal person's price range.

CASCADE LOUNGE AT LOEWS VENTANA CANYON RESORT

7000 N. Resort Dr., 520/299-2020,
www.loewshotels.com
HOURS: Sun.-Thurs. 2-10 P.M., Fri.-Sat. 2 P.M.-midnight
COST: Generally no cover
Map 4

Eminently tasteful and upscale, with warm and earthy colors, thick and comfortable furniture, low, flattering lighting, and 30-foot windows

TEQUILA: A SHORT GUIDE

Tucson's best restaurants are its many authentic Mexican eateries, and many of them offer hundreds of different kinds of tequila, an alcohol made in the state of Jalisco, in a city called Tequila. Tequila is made exclusively from just one species of the agave plant, the blue agave. Another drink, mezcal, is made from 100 percent agave, but is prepared in a different way than tequila, giving it an earthier, almost "dirty" taste that some borderlanders prefer over the more popular and widely available tequila. The southern Mexican state of Oaxaca (pronounced wa-HA-kah) is known for producing superior mezcal, but it is also made in other regions of Mexico; whereas tequila, by law, is made only in Jalisco. A simple rule to go by is this: All tequila is mezcal, but not all mezcal is tequila. Mezcal is probably best known in the United States as the drink with the worm at the bottom of the bottle. Contrary to myth, the worm has no hallucinogenic properties (trust me—I've eaten dozens of them). Not too many restaurants and bars in the Old Pueblo serve mezcal, although you can usually find one or two brands at some of the better-stocked liquor stores in Tucson. Try **The RumRunner** (3131 E. 1st St., 520/326-0121, www.rumrunner.com, Mon. 11 A.M.-7 P.M., Tues.-Sat. 11 A.M.-10 P.M., Sun. noon-6 P.M.) on

Speedway Boulevard east of Tucson Boulevard, or **Plaza Liquors** (2642 N. Campbell Ave., 520/327-0452, Mon.-Sat. 10 A.M.-9 P.M.) on Campbell just north of Grant Road. Of course, if you make a short drive to Nogales, Sonora, Mexico's tourist area just across the border, there are many stores that sell Oaxacan mezcal.

As for tequila, there are several different kinds to choose from, not to mention myriad brands. If you're having a margarita, a popular tequila-based cocktail with lime juice and other flavors, it's not overly important that it be made with the most expensive, best tequila (although it certainly doesn't hurt). Usually an **oro** (gold) tequila, which has colors and flavors added to it, will do. If you're a bit confused by all the different kinds of tequila available, remember: **Blanco** (white or silver) tequila is bottled less than 60 days after being distilled in stainless-steel barrels; **reposado** (rested) has been aged anywhere from two months to one year in oak barrels; and **añejo** (aged) has been aged for at least one year. If you want to drink your tequila straight (with a bit of lime and salt added), it's best to choose a brand made from 100 percent agave, with no sugars or other ingredients added. Or just ask your bartender—they are usually very nice, understanding people.

offering commanding views from Ventana Canyon's high perch in the Catalina Foothills, the Cascade Lounge is one of Tucson's most romantic night spots. They offer a nightly happy hour with affordable drinks and small plates (5:30–7:30 P.M.), and there's music Wednesday–Saturday.

CHE'S LOUNGE
350 N. 4th Ave., 520/623-2088, www.cheslounge.com
HOURS: Daily noon-2 A.M.
COST: Generally no cover
Map 2

Not exactly a hangout for revolutionaries in the Che Guevara mode, Che's Lounge is instead a small, inviting hangout for a vast array of 4th Avenue denizens, from college kids to 40-somethings. They don't charge much for their drinks, and if you're broke you can always find somebody with $1 to buy you a PBR or one of the round-robin of $1 drafts they serve nightly. Bands set up in the cramped corners most weekend nights, and there are a few classic arcade games scattered throughout and an excellent, fully stocked juke.

ELLIOTT'S ON CONGRESS
135 E. Congress St., 520/622-5500,
http://elliottsoncongress.com
HOURS: Mon.-Sun. 11 A.M.-2 A.M.
COST: Generally no cover
Map 1

This cozy and hip downtown bar and restaurant is the place to go for infused vodka; they offer dozens of house-infused varieties with flavors that, at first glance, seem a bit nonsensical: jalapeño, habanero, green bell pepper, horseradish, etc. Always try it before you scoff, though; the best time to do so is during the daily happy hour (4–7 P.M.), during which the unique concoctions are just $3. The food here is worth a trip in itself (try the duck sliders or the vodka pasta), and the unique appetizers, perfect companions for your distilled delights, include

the Jalapeño Board: open-faced jalapeño peppers baked with several cheeses, shrimp, and bacon, drizzled with sweet agave.

KON TIKI
4625 E. Broadway Blvd., 520/323-7193,
www.kontikitucson.com
HOURS: Mon.-Thurs. 11 A.M.-1 A.M., Fri.-Sat. 10 A.M.-2 A.M., Sun. 10 A.M.-midnight
COST: Generally no cover
Map 3

The ancient recipe of fruit juice mixed with booze is at the heart of this retro-realistic spot on Broadway Boulevard, a favorite among the Arizona tiki-culture crowd since it opened way back in 1963. The drinks at Kon Tiki are a far cry from a red plastic cup full of "jungle juice" ladled out in some dorm room, however. Even if you claim to be a shot-and-beer type, it's hard to resist escaping to Kon Tiki's cool, dark interior to sip away at happy hour (when tasty pupus, with amazing booze-soaking power, are half price), trying something pink, something blue, something red, something frozen, something served in a Polynesian-style bowl bigger than your head. Make sure to say hello to the huge, languid iguana hanging out behind glass.

MUSIC BOX LOUNGE
6951 E. 22nd St., 520/747-1421
HOURS: Mon.-Sat. 11 A.M.-2 A.M., Sun. 11 A.M.-9 P.M.
COST: Generally no cover
Map 6

A fun place to hang out on the far east side, the Music Box offers all the games and events that the contemporary bargoer has come to expect: karaoke, beer pong, Wii, and a DJ spinning top-40 dance hits on Friday and Saturday nights. The drinks are cheap, with well and domestic beers usually under $3. There's a nice smoking patio, and the place has a friendly, regulars' vibe. They serve chili dogs and burgers throughout the night.

TUCSON'S CASINOS

Near Tucson are three casinos owned and operated by Native American tribes, and all of them offer slots, poker, blackjack, and plenty of other games of chance to separate you from your money. Though it's not exactly Vegas, the "Indian casinos," as most locals call them, are generally clean and fun places to spend your time. The completely rebuilt **Desert Diamond Casino & Hotel** (7350 S. Nogales Hwy., 520/294-7777 or 866/332-9467, www.desertdiamondcasino.com) has excellent accommodations and several restaurants on-site—including a steak house and Vegas-style all-you-can-eat buffet. The hotel-casino, operated by the Tohono O'odham, also has the **Monsoon Nightclub,** which brings in a mixed crowd of dancing revelers that skews a bit older than other dance clubs in town.

About 20 miles south of downtown Tucson, along I-19, the O'odham operate a second **Desert Diamond Casino** (520/294-7777, www.desertdiamondcasino.com) near the small bedroom town of Sahuarita and just a hop and a skip to the retirement community of Green Valley. As such, you're likely to see a few retirees hanging around the blackjack tables,

poker tournaments, and slots spending their Social Security checks. The New American cuisine served at the elegant **Agave Restaurant** (Mon.-Thurs. 11 A.M.-10 P.M., Fri.-Sat. 11 A.M.-11 P.M., Sun. 11 A.M.-7 P.M.) is always tasty, and the all-you-can-eat buffet is delicious, fresh, and stocked with more food than anybody needs. There's also a constant stream of talent moving through the **Diamond Entertainment Center,** an intimate concert theater that has hosted top-name acts like Willie Nelson and Bob Dylan.

A Mediterranean-influenced funland with poker, slots, bingo, blackjack, and keno, **Casino del Sol** (5655 W. Valencia Rd., 800/344-9435, www.casinodelsol.com) is operated by the Pascua Yaqui. About 17 miles southwest of downtown Tucson, the casino offers delicious high-end continental cuisine at **Bellissimo** (daily 5-11 P.M.) and live music in the **Paradise Bar and Lounge.** Check the website for the schedule of bands playing at the intimate **Anselmo Valencia Tori Amphitheater,** which welcomes national touring acts, many of them stars from the 1960s, 1970s, and 1980s.

THE PLAYGROUND BAR & LOUNGE
278 E. Congress St., 520/396-3691,
http://playgroundtucson.com
HOURS: Mon.-Fri. 4 P.M.-2 A.M., Sat.-Sun. noon-2 A.M.
COST: Generally no cover
Map 1

The premier downtown desert-hipster hangout with a lost childhood theme, the best thing about the Playground, besides its deep stylishness, is its spectacular rooftop patio with panoramic views of the city—the perfect place to sip a margarita or a martini while the sun dips away in the cool of the evening. Twentieth-century nostalgia and a kind of slacker-intellectual ethos pervade here: DJs playing only vinyl,

"show and tell" lectures on local issues, scarf-wearing fans gathering to watch FIFA soccer games. Often there's a shoe-gazing local band playing on one floor while an energetic DJ entertains on another. They offer cheap drinks during "recess" (Mon.–Fri. 4–7 P.M.).

SCOTT & CO.
49 N. Scott Ave., 520/624-4747, www.47scott.com
HOURS: Mon.-Sat. 6 P.M.-close
COST: Generally no cover
Map 1

A tiny, outwardly nondescript speakeasy-style bar on downtown's Scott Avenue, the emphasis here is on the drink in your hand. The expert

Scott & Co. has a speakeasy vibe.

bartenders at Scott & Co., which is connected to the excellent restaurant **47 Scott** (47 N. Scott Ave., 520/624-4747, Mon.–Fri. 4 P.M.–close, Sat.–Sun. 10 A.M.–close) next door, take their jobs very seriously. The menu of unique and creative drinks—many of them updated twists on classic cocktails (e.g., the Sonoran Old Fashioned: *añejo* tequila, bacanora, agave nectar, bitters, and grapefruit)—changes often, but the ingredients are always top shelf and house-made. Don't pass up the chance to have the bartender make you a custom drink based on an interview about your preferences. This place is not appropriate for large, loud parties; it's more a romantic throwback to the days when drinking cocktails was serious business.

SKYBAR
536 N. 4th Ave., 520/622-4300,
www.skybartucson.com

HOURS: Daily 9 A.M.–2 A.M.
COST: Generally no cover
Map 2

Skybar is the best bar on 4th Avenue, perhaps in the whole of Tucson. Powered by the sun and situated next door to a pizza place that will walk your pie over and drop it on the bar, this welcoming, comfortable, and fun bar is the ideal place to waste your life away. Live bands shake the place most nights, and there's a small dancing space if the mood strikes. However, it's difficult, especially after a few martinis, to take your eyes off the big screens showing live shots of the cosmos as seen through the bar's own telescope. The crowd is the typical 4th Avenue mixture of local rockers, college-age hipsters, and that certain set of Old Pueblo old folks who won't stay home when there's a rock band playing somewhere in the desert city.

SMOKE CIGAR PATIO AND BAR
2959 N. Swan Rd., 520/327-7463,
www.metrorestaurants.com
HOURS: Mon.–Thurs. 11:30 A.M.–9 P.M.,
Fri. 11:30 A.M.–10 P.M., Sat. 5–9 P.M., Sun. 5–8 P.M.
COST: Generally no cover
Map 3

This very comfortable and stylish climate-controlled smoker's patio-lounge is at McMahon's Prime Steakhouse. The steak house isn't among my recommendations, but if you're a smoker looking for fellow travelers and a high-end place to relax with a drink, an appetizer, and a clean ashtray at the ready, this is the place for you. It's a bit pricey all around, but they offer daily drink and food specials, and a happy hour (Mon.–Fri. 3–7 P.M.). The cigar selection runs from as low as $2.50 to as high as $36, with most falling in the $8–15 range. While nearly all of Tucson's bars have added enclosed climate-controlled patios since an ordinance banned smoking in bars otherwise, this is by far the nicest.

NIGHTLIFE

© TIM HULL

Wine Bars

ARMITAGE WINE LOUNGE AND CAFE
2905 E. Skyline Dr., Ste. 168, 520/682-9740,
www.armitagewine.com
HOURS: Mon.-Fri. 11 A.M.-11:30 P.M.,
Sat.-Sun. 10 A.M.-midnight (lounge open later)
COST: Generally no cover
Map 4

Located in the upscale La Encantada shopping
center in the Foothills, Armitage has ambience
to spare, a deep wine list, delicious fare, and
excellent cocktails (their martinis are especially
good) for those in your party who don't prefer the grape. They offer wine tastings (Tues.
6–8 P.M.) and happy hour (daily 4–7 P.M. and
10 P.M.–close). To truly sample Armitage's cel-
lar, try a few of their flights.

CATAVINOS
3063 N. Alvernon Way, 520/323-3063,
www.catavinoswines.com
HOURS: Tues.-Wed. 11 A.M.-6 P.M.,
Thurs.-Sat. 11 A.M.-8 P.M.
COST: Generally no cover
Map 3

This locally owned cozy wine shop and tasting
room on Alvernon Way is the most affordable
destination in town for wine lovers, with hundreds of great wines from around the globe offered for under $15 a bottle. The themed wine
tastings (Thurs.–Sat. 4–8 P.M.) feature a different flight of six wines every week, and include
cheese and crackers for just $10 per person ($8 if
you buy a bottle for $10 or more). CataVinos also
features a rotating gallery of local and regional
art to look at while you're worshipping the grape.

NIGHTLIFE

ARTS AND LEISURE

Tucson is an active, outdoorsy, sunburned place. On any given day, you'll see Tucsonans decked out in colorful, skin-tight Lycra outfits, pedaling with all their might up and down the steep mountain roads and along the bike routes through the city; you'll also see them hiking on desert trails among the saguaro forests, and exploring the sky island mountain ranges that encircle the valley. If you're coming to Tucson to find some similar action, you won't have to look far.

Tucson is also a cultural center; it is the cultural capital of Arizona, and one of the top art towns in the Southwest. There are scores of galleries and museums in town, and, contrary to popular opinion, not all of them are dedicated exclusively to paintings of cowboys and Indians and howling coyotes. The festival seasons in Tucson are pretty much the opposite of everywhere else. There's little going on here in the summer, but come February suddenly the calendar is full with arts fairs, cultural festivals, and sporting events.

Let's say you want to get some exercise but you don't feel like jogging or biking or walking in the wild desert. Fear not, for as much as I've tried to show that Tucson is indeed an exotic city with a wholly unique setting, the truth is that much of the town is as normal and American as can be. That means there are myriad green-grass parks within easy distance of all the neighborhoods. Here you can play all the tennis, golf, and pick-up basketball that you want, only you don't have to take it inside when the summer ends.

© TIM HULL

HIGHLIGHTS

LOOK FOR 【 TO FIND RECOMMENDED ARTS AND ACTIVITIES.

© TIM HULL

The Loft Cinema

【 **Best Place to Brush Up on Tucson's History:** Visit the **Arizona Historical Society Downtown Museum** to learn about the history of Tucson's city center from the dusty-street territorial days to the advent of suburban sprawl in the 1960s (page 107).

【 **Best Contemporary Art Gallery: Etherton Gallery** concentrates on photography—from the classic 19th-century chroniclers of the West to today's shutterbugs, as well as regional and local artists of the highest caliber (page 111).

【 **Best Southwestern Art Gallery:** At the **Mark Sublette Medicine Man Gallery** you can view all the famous images and tropes from the Southwest's history beside the best interpretations of the region by today's artists (page 112).

【 **Best Live-Music Venue:** Open since 1920 and over the years a vaudeville house, a silent movie theater, and a porn theater, **The Rialto** now operates as a nonprofit organization showing the best concerts in town (page 114).

【 **Best Movie Theater: The Loft Cinema,** a nonprofit art house, shows the best in contemporary and classic cinema, along with craft-brewed beers and gourmet pizza (page 117).

【 **Best Festival:** Make sure you're hungry when you attend the annual multicultural **Tucson Meet Yourself** festival at downtown's El Presidio Park. Members of dozens of cultural clubs—from Colombians to Navajos—cook up and sell their national cuisine (page 121).

【 **Best Urban Park:** The cool green grass, duck ponds, shade trees, and state-of-the-art playgrounds at **Gene C. Reid Park** will make you forget you're in a desert (page 125).

【 **Best Hiking in the Mountains:** About an hour's drive from Tucson's downtown, **Mount Lemmon hiking trails** are green, lush, and about 10 degrees cooler than the desert floor far below (page 133).

【 **Best Hiking in the Desert: Tucson Mountain Park** is a huge public park west of downtown that has dozens of desertland trails with some of the largest saguaro forests in the world (page 135).

【 **Best Mountain Biking:** A fantastic system of single-track trails on a swath of scrubby state-trust land southeast of midtown, the **Fantasy Island biking trails** are indeed a mountain biker's dream come true (page 137).

The Arts

The creative class is well represented in Tucson. Indeed, there are probably more artists and artisans living in or near the Old Pueblo than in any other Arizona locale save the Navajo and Hopi Reservations. Many of the top galleries in Tucson also have sister galleries in Santa Fe, New Mexico, or in Sedona in Northern Arizona. You don't have to appreciate the sometimes overly romantic depictions of the famed Old West to enjoy looking at art in Tucson. There are all kinds of galleries, especially in the downtown area, that show art from a more experimental, contemporary Southwest, and there are few cowboys left these days. But if you do love Western and Southwestern art, from the conservative to the experimental, there are few better places to be. Head to the foothills neighborhood around Campbell and Skyline for galleries showing the best of the genre.

MUSEUMS

You'll find the largest and best of the city's museums in the *Sights* chapter. Described here are some of Tucson's smaller, more specific museums, for those with an interest in Arizona history, mining history, rodeo, archaeology, trains, photography, art, and other subjects.

◀ ARIZONA HISTORICAL SOCIETY DOWNTOWN MUSEUM

140 N. Stone Ave., 520/770-1473,
www.arizonahistoricalsociety.org
HOURS: Tues.-Fri. 10 A.M.-4 P.M.
COST: $3 adult, $2 student 12-18 and senior
Map 1

Until shopping malls began to proliferate in midtown starting in the 1960s, downtown Tucson was the commercial and social heart of the city, a fact that this small museum celebrates. While there are ongoing attempts to revitalize downtown through a project called Rio Nuevo, it's unlikely the once-bustling mixed-use area will ever return to its former glory, when locally owned department stores, barber shops, boutiques, hotels, restaurants, and

theaters lined the narrow streets, the sidewalks crowded with people working, shopping, living, and playing all within the same few blocks. The museum, tucked away in a few rooms off the lobby of the Wells Fargo building on Stone Avenue—a still-busy, business-minded downtown district crowded on the weekdays but largely deserted after 5 P.M. Friday—shows artifacts from the early days of downtown to its desertion, with large, rare photographs and saved ephemera from different eras of the city's history. An especially interesting installation tells the history of the Dillinger gang's capture in Tucson in the 1930s.

ARIZONA HISTORICAL SOCIETY MUSEUM

949 E. 2nd St., 520/628-5774,
www.arizonahistoricalsociety.org
HOURS: Mon.-Sat. 10 A.M.-4 P.M.
COST: $5 adult, $4 student
Map 2

Just south of the Main Gate wall along North Campus Drive is the largest of the Arizona Historical Society's three Tucson museums. Exhibits include a full-scale reproduction of the cramped canvas-tent homes early miners lived in and a walk through a dark underground mine. There's also an old Studebaker on display; this make of car was once so popular with Arizona's sheriffs that the car company sent an author to the young state to write a public relations pamphlet that included exciting stories of frontier law enforcement. This is an interesting stop for Arizona history buffs, and there are several hands-on exhibits for the kids.

ASARCO MINERAL DISCOVERY CENTER

1421 W. Pima Mine Rd., Sahuarita, 520/625-8233,
www.mineraldiscovery.com
HOURS: Tues.-Sat. 9 A.M.-5 P.M.
COST: Exhibitions free, mine tour $8 adult,
$5 child 5-12
Map 8

The Discovery Center explains, using exhibits,

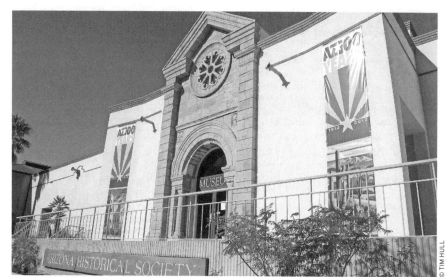

© TIM HULL

Arizona Historical Society Museum

old mining equipment, and films, how all the huge piles of dirt flanking the valley's west side got there. The copper in the Santa Cruz Valley is of the porphyry variety, meaning it's very low grade and takes a lot of earth moving to get at; a one-hour bus tour offered five times a day on Tuesday, Thursday, and Saturday will take you up into the hills to the sprawling Mission Mine to show you how it's done. From the bus you'll see the vast pit and the post-apocalyptic landscape created by large-scale copper mining, and you'll drive through a working mill. Back at the Discovery Center there's a gift shop that sells souvenirs.

CENTER FOR CREATIVE PHOTOGRAPHY
1030 N. Olive Rd., 520/621-7968,
www.creativephotography.org
HOURS: Mon.-Fri. 9 A.M.-5 P.M., Sat.-Sun. 1-5 P.M.
COST: Free
Map 2

UA's Center for Creative Photography has one of the largest photography collections in the world; it holds the archives of Ansel Adams,

Edward Weston, and dozens more major artists. The center mounts a few exhibitions a year, so it's a good idea to check the website in advance to see what's on display. You can even make an appointment to personally view a few of the 80,000 prints accessible to the public.

FORT LOWELL MUSEUM
2900 N. Craycroft Rd., 520/885-3832,
www.arizonahistoricalsociety.org
HOURS: Fri.-Sat. 10 A.M.-4 P.M.
COST: $3 adult, $2 child under 18
Map 3

This small museum is dedicated to the stories of the Apache wars of the late 19th century. There are still a few crumbling adobe ruins left behind that give a sense of what the fort was like just before it was abandoned in 1891, after the end of the struggle between the army and various Apache tribes. Displays inside the reconstructed commanding officer's quarters tell the whole history of those wars and show what life was like then, with pictures, artifacts, and text.

GADSDEN-PACIFIC DIVISION
TOY TRAINS OPERATING MUSEUM

3975 N. Miller Ave., 520/888-2222,
www.gpdtoytrainmuseum.com
HOURS: Sept.-June second and fourth Sun. of the
month 12:30-4:30 P.M., closed July and Aug.
COST: Free
Map 5

This North Side toy-train museum is open
only rarely, but if you're an enthusiast of miniature trains you'll want to see it. The museum's main warehouse building features several
large, intricate toy-train cities, and there's a
historic caboose waiting in retirement on the
grounds. The museum isn't open in July and
August, and it's only open to the public two
weekends a month otherwise, so it's a good idea
to call ahead if you want to visit. It's located
two blocks west of Price and Romero Roads,
on Miller Avenue.

INTERNATIONAL WILDLIFE MUSEUM

4800 W. Gates Pass Rd., 520/629-0100,
www.thewildlifemuseum.org
HOURS: Mon.-Fri. 9 A.M.-5 P.M., Sat.-Sun. 9 A.M.-6 P.M.
COST: $8 adult, $3 child 4-12
Map 5

As you drive west toward Gates Pass and the
Tucson Mountains, off on the north side of
the road, partly obscured by the thick desert,
a large castle-esque building holds the impressive taxidermy collection of this private,
nonprofit natural-history museum. There are
more than 400 stuffed and preserved mammals, birds, insects, and spiders here, including "Big Terror," a stuffed tiger who still looks
a bit hungry. The mighty beast was killed in
1969 in India, after he'd reportedly devoured
between 8 and 12 people. This is a fun and
educational place to bring kids, but if you have
limited time I'd recommend skipping it in
favor of the Arizona-Sonoran Desert Museum
a few miles up the road, where the mountain
lions, rattlesnakes, beavers, and scorpions are
all indigenous—and alive.

MINI TIME MACHINE MUSEUM
OF MINIATURES

4455 E. Camp Lowell Dr., 520/881-0606,
www.theminitimemachine.org
HOURS: Tues.-Sat. 9 A.M.-4 P.M., Sun. noon-4 P.M.
COST: $9 adult, $6 child
Map 3

Built by passionate collectors of all things
miniature, this charming museum in midtown is a great place to take kids, who generally find all the tiny objects and detailed
dioramas endlessly fascinating. They'll also
like the Enchanted Tree, with its big face and
fairytale trunk-life. The museum has a permanent collection of nearly 300 miniatures,
both contemporary and antique, and presents
special exhibits from time to time that explore
a particular theme or style in depth and, of
course, in miniature.

SOUTHERN ARIZONA
TRANSPORTATION MUSEUM

414 N. Toole Ave., 520/623-2223,
www.tucsonhistoricdepot.org
HOURS: Tues.-Thurs. 11 A.M.-3 P.M., Fri.-Sat.
10 A.M.-4 P.M., Sun. 11 A.M.-3 P.M.
COST: Free
Map 1

When the railroad reached the isolated town
of Tucson in the 1880s, it transformed the city
and the region. This small museum at the refurbished old rail depot downtown explains all
the myriad ways the railroad, and later the car
and the interstate system, changed Tucson and
the Southwest, opening it up to visitors and
settlers and linking it more with the United
States rather than with Mexico, as it had
been before the train's arrival. There's a life-
like statue of Wyatt Earp and Doc Holliday
nearby, and a plaque that tells the story of a
bit of revenge and/or murder that went down
here back in the old violent days. Also, an old
locomotive of the kind that used to haul goods
and folks across the nation is preserved and
on display.

ARTS AND LEISURE

TUCSON CHILDREN'S MUSEUM

200 S. 6th Ave., 520/792-9985,
www.tucsonchildrensmuseum.org
HOURS: Tues.-Fri. 9 A.M.-5 P.M., Sat.-Sun. 10 A.M.-5 P.M.
COST: $8 adult, $6 senior and child 2-18
Map 1

My favorite thing about the Tucson Children's Museum is the historic downtown Carnegie Library building it's been housed in since 1991. But if you have kids, you're sure to appreciate the creativity and attention to detail of the operators of this nonprofit interactive learning center. There are 12 permanent exhibits here, all of them hands-on and featuring some kid-mesmerizing subject like dinosaurs, electricity, ocean life, or trains. There's also an "enchanted rainforest" geared toward preschoolers. It's not always easy to find parking because the museum has no lot of its own. There are metered spaces around the museum, and $1 in change will get you about two hours during the week; on weekends parking is free.

TUCSON RODEO PARADE MUSEUM

4823 S. 6th Ave., 520/294-3636,
www.tucsonrodeoparade.org
HOURS: Jan.-Apr. Mon.-Sat. 9:30 A.M.-3:30 P.M.
(hours vary during rodeo week in Feb.)
COST: $10 adult, $2 child
Map 7

In a circa-1918 hangar on the south side, a fabled "surrey with the fringe on top" used in the 1955 film *Oklahoma*—filmed in the Santa Cruz Valley south of Tucson—is preserved in near-mint condition along with scores of other original buggies and wagons from the days before the internal combustion engine took over the world. Many of the buggies and wagons are hitched up to horses and rattled through the streets in late February during the annual Rodeo Parade, the longest nonmotorized parade in the nation. Other highlights include a carriage once owned by industrialist Andrew Carnegie; a U.S. Army freight wagon from the days when the army occupied the Arizona Territory; and a carriage that was used for a time by Emperor Maximilian, whom the French set up as their puppet leader of Mexico

in 1864. There's also a re-creation of what Tucson's main street might have looked like in the 19th century, including a blacksmith shop and a bunkhouse.

VISTA DEL RIO CULTURAL RESOURCE PARK

7575 E. Desert Arbors St., 520/791-4873
HOURS: Daily dawn-dusk
Map 6

Before the Spanish arrived in Southern Arizona, before the Mexicans, before the Americans, even before the Tohono O'odham and the Apache ruled this desert, it was home to the Hohokam people, arid-land farmers who lived in the Sonoran Desert's river valleys, building a highly complex culture that survived for centuries. Though the Tucson Valley doesn't have any spectacular Hohokam ruins on the order of Casa Grande (just off I-10 halfway between Tucson and Phoenix), this four-acre east-side archaeological park preserves the humbler ruins of a village occupied by the Hohokam from about A.D. 1000 to 1150. Even if you're less than fascinated by the dirt-mound ruins, this is a quiet and peaceful park with walking paths and sitting areas, perfect for relaxation and contemplation among the ghosts of a long-lost nation.

GALLERIES

CONRAD WILDE GALLERY

439 N. 6th Ave., 520/622-8997,
www.conradwildegallery.com
HOURS: Tues.-Sat. 11 A.M.-5 P.M.
Map 2

An emphasis on abstraction and the mysterious power of color pervades this downtown gallery. Emerging and established artists have common cause here, but most of the colorful, challenging work is by artists (many of them regional) with long resumes. Collectors especially shouldn't miss popping into Conrad Wilde if they are in town. Contemporary paintings, sculpture, and works on paper are all well represented, and the works often have an experimental quality that will make you scratch your head and lose your breath at the same time.

🄲 ETHERTON GALLERY

135 S. 6th Ave., 520/624-7370,
www.ethertongallery.com
HOURS: Tues.-Sat. 11 A.M.-5 P.M.
Map 1

Etherton is one of the city's finest galleries and is routinely voted among the best in town in the Old Pueblo's many polls. The downtown gallery, located in the historic Oddfellows Building, concentrates on photography—from the classic 19th-century chroniclers of the West to today's interpreters—and regional and local artists of the highest caliber. The **Temple Gallery** (330 S. Scott Ave., 520/624-7370, Mon.-Fri. 10 A.M.-5 P.M.) at the Temple of Music and Art is also managed by Etherton Gallery and features new work by local artists.

GALLERY ROW AT EL CORTIJO

3001 E. Skyline Dr., www.tucsongalleryrow.com
HOURS: Vary per gallery
Map 4

The best of the contemporary art galleries at Gallery Row at El Cortijo, a collection of five art galleries at 3001 East Skyline at Campbell, is the **Wilde Meyer Gallery** (3001 E. Skyline Dr., Ste. 115, 520/615-5222, www.wildemeyer. com, Mon.-Wed. and Fri. 10 A.M.-5:30 P.M., Thurs. 10 A.M.-7 P.M., Sat. 10 A.M.-6 P.M., Sun. noon-5 P.M.). Wilde Meyer truly has some of the best paintings in town and features a large and eclectic selection of contemporary paintings, many but certainly not all by artists dealing with the past, present, and future of the Southwest. Another gallery worth a pop-in here is **The Max Gallery** (3001 E. Skyline Dr., Ste. 127, 520/529-7349, www.themaxgallery. com, Tues.-Thurs. 10 A.M.-5:30 P.M., Fri.-Sat. 10 A.M.-7 P.M., Sun. 11 A.M.-4 P.M.), showing paintings and sculptures about the West and its many myths, legends, and iconic landscapes. There are also a few galleries worth perusing in the shopping center just to the south of Gallery Row along Skyline.

GALLERY WEST FINE AMERICAN INDIAN ART

6420 N. Campbell Ave., 520/529-7002,
www.indianartwest.com
HOURS: Mon.-Sat. 10 A.M.-4 P.M.
Map 4

A tiny gallery featuring Native American art

Gallery Row at El Cortijo

© TIM HULL

ARTS AND LEISURE

and artifacts from the 19th and 20th centuries, Gallery West, one of three excellent galleries of Western art that look out on a shady courtyard at Campbell and Skyline, features Tohono O'odham baskets, Hopi and Pueblo pottery—including rare Hopi tiles—kachinas from the 1950s and 1960s, and Navajo and Pueblo jewelry. They also sell unique reprints of the original 1886 photograph of Geronimo and Chiricahua Apache Chief Naiche by Tombstone photographer C. S. Fly—the only photographer to have photographed these infamous Apache warriors while they were on the run from the U.S. Army. A large (44" x 72") framed digital pigment print reproduced from the original first-generation photograph will set you back about $1,500 (although a small—23" x 28"—unframed reproduction runs as low as $250).

JOSEPH GROSS GALLERY AT THE UA SCHOOL OF ART

University of Arizona campus, 1031 N. Olive Rd. 520/626-4215, http://web.cfa.arizona.edu/galleries
HOURS: Mon.-Fri. 9 A.M.-4 P.M.
Map 2

A small gallery on the UA campus, the Joseph Gross Gallery, and its sister the Lionel Rombach Gallery, both free to the public, exhibit works by UA faculty, students, and various regional, national, and international artists working in a variety of media. The work featured here is usually some of the most experimental and cutting edge to be seen in the Old Pueblo, especially during the annual Master of Fine Arts Thesis show in April and May.

MADARAS GALLERY

Gallery Row, 3001 E. Skyline Dr., 520/615-3001, www.madaras.com
HOURS: Mon.-Sat. 10 A.M.-6 P.M., Sun. 11 A.M.-5 P.M.
Map 4

Diana Madaras is among Southern Arizona's most successful and popular artists; her watercolors and acrylics, a mixture of playful realism and expressionistic color, have earned her high-profile commissions—including paintings hanging at the Westin La Paloma, Loews

Ventana Canyon, and Mirival—a little bit of fame, and enough money to sustain not just one but two local galleries that feature her work exclusively. The second gallery location is in midtown (1535 E. Broadway Blvd., 520/623-4000). Her style is instantly recognizable once you see it for the first time, and her various whimsical and romantic interpretations of Southwestern landscapes, people, and culture represent her best work.

MARK SUBLETTE MEDICINE MAN GALLERY

6872 E. Sunrise Dr., 520/722-7798, www.medicinemangallery.com
HOURS: Late Nov.-Apr. Mon.-Sat. 10 A.M.-5 P.M., Sun. 1-4 P.M.; May-Sept. Tues.-Sat. 10 A.M.-5 P.M.; Oct.-late Nov. Mon.-Sat. 10 A.M.-5 P.M.
Map 4

For anyone enraptured by the classic art of the Southwest—from the photographs of Edward Curtis to the modernist illustrations of Maynard Dixon; from the ceremonial kachinas of the Hopi people to the elegant yellow-brown pottery of Nampeyo—Mark Sublette's Medicine Man Gallery is an absolute must-visit. The huge gallery also features the **Maynard Dixon Museum,** with a wide selection of often obscure paintings, illustrations, and ephemera from throughout the great artist's career. There's also a contemporary art gallery here featuring the best in new Western art by the likes of the fabulous Navajo artist Shonto Begay.

MOCA TUCSON

265 S. Church Ave., 520/624-5019, www.moca-tucson.org
HOURS: Wed.-Sun. noon-5 P.M.
COST: $8
Map 1

True to a long tradition of repurposing old buildings in downtown Tucson, this exhibit space used to be a fire station. MOCA puts on several exhibits each year, mixing paintings, photography, and installations—with a seeming preference for the latter. When they say contemporary here they really mean it: You

MAYNARD DIXON: MASTER PAINTER OF THE TUCSON VALLEY

Maynard Dixon (1875-1946) was a popular artist and illustrator who mixed the Southwest's exotic landscapes and peoples with the aesthetic tropes of modernism. He lived and painted in Tucson in the 1930s and 1940s with his wife, the photographer Dorothea Lange.

Dixon had a very successful career as an illustrator for magazines, books, and advertising—he was there among the leading lights of the Golden Age of Illustration like Wyeth, Parrish, and, especially, Remington—before settling down to paint the desert and its peoples fulltime. In his commercial work he wandered, as many illustrators do, among realism, fantasy, and stereotype, and his paintings, mostly oils and watercolors, similarly teeter back and forth between pure recordings of bouncing-light landscapes and an almost social realism in some of his portraits of Native Americans.

Others of his paintings are mythic and border on a kind of romantic fantasy. In 1922, two decades after he first visited Arizona, Dixon lived at Walpi on First Mesa, in the land of Hopi Indians in northeastern Arizona, for four months. His hosts were "two Hopi snake priests, Namoki and his blind brother Loma Himna." One of the more powerful and evocative of Dixon's paintings from this era is *The Witch of Sikyatki*, an arresting scene from Hopi mythology in which the titular witch is locked in an unnerving glance at the viewer.

In Tucson, Dixon primarily painted the desert landscape, and I don't think anybody painted it better. The overwhelming feeling one gets after spending time with Dixon's work is one of being overwhelmed—by jutting rock, by deep canyons, by endless blue sky. In his paintings, the desert is nearly always much bigger than the people in it. And that's as it should be.

"Maynard Dixon's love for the simplified forms and colors in the west he wandered, explored and mined for subject matter, is what distinguishes him from other Western artists and makes him essential in every sense of the word," says a recent catalogue for the prestigious Scottsdale Art Auction, in which Dixon's painting *Prairie Mother* was expected to go for between $150,000 and $200,000. "It is Dixon," the catalogue continues, "who bridges modernism and the characteristic realism of Western art."

Here in the Old Pueblo, Dixon's work is very popular. In 2008 the Tucson Museum of Art put on the largest single show of his work ever, collecting each of Dixon's Arizona paintings in one place for the first time. At the essential **Medicine Man Gallery in Tucson,** there's a permanent display of much of Dixon's work collected at the Maynard Dixon Museum. The gallery's owner, Mark Sublette, also presents a lot of information on Dixon's life and many images of his work at www.maynarddixon.org.

---

will see art done this afternoon by working, struggling, and inspired artists confronting aesthetic and social themes in all kinds of interesting and confusing ways. Check the website before going for information on the most recent exhibits.

OBSIDIAN GALLERY

410 N. Toole Ave., 520/577-3598,
www.obsidian-gallery.com
HOURS: Wed. and Fri.-Sat. 11 A.M.-6 P.M.,
Thurs. 11 A.M.-8 P.M., Sun. 11 A.M.-2 P.M.
`Map 1`

You won't find many Southwestern cliches here. Obsidian, in the historic depot on Toole Avenue, features the best in contemporary fine arts and crafts by local and national artists with their feet firmly planted in imaginary worlds both parallel and counter to this one. There is much ironic whimsy in the crafts here, and also some nearly shocking beauty. The paintings stand out even in a forest of sculptures and ceramics, and seem to have been chosen, like all the art in this essential Tucson gallery, by a finely tuned and eclectic eye.

PLATFORM GALLERY

439 N. 6th Ave., 520/248-4500, www.platformart.com
HOURS: Thurs.-Sat. noon-4 P.M.
Map 2

This contemporary art gallery is in the warehouse arts district on the corner of 6th Avenue and 6th Street and offers a heady mix of paintings, drawings, photographs, and sculptures by emerging and established artists from the Southwest. Here, as in many of Tucson's contemporary art spaces, you'll find artists dealing with the region, and the history of the region's art, in exciting new ways. The owners seem to prefer a mixture of representation and abstraction, and the old utilitarian building (it looks like it might have been a gas station at one time) has been refurbished into something wonderful.

SANDERS GALLERIES

6420 N. Campbell Ave., 520/299-1763,
www.sandersgalleries.com
HOURS: Mon.-Sat. 10 A.M.-5 P.M.
Map 4

One of three longtime galleries looking out on a lush enclosed courtyard overlooking the valley at Campbell and Skyline, Sanders, like its neighbor Settlers West, features the kind of work that often appears in the magazine *Art of the West:* contemporary regional, national, and international artists, many of whom use as their subject matter scenes of Native American life; thrilling landscapes featuring mostly unspoiled Western scenes; and detailed, ultra-realistic portraits of iconic Western animals—mountains lions, bobcats, mustangs, and the like.

SETTLERS WEST GALLERY

6420 N. Campbell Ave., 520/299-2607,
www.settlerswest.com
HOURS: Mon.-Sat. 10 A.M.-5 P.M.
Map 4

For 30 years Settlers West has shown the best in contemporary and classic Western art. The paintings and sculptures depict romantic, even idealized, scenes of Native American life, many of them non-Southwestern. Wildlife art, depictions of cowboy culture, and landscapes filled with deserts, cacti, and red-rock canyons abound. This is not the place to find experimental or even modernist work—it's all pretty traditional, but always of the highest quality.

CONCERT VENUES

ANSELMO VALENCIA TORI AMPHITHEATER

Casino del Sol, 5655 W. Valencia Rd., 520/838-6700,
box office 520/838-6400, www.avaconcerts.com
Map 8

Where else are the likes of Queensryche or Frankie Valli and the Four Seasons going to play when they come to Tucson, the Rialto? Don't be absurd. They're too big to be contained by a roof. We can thank the proliferation of midsize outdoor venues like the 4,470-seat Anselmo Valencia Tori Amphitheater for keeping undead doo-woppers and the skeletal remains of bands we really liked when we were 13 on the touring circuit. This is Southern Arizona's largest concert venue, with six corporate boxes, nearly 2,000 seats, and a lawn for the rest of us.

FOX TUCSON THEATRE

17 W. Congress St., 520/624-1515,
www.foxtucsontheatre.org
HOURS: Box office Tues.-Fri. 11 A.M.-6 P.M., Sat.-Sun. two hours before performance
Map 1

From the 1930s to the 1970s, the Fox was the place to go in Tucson to see Hollywood's latest offering, and the theater's art deco style nearly matched the glamour on the screen. Along with many other once-famous and much-used buildings in downtown, the Fox fell into disrepair until the late 1990s, when a group formed to raise money to refurbish the old movie house. Now the theater, beautifully restored to its original grandeur, shows classic films several times a month and hosts concerts and events.

◖ THE RIALTO

318 E. Congress St., 520/740-1000,
www.rialtotheatre.com
HOURS: Box office Mon.-Fri. noon-6 P.M.
Map 1

A cool old theater with a balcony, The Rialto

© TIM HULL

The Rialto

regularly hosts the best alt-rock and alt-country touring bands—acts like Ryan Adams, Son Volt, the Drive-By Truckers, and Shooter Jennings. Across Congress Street from the Hotel Congress downtown, the theater originally opened in 1920. Now it operates as a non-profit organization showing the best concerts in town. If you're a serious fan of music—rock, hip-hop, alternative rock, and alt-country—don't come to Tucson without checking the Rialto's website first; you just might find that there's someone coming that you want to see.

TEMPLE OF MUSIC AND ART
330 S. Scott Ave., 520/622-2823,
www.arizonatheatre.org
Map 1

A group of music-loving Tucsonans called the Saturday Morning Music Club saw to the construction of this wonderful Spanish colonial revival theater downtown, on the edge of the historic Armory Park neighborhood. The theater, known for its stylish interior and excellent acoustics, drew top-name musicians to the Old Pueblo for years. Bands and soloists still play here from time to time, but mostly it is the main stage for the **Arizona Theatre Company**

(box office 520/622-2823), which puts on excellent regional productions of top-shelf plays and musicals here and in Phoenix.

PERFORMING ARTS
ARIZONA FRIENDS OF CHAMBER MUSIC
Leo Rich Theater, 260 S. Church St., 520/577-3769,
www.arizonachambermusic.org
COST: $30 adult, $10 student
Map 1

This dedicated group of local chamber-music enthusiasts brings the world's top musicians to the intimate Leo Rich Theater at the Tucson Convention Center, and in March presents a festival's worth of the new sounds of various known and unknown small ensembles from all over.

ARIZONA OPERA
Tucson Convention Center Music Hall,
260 S. Church St., 520/293-4336,
www.azopera.com
COST: Ticket prices vary based on production
Map 1

It's not Santa Fe, but the Arizona Opera Company presents some of the best regional opera in the country October–April at the Tucson Convention Center Music Hall. There's usually not a lot of experimenting going on—you'll get the classics that you've heard of, done well. A night out at the opera in Tucson is a good chance to see the city's diversity of style: You'll see a few people in black tie and flowing gowns, and others in jeans and flip-flops. Like the Arizona Theatre Company's productions, operas usually premiere in Tucson and then move on to Phoenix.

ARIZONA REPERTORY THEATRE
University of Arizona School of Theatre Arts,
520/621-7008, http://tftv.arizona.edu/season
COST: $28 adult, $26 senior, $19 student
Map 2

The training company for the UA's School of Theatre Arts necessarily puts on a short season of top-name dramas and comedies—works by Neal Simon, Shakespeare, William Inge, and the like, performed earnestly if not always expertly. The UA Fine Arts box office is located at 1025 North Olive Road, near the southeast corner of Park Avenue and Speedway Boulevard.

ARIZONA THEATRE COMPANY

Temple of Music and Art, 330 S. Scott Ave., 520/622-2823, www.arizonatheatre.org
COST: Ticket prices vary based on production
Map 1

The state's flagship troupe puts on an entertaining season of plays September–May. Most productions debut at the beautiful Temple of Music and Art in Tucson and then move on to Phoenix. Lately the company, like most other regional nonprofits, has been choosing material with somewhat obvious toe-tapping, audience-pleasing potential. Tucson's many ex-hippie boomers were overjoyed with a recent revival of *Hair,* and other recent productions have depicted the lives and music of Janis Joplin, Billie Holiday, and Hank Williams.

BEOWULF ALLEY THEATRE COMPANY

11 S. 6th Ave., 520/882-0555, www.beowulfalley.org
COST: $20 adult, $18 senior, $8 student
Map 1

This theater company presents three or four plays every season, typically quite well done and accessible; many of the works are Arizona premieres of off-off-Broadway shows by contemporary playwrights. At Beowulf, as it is with most of the small theater companies in Tucson, one gets the sense that the players love and need theater in a way that most of us don't understand, and that they would be performing the same play in the same way even without an audience. You can't ask for more than that out of a night at the intimate, somewhat charming Beowulf Alley Theatre.

BORDERLANDS THEATER

El Centro Cultural de las Americanas, 40 W. Broadway Blvd., 520/882-7406, www.borderlandstheater.org
COST: $10.75-24.75
Map 1

Borderlands, as its name implies, concentrates on theater that explores regional issues and lifestyles, especially Mexican American and border-region culture. They usually produce between three and six plays a season, some of them by homegrown playwrights, at various small venues around town.

GASLIGHT DINNER THEATRE

7010 E. Broadway Blvd., 520/886-9428, www.thegaslighttheatre.com
HOURS: Box office Mon.-Thurs. 10 A.M.-8 P.M., Fri.-Sat. 10 P.M.-10 P.M., Sun. noon-8 P.M.; showtimes Tues.-Thurs. 7 P.M., Fri.-Sat. 6 P.M. and 8:30 P.M., Sun. 3 P.M. and 7 P.M.
COST: $17.95 adult; $15.95 senior, student, and active military; $7.95 child 2-12
Map 6

It's certainly not high art, but the melodramas and family comedies put on at this east-side dinner theater are typically fun and often hilarious. The shows change every few months and are usually on the order of the *Ballad of Two-Gun McGraw, or Just Horsin' Around* and *On the Road to the North Pole, or The Snow Must Go On.* The shows last about two hours, and the "dinner" is a pretty good pizza pie ordered and delivered from Grandma Tony's next door. Kids will invariably like the shows; if the adults need a little help getting into it, a modest selection of beer and wine is served.

INVISIBLE THEATRE

1400 N. 1st Ave., 520/882-9721, www.invisibletheatre.com
COST: $22-45
Map 2

For nearly 40 years the Invisible Theatre has been offering popular productions of the classics, off-Broadway touring productions, and locally created plays as well. The theater itself is an old building that used to hold a laundry but now holds 80 seats and an intimate stage.

RHYTHM & ROOTS CONCERT SERIES

Various venues, 520/319-9966, www.rhythmandroots.org
COST: Ticket prices vary based on performance
This series brings roots musicians—blues, folk,

bluegrass, zydeco, and some bluesy-country rock—to Tucson. Concerts are held at various locations in the downtown area, such as Old Town Artisans, the Lost Barrio, and other places. The music is always good, and the series is responsible for bringing some little-known legends to the Old Pueblo. If you're a fan of the genre(s), you'll want to get the latest scoop from the website before coming to town.

ROGUE THEATRE
300 E. University Blvd., 520/551-2053, www.theroguetheatre.org
COST: $20
`Map 2`

The only company in Tucson doing the likes of Pirandello and Genet as a regular rule, the Rogue Theatre puts on about four or five productions a year. You will usually get your money's worth as long as you are looking to be challenged, entertained, and inspired.

TUCSON SYMPHONY ORCHESTRA
Tucson Convention Center Music Hall, 260 S. Church St., 520/882-8585, www.tucsonsymphony.org
COST: Ticket prices vary based on production
`Map 1`

More than 80 years old, this orchestra holds concerts September–May at the Tucson Convention Center Music Hall, with the familiar mixture of classics and pops, from Stravinsky to Bugs Bunny. The orchestra is impeccable most nights, and well worth seeing and hearing—certainly one of the better mid-size orchestras in the Southwest.

CINEMA
◖ THE LOFT CINEMA
3233 E. Speedway Blvd., 520/795-7777, www.loftcinema.com
COST: $9.25 adult, $6.75 child 12 and under,

$6.75 Mon.-Fri.. before 6 P.M.
`Map 3`

The nonprofit arts organization that runs this landmark theater on Speedway books thoughtful and entertaining films, showing not only the best of today's art-house flicks but also classics and cult films, and you can buy a microbrew and a slice of pizza to go with all the soul searching on the screen. The theater regularly puts on special events with directors, screenwriters, and actors, as well as festivals and one-night-only showings, so it's a good idea to check out the website if you're a traveling cinephile.

COMEDY
LAFFS COMEDY CAFFE
2900 E. Broadway Blvd., 520/323-8669, www.laffstucson.com
HOURS: Thurs. 8 P.M., Fri. 8 P.M. and 10:30 P.M., Sat. 7 P.M. and 9:30 P.M.
COST: $10-15
`Map 3`

Touring comics from around the country stop in for a set or two at Laffs Comedy Caffe near Broadway and Country Club. There's usually a fun time to be had here—the local-comic emcees are amusing and the touring pros kill more often than not. The staff herds showgoers into a small lounge before each show, and it's easy to forget that the two-drink (or food item) minimum doesn't start until the show does. The full bar serves a range of beers in cans and bottles, and several delicious and insidious high-octane special drinks with names like the Giggler and Laff's Punch. The kitchen serves a full menu of appetizers, grill-style entrées, and desserts, but this is not an ideal place to eat your supper. Calling ahead for a reservation is a good idea but not typically necessary. They may ask you to share your table once the show starts in an effort to fill up the room, but you can just politely say no and they won't ask again.

ARTS AND LEISURE

Festivals and Events

SPRING
ARIZONA INTERNATIONAL FILM FESTIVAL

The Screening Room, 127 E. Congress St.,
520/882-0204, www.filmfestivalarizona.com
COST: $6-8 single tickets
Map 1

For 10 days beginning in mid-April, film-makers and film lovers from around the world come to Tucson to watch and celebrate independent cinema. This popular local film festival is approaching its third decade, and the most recent event premiered movies from Bolivia, Japan, Germany, South Africa, and even the good old U.S.A. The best films screened at the festival, which takes place at downtown's tiny Screening Room and sometimes at other venues around town, are the entrants in the annual Reel Frontier Film and Video Contest.

4TH AVENUE STREET FAIRS

4th Ave., 520/624-5004, www.fourthavenue.org
COST: Free
Map 2

Artists, artisans, street performers, food-booth proprietors, and thousands of Tucsonans converge on 4th Avenue twice a year for this popular event. The street closes down and hundreds of white tents go up, selling jewelry, paintings, photographs, leather goods, glass art, and all kinds of other items you never knew existed. The best part of the two annual street fairs is seeing all the street performers—mostly fiddle and guitar bands and folksingers vying for attention, but there are also usually a few adorable little kids with their violins hoping for a few bucks tossed in their case. It's a crowded, greasy-food good time every year. Usually the spring fair, toward the end of March, is the more popular, what with the gorgeous weather and all. The winter fair is in December.

LA FRONTERA TUCSON INTERNATIONAL MARIACHI CONFERENCE

504 W. 29th St., 520/838-3908,
www.tucsonmariachi.org
COST: Admission varies according to event
Map 1

Mariachi music is an important part of Tucson's soundtrack; it can be heard everywhere—in one restaurant or another just about every night of the week, and pretty much at any festival or event that draws more than three people. Many public schools in the Old Pueblo offer mariachi classes as part of their music curricula. It's not surprising, then, that one of the most popular annual gatherings of mariachi enthusiasts and professionals takes place in Tucson every April. The weeklong event features concerts and workshops and a final-day fiesta at the Reid Park bandshell—the easiest and least expensive way to take part ($5 adult, free child under 12). Otherwise check the website for performance times, venues, and prices (tickets tend to sell out early).

PIMA COUNTY FAIR

Pima County Fairgrounds, 11300 S. Houghton Rd.,
520/762-9100, www.pimacountyfair.com
COST: $7 adult, $2 child 6-10, $5 parking
Map 5

For 10 days every year beginning in mid-April, myriad cowboys, country folk, 4-H geniuses, and cotton-candy kids converge on the Pima County Fairgrounds southeast of Tucson, where they show off their pigs and goats and prize bulls, their roses, jams, and pumpkins-on-steroids, their gullibility and screaming skills, and quite often the contents of their stomachs. In short, it's the county fair, an ancient American ritual that is different in Southern Arizona only in that there are usually quite a number of families up from Sonora in attendance. The free concerts usually feature one or two superstar Mexican groups along with a few mid-level American country acts.

SPRING ART FAIR

Tucson Museum of Art, 140 N. Main Ave.,
520/624-2333
COST: Free
Map 1

The last weekend in March brings artisans from around the region to the Tucson Museum of Art. You'll find one-of-a-kind handmade treasures and unique decorative items here, and both the fair and entrance to the museum are free. There's a similar market in the fall—a good chance to buy unique holiday presents.

TUCSON FOLK FESTIVAL

El Presidio Park, 160 W. Alameda St., 520/792-6481,
www.tkma.org
COST: Free
Map 1

The Tucson Kitchen Musicians, a longtime group of folkies and other musical types in Tucson, put on this excellent showcase of local and regional folk and blues music every year in downtown El Presidio Park. It's a chance to discover all the talented singer-songwriters working in the folk, acoustic, and roots traditions in the Old Pueblo, and much of the festival is usually broadcast on KXCI, Tucson's community radio station. There are always a few food booths set up, and the whole event is popular and crowded with families and kids.

UA SPRING FLING

Rillito Downs, 1st Ave. and River Rd., 520/621-5610,
www.springfling.arizona.edu
COST: $5 adult and child over 7, free UA students and active military, $5 parking
Map 4

Instead of showers, which don't usually return to the desert until July or August, April brings the University of Arizona's annual fund-raising carnival to the Old Pueblo. A popular local tradition since 1974, the event features carnival rides, food booths, games, and displays operated by various UA clubs and organizations in need of funding. The revelry lasts for four nights at the beginning of April, each one usually crowded with UA students, families, and packs of wild teenagers.

WA:K POWWOW

Mission San Xavier del Bac, 1950 W. San Xavier Rd.,
Tucson, 520/294-5727
COST: Free
Map 8

The Tohono O'odham were dry-farming and gathering juicy saguaro fruit in the Tucson valley long before the Spanish arrived, and they were often considered friendly allies to the Spanish, Mexicans, and Americans, all of whom fought viciously with the Apache, who were the historic enemies of the "Desert People" as well. During the second weekend in March, the O'odham, formerly called the Papago, gather at the large open plaza at San Xavier del Bac for a cultural festival featuring traditional dancing, drumming, arts and crafts, native foods, and other activities.

SUMMER
CINCO DE MAYO

Kennedy Park, La Cholla Blvd. and Ajo Way,
520/292-9326
COST: Free
Map 7

That fateful day when Mexican soldiers routed an army of adventuring, occupying French at the battle of Puebla (May 5, 1862) is celebrated in the Old Pueblo in various ways. For most of us, the many supermarket markdowns on Mexican beer, corn chips, and salsa are enough to get us in the mood; others head over to South Tucson's Kennedy Park for a colorful fiesta featuring mariachi, traditional dances, folk arts, concerts, and, of course, heaps of Mexican cuisine.

DÍA DE SAN JUAN

Mercado San Agustin, 100 S. Avenida del Convento,
520/665-8618
COST: Free
Map 6

On June 24 the overheated populous prays for rain during a free festival celebrating John the Baptist and the saint's historical relationship with the desert's summer rainy season. The tradition of celebrating the Baptist's birthday came to the region with the Spanish in

ARTS AND LEISURE

the 1600s, and over the centuries was imbued with more localized and indigenous meanings. The event features a parade, food booths, mariachi, and native dancing meant to inspire the summer rains to visit the dry, hot pueblo.

HA:SAN BAK: SAGUARO HARVEST CELEBRATION

Colossal Cave Mountain Park,
16721 E. Old Spanish Trail, Tucson, 520/647-7121,
www.colossalcave.com
COST: $5 per vehicle
Map 8

Many, if not most, Tucsonans have at least one saguaro within a few feet of their front door, yet few of them see the ubiquitous cactus as a source of sustenance. The Tohono O'odham, on the other hand, have constructed a large part of their culture around the comings and goings of the saguaro's red fruit, and over centuries in the desert have devised myriad uses for every part of the great cactus-tree. In late June, as the annual harvest is in full swing, native volunteers give workshops on the uses and wonders of the saguaro at Colossal Cave Mountain Park near Vail, including making a batch or two of saguaro syrup and other delicacies.

IRONWOOD FESTIVAL

Tucson Audubon's Mason Center, 3835 W. Hardy St.,
Tucson, 520/744-0004, www.tucsonaudubon.org
COST: Festival free, $5 for admission to Ironwood Jam
Map 8

In early May, just when the sun starts in with the attitude, Tucson's self-professed tree huggers gather at the Audubon Society's Mason Center (near Arthur Pack Regional Park) northwest of town to celebrate the long-lived ironwood tree (protected at nearby Ironwood National Monument), and the key role it plays in the desert's astonishingly diverse ecosystem. The festival features fun and educational activities like guided bird walks, natural history displays and lectures, and, once the sun dips away a bit, a lineup of folk-rock bands at the Ironwood Jam ($5).

JUNETEENTH FIESTA

Kennedy Park, La Cholla Blvd. and Ajo Way,
520/617-7385, www.youthtogether.org/juneteenth
COST: Free
Map 7

Tucsonans celebrate the nation's oldest African American holiday with a two-day festival at the south side's Kennedy Park. The fun begins on June 18 and continues the next day, known as Juneteenth, the day that far-flung slaves in Galveston, Texas, finally learned that they'd been set free, two years after President Lincoln issued the Emancipation Proclamation. The annual event, now in its fourth decade, features food booths, live music and other entertainment, and loads of stuff for the kids.

FALL

ALL SOUL'S PROCESSION

Various downtown locations,
www.allsoulsprocession.org
COST: Free
Map 1

Something like 20,000 people participate in this unique local tradition, now 20 years old, based on the rites and folk art of Mexico's Day of the Dead. A local arts collective organizes the colorful and creative nonmotorized parade through downtown, featuring giant puppets and other Mexican-inspired folk arts handmade by participants. The whole thing culminates in a big ceremonial fire and a "dance of the dead." The All Soul's Weekend (the first full weekend of November), with the parade and bonfire its finale, features several like-minded events, such as arts shows, poetry readings, and a kids' parade.

EL TOUR DE TUCSON

Perimeter Bicycling Association of America,
2609 E. Broadway Blvd., Tucson, 520/745-2033,
www.pbaa.com
COST: Free for spectators; entrance fees vary for riders
Map 8

The Tucson-based nonprofit PBAA puts on several road-bike races in Southern Arizona that raise millions for local charities and bring tough, wiry bicyclists to Tucson from all over the world. The most popular of these is the Tour de Tucson in late November, when the weather here is more like spring than fall. The main 109-mile route takes riders all over the Tucson valley, up into the foothills and mountains and back, as thousands of spectators line portions of the route cheering and holding up signs to egg on the exhausted cyclists. The tour typically draws more than 9,000 riders and includes shorter routes of 80 miles, 67 miles, 35 miles, and even a 4-mile fun ride for kids and families. Another popular local PBAA event is the **Tour of the Tucson Mountains** in late April, with 70- and 27-mile courses, and in October the group puts on the **Cochise County Cycling Classic,** with 45-, 92-, and 157-mile routes, and even an insane 252-mile route that requires riders to have a backup crew.

a classic car at Tucson Meet Yourself

DAVID JEWELL © METROPOLITAN TUCSON CONVENTION & VISITORS BUREAU

OKTOBERFEST

Hi Corbett Field, 3400 E. Camino Campestre, www.tucsonoktoberfest.org
COST: $3
`Map 3`

Beer and sausage are year-round necessities for many of us, but these and other German imports take center stage at midtown's Hi Corbett Field in early October. Tucson's Oktoberfest takes place over four days and evenings and features scores of arts and crafts booths and food and beer vendors, along with a polka band or 20. A dance always breaks out, and there is a lot for the kids to do. The only thing that separates this local Oktoberfest from one in, say, Wisconsin, is that here you don't need a coat and gloves.

TUCSON MEET YOURSELF

El Presidio Park, 160 W. Alameda St., 520/792-4806 or 520/621-4046, www.tucsonmeetyourself.org
COST: Free
`Map 1`

With so much written and filmed about the usual suspects of Southwestern history, it's easy to forget that Tucson is as multicultural as a city can be, albeit on a rather smaller scale than most. Tucson Meet Yourself, an annual festival held October 10–12 at El Presidio Park downtown, shows off just how diverse the city is. If you're going, go hungry. Dozens of cultural clubs—from Colombians to Danes to Koreans to Irish to Poles, Russians, Navajo, and more—cook up and sell their national cuisine, making it possible to have catfish, sweet-potato pie, roasted corn, fry bread, and pickled herring all in one meal. The festival also features folk-art demonstrations.

WINTER

ACCENTURE MATCH PLAY

Ritz-Carlton Golf Club at Dove Mountain, www.worldgolfchampionships.com
COST: $99 week pass (includes parking pass); free for children under 18 and military
`Map 8`

In late February the keen eyes of the professional golf world are focused squarely on Tucson when Tiger Woods comes to town, bringing along the world's top 64 golfers to battle it out for an oversize $8 million check. Tiger made his 2009 return to professional golf at this popular tournament, which has top golfers competing

ARTS AND LEISURE

for each hole instead of an entire round. The international press descends on the ultra-high-end Dove Mountain golf resort northwest of midtown, and tickets aren't too easy to come by.

DILLINGER DAYS

Hotel Congress, 311 E. Congress St., 520/622-8848, www.hotelcongress.com

COST: Admission varies according to event

Map 1

In 1935 the small little-known desert town of Tucson made international news when the infamous Dillinger gang, and later the public enemy himself, was captured here after a fire

at the Hotel Congress, where most of the gang members were lying up for the night. Now, in late January every year, various downtown institutions, especially Hotel Congress, celebrate that fateful night with a gala event, reenactments of the capture, lectures, tours, old movies from the time, and much more.

FIESTA DE LOS VAQUEROS

4823 S. 6th Ave., 520/741-2233, www.tucsonrodeo.com

COST: Most seats $12-26

Map 7

One of the Old Pueblo's most popular annual

THE DAY OF THE DEAD

PUBLIC DOMAIN/LIBRARY OF CONGRESS PRINTS AND PHOTOGRAPHS DIVISION

Calavera Oaxaqueña (Calavera from Oaxaca), by José Guadalupe Posada, 1910

Here in the borderlands it's difficult to find a boutique, gift shop, or gallery these days that doesn't sell *calaveras* (skeletons doing human things), whether on statues, paintings, T-shirts, or all manner of other consumer goods featuring the Day of the Dead aesthetic. Generally these art objects re-create the work, or at least the spirit of the work, of José Guadalupe Posada, a late 19th- and early 20th-century Mexican printmaker and illustrator whose broadsides and newspaper illustrations em-

ployed the *calavera* and Day of the Dead traditions in social commentary. While Posada's work had the immediacy of journalism, it has outlasted its original intent and is more popular today than ever before. His style, and his overt political commentary, influenced the likes of Diego Rivera and other Mexican muralists of the first half of the 20th century.

To see Posada's famous broadsides in the original, as they were distributed on the streets of Mexico City, check out the University of New

events (local school kids get two "rodeo days" off every year), the "Celebration of the Cowboys" began way back in 1925 and is today one of the top 25 outdoor rodeos in the nation. Something like 50,000 people head to the south side over eight days every February (usually beginning around February 20) to watch the dramatic bull riding, steer wrestling, women's barrel racing, and more, and to eat a few tons of barbecue beef and pork. The rodeo typically draws more than 600 contestants, among them the best riders, ropers, and cow-wrestlers in the world, who compete for $320,000 in prize money.

LA FIESTA DE TUMACÁCORI

Exit 29 on I-19 South, Tumacácori National Historic Park, Tumacácori, 520/398-2341, www.nps.gov/tuma
COST: $3
Map 8

During the first full weekend in December, Mission Tumacácori, about six miles south of Tubac along the frontage road, hosts a festival featuring dozens of food vendors and craft booths, live music, kids' activities, and a traditional mariachi mass celebrated in front of the ruin of the 17th-century mission, which was founded, like its sister to the north, San Xavier del Bac, by Padre Kino during his legendary

Mexico's digital collection online at http://econtent.unm.edu/cdm.

The Day of the Dead, or El Día de los Muertos, falls on November 2, but the celebrations begin on November 1 or even before that. It is roughly meant to coincide with the traditional Catholic holidays of All Saints Day and All Souls Day, but the tradition, most anthropologists believe, is far older than the Spanish conquest of Mexico. Indeed it is, like most New World rites, an amalgam of pre-Columbian and Spanish traditions whose origins reach far back into the mist.

At its heart, the holiday is an explicit admittance that death and the dead have a profound influence on the living, and that the two camps coexist side by side, always. The details of the celebrations vary from region to region, from town to town, from big cities to rural areas. Generally they include feasts, often laid out in graveyards, with a dead relative's favorite dishes prepared and set aside. There are parades and marches, candles and altars, sugar skulls, sweetbreads shaped like skulls and skeletons, and, of course, calaveras galore.

For many years the Day of the Dead has been marching north, so much so that it now rivals Cinco de Mayo as the southwestern Anglo's favorite Mexican import. The spectacles surrounding the holiday have always been a subject of fascination for tourists, especially those from the United States. As far back as the

1970s, Mexican observers were complaining that in places like Mixquic and Pátzcuaro, towns famous for their Day of the Dead celebrations, "cameras had come to outnumber candles in the cemeteries."

Day of the Dead is not so much a holiday as a year-round way of looking at the world. This way of looking at the world, for me, comes directly from Posada's work. The calavera, especially as it was presented by Posada, is a reminder that we are all mere skeletons; we are all the walking dead, and everything we do and say in this world will one day be forgotten. No matter how much money we have (and Posada's frequent target, along with those in political power, was the rich), no matter how much power we have, we are all equally bones underneath, and we will soon enough be gone. Death is not absent from your life until it comes for you. It is there walking beside you all the time, so you might as well give death its due, and a holiday too.

Usually, throughout November there's a traditional Day of the Dead altar at Tolteca Tlacuilo in the **Old Town Artisans complex** (186 N. Meyer, 520/623-5787, 9:30 A.M.-5:30 P.M.); and the **Tucson Museum of Art** (140 N. Main Ave., 520/624-2333) typically celebrates the ancient rite with a family event on November 2, with the usual music, food, arts and crafts, an altar, and a parade and big-head puppets.

ARTS AND LEISURE

forays into the Santa Cruz Valley. During the festival, admittance to the national park is free.

SOUTHWEST INDIAN ART FAIR

Arizona State Museum, 1013 E. University Blvd., 520/621-6302, www.statemuseum.arizona.edu
COST: $10
`Map 2`

This major event brings Native American artists and the people who love their work to Tucson from all over the Southwest. White-roofed booths sprawl out on the lawn in front of the Arizona State Museum on the UA campus, while the smell of fry bread and other delicious, decadent foods fills the air. Artists from Navajoland, from Hopi, from the pueblos of the Rio Grande Valley, and elsewhere bring their fetishes, kachinas, paintings, squash-blossom belt buckles, and other items to sell and talk about. It's a great chance to buy something unique and meaningful and to meet the artist who made it so.

TUBAC FESTIVAL OF THE ARTS

Tubac, 520/398-2704, www.tubacaz.com/festival.asp
COST: Free
`Map 8`

For four days in early February the population of the tiny historic village of Tubac, about 45 minutes south of Tucson on I-19, swells tenfold, as hundreds of roaming artists and artisans set up their white tents and offer their unique and often strange visions and creations. Thousands flock from all around—Tucson, Green Valley, and Nogales—to stroll through the village's few streets, ducking in and out of all the crafty shops, eating grilled and fried

food, and generally enjoying a 70-degree blue-sky day in late winter.

TUCSON GEM, MINERAL & FOSSIL SHOWCASE

Various locations, 520/322-5773, www.tgms.org
COST: $10
`Map 1`

The grand dame of Tucson's "golden month," the Gem Show brings visitors from all over the globe to the desert for one of the most popular and prestigious events of its kind. If you're into gems, minerals, fossils, and rocks, you probably know about it already. If your interest is more casual, however, the most affordable and easiest way to join in the fun is to go to the huge Main Show at the Tucson Convention Center on the second full weekend of February, where you'll likely be astounded by the otherworldly colors and patterns in all those mysterious rocks.

WINTERHAVEN FESTIVAL OF LIGHTS

Fort Lowell Rd. and Country Club Dr., Winterhaven, www.winterhavenfestival.org
COST: Donation of canned food recommended
`Map 3`

Every December for the past 60 years or so, the Winterhaven neighborhood—a tree-lined, relatively upscale enclave in midtown—has draped itself in lights for the benefit of the local food bank. After the sun goes down, residents invite the public to walk their pleasant streets and take in the show; vendors sell trolley and wagon rides around the neighborhood and various edible holiday treats, and sometimes it's even a bit cold. You might just mistake the whole scene for a sign of winter.

Sports and Recreation

PARKS

ABRAHAM LINCOLN REGIONAL PARK

4325 S. Pantano Rd., Tucson, 520/791-4873, www.tucsonaz.gov/parksandrec
HOURS: Daily 6 A.M.–10:30 P.M.
COST: Free

`Map 8`

A 191-acre desert park in southeast Tucson near Davis-Monthan Air Force Base, Lincoln Regional Park features some of the best sand-volleyball courts in town, as well as softball fields, walking trails, a fitness center and swimming pool, playgrounds, picnic ramadas, and more. The lush riparian **Atturbury Bird and Animal Sanctuary** in the lower section of the park features a mile-long loop trail through a water-inspired desert landscape with all kinds of birds and other creatures flitting and scuttling about.

ARTHUR PACK REGIONAL PARK

9101 N. Thornydale Rd., Tucson, 520/877-6000, www.pima.gov/nrpr/parks
HOURS: Daily 7 A.M.-10 P.M.
COST: Free
Map 8

A large Pima County–run desert park on the far northwest side of town, Arthur Pack Regional Park has walking trails, picnic areas with shady ramadas, lighted soccer and baseball fields, basketball courts, and an excellent playground. Also on-site is the **Crooked Tree Golf Course** (520/744-3322), a public course with fantastic views of the mountains and the sweeping desert. This park is different from those inside the city in that it has more of a wild desert feel while still offering all the amenities.

BRANDI FENTON MEMORIAL PARK

3482 E. River Rd., www.brandifentonmemorialpark.org
HOURS: Park daily 7 A.M.-10 P.M.; visitor center Tues.-Fri. 10 A.M.-4 P.M.
COST: Free
Map 4

Kids love the clean and well-designed "splash pad" at beautiful Brandi Fenton Park between River Road and the Rillito, and it's a worry-free good time for parents as well. Just push the button and for 15 minutes at a time cool water sprays out of fountains, falls from buckets, and bubbles and sprays up out of the ground, allowing water-resistant tykes to get the hang of a wet face before tackling the pool. The splash pad is open mid-April–October 31, and it's free. It's akin to the old lawn-sprinkler method of summertime cooling off, only much better. The park also has covered basketball courts, picnic tables, and more.

GARDEN OF GETHSEMANE/ FELIX LUCERO PARK

602 W. Congress St., 520/791-4873, www.tucsonaz.gov/parksandrec
HOURS: Daily 6 A.M.-10:30 P.M.
COST: Refundable deposit and access keys required; call for information
Map 1

On the west bank of the Santa Cruz River downtown, this strange, peaceful sculpture garden holds several handmade religious statues created by Felix Lucero in the 1940s, along with a green and cool spread of vegetation. The concrete sculptures—Jesus in his tomb, a depiction of the Last Supper, and more—were the result, according to the *Arizona Daily Star,* of a battlefield promise the late Lucero made to his God during World War I. Lucero moved to Tucson in 1938 and lived in a handmade shack under a bridge near what is now the park while sculpting the statues using riverbed sand and concrete. You might see a few people praying here, as it's a very calm and obviously inspiring little sanctuary.

◖ GENE C. REID PARK

900 S. Randolph Way, 520/791-4873, www.tucsonaz.gov/parksandrec
HOURS: Daily 6 A.M.-10:30 P.M.
COST: Free
Map 3

This 131-acre greenscape on the southern end of midtown is probably the city's favorite non-desert playground, with plenty of imported-tree shade and cool bermuda grass for lounging and forgetting. The park has, among dozens of other attractions, two small duck-topped lakes (no swimming), a bandshell and amphitheater for concerts under the stars, and an off-leash dog park. The playground equipment is all cool submarine-style passageways, twisting slides, fire poles, and sky-reaching swing sets, and several layers of soft wood chips and some bouncy outdoor foam flooring provide for soft landings. Hi Corbett Stadium is located on the park's grounds, as are the Reid Park Zoo, a large modern recreation and aquatics center, a tennis facility, and a golf course.

ARTS AND LEISURE

SOUTHERN ARIZONA'S BIRDS

Southern Arizona is a mecca for bird enthusiasts, who stalk the region's sky island mountain ranges looking for rare subtropical birds like the **elegant trogan**, a green, red, white, and black bird related to the jungle-loving quetzal. A good guide to get is *Finding Birds in Southeast Arizona*, published by the Tucson Audubon Society and available at its Nature Shop (520/629-0510). If you want to find out which rare birds are making appearances in the area, call the **Rare Bird Alert** (520/798-1005).

Of course not all of the hundreds of bird species in Southern Arizona are rare. Some of the more common avian species you're likely to see around the desert are the small flitting **cactus wren,** which lives among the spiky plants and is the Arizona state bird, and the tall **road runner,** which may be the state's most recognizable bird. The **red-tailed hawk** proliferates in the desert sky, hunting rodents. Look for them perched and watching atop telephone poles along the highways. Water birds, including the elegant **great blue heron,** hang around the state's riparian areas, and **wild turkeys** are somewhat common in oak and pine woodlands. One of the most common birds in the desert is the **Gambels quail,** which can often be seen crossing streets followed by a ragged line of tiny offspring. The **turkey vulture** is constantly soaring slowly in the ever-blue dryland sky. Various owl species are common in the woodlands and the deserts, and the **gila** and the **acorn woodpecker** are always tapping away at some tree, saguaro, or woodland home.

HIMMEL PARK

1000 N. Tucson Blvd., 520/791-4873, www.tucsonaz.gov/parksandrec
HOURS: Daily 6 A.M.-10:30 P.M.
COST: Free
Map 3

The Sam Hughes neighborhood is one of midtown's finest, so it stands to reason that its park, a 26-acre grass-covered shade space near Tucson and Speedway Boulevards, is one of the best around. It's crowded with palm and olive trees, and has tennis courts, basketball hoops, playground equipment, and a public pool originally designed in 1936, when the public pool was a very important local institution. On weekends you can usually catch a league soccer match or two here.

MORRIS K. UDALL PARK

7290 E. Tanque Verde Rd., 520/791-4873, www.tucsonaz.gov/parksandrec
HOURS: Daily 6 A.M.-10:30 P.M.
COST: Free
Map 6

Named for one of Arizona's best-loved politicians and environmentalists (not to mention secretary of state during the Kennedy administration and onetime presidential candidate), "Mo" Udall, this east-side park is among the best in the city. With 172 acres and a commanding view of the Santa Catalinas, the park features a dog-walking area, human walking and running trails, sports fields, picnic ramadas, a playground, bocce courts, horseshoe pits, sand-volleyball courts, tennis courts, an amphitheater, and much more.

SANTA CRUZ RIVER PARK

South from Grant Rd. to 29th St.
HOURS: Daily 6 A.M.-10:30 P.M.
COST: Free
Map 1

There is neither river nor park here, some might say, but still it's as good a vantage as any other from which to view what remains. The Santa Cruz, like most Southwestern desert rivers, was never a deep, swollen river, but it at least had a perennial flow. It sustained a few different indigenous communities for eons, and was the green, cool home of beaver, otter, native fish species, and all manner of wild riparian life. Now look at it. It's not *all* our fault;

the region is prone to long droughts, and most desert rivers have wildly fluctuating, even intermittent, flows. But it was largely the pumping of groundwater throughout the region that sent the river underground for good a few generations ago. Every now and then, if the late-summer monsoon comes on blessedly strong, the water rises and flows past this pleasant man-made green space just west of downtown, where you can ride your bike or take an early-morning jog, or just gaze at the dry, rocky bed.

GYMS AND HEALTH CLUBS
LIGHTHOUSE/CITY YMCA

2900 N. Columbus Blvd., 520/795-9725,
www.tucsonymca.org/lighthouse
HOURS: Mon.-Thurs. 5:30 A.M.-9 P.M., Fri.
5:30 A.M.-8 P.M., Sat. 7 A.M.-7 P.M., Sun. 9 A.M.-7 P.M.
COST: Non-members (over 22 years old) $10/day
Map 3

This clean and well-kept YMCA facility on Columbus is on the grounds of the City of Tucson's McCormick Park, so after you're done with pilates or swimming laps or punishing yourself on the stair-stepper, you can have a cookout and a softball game. The outdoor pool here is huge and refreshing, at least before July—then you feel like a tea bag dipping in. At any rate, the Lighthouse facility has everything one expects from a YMCA facility, and then some. If you're a member of the YMCA in another city, you can use any Tucson YMCA facility five times a month for free. If you want to use it more, it'll cost you $5 per day.

LOHSE FAMILY YMCA

60 W. Alameda St., 520/623-5200,
www.tucsonymca.org/lohse
HOURS: Mon.-Fri. 5:30 A.M.-8 P.M., Sat. 8 A.M.-6 P.M.
COST: Non-members (over 22 years old) $10/day
Map 1

Tucson has some of the best YMCA facilities in the region, all of them bustling and clean, inviting and up-to-date. The Lohse Family branch downtown has everything any fitness freak would want: weight machines, cardio equipment, a huge basketball court, free

weights, an indoor running track, aerobics and yoga studios, and a six-lane covered and heated swimming pool. There's a parking garage ($2 per hr.) right next door and metered parking on the street. If you're a member of the YMCA in another city, you can use any Tucson YMCA facility five times a month for free. If you want to use it more, it'll cost you $5 per day.

MID-VALLEY ATHLETIC CLUB AND WELLNESS CENTER

140 S. Tucson Blvd., 520/792-3654,
www.mvactucson.com
HOURS: Mon.-Thurs. 5 A.M.-10 P.M., Fri. 5 A.M.-8:30 P.M.,
Sat. 7 A.M.-7 P.M., Sun. 9 A.M.-7 P.M.
COST: $10/day
Map 3

A comfortable, clean, and welcoming club near Broadway and Tucson Boulevards, Mid-Valley has all kinds of up-to-date workout and weight machines, pilates and aerobics classes, an excellent pool, and an in-house spa where you can get a massage, a manicure, a pedicure, or a new hairstyle instead of working out. If you're just visiting, you can buy a $10-per-day guest pass and use all the facilities, or it's $70 for a month to reward and punish yourself in equal measure.

MORRIS K. UDALL RECREATION CENTER

7200 E. Tanque Verde Rd., 520/791-4931,
www.tucsonaz.gov/parksandrec
HOURS: Mon.-Fri. 6 A.M.-8 P.M., Sat. 8 A.M.-4 P.M.
COST: $2/day for residents, $3/day for nonresidents
Map 6

Located on the grounds of the huge east-side Morris K. Udall Regional Park, this clean and popular city-run recreation center has it all—a weight room, cardio equipment, a walking track, three handball and racquetball courts, pool tables, an open gym where people play basketball, volleyball, and badminton, and much more. There's also a seniors' club with all kinds of social and sports activities, and a long schedule of kids' activities like nighttime basketball games and more.

ARTS AND LEISURE

PRACTICING CAUTION IN TUCSON'S HEAT

Arizona's incessant sun can quickly become a dangerous threat to your health. Stay in the shadows, covered from head to toe. If you're not willing to do this, then at least wear a hat with a wide brim, use high-number sunscreen, cover your neck, and wear long sleeves. This applies not only to backcountry desert adventurers and hikers; mere sight-seers, especially children, are susceptible to sun- and heat-related health issues—more so, in fact: The less fit you are, the higher the danger.

If you get a sunburn, stay out of the sun, and try to keep cool and hydrated. There are dozens of over-the-counter balms available, but simple aloe also works well. A popular home remedy is to gently dab the burned areas with vinegar. The best way to avoid sunburn is to stay out of the sun; barring that, cover up and follow common sense. Children and those with fair skin should be even more cautious.

Hikers, shoppers, sightseers, golfers, and anybody else exerting themselves under high-heat conditions should watch out for **dehydration.** When your body becomes depleted of fluids, you'll notice first that you are not urinating regularly and your saliva has dried up. You may become irritable and confused; your skin may turn gray and your pulse race. Children can become dehydrated quickly. The best way to avoid dehydration is to limit your exertion during the hottest part of the day and to drink a lot of water. If you feel the symptoms of dehydration coming on, get to a cool, comfortable place, take in fluids, and rest.

Hikers should take along a few packets of electrolyte powder—these can be lifesavers. If you exert yourself in the heat and sun and fail to replace the fluids flowing out, your body can become depleted of both electrolytes and fluids. Such is the path to **heat exhaustion,** a dangerous condition that can turn fatal if not treated. You begin to feel nauseated, dizzy, and weak, and your muscles cramp. If you experience any of these symptoms, get to a cool, comfortable place quickly and drink water and something with sodium and potassium in it.

Heat stroke, sometimes called sun stroke or heat hyperpyrexia, is a severe, dangerous health threat that is frequently fatal and changes a victim's health significantly and irrevocably. Heat stroke occurs when the body's temperature-regulating capacity fails; this can be caused by either relatively short exposure to extremely high heat—like, say, a short, strenuous run on a 105-degree July afternoon—or prolonged exposure to relatively high temperatures, as in a 15-mile hike in 90-degree heat. And that's only if you're in good shape; it would take far less to cause heat stroke in most of us. The first and most important sign of heat stroke is a lack of sweating. If you stop sweating in a situation where you *should* be sweating, take notice. Your heart rate will speed up noticeably, and your skin will become dry; you'll get a headache and become confused. At its worst, heat stroke leads to unconsciousness, convulsions, and death. Once you notice you're not sweating, you must get help immediately: Get to an emergency room as soon as possible.

The mountains in Southern Arizona reach up to 10,000 feet. A few of the state's mountain towns sit between 5,000 and 8,000 feet above sea level. Lowlanders in relatively good shape may get headaches, a little dizziness, and shortness of breath while walking around Mount Lemmon or other mountains in the region, but very few will experience serious **altitude sickness**—the result of not getting enough oxygen, and therefore not enough blood flow, to the brain. Take it easy in the higher elevations if you begin to feel tired and out-of-breath, dizzy, or euphoric. If you have heart or lung problems, you need to be more aware in the higher elevations; the best thing to do is to get a prescription for oxygen from your doctor and carry it with you if you plan on spending a lot of time in the mountains.

NORTHWEST YMCA

7770 N. Shannon Rd., Tucson, 520/229-9001,
www.tucsonymca.org/northwest

HOURS: Mon.-Fri. 5 A.M.-10 P.M., Sat. 5 A.M.-8 P.M.,
Sun. 10 A.M.-8 P.M.

COST: Non-members (over 22 years old) $10/day

Map 4

A gleaming 35,000-square-foot exercise center
on the northwest side, the Northwest YMCA
features a huge heated pool for lap swimming,
and a separate pool area with a slide for the kids.
It has clean and well-lit exercise rooms with all
the latest cardio and weight-training machines,
a large gym for pick-up games, an aerobics
room, very clean and comfortable locker rooms,
and a day-care area where you can leave the kids
while you get in shape. If you're a member of the
YMCA in another city, you can use any Tucson
YMCA facility five times a month for free. If
you want to use it more, it'll cost you $5 per day.

RANDOLPH RECREATION CENTER

200 S. Alvernon Way, 520/791-4560,
www.tucsonaz.gov/parksandrec

HOURS: Mon.-Fri. 6:30 A.M.-8 P.M., Sat. 8 A.M.-4 P.M.

COST: $1.50 per day for residents, $2 for nonresidents

Map 3

One of four large regional recreation centers
operated by the City of Tucson, the Randolph
Center at Reid Park has a weight room and
fitness center, a gym for basketball and volleyball, a gymnastics room, aerobics classes, and
even a pottery studio with a kiln. Nonresidents
can use the weight and fitness machines and
the gym for a mere $2 per day (for kids under
18 it's $1). There's an outdoor pool that's only
open during the summer, and a two-mile outdoor walking-running-biking-rollerblading
track that takes you around the entire sprawling midtown park.

TUCSON RACQUET & FITNESS CLUB

4001 N. Country Club Rd., 520/795-6960,
www.tucsonracquetclub.com

HOURS: Daily 24 hours

COST: $10 daily fee

Map 4

A 20-acre oasis for all things active and

health-conscious near the dry Rillito River, this
tennis and fitness club opened in 1967 and is
still the city's finest. The club, which is always
open, has 33 lighted tennis courts and 11 indoor racquetball and handball courts. It has two
large heated pools and a state-of-the-art cardio
and weight center. Staff members offer pilates,
aerobics, tae kwan do, and Thai yoga classes,
and there's a restaurant with all kinds of healthful eats and a full-service spa. Out-of-towners,
or curious townies, can use all the facilities for
$10 per day.

GOLF

It's not easy to justify the existence of golf courses
in the arid Southwest, at least not from a perspective that recognizes the region's rather obvious
resource deficiencies. It is, however, somewhat
easier from the average golfer's point of view,
for whom the region's primary deficiency—its
aridity—is instead its greatest attribute, allowing
one to play 36 holes on Thanksgiving morning
with visiting relatives. And so the courses proliferate. The City of Tucson operates five public
courses in town, all of them excellent, though
older and less dramatic than most of the resort
and private courses invading the desert. The
City's somewhat humbler courses come with
the added benefit of being ecologically defen-
sible: They are all irrigated with reclaimed water.
The City maintains a helpful website (www.tuc-
soncitygolf.com) where you can see maps of all
the courses, get rates (they are generally quite
low, ranging $15–70 for 18 holes depending on
premiums, season, time of day, and residency),
and book tee times. All of the city courses have
clubhouses, lighted driving ranges, carts, pros,
and pro shops.

RANDOLPH GOLF COURSE AND DELL URICH GOLF COURSE

600 S. Alvernon Way, 520/791-4161,
www.tucsoncitygolf.com

HOURS: Daily 5 A.M.-7 P.M.

COST: $23-72 for 18 holes (price depends on
season and residency)

Map 3

These side-by-side courses at midtown's Reid

golf at Reid Park

Park are the two most popular in Tucson's municipal system. Randolph, the city's flagship course and the longest at 6,500 yards from the regular tees, has been the site of numerous PGA and LPGA tournaments, and is green, spacious, and tree lined. Dell Urich, a par-70 course a bit to the south of Randolph, was opened in 1996 and is probably the most popular in town. Both make for easily accessible and relatively inexpensive in-town play year-round.

SWIMMING
CITY OF TUCSON AQUATICS PROGRAMS
Various locations, 520/791-4245 or 520/791-5352, www.tucsonaz.gov/parksandrec/aquatics.php
HOURS: Vary based on location
COST: $2 adult, $1 child

Long before air-conditioning became generally available, and before many middle- and upper-class Tucsonans began digging their own backyard pools, the publicly funded swimming hole was a very important Old Pueblo institution. It still is, though to a lesser extent than it was in, say, the 1930s and 1940s. The City of Tucson operates 27 public pools all over town. Most of them are only open from May to August, when you almost need a tepid-water pool available to stay sane in the desert. Nine city pools stay open year-round and are heated. The cost to swim is nominal, and you're likely to make a few friends poolside. The best place to find the nearest city pool is the city's comprehensive website. Most of the city pools have scheduled hours for kids and for lap swimming and other special activities. There are always lifeguards on duty.

TENNIS
FORT LOWELL TENNIS CENTER
2900 N. Craycroft Rd., 520/791-2584, www.fortlowelltennis.com
HOURS: Daily 6 A.M.–10:30 P.M.
COST: $2.50 day, $10 night
Map 3

The tennis center at Fort Lowell Park—where the Apache-fighting U.S. soldiers once lived long ago—has eight courts and offers a slew of leagues, tournaments, and classes throughout the year. It's a good idea to call ahead for a reservation as the courts here get regular and heavy use. There's a busy director-pro here to coordinate everything, and the Santa

© TIM HULL

Catalinas loom large and beautiful over the smooth courts.

HIMMEL PARK TENNIS CENTER

1000 N. Tucson Blvd., 520/791-3276
HOURS: Daily 6 A.M.-10:30 P.M.
COST: $2.50 per person for 1.5 hours
Map 3

The eight older and slightly scuffed-up courts at the Sam Hughes neighborhood's Himmel Park offer a bit more laid-back atmosphere for tennis than the huge, serious Randolph Center. You can call ahead and reserve a court, but often you can just show up and there'll be one available. There are several leagues that play here so you might want to call and check before showing up, especially on weekends.

REFFKIN TENNIS CENTER

50 S. Alvernon Way, 520/791-4896,
www.reffkintenniscenter.com
HOURS: Daily sunrise-9:30 P.M.
COST: $2.50 per person for 1.5 hours
Map 3

The Southwest's largest public tennis facility, this huge gathering of courts, pros, and nets at the corner of Broadway and Alvernon—the northeast corner of sprawling Reid Park—offers 25 lighted tennis courts and 10 lighted racquetball courts. You really must call ahead to reserve a court—it's a very popular place. And, if you're here in the summer, you have to get on the court very early, or after dark, to avoid the heat.

YOGA

TUCSON YOGA

150 S. 4th Ave., 520/988-1832, www.tucsonyoga.com
HOURS: Mon.-Wed. 7 A.M.-8:30 P.M.,
Thurs. 7 A.M.-8 P.M., Fri. 7 A.M.-7 P.M., Sat. 9 A.M.-12:15 P.M.,
Sun. 9 A.M.-8:30 P.M.
COST: $6 per class or $45 per month for
unlimited classes
Map 1

This downtown yoga center offers inexpensive and professionally led classes throughout the day and evening (usually the last class starts around 7 P.M., earlier on weekends). A favorite among Tucson's yogis—it's been voted the best

yoga studio in town several times by readers of the *Tucson Weekly*—Tucson Yoga presents at least two or three "basic yoga" classes per week for beginners, as well as classes for experts and everyone in between. They also offer several wellness and spirituality classes and events throughout the month.

GUIDED AND WALKING TOURS

KRUSEARIZONA TOURS

Citywide, 520/625-8365, www.krusearizona.com
COST: $15 per person

Among the few walking tours offered of the Old Pueblo's historic downtown neighborhoods and sights, Alan Kruse's KruseArizona Tours are by far the best. Friendly, animated, and extremely well-versed in the long, fascinating history of Tucson, Kruse dons the typical garb of a frontier teacher to take on the guise of John Spring, the second public-school teacher in Tucson circa 1870. The tours are offered in the mornings throughout the week and on Saturdays; they last about two hours, taking you through Barrio Histórico, the El Presidio neighborhood, and all around downtown. He also offers "twilight tours" April–June to avoid the heat of the day.

THE PRESIDIO TRAIL

Starts at Church Ave. and Washington St., Tucson
Presidio Trust for Historic Preservation, 520/748-2837,
www.tucsonpresidiotrust.org
COST: Free
Map 1

Put together by the Tucson Presidio Trust for Historic Preservation, the Presidio Trail is an interesting and fun self-guided walking tour of downtown's historic neighborhoods and landmarks. The 2.5-mile walk is designed as a loop and takes you past 23 historically significant sites, most of them marked by plaques. The walk begins and ends at the intersection of Church and Washington Streets, right where the original presidio once stood. The Presidio Trust has put together a complete guide to the trail, with a cartoon map that shows the entirety of downtown Tucson's landmarks better than any other—reading the charmingly drawn map is half the fun. The map is available for free at the **Tucson Visitor Center** at **La Placita Village** (110 S. Church Ave., 800/638-8350, Mon.–Fri. 9 A.M.–5 P.M., Sat.–Sun. 9 A.M.–4 P.M.).

SKATE PARKS
RANDOLPH CENTER SKATE PARK
200 S. Alvernon Way, 520/791-4560
HOURS: June-July Mon.-Sat. 8 A.M.-4 P.M., Aug.-May Mon.-Fri. 2 P.M.-sundown
COST: Free
Map 3

If you need to shred to live, then grab your board or your skates and head over to Reid Park and the Randolph Center Skate Park, with vertical props, rails, and a host of ramps in an enclosed 20,000-square-foot asphalt site. Call ahead for hours; it's not always open. **Catalina High School** (E. Pima St., 520/791-4873), near Pima Street and Dodge Boulevard, also has a fenced-in outdoor roller rink and a skate park that can be used by the general public after school hours.

HIKING
Tucson and its surrounding sky island ranges have excellent hiking trails for all experience levels. Desert trails tend to be rather flat and rocky, while the mountain trails are steep and usually offer some spectacular views. I don't recommend hiking in the desert during the height of summer. If you really must, start early in the morning and try to be done by noon. Always take water and salty snacks with you on the trail, always wear a hat, and stay alert to signs of dehydration and heat exhaustion/stroke. If you're hiking in Sabino Canyon or in other areas of the desert that typically receive runoff from the towering mountains above during the rainy season in July and August, remember that just because it's not raining in the desert doesn't mean it isn't raining in the mountains. And rain in the mountains invariably washes down to the desert, sometimes catching lowland hikers unaware and sweeping them off to their deaths. If the trails and hiking areas listed here aren't enough for you, check out local hiking expert Betty Leavengood's *Tucson Hiking Guide.*

FOREST INFORMATION

Most of the public lands around Tucson and Southern Arizona are administered by **Coronado National Forest.** The forest's main office in Tucson (300 W. Congress St., 520/388-8300, www.fs.usda.gov/coronado, Mon.-Fri. 8 A.M.-4:30 P.M.) can direct you to a specific field office.

Public wildlands that aren't administered by the U.S. Forest Service are usually administered by the **Bureau of Land Management** (12661 E. Broadway Blvd., 520/258-7200, www.blm. gov, Mon.-Fri. 8 A.M.-4 P.M.).

If you have any trouble with wild animals or need to report a poaching incident, call the **Arizona Game & Fish Department** (555 N. Greasewood Rd., 520/628-5376, www.azgfd. gov, Mon.-Fri. 8 A.M.-5 P.M.).

A good place to get advice and topo maps is the **Arizona Geological Survey** (416 W. Congress St., Ste. 100, 520/770-3500, www. azgs.az.gov, Mon.-Fri. 8 A.M.-5 P.M.

A quick word of warning: The forests, deserts, and grasslands of the Coronado National Forest are extremely susceptible to wildfire, especially in the dry summer months. In fact, fire and smoking restrictions often go into effect early in the summer, if not before, and those who don't follow these restrictions to the letter are liable to end up with a stiff fine or, even worse, a burned-down forest on their conscience. In the worst cases, some forest areas are closed completely during the height of the wildfire season. If you see a wildfire in the forest, call the Coronado National Forest (520/670-4522) to report it.

You can find it online and at many local bookstores.

THE ARIZONA TRAIL

Various trailheads around Southern Arizona, www.aztrail.org

COST: Free

Map 8

The Arizona Trail is a nearly 800-mile network of mostly existing trails that one could follow on foot, horse, or mountain bike (if you want to carry your bike through the Grand Canyon and other federal wilderness areas along the way), from the border with Mexico to the border with Utah. There are 43 different "passages" that make up the trail, each between 11 and 35 miles; more than a dozen of these are in Southern Arizona, within easy reach of Tucson. The trail through Southern Arizona traverses all of the region's biomes, from the scrubby desert to the dry grasslands to the cool, green mountains—it's a great way to get to know all the natural wonders around Tucson. The non-profit Arizona Trail Association is responsible for upkeep and trail building, and their website has a complete map and detailed description of the trail.

MADERA CANYON HIKING TRAILS

Madera Canyon Rd., east of Green Valley, 520/281-2296

Map 8

The most popular trail to the top of Mount Wrightson, the 10,000-foot peak of the Santa Rita Mountains, is the 10.8-mile round-trip Old Baldy Trail, which is fairly steep but much shorter than the more gradual, 16-mile round-trip Super Trail. Both trails are well marked, heavily used, and start near the Mount Wrightson Picnic Area at the top of Madera Canyon. Both trails also take you over Josephine Saddle, at about 7,000 feet, and Baldy Saddle at more than 8,000 feet, just below the peak, which make good places to stop and rest. At Josephine Saddle, make sure to look at the makeshift memorial to a group of Boy Scouts that got caught in a snowstorm

on the mountain in the 1950s and never returned. If you're coming up the Super Trail, stop and rest at Sprung Spring just before you reach the saddle, which has delicious mountain water trickling from a spigot. To see the lushness that a little trickling water can inspire, hit the 5.8-mile Bog Spring–Kent Spring Loop, which leads over some old mining roads in the lower reaches of the canyon on to some fairly steep and skinny trails along a windswept ridge, providing pretty spectacular views of the valley below. The trail eventually leads deep into the forest, where sycamores thrive on the edges of green and spongy clearings. Also try the 4.4-mile one-way Nature Trail, a strenuous but easy way to see the entire canyon, from the desert grasslands at its entrance at the Proctor Parking Area, where you can pick up the trail, all the way up to the woodlands at the top. Small signs along the way point out notable flora and fauna, and the highest point on the trail, high above the canyon floor, offers a unique perspective. The trails are managed by managed by the Coronado National Forest's **Nogales Ranger District** (303 Old Tucson Rd., Nogales).

🄲 MOUNT LEMMON HIKING TRAILS

Coronado National Forest, 520/670-4522, www.fs.usda.gov/coronado

COST: $5 per vehicle

Map 8

The dozens of trails around and on 9,157-foot Mount Lemmon, about an hour's drive up the winding Sky Island Scenic Byway from central Tucson and into another world entirely, are beloved among all those Tucsonans sweating away in the hot valley down there, dreaming of a weekend day spent scrambling around the evergreen forests and cool streams up on the mountain. Since there are so many trails to choose from (many of them lead into and branch off one another), you might consider the following eight-mile loop composed of portions of several trails, which is designed to take you through some of the best areas the mountain has to offer.

At Summerhaven, turn onto the Sabino

JUAN BAUTISTA DE ANZA NATIONAL HISTORIC TRAIL

The Juan Bautista de Anza National Historic Trail, popularly known as the Anza Trail, traces the route the Basque explorer took in 1776 while leading some 240 immigrants west to Alta California to establish a presidio and settlement.

The trail will eventually run from Culiacán, Mexico, to San Francisco, about 1,200 miles over mostly rugged and arid territory.

A rather lush section of the trail, following the Santa Cruz River from the presidio at Tubac to the mission at Tumacácori, is already one of the more popular hikes in the valley. The 4.5-mile one-way trail, which can be picked up at well-marked trailheads at the mission and the presidio, provides an intimate look at the riparian habitat along the river, a shady greenway crowded with cottonwoods.

The trail isn't exactly pristine, however.

Hikers and horseback riders are likely to see the left-behind evidence of illegal immigration along the trail, and the river itself flows with reclaimed wastewater. Still, it's a beautiful route, and this mostly flat, easy trail is a great option for families.

There's also about a four-mile one-way stretch of the trail near Rio Rico, following the river and winding through mesquite forests. To reach this section of the trail, head south on I-19 to exit 17, Rio Rico/Yavapai Drive. Head north and cross the Santa Cruz, then turn left onto a gravel road and look for the trailhead sign.

A mostly paved section of the Anza Trail runs near downtown Tucson, along the dry riverbed west from Silverlake to Columbus Park, while other stretches are planned for the near future in Green Valley, Canoa Ranch in the Santa Cruz Valley, and northern Pima County.

Canyon Parkway and follow it down to **Marshall Gulch;** leave your car at the small streamside parking lot. Start on Trail #3 (Marshall Gulch Trail), behind the bathrooms, and follow it up through the shady forest for 1.2 miles to Marshall Saddle, at 7,920 feet. At Marshall Saddle branch off to the left on Trail #44 (Wilderness of Rocks Trail), which will take you down about 700 feet into the beautiful **Wilderness of Rocks** for 1.7 miles. At the junction, take Trail #12 (the Lemmon Rock Lookout Trail) as it rises and rises for about 2 miles to near the very peak of Mount Lemmon, at 9,157 feet, where you'll be among metal towers essential to life down below. Along the way you can stop off at the Mount Lemmon Lookout, which offers one of the best views in the region. You'll see the ski lift near the top, but don't get on. Instead, hike along **Radio Ridge** using the Mount Lemmon Trail (Trail #5) for a mile or so to its junction with Trail #93 (Aspen Trail), then follow that downhill for 1.3 miles to find yourself back at Marshall Saddle—then

it's 1.2 miles back to the car. The climbs on this loop can be a bit brutal, but you're definitely rewarded for the effort. For information on other trails and more suggestions on which ones to try, stop by the Palisades Visitor Center on your way up the hill. There you can talk to rangers and pick up a map of the trail system.

SAGUARO NATIONAL PARK WEST
Red Hills Visitor Center, 2700 N. Kinney Rd., 520/733-5158, www.nps.gov/sagu
COST: $5 individuals, $10 per vehicle
Map 5

Both sections of Saguaro National Park offer excellent desert hiking. In the Tucson Mountains district west of town, a strenuous but beautiful hike up to 4,687-foot Wasson Peak, the highest in the Tucson Mountains, is a great way to spend a Sonoran Desert morning. You can get there by picking up the King Canyon Trail just across Kinney Road near the Arizona-Sonora Desert Museum. It's about 3.5 miles to the top of the peak, hiking on switchbacks though typical bajada desert; then you can make it a loop by heading down the Hugh Norris Trail to its junction with the Sendero Esperanza Trail and taking the Gold Mine Trail back to the car. The whole adventure is about 7.5 miles total. There are certainly easier and less steep trails around the park as well. An easy one to take with kids is the 0.5-mile Signal Hill Petroglyphs Trail, which features a modest climb to a collection of boulders with several petroglyphs on display. If you continue on from here the flat, easy trail takes you through some wonderful desert with a good chance to see wildlife. In the park's eastern section, at the base of the Rincon Mountains, there are several 3–5-mile loop hikes that will take you through all of the best parts of the sprawling cactus forests; for a short 2-mile round-trip walk, the Cactus Forest Trail is an easy, mostly flat trail among the green-armed giants. The visitors centers at both the western and eastern sections have complete trail guides and rangers on duty who can help you decide the best routes, and the park's website has detailed maps and trail guides as well.

◾ TUCSON MOUNTAIN PARK

Enter at Gates Pass Rd., 10 miles west of downtown, www.pima.gov/nrpr/parks
COST: Free
Map 5

Some of the best desert hiking in the region can be found at this sprawling saguaro-crowded park west of the city. Here the trails are rocky and sandy, moderately flat, and thickly lined with desert vegetation. The nearly 5-mile round-trip **Brown Mountain Trail** leads through a cactus forest along the sandy bottomlands between the mountains, then rises sharply to a ridgeline that looks out on the hard country all around. You can access the trailhead at the Brown Mountain Picnic Area or the Juan Santa Cruz Picnic Area, both a bit southeast of the Arizona-Sonora Desert Museum off Kinney Road. Just before you reach the valley after the steep descent from Gates Pass, there's a parking lot and trailhead where you can pick up the 5.5-mile **David Yetman Trail,**

named for the host of the PBS show *The Desert Speaks.* There's another trailhead at Camino de Oeste—and if you leave a car at both ends you won't have to do a more-than-10-mile there-and-back trudge. Pima County's Natural Resources Department keeps a map of the trails around Tucson Mountain Park on their website.

TUMAMOC HILL TRAIL

1675 W. Anklam Rd., www.tumamoc.org
COST: Free
Map 5

For a moderately strenuous climb on smooth asphalt road just a few miles west of downtown, head over to the entrance to the University of Arizona's desert laboratory on Tumamoc Hill (where scientists have been studying the Sonoran Desert for more than 100 years). The gradual rise up the entrance road to the top of the historic hill overlooking Tucson is a 3.1-mile round-trip walk, with an elevation gain of about 730 feet. It's a popular route for Tucsonans looking for some early-evening exercise, and the view from the top can't be beat. A sign at the entrance says that hikers are not allowed on the road Monday–Friday 7:30 A.M.–5:30 P.M. That doesn't mean that you have to wait until Saturday morning, though. Many hikers head up in the evening; bring a flashlight with you because, depending on how in shape you are, the round-trip could take up to three hours. Make sure to stay on the roadway at all times—there are long-term experiments going on in the desert around the route that could be ruined if trampled on or otherwise disturbed. Outside of a small private home at the beginning of the road up the mountain, look for the homemade shrine with a sign encouraging visitors to stop and look. To get to the entrance, head west on Speedway Boulevard from downtown, under I-10 to Silverbell Road. Turn south on Silverbell and drive a short way to West Anklmam Road and turn west; the trailhead is on the left. There is no parking at the trailhead, so either get dropped off or park at nearby St. Mary's Hospital.

VENTANA CANYON TRAIL

Trailhead: Loews Ventana Canyon Resort parking lot, 7000 N. Resort Dr.

COST: Free

Map 4

This tough, steep, 13-mile round-trip hike into the Santa Catalina Mountains isn't for the casual hiker, though of course you don't have to go the whole way. The trail ends at the titular *ventana* (window in Spanish), an approximately 15-foot-high, 25-foot-wide, naturally worn hole in a jutting rock slab. The trailhead is at the parking lot of the Loews Ventana Canyon Resort in the foothills and is open and accessible to the public during the day. A full day's hike here, or just a few miles up into the steep slopes of the front range, provides a chance to see the desert at its best.

BIKING

Biking, whether of the sleek road or the tough mountain variety, is hugely popular in the Old Pueblo. For years Tucson and Pima County have been recognized as very bike-friendly areas; the region is the only in Arizona to obtain a gold-level ranking from the League of American Bicyclists, and there are something like 630 miles of dedicated bike paths throughout the city and county. The **Tucson Visitor Center** downtown at **La Placita Village** (110 S. Church Ave., 800/638-8350, Mon.–Fri. 9 A.M.–5 P.M., Sat.–Sun. 9 A.M.–4 P.M.) offers free maps to many of the bike paths and trailheads here, or you can download the most up-to-date version at www.dot.co.pima.az.us/tpcbac, the website of the very active Tucson–Pima County Bicycle Advisory Committee.

Bike Rentals and Shops
BROADWAY BICYCLES

140 S. Sarnoff Dr., 520/296-7819, www.broadwaybicycles.com

HOURS: Mon.-Fri. 10 A.M.–6 P.M., Sat. 9 A.M.–6 P.M., Sun. 11 A.M.–4 P.M.

COST: $30-50 per day, $150-250 for seven days

Map 6

The friendly folks at Broadway Bicycles, off Broadway Boulevard just west of the popular road-bike route on Old Spanish Trail, rent top-brand (Trek and Fisher) late-model road bikes and mountain bikes, and give out good advice about the best rides and trails in and around Tucson. They also have an expert service department and a full stock of top-of-the-line road and mountain bikes, helmets, clothing, and other equipment.

CYCLE TUCSON

520/245-6011, www.cycletucson.com

COST: $50 per day, $120 for three days, plus various packages and specials

The couple that owns this local bike rental and guide service have a combined 35 years in the cycling industry, so they know what they're talking about. They provide rental road and mountain bikes, and they'll help you decide where to go (or even take you out themselves). Moreover, they bring the bikes to you, take you out to the trail or route, and then pick you up at sunset. They prefer Cannondale road bikes, mountain bikes, and hybrids.

ORDINARY BIKE SHOP

311 E. 7th St., 520/622-6488, www.ordinarybikeshop.com

HOURS: Mon.-Fri. 9 A.M.-7 P.M., Sat. 8 A.M.-5 P.M.

Map 2

Located downtown on 7th Street near 4th Avenue, Ordinary Bikes has been voted the best bike shop in Tucson by the bike-loving readers of the local alternative weekly for nearly a decade straight. The guys here are friendly and helpful, and their service department will fix just about any problem your bike is having. They don't rent bikes, but they do sell used ones from time to time. They have a good selection of new mountain and road bikes, including brands like Bianca, Raleigh, and Diamondback, along with a limited selection of clothing and other equipment.

Bike Trails and Routes
BRAD P. GORMAN MEMORIAL BIKEWAY

Catalina Hwy. to Santa Catalina Mountains

COST: Free

Map 8

A favorite route for road bikers is the long, hard

climb up the Catalina Highway, also called the Brad P. Gorman Memorial Bikeway, into the cool heights of the Santa Catalina Mountains. The route is about 38 miles from midtown to the village of Summerhaven, and most of it is uphill. Take Tanque Verde Road to the Catalina Highway, and pedal as hard as you can. Make sure to watch the cars along the road carefully; some of the day-trippers to the mountains will be too busy checking out the views to notice you on your bike.

DAN YERSAVICH MEMORIAL BIKEWAY

Broadway Blvd. to Saguaro National Park East, along Old Spanish Trail

COST: Free

Map 6

A popular road-bike ride on a warm weekend morning is the Dan Yersavich Memorial Bikeway along Old Spanish Trail from Broadway Boulevard to Saguaro National Park East (about 6 miles). You can ride among the saguaros on Cactus Loop Road or you can continue on the route for another 12 miles to Colossal Cave Mountain Park. Most of the route has a bike lane, but be sure to look out for traffic along the way.

◖ FANTASY ISLAND BIKING TRAILS

S. Harrison Rd. at E. Irvington Rd., Tucson

COST: Free

Map 8

While none of the trails and loops at Fantasy Island is very long, they are all fun and relatively easy—it's a great place for beginners and novices to ride. There's a detailed trail map set up at the entrance. Be careful not to stare too much and lose your balance while passing all the strange junk-art objects set up along the trails. You need to purchase a permit to recreate on state-trust land in Arizona, and you should always have it with you while you're riding just in case. To purchase one ($15 for a year), go to www.land.state.az.us.

50-YEAR TRAIL

Trailhead: parking lot on Golder Ranch Rd., Tucson

COST: Free

Map 8

Some of the best desertland single-tracks in Southern Arizona can be found about 25 miles north of Tucson in the Golder Ranch area. A series of rocky, undulating trails through desert, the 50-Year Trail is great fun for experts and beginners alike. You'll need your state-trust land permit for this ride (although I've never seen anybody out there checking permits or anything). Take Oracle Road north through Oro Valley and turn right on Golder Ranch Road; follow it until you get to a dirt parking lot and a cattle guard. The trail is just beyond the cattle guard.

MOUNT LEMMON BIKING TRAILS

Palisades Visitor Center, milepost 19.9 on Catalina Hwy.

HOURS: Daily 8:30 A.M.–4:30 P.M.

COST: $5

Map 8

If you're not into desert-country mountain biking, head up the Sky Island Scenic Byway to the wooded and green Mount Lemmon and its many difficult, steep, and rocky trails. Consider the **Aspen Draw** (summer only), a popular and technical route, or the **Milagrosa Trail, Green Mountain,** and the **Molino Trail.** Stop at the Palisades Visitor Center on your way up the mountain for a trail map. The air up on the mountain, which rises beyond 9,000 feet, is cooler and thinner, so remember that you probably won't be in top riding condition up here unless you're used to high altitudes. You can also get information about Mount Lemmon biking trails at the Coronado National Forest Santa Catalina Ranger District (5700 N. Sabino Canyon Rd., 530/749-8700, www.fs.fed.us/r3/coronado, Mon.–Fri. 8 A.M.–4:30 P.M., Sat.–Sun. 8:30 A.M.–4:30 P.M.).

RILLITO PARK BIKE ROUTE

Craycroft Rd., following the Rillito River

COST: Free

Map 4

This flat and easy 11-mile route following the sandy-bottomed Rillito is a great route for exercise and commuting across the north end of Tucson. Sure the river is dry on top, but it's still a relatively green and shady route. For north-end bike commuters it's a kind of east–west freeway—one with bunnies and lizards always popping out to keep you sharp. The path runs from near I-10 all the way to Craycroft Road, and along the way it passes several parks, always hugging the parched riverbed, colored here and there with seeping lushness.

STARR PASS BIKE TRAIL

Tucson Mountain Park, start at parking lot on Clearwell Rd.
COST: Free
Map 5

An eight-mile single-track loop through rocky desert, Starr Pass is a tough ride but fun and beautiful, with sweeping views of the valley below. To get to the trailhead, go west from downtown on St. Mary's Road past Pima College (it turns into Anklam Rd.) to Players Club Drive and turn left, heading to a four-way stop with Starr Pass Boulevard, where you turn left again. Take the first right onto dirt Clearwell Road and park in the parking lot. The Starr Pass Trail hooks up with the Yetman Trail, which is also a good ride, as are most of the rocky, challenging up-and-down single-tracks and old dirt roads in the Tucson Mountains and the cactus-crowded valleys below them.

3RD STREET BIKE ROUTE

Start at 3rd St. at Wilmot Rd.
COST: Free
Map 2

This bike route is an easy, flat way to get from midtown to downtown on a bike. It goes from Wilmot Road on the eastern edge of midtown all the way through the University of Arizona to downtown. The route is designed to avoid high-traffic areas, and most of the time you'll be cruising along empty (except for your biking compatriots) and quiet residential streets. When you go through campus, make sure to follow all of the bike-riding traffic rules.

HORSEBACK RIDING

The horse has been an integral part of daily life in Tucson and Southern Arizona since the Spanish introduced the beast to the Southwest back in the 1500s. The new, useful animal transformed the lives and cultures of the native peoples here virtually overnight, and still today there is a distinct subculture of "horse people" in the Old Pueblo whose lives are dedicated to the care and enjoyment of the equestrian kind. There are quite a few such people who will rent you a usually friendly, docile horse and guide you and your new friend deep into the desert on trails once traversed by conquistadores, cowboys, and Indians. Most places require that kids be at least six years old to ride, and most have a 230-pound maximum weight limit, but call ahead to make sure. Spring rides are the best, obviously, especially when the desert's in bloom. Summer is different—go early in the morning or book one of the fun evening or nighttime rides many places offer. Always wear long pants and closed-toed shoes, and always bring a hat, though it doesn't necessarily have to be the cowboy type.

PANTANO RIDING STABLES

4450 S. Houghton Rd., 520/298-8980, www.horsingaroundarizona.com
HOURS: Winter daily 8 A.M.-5 P.M., summer daily 8 A.M.-noon and 4-6:30 P.M.
COST: $35 for 1 hour, $45 for 1.5 hours, $65 for 2 hours, $50 for sunset ride
Map 8

About 13 miles southeast of town, out in the shaggy cactus-and-scrub desert not far from Saguaro National Park East, the friendly folks at Pantano Riding Stables will take you out and make you feel like a real cowboy. Along with the usual one- to two-hour trail rides, they offer a fun "campfire ride" where you can dine under the stars as if you're working some kind of roundup. The desert out this way is beautiful and thick, and if you go when the cacti are blooming you are in for a spectacular show. It's a good idea to call ahead for a reservation.

PUSCH RIDGE RIDING STABLES

13700 N. Oracle Rd., 520/825-1664, www.puschridgestables.com
HOURS: Daily 8 A.M.-4 P.M.
COST: $40 one hour, $60 two hours, $50 sunset ride
Map 8

In the northwest foothills of the Santa Catalina

© TIM HULL

Horseback riding is a must for those who want the full Southwestern experience in Tucson.

Mountains, about 20 miles northwest of town near Catalina State Park, Pusch Ridge Riding Stables go out on fun desertland trail rides every hour on the hour 8 a.m.–3 p.m. every day. During the busy spring season, rides typically include about 6–8 riders and a guide. The "moonlight rides" here are particularly enchanting, making one feel a bit like an outlaw on the run. These last 1.5 hours and cost $60 per person with a minimum of four riders. They also offer half-day ($100 pp) and full-day ($160 pp) rides, and private rides ($85 per hour). Call ahead for reservations, especially on the weekends.

BALLOONING
SOUTHERN ARIZONA BALLOON EXCURSIONS
537 W. Grant Rd., 520/624-3599,
www.tucsoncomefly.com
HOURS: Daily, weather permitting
COST: $175 per person
`Map 4`

For more than 25 years this local family-owned company has been taking people high into the blue, cloudless skies over Tucson for a glimpse of the desert from above. For the hour-long rides, offered every day that weather permits (no rain and no strong winds), they'll fill their big balloons for a drift over the Tucson Mountains and the Avra Valley. Depending on the day, you will likely be in a basket with just a few other people or up to eight. The price includes a champagne brunch upon landing, a certificate, and two pictures. Make sure to bring a hat. Calling ahead to make a reservation is a must.

SPECTATOR SPORTS
FC TUCSON
Kino Sports Complex, Field No. 5, www.fctucson.com
COST: $12
`Map 7`

Tucson's scrappy Premier Development League soccer team is a lot of fun to watch. Games are played during a late-spring, early-summer season; you can buy your ticket at the gate. It's kind of a cross between MLS and AYSO, with a loud and dedicated group of chanters called the "Desert Pricks" adding big league atmosphere for a crowd of folks sitting on the sidelines in lawn chairs. Otherwise there's the bleachers. A few vendors sell beer and soda and hot dogs, including the Sonoran variety. The action on the field is usually quite exciting, as promising young talents compete furiously for a future in the beautiful game.

SOUTHWESTERN INTERNATIONAL DRAGWAY

12000 S. Houghton Rd., Tucson, 520/762-9700, www.sirace.com
COST: Varies depending on event
Map 8

This dragway about 20 miles southeast of midtown, near the Pima County Fairgrounds, hosts a plethora of drag-racing events throughout the year, from professional races with the sport's big names to weekend-morning high-school races and other amateur events. There's seating here for more than 6,000, and it's always fun to sit in the sun (with a hat on, of course) and watch the cars burn up their rubber on the already near-melting blacktop.

TUCSON RACEWAY PARK

11955 S. Harrison Rd., Tucson, www.tucsonracewaypark.com
COST: $10 adult; $7 active military, senior, child; free for children under 8
Map 8

This small track about 20 miles southeast of

midtown, at the Pima County Fairgrounds, puts on street stock, late model, spectator drag, modified, Pro 4, factory stock, and Hornet races throughout the year, along with a host of special events and driving schools.

UNIVERSITY OF ARIZONA SPORTS

McKale Center, 520/621-2287, www.arizonaathletics.com
COST: Varies depending on event
Map 2

The biggest sports draw in the region are the teams of the University of Arizona. With perennial powerhouses in basketball, volleyball, and baseball, and a Pac-10 football team that is usually expected to hold its own in a tough division, there's always something to cheer for on campus. UA basketball is traditionally the top sport not only on campus but in all of Southern Arizona; for years, as now-retired coach Lute Olsen was always leading the team to the final days of the NCAA tournament every March, the whole town caught the madness en masse. With the Lute era over, it remains to be seen if the team will be as popular locally as it once was, but don't expect getting tickets to be easy regardless of who is coaching. UA basketball is still the top sports draw in town, and is likely to remain that way for the time being.

SHOPS

David Puddy asked it on the television show *Seinfeld:* "What can you get at the Gap in Rome that you can't get at the Gap on 5th Avenue?" Use this as your mantra while shopping in Tucson and Southern Arizona. The Old Pueblo has all the chains, more so than most midsize cities. But if you spend your time at the Gap you're going to miss a unique shopping experience—a chance to find that treasure that has eluded you, to return home with an authentic artifact.

You'll find merchants with Mexican imports, folk arts, Western Americana, and Indian jewelry; boutiques with clothes you'll find nowhere else; and galleries featuring the work of artists from Tucson and the rest of the world. Take a short drive south to Tubac—an artist's village that caters to, or better yet exists for, the discriminating treasure hunter—then on across the border to Nogales, Sonora, and you'll find items you never knew you had to have. A brief scenic journey east and you're among the antiques stores and artisan boutiques of old-town Bisbee. Fear not: Shopping in Southern Arizona isn't just for the moneyed. There are finds for everyone, and for every budget.

If you're looking for that truly Southwestern gift or souvenir to take home, there are many places to find such items. Some of the most popular items that just scream "Tucson" are the many Day of the Dead *calaveras* available throughout the borderlands; and, of course, anything with the beloved visage of the Virgin of Guadalupe will remind you of your time in the desert every time you look at it. There are also many antiques and resale stores here stocked with the former possessions of all those retirees who came to the desert to live out their final days in free and easy style.

HIGHLIGHTS

LOOK FOR ❨ TO FIND RECOMMENDED SHOPS.

© TIM HULL

Bookmans

❨ **Best Bookstore:** Book lovers can't miss **Bookmans,** a popular Southern Arizona chain with an amazing inventory and used books at less than half the original price (page 144).

❨ **Best Music Store:** The East Speedway Boulevard location of **Zia Record Exchange** is stocked full with an eclectic mixture of brand-new and gently used CDs, often for prices similar to, if not below, the big national chains (page 145).

❨ **Best Thrift Store:** "Vintage clothing for New Bohemians" is how the founder of **Buffalo Exchange** describes her first store, a popular Tucson original that spawned a nationwide chain (page 148).

❨ **Best Shopping District:** With over 100 mostly locally owned stores, restaurants, boutiques, bars, clubs, and coffeehouses, the tree-lined **4th Avenue** district downtown is the perfect place to shop, eat, and drink the day away (page 153).

❨ **Best Upscale Shopping:** Tucson's answer to the famous high-end shopping mecca of Scottsdale, **La Encantada** is an elegant outdoor mall in the foothills, offering all the most posh chains and a few local boutiques as well (page 153).

❨ **Best Antiques:** Prepare to spend hours in the **Speedway Antiques District,** where the best of the handful of antiques shops is Copper Country Antiques, a huge antiques warehouse with Western- and Southwestern-themed treasures and much, much more (page 157).

❨ **Best Place to Buy Folk Art:** Arizona's first settlement, **Tubac** is now an artist's colony and shopping village with more than 100 shops and galleries, many of them selling Mexican and South American imports (page 157).

❨ **Best Gifts from the Desert:** Take a piece of the Sonoran Desert home with you from **Native Seeds/SEARCH,** where you'll find unique items from and about the desert, including videos, books, crafts, and heirloom seeds (page 159).

❨ **Best Native American Arts:** The oldest Native American arts shop in Tucson, **Bahti Indian Arts** sells some of the finest examples of Navajo, Hopi, and Pueblo textiles, kachinas, jewelry, basketry, pottery, paintings, and sculptures in the region (page 162).

Antiques

COPPER COUNTRY ANTIQUES
5055 E. Speedway Blvd., 520/326-0167,
www.coppercountryantiques.com
HOURS: Mon.-Sat. 10 A.M.-6 P.M., Sun. 11 A.M.-5 P.M.
Map 3

Just head east on Speedway Boulevard past Alvernon and look for the building with the winged buffaloes on its roof. There's definitely something a little off center going on at this huge midtown antiques mall; I once saw a homemade sign taped onto their regular sign that said, "will trade antiques for alfalfa hay." Inside they've got all the usual Western- and Southwestern-themed treasures, along with mini-stores dedicated to mid-century modern furniture, war memorabilia, old golf clubs, antique jewelry, and much more. Prepare to spend hours in here. Don't worry about missing lunch, though; there's a casual little bistro inside.

TOM'S FINE FURNITURE AND COLLECTIBLES
5454 E. Pima St., 520/795-5210
HOURS: Mon.-Sat. 10 A.M.-5 P.M., Sun. 11 A.M.-4 P.M.
Map 3

A labyrinthine store on Pima near Craycroft, Tom's is crammed to the rafters with furniture, antiques, knickknacks, home decor items, and scores of strange, unclassifiable artifacts; there doesn't seem to be any theme here, just rooms of stuff, much of it expensive. I saw a dusty pair of original high-dollar Eames lounge chairs next to a cigar-store Indian next to a Victorian dressing table and on and on—it's a great place to get lost for a while.

Bath, Beauty, and Spas

ELIZABETH ARDEN RED DOOR SALON
3666 E. Sunrise Dr., 520/742-7866,
www.reddoorspas.com
HOURS: Sun. 9 A.M.-7 P.M., Mon.-Wed. 9 A.M.-8 P.M., Thurs.-Sat. 8 A.M.-8 P.M.
Map 4

Just walking into Tucson's version of the world-famous Red Door Salon, at the Westin La Paloma Resort and Spa lowers your pulse by a few beats, and staff are professional and friendly. They offer just about any massage, facial, or other procedure you're looking for, but it will cost you: The lowest price for a half day or so of pampering is around $350.

GADABOUT SALON AND SPA
3201 E. Speedway Blvd., 520/325-0000,
www.gadabout.com
HOURS: Tues., Thurs., and Fri. 7 A.M.-8 P.M., Wed. and Sat. 7 A.M.-6 P.M.
Map 3

Get a cut, style, massage, mani-pedi, wax, or even a full day of outlandish body-pampering at this branch of this locally owned salon and spa empire.

HASHANI SPA
3800 W. Starr Pass Blvd., 520/791-6117,
http://spa.jwmarriottstarrpass.com
HOURS: Hours vary; call ahead for information.
Map 5

Named for the iconic saguaro cactus so prevalent in its resort location, Hashani is an upscale oasis of relaxation and rejuvenation. The setting, at Starr Pass Resort, is highly inspiring, especially when seen from a glassy pool overlooking the desert. They offer an array of massages (50 min. $150) and facials and other treatments, including the Arizona-themed "copper peptide firming facial" ($130), and the creosote purifier ($135), which taps into the famed healing properties of this ubiquitous desert bush. They recommend making reservations at least two weeks ahead.

SONORAN SPA

245 E. Ina Rd., 520/917-2467,
http://westwardlook.com/Tucson-spa-resort
HOURS: Daily 8 A.M.–9 P.M.
Map 4

Visit the Westward Look Resort's sumptuous Sonoran Spa after a day spent in the unrelenting desert sunshine. They offer an Arizona Aloe Wrap (60 min. $109) specifically for natives (and those who have gone native) with "sunburned, dry or stressed skin." One assumes that the relatively high cost of the treatment prevents a long line from forming every day. They also offer a Native American–inspired blue corn scrub, and several "ancient desert rituals" (60 min. $129) meant to relax and refresh even the most frenzied of desert subjects.

TREEHOUSE THAI MASSAGE SPA

148 S. 4th Ave., 520/622-8895,
www.arizonamassageworkshops.com
HOURS: Tues.-Fri. 9 A.M.–8 P.M., Sat. 10 A.M.–6 P.M.
Map 1

This delightful 4th Avenue spa, a local favorite, specializes in Thai massage ($99 for 2 hrs., $139 for 3 hrs.). Each relaxing, refreshing session includes a foot bath, herbal sauna, and tea. This is an affordable and welcoming place, and the perfect place to escape the pressures of the day under the expert hands of a practitioner well versed and studied in an ancient form of deep healing.

Books and Music

ANTIGONE BOOKS

411 N. 4th Ave., 520/792-3715,
www.antigonebooks.com
HOURS: Mon.-Thurs. 10 A.M.–7 P.M.,
Fri.-Sat. 10 A.M.–9 P.M., Sun. noon–5 P.M.
Map 2

A 4th Avenue institution that's now solar powered, and one of the last independent bookstores in town selling primarily new books, Antigone can get away with it by concentrating on a niche: books about women. There always seems to be some signing or reading going on here, and you'll find an unprecedented selection of books about social justice, gender issues, environmentalism, and left-leaning politics. They also offer a large selection of cards, posters, and book-related merchandise.

◖ BOOKMANS

6230 E. Speedway Blvd., 520/748-9555,
www.bookmans.com
HOURS: Daily 9 A.M.–10 P.M.
Map 6

Book lovers can't miss Bookmans, a Southern Arizona original with an inventory to rival the local Barnes & Noble—only the books here are gently used and less than half the price. There are three Bookmans stores in Tucson, all of them featuring thousands of used books, CDs, videos, DVDs, and video games, but the relatively new Speedway location has become the firm's flagship store. Prices are cheap compared to smaller boutique-style used-book stores, and the selection is absolutely without compare. This is one of the Southwest's best used-book stores. The other two Bookmans locations are on 1930 East Grant Road (520/325-5767) and 3733 West Ina Road (520/579-0303).

THE BOOK STOP

214 N. 4th Ave., 520/326-6661,
www.bookstoptucson.com
HOURS: Mon.-Thurs. 10 A.M.–7 P.M.,
Fri.-Sat. 10 A.M.–10 P.M., Sun. noon–5 P.M.
Map 2

One of the last independent bookstores in Tucson, The Book Stop has been around since the late 1960s, but it's only been on 4th Avenue for a few years. They've got a spectacular selection of used and out-of-print books, including

Antigone Books is a solar-powered bookshop on 4th Avenue.

a substantial section on the Southwest. The books are a bit pricey in comparison to the bigger Bookmans, but when you're inside this classic store you feel a million miles away.

CLUES UNLIMITED

3146 E. Fort Lowell Rd., 520/326-8533,
www.cluesunlimited.com
HOURS: Tues.-Sat. 10 A.M.-6 P.M.

Map 3

Mystery and crime fiction is all they do at Clues Unlimited, a small but very intelligently stocked niche bookstore. They sell an unmatched selection of British imports (everybody knows the Brits write the best mysteries), and there's always some signing or reading featuring crime writers both new and established. A visit here should really be a priority for fans of the genre, or for anyone curious to see what the nearly extinct, locally owned retail bookstore looks like.

ZIA RECORD EXCHANGE

3370 E. Speedway Blvd., 520/327-3340,
www.ziarecords.com
HOURS: Sun.-Thurs. 10 A.M.-10 P.M.,
Fri.-Sat. 10 A.M.-midnight

Map 3

This Arizona and Nevada chain's claim to be "the last real record store" is, sadly, quite true—at least in these arid parts. For a few generations Zia sold an excellent selection of vinyl, and cassettes both new and used, to all the state's rock and rollers. These days the cassettes are no longer stocked much, but the store's Speedway Boulevard location is stocked full of CDs, vinyl, and DVDs of all stripes, still a mixture of the brand-new and the gently used, and often for prices similar to, if not below, the big chains. There's a second location in Tucson (3655 N. Oracle, 520/887-6898).

© TIM HULL

SINGING WIND BOOKSHOP

Take a short, scenic drive north of Benson, a small town east of Tucson, to the verdant ranching country and you'll find an unexpected destination for bibliophiles, or anyone interested in how a bookstore can thrive for more than 30 years in a relatively secluded ranch house.

Winifred Bundy's **Singing Wind Bookshop** (700 W. Singing Wind Rd., 520/586-2425, daily 9 A.M.-5 P.M., including most holidays) opened 33 years ago in the ranch house where Bundy has lived for 52 years. She still lives in the house, and she's likely to come out and show you around in her stocking feet. Make sure to get the tour, as the stock (mostly new books, with an emphasis on Southwestern and Western themes) is organized according to a slightly individualistic code, and Winifred is a great source for recommendations.

She learned about the Southwest from the great Lawrence Clark Powell, and now publishes several one-of-a-kind editions of his work and also sells tapes of conversations with Pow-

ell accompanied by music from Tucson band Calexico. If you plan to buy any books—and it's difficult, many find, to drive all the way out there and not purchase something, as there's simply too much great stuff that can't be found elsewhere—take cash or a checkbook; Winifred says she doesn't "mess with credit cards." She encourages book lovers to bring lunch and have a picnic on the ranch, and don't miss saying hello to the mule and beautiful white horse who share a pasture along the road leading to the shop. A well-stocked children's reading room makes this a great family destination, especially when Winifred's friendly dog comes out from the back room looking to play.

From the tiny town of Benson, along I-10 about 40 miles east of Tucson, take 4th Street (the main drag) to Ocotillo Road, then head north about three miles to Singing Wind Road, a dirt road. Turn east (right) onto the road, drive to a green gate (it may or may not be open; if it isn't, open it yourself), and continue about a quarter of a mile to the ranch house.

Boutique Grocery and Liquor Stores

Tucson has many industrial-size supermarkets—Fry's, Safeway, Basha's (an Arizona chain), Costco, and more. It also has its fair share of the smaller market chains like Trader Joe's, Sprouts, and, of course, Whole Foods. The best local places to shop for delicacies, delectables, and spirits, however, are the many locally owned (or at least Arizona-based) boutique groceries, delis, and liquor stores. The best of these are gathered here.

AJ'S FINE FOODS

2805 E. Skyline Dr., 520/232-6340,
www.ajsfinefoods.com
HOURS: Daily 6 A.M.-9 P.M.
Map 4

This high-end grocery store at the foothills' La Encantada is truly a "purveyor of fine foods,"

with all kinds of boutique-style foods and imported delicacies available, as well as a good restaurant with outdoor seating.

FOOD CONSPIRACY CO-OP

412 N. 4th Ave., 520/624-4821,
www.foodconspiracy.org
HOURS: Daily 8 A.M.-10 P.M.
Map 2

This beloved local co-op has been located on busy, bohemian 4th Avenue downtown for years; the produce is all organic, and they stock "as much seasonal, local produce as possible." They also have all kinds of special-diet selections (gluten-free, dairy-free, vegetarian, macrobiotic, low-fat, low-sodium, unrefined foods, etc.) and a good assortment of international foods.

Food Conspiracy Co-Op

PLAZA LIQUORS

2642 N. Campbell Ave., 520/327-0452

HOURS: Mon.-Sat. 10 A.M.-9 P.M.

Map 3

A perennial winner for best liquor store in town in the *Tucson Weekly*'s Best of Tucson poll, Plaza Liquors is an essential stop for beer lovers. They have the absolute best selection of beer in the Old Pueblo, with hundreds of varieties from all over the world sold by the bottle or can. The small, rather cramped store on busy Campbell Avenue also has a great selection of spirits and wines, and very friendly and helpful staff.

RINCON MARKET

2513 E. 6th St., 520/327-6653, www.rinconmarket.com

HOURS: Mon.-Fri. 7 A.M.-9 P.M., Sat. 7 A.M.-8 P.M., Sun. 8 A.M.-8 P.M.

Map 3

In midtown's Sam Hughes neighborhood, Rincon Market is one of the last old-school neighborhood grocery stores in Arizona. They have an excellent butcher, and they sell a lot of kosher foods and prepared dishes, including the best roast chicken in town. The deli here is always good, and they've got a salad bar and a good produce selection. Perhaps the best time to visit the Rincon Market is on the weekend, when they open their **breakfast bar** (Sat. 7 A.M.-noon, Sun. 8 A.M.-1 P.M.), featuring a made-to-order omelet bar, Belgian waffles, and eggs Benedict (Sun. only).

THE RUMRUNNER

3131 E. 1st St., 520/326-0121, www.rumrunnertucson.com

HOURS: Mon. 11 A.M.-7 P.M., Tues.-Sat. 11 A.M.-10 P.M., Sun. noon-6 P.M.

Map 3

This popular midtown liquor store has an excellent selection of wines and spirits from all over the world. Even if you're looking for something a bit obscure, they are bound to have it here. Inside, **The Dish Bistro-Bar** (520/326-1714, www.dishbistro.com) serves up a mean bowl of mussels—the perfect accompaniment to a few glasses of the wine you just picked out.

17TH STREET MARKET

840 E. 17th St., 520/792-2588,
www.seventeenthstreetmarket.com
HOURS: Mon.-Sat. 10 A.M.-6 P.M.
Map 1

Located in the old warehouse district near downtown's Armory Park neighborhood, this store has a bit of a warehouse feel to it, naturally. It's quite large, and is stacked to the rafters with all manner of food, much of it international in flavor. They have an especially large selection of Asian foods, and excellent always-fresh produce, meats, and seafood. There's also a music shop located inside the store where they sell a great selection of work by Tucson musicians.

Children's Stores

THE KID'S CENTER

1725 N. Swan Rd., 520/322-5437,
www.e-kidscenter.com
HOURS: Mon.-Sat. 9 A.M.-5:30 P.M.
Map 3

The Kid's Center doesn't really look like a toy store from the outside, but more like a school or day-care center, in keeping with its rather scholastic-sounding name. And while there is definitely an emphasis on thoughtful play here, kids from babies to early teens will likely peel away upon entering and commence nosing around and poking through this store's myriad books, science kits, dress-up costumes, puzzles, stuffed animals, toy horses, puppets, art supplies, musical instruments, games, and more, most of them uncommon and boutique-brand items that you don't usually find at the big boxes.

MILDRED AND DILDRED TOY STORE

2905 E. Skyline Dr., 520/615-6266,
www.mildredanddildred.com
HOURS: Mon.-Sat. 10 A.M.-8 P.M., Sun. 11 A.M.-6 P.M.
Map 4

Probably the highest of the high-end toy shops in the Old Pueblo, this cute, playful little boutique at the upscale La Encantada in the foothills sells fun toys, games, and other kids' stuff that you likely won't see too many other places—certainly not at Toys"R"Us and the like. Many of the toys here are imported, others are made from recycled products, and others are just weird and fun.

Clothing and Shoes

◖ BUFFALO EXCHANGE

2001 E. Speedway Blvd., 520/795-0508,
www.buffaloexchange.com
HOURS: Mon.-Sat. 10 A.M.-8 P.M., Sun. 11 A.M.-7 P.M.
Map 2

Buffalo Exchange has spread to college towns and hipster enclaves from Tempe to Brooklyn, but it all started in midtown Tucson in the early 1970s. At the original store you can still find some gently used or even new higher-end brands here for significantly less than retail, plus a large selection of previously worn shoes and jewelry and other items. Or, you can bring in your unwanted duds and maybe get some cash. There's also a Buffalo Exchange downtown (250 E. Congress St., 520/882-2939, Mon.-Sat. 11 A.M.–7 P.M.), and one on the East Side (6212 E. Speedway Blvd., 520/882-8392, Mon.–Wed. 10 A.M.–6 P.M., Thurs.–Sat. 10 A.M.–7 P.M., Sun. 11 A.M.–6 P.M.).

DESERT VINTAGE AND COSTUME

636 N. 4th Ave., 520/620-1570
HOURS: Mon.-Sat. 11 A.M.-6 P.M., Sun. noon-5 P.M.
Map 2

This popular thrift store on 4th Avenue isn't

Buffalo Exchange has fashionable used clothing for sale at multiple locations.

very big, but it's well stocked with clothes from bygone eras. You can find anything you need here to dress up like a disco king or a private eye circa 1945. There are hats, boas, and pass-on jewelry galore. This is one of a few good thrift stores along 4th Avenue; all are stocked with the left-behind fashions of millions of snowbirds, retirees, and longtime natives.

J. GILBERT FOOTWEAR

7041 N. Oracle Rd., 520/531-8385,
www.jgilbertfootwear.com
HOURS: Mon.-Sat. 10 A.M.-5:30 P.M.
Map 4

You probably wouldn't want to wear your high-dollar fancy J. Gilbert boots to the rodeo or out honky-tonkin' (unless you *want* to get them scuffed and dirty), but nobody's better at selling footwear molded from the skin of baby buffaloes, gators, caimans, and ostrich. The upscale Casas Adobes Plaza in the foothills has the only J. Gilbert this side of Scottsdale, so check it out and place a special order—they even make them out of python.

MAYA PALACE

7057 N. Oracle Rd., 520/575-8028,
www.mayapalacetucson.com
HOURS: Mon.-Fri. 10 A.M.-6 P.M., Sat. 10 A.M.-5:30 P.M.,
Sun. noon-5 P.M.
Map 4

Fashionable women will want to peruse this high-end clothing store featuring fashions from around the world for work, play, and even formal occasions (their stock of wedding dresses contains many you won't see anywhere else). There's a concentration here on a sartorial globalization, hence the name, and they also stock an ever-changing array of imported gifts and accessories from all over the globe. In addition to this store at the upscale Casas Adobes Plaza in the foothills, the popular Maya Palace has locations at El Mercado (6332 E. Broadway Blvd., 520/748-0817) and Plaza Palomino (2960 N. Swan Rd., #133, 520/325-6411), both open the same hours as the store in the foothills.

Home Furnishings

ANTIGUA DE MEXICO

3235 W. Orange Grove Rd., 520/742-7114,
www.antiguademexico.us
HOURS: Mon.-Sat. 10 A.M.-5:30 P.M.
Map 4

If you're looking to turn your home into a faux
Spanish hacienda, there are few better places
in the Old Pueblo to shop than Antigua de
Mexico. Here you'll find all the usual beautiful and romantic suspects: colonial furniture
from Mexico and South America, tinwork,
Oaxacan folk art, glassware, Talavera, and
even silver jewelry imported from Mexico and
elsewhere. There are a lot of stores like this
in Tucson, Tubac, and across the border in
Nogales, Mexico, but Antigua de Mexico has
been family owned for more than 30 years, and
they have all you need in one place.

BON BOUTIQUE

3022 E. Broadway Blvd., 520/795-2272,
www.bon-boutique.com
HOURS: Mon.-Sat. 10 A.M.-6 P.M.
Map 3

This enchanting, eclectic store sells a mix of
home decor, clothes, books, garden supplies,
knickknacks, and seemingly just about anything else that appeals to the owners, who have
a playful but always elegant, intelligent, and
classic sense of style. You will likely spend a
good deal of time in here if you're the kind of
shopper that likes to be surprised and intrigued
at every corner.

MEXICAN TILE AND STONE CO.

1148 E. Broadway Blvd., 520/622-4352,
www.mexicantileandstone.com
HOURS: Mon.-Fri. 8 A.M.-4 P.M., Sat. 10 A.M.-2 P.M.
Map 2

This midtown store has all you need to give
your home that Old Pueblo look, selling
all kinds of imported and handmade tiles,
Talavera sinks, copper items, and all the other
special aesthetic touchstones that make the
Tucson style so unique. If you can't quite get
a grip on what the favored Southwestern design is among those who can afford it, this is
the place to peruse. After a few minutes, you're
bound to get it.

ORIGINATE

526 N. 9th Ave., 520/792-4207,
www.originatenbm.com
HOURS: Tues.-Fri. noon-6 P.M., Sat. noon-4 P.M.
Map 2

Tucson has been going through a kind of green
revolution in recent years, and nowhere has this
revolution taken off more thoroughly than
in the downtown neighborhood of Dunbar
Springs, where you'll see a lot of rain-har-
vesting, xeriscape, community gardens, solar
panels, bicyclists, and alternative building tech-
niques. It's also where you'll find this unique
shop, which sells all kinds of green building
materials and recycled materials. It's definitely
worth a look for anybody interested in the cutting edge of green living.

Maps and Outdoor Gear

SUMMIT HUT

5045 E. Speedway Blvd., 520/325-1554 or
800/499-8696, www.summithut.com
HOURS: Mon.-Fri. 9 A.M.-8 P.M., Sat. 9 A.M.-6:30 P.M.,
Sun. 9 A.M.-5 P.M.
Map 3

This locally owned outdoor gear shop has all
you need to outfit yourself for a wild desert
adventure. You'll find outdoor clothing and
backpacking equipment like top-brand back-
packs, tents, featherlight stoves and sleeping
pads, Chaco sandals, hiking shoes, and other
must-have desert-rat gear, plus a large selection of
mountaineering equipment. They also sell topographical maps and hiking guides, and there
are often lectures and workshops on the local

and regional wildlands at both the midtown and northwest locations. Their prices aren't exactly low, but you can usually find some great sales. There is another Summit Hut location in the foothills (4605 E. Wetmore, 520/888-1000).

TUCSON'S MAP & FLAG CENTER

3239 N. 1st Ave., 520/887-4234,
www.mapsmithus.com
HOURS: Mon.-Sat. 9 A.M.-5:30 P.M.
`Map 3`

A good selection of Southern Arizona maps, trail guides, and travel books can be found at this midsize store on 1st Avenue; they also stock maps and guides for Arizona and the rest of the world. There is a variety of globes available here, along with flags from nations the world over. They have a decent selection of topographical maps of the region and elsewhere. The prices here are generally on par with the big chain bookstores, which are the only other places in town where you'll find even close to the number of useful guides and road maps that they sell here.

Open-Air Markets

With its year-round growing seasons (save, perhaps, for a few of the hottest months in summer), the Tucson area and Southern Arizona is cultivating an increasingly active appetite for locally grown produce. While you can find vegetables, fruits, eggs, meats, coffee, and other edibles produced in the region at a few Tucson grocery stores, the best place to sample the local land's bounty is at one of the many year-round farmers markets held throughout the week at various points around the Old Pueblo.

COMMUNITY FOOD BANK FARMERS MARKET

3003 S. Country Club Rd., 520/622-0525,
www.communityfoodbank.com
HOURS: Tues. 8 A.M.-noon
`Map 7`

Every Tuesday the **Southern Arizona Community Food Bank** (between Ajo Way and 36th St.) sets up a small farm stand–style market with fresh vegetables and eggs from the food bank's community demonstration garden and elsewhere.

DOWNTOWN FARMERS MARKET AND ARTS AND CRAFTS MERCADO

101 N. Stone Ave., 520/326-7810
HOURS: Wed. 8 A.M.-1 P.M.
`Map 1`

On the plaza at the Joel V. Valdez Main Library every Wednesday, the Downtown Farmers Market features dozens of booths and tables selling locally grown produce and other foodstuffs, as well as arts and crafts by local artists and artisans. There's even usually a psychic on hand.

EL PRESIDIO MERCADO

255 W. Alameda St. at Church Ave., El Presidio Park, 520/326-7810
HOURS: Fri. 9 A.M.-2 P.M.
`Map 1`

Every Friday El Presidio Park downtown is taken over by farmers and artisans selling their vegetables and fruits, coffees, meats, and other homegrown, organic, and healthy alternatives to the age-old supermarket paradigm. All the usual stuff can be found here—from chiles to melons to honey to freshly made tamales and tortillas.

RINCON VALLEY FARMERS & ARTISANS MARKET

12500 E. Old Spanish Trail, Tucson, 520/591-2276
HOURS: Summer Sat. 8 A.M.-1 P.M.,
winter Sat. 9 A.M.-2 P.M.
`Map 8`

On Saturday year-round, folks living in the east-side Rincon Valley set up their homegrown delectables and fresh-roasted coffee and arts and crafts on a lot about four miles east of Saguaro National Park East. It's a beautiful drive, and it's fun to combine a stop at the market with a slow, easy desert trip out to the national park.

SANTA CRUZ RIVER FARMERS MARKET
100 S. Avenida del Convento, 520/461-1110,
www.mercadosanagustin.com
HOURS: Summer Thurs. 4-7 P.M.,
winter Thurs. 3-6 P.M.
Map 5

One of the better farmers markets in town, the west side's Santa Cruz River Farmers Market takes place in the late afternoon on Thursday at Mercado San Agustin. Here you can find all kinds of fresh vegetables, fruits, and meats in season, as well as prepared Mexican favorites and other delicacies.

ST. PHILIP'S SATURDAY FARMERS MARKET
4380 N. Campbell Ave., 520/603-8116
HOURS: Sun. 9 A.M.-1 P.M.
Map 4

Probably the Old Pueblo's favorite farmers market, St. Philip's Farmers Market at St. Philip's Plaza in the foothills draws a crowd every Saturday with all the usual fresh seasonal vegetables and fruits, fresh-ground organic coffee, and all manner of other artisanal foods and delicacies, not to mention a fair bit of socializing and meeting of new friends and locavore compatriots.

Shopping Districts and Centers

BROADWAY VILLAGE
2926 E. Broadway Blvd., 520/321-0392
HOURS: Vary according to shop
Map 3

A charming little collection of shops and a restaurant at Broadway Boulevard and Country Club, Broadway Village was designed by Josias Joesler in his always recognizable hybrid of revival styles. There are several home decor stores here, and a few boutiques offering clothing, gifts, and items unique to the region. There are also a few colonial-style furniture stores and other shops worth looking at in the general vicinity between Campbell and Country Club along Broadway Boulevard.

CASAS ADOBES PLAZA
7001-7153 N. Oracle Rd., 520/299-2610,
www.casasadobesplaza.com
HOURS: Mon.-Sat. 10 A.M.-6 P.M., Sun. 11 A.M.-4 P.M.
Map 4

This longtime favorite shopping center of the foothills crowd has six restaurants, including Bluefin and Wildflower, two of the city's best, and a wonderful Spanish colonial style with lots of fountains and patios. There are several decidedly upscale shops and boutiques here, including Maya Palace, a high-end purveyor of designer women's clothing from around the world, with three Tucson locations. Many of the stores here sell top-shelf Southwestern styles and gifts, and there's a Whole Foods as well.

CAT MOUNTAIN STATION
2740 S. Kinney Rd., 520/578-8795 or 520/838-3779,
www.catmountainstation.com
HOURS: Vary according to shop
Map 5

About a half-hour drive southwest of downtown, this refurbished 1950s shopping plaza, with its cobblestone courtyard and trickling fountain, offers a tasteful resting spot for desert explorers out for a day in Tucson Mountain Park, the Sonoran Desert Museum, and Saguaro National Park. Close to all of those attractions, Cat Mountain Station is worth a stop before heading back to town: rest up, have lunch, and peruse **Cat Mountain Emporium and Furniture Annex,** a 4,500-square-foot consignment mall, featuring antiques and vintage items, arts and crafts, and imported folk art. **Affairs of the Art Gallery** is a co-op featuring the work of local artisans, where you'll find truly one-of-a-kind paintings, jewelry, greeting cards, and other items—all in that distinctive Tucson mood. Then head over to

Studio S'Evans, a framing shop and fine art and craft gallery where you're likely to spot something heretofore unknown that you cannot now live without.

THE FOOTHILLS MALL

7401 N. La Cholla Blvd., Tuscon, 520/219-0650, www.shopfoothillsmall.com

HOURS: Mon.-Sat. 10 A.M.-9 P.M., Sun. 11 A.M.-6 P.M.

`Map 4`

This sprawling north-side mall has more than 90 stores, many of them designer outlets. Here you'll find the Nike Factory Store, Saks Fifth Avenue Off 5th, a Levi's Outlet, and many more—plus, there's no city sales tax. There are also a number of food court–style restaurants, the usual mall chains, a multistory Barnes & Noble, and Thunder Canyon Brewery, where you can get a well-crafted pint and some tasty appetizers (half off Mon.–Fri. 3–7 P.M.) after your spending spree.

◖ 4TH AVENUE

4th Ave. between University Blvd. and Toole Ave.

HOURS: Vary according to shop

`Map 2`

Pretty much the opposite of nearby Main Gate Square, nearly all the shops along 4th Avenue (there are about 100 of them) are locally owned and sell items preferred by bohemian types and the thrift-store-chic crowd. There are also jewelry stores, smoke shops, two bookstores, and numerous coffeehouses, restaurants, and watering holes. You could spend all day shopping up and down the avenue, eating and drinking along the way. This is the place to find a unique gift or some treasure that you can only get in Tucson.

GRANT ROAD ANTIQUES DISTRICT

Grant Rd. between Campbell Ave. and Craycroft Rd.

HOURS: Vary according to shop

`Map 3`

There are more than half a dozen antiques and resale shops on both sides of Grant Road between Campbell and Craycroft, the best of which is the **American Antique Mall** (3130 E. Grant Rd., 520/326-3070,

www.americanantiquemall.com, Tues.–Sat. 10 A.M.–5 P.M.). A visit here will give you a good idea of the kinds of antiques, collectibles, and generally interesting junk available at most of the Old Pueblo's resale places—a crowded mix of cowboy-life and Southwestern collectibles and kitsch; Native American jewelry and artifacts (not all of them authentic); furniture from the common to the rare, the handmade and the colonial, the retro and the modern; old, but not necessarily collectible, books (a *lot* of Westerns); and all the varied possessions and ephemera left behind by several generations of snowbirds and retirees who spent their final days warm and content in the desert.

◖ LA ENCANTADA

2905 E. Skyline Dr., Ste. 279, 520/615-2561, www.laencantadashoppingcenter.com

HOURS: Mon.-Wed. 10 A.M.-7 P.M., Thurs.-Sat. 10 A.M.-8 P.M., Sun. 11 A.M.-6 P.M.

`Map 4`

Tucson's answer to the high-end shopping centers that abound in Scottsdale, just a hundred miles or so up I-10, La Encantada offers all the most posh chains and a few local boutiques as well. It's a two-level outdoor mall, so during the summer, walking from Bebe to Tiffany & Co. and then back to Louis Vuitton will be a bit uncomfortable. Also here is Crate and Barrel, The Apple Store, a boutique toy store, and the only-for-the-too-rich Muttropolis Dog & Cat Boutique. There are several good places to eat and drink here after a hard day of shopping.

LA PLACITA

110 S. Church Ave., 520/903-9900

HOURS: Vary according to shop

`Map 1`

There are a few shops worth visiting in this multicolored Mexican-style plaza downtown, as well as several restaurants and the **Tucson Visitor Center** (100 S. Church Ave., 520/624-1817, Mon.–Fri. 9 A.M.–5 P.M., Sat.–Sun. 9 A.M.–4 P.M.), which has all kinds of literature and information on what to do and how to do it in Southern Arizona. La Placita is a great place to sit back and enjoy an invariably

high-end shopping in the shadow of the Santa Catalina Mountains at La Encantada

beautiful Tucson day, and there's often something going on in the courtyard, whether it's a free lunchtime concert or a classic movie shown outdoors at night. Don't miss checking out the 1880s gazebo just off the grassy courtyard.

LA PLAZA SHOPPES

6530 E. Tanque Verde Rd.
HOURS: Vary according to shop
Map 6

A small group of stores on the east side just across Tanque Verde from Trail Dust Town, La Plaza Shoppes has a few boutiques and galleries worth a look. There are also three or four good restaurants in and around this small red-brick strip. Make sure to stop into **Covington Fine Arts Gallery** (Ste. 140, 520/298-7878, Tues. and Thurs.–Sat. 10 A.M.–3 P.M., Wed. by appointment), especially if you're looking for art outside the Southwestern aesthetic so prevalent in Tucson. Covington doesn't have much in the way of the usual cowboy and Indian art, but they carry an impressive selection of American and European paintings and prints ranging from the early 19th century to the 1950s.

LOST BARRIO

200 S. Park Ave, 520/461-1341,
www.lostbarriotucson.com
HOURS: Vary according to shop
Map 2

A series of rustic old warehouses tucked away on Park Avenue just before you enter downtown from Broadway, the Lost Barrio has nearly a dozen shops selling handcrafted and imported furniture, folk arts, antiques, and home decor. Several of the stores sell Mexican and colonial-style furniture and antiques, of course, while others offer treasures from Africa, Asia, and elsewhere. The oldest and best of the stores here is **Rustica** (520/623-4435, www.rustica-tucson.com, Mon.–Sat. 11 A.M.–4 P.M., Sun. noon–4 P.M.), which has gorgeous Mexican and Peruvian furniture and Talavera pottery.

La Placita

You could easily spend several hours exploring these stores and fantasizing about each room of your ideal Southwestern-style bungalow in the desert.

MAIN GATE SQUARE

University Blvd. and Euclid Ave., 520/622-8613, www.maingatesquare.com

HOURS: Vary according to shop

`Map 2`

Here you'll find shopping for the college crowd and those who want to dress young. American Apparel, Urban Outfitters, and the like can be found here, as well as a few homegrown stores. Coffeehouses and lunch spots make this a good place for shopping while eating. Main Gate Square is right next to the University of Arizona and so is frequented by students. There are 52 stores and restaurants on this block. Be careful about parking; instead of braving the back-in-only metered parking, go to the Main Gate Parking Garage (815 E. 2nd St.) and leave your car in shade and safety.

MONTEREY COURT

505 W. Miracle Mile, 520/207-2129, www.montereycourtaz.com

HOURS: Vary according to shop

`Map 4`

The "Neon District" along Miracle Mile, just north of downtown, long ago lured car-bound tourists with its Southwestern-style motor lodges and mid-century commercial optimism. The coming of the interstate knocked the neighborhood down for years, and until recently it was known as a place of vice and crime. There's been a slow resurgence of the area, and this small collection of boutiques set up in a wonderfully remodeled 1940s motor lodge has played a big part. You won't find any corporate chains here—far from it. It's all locally owned and locally oriented, right down to the courtyard stage welcoming local bands. For your folk art and Mexico-inspired decoration needs, there's **Hacienda Bellas Artes.** Looking for a book bag decorated with a classic illustration from Victorian literature? Check

© TIM HULL

Monterey Court is leading the charge to reform the Miracle Mile neighborhood.

out the **Dragon's Spark.** Also don't miss the mosaic art at **Gone To Pieces,** the locally inspired gifts and handmade treasures at **Small Miracle Craft Mall,** and much more.

OLD TOWN ARTISANS

201 N. Court Ave., 520/623-6024,
www.oldtownartisans.com
HOURS: Sept.-May Mon.-Sat. 9:30 A.M.-5:30 P.M.,
Sun. 11 A.M.-5 P.M.; June-Aug. Mon.-Sat. 10 A.M.-4 P.M.,
Sun. 11 A.M.-4 P.M.
`Map 1`

Even if you don't have any room in your budget for pottery, Mexican folk arts, and turquoise jewelry, you should still find time to visit this shady, historic spot across from the Tucson Art Museum downtown. Six shops and galleries are gathered in the 150-year-old adobe structure, each one opening onto the verdant

Mexican-style courtyard with a fountain and tables. There's a great restaurant here as well, and there are often festivals and live music going on in the courtyard, which is a great place to sit and rest with a beer. The import shop **Tolteca Tlacuilo** (520/623-5787, www. toltecatlacuilo.com, June–Sept. 15 Mon.–Sat. 10 A.M.–4 P.M., Sun. 11 A.M.–4 P.M., Sept. 16–May Mon.–Sat. 9:30 A.M.–5:30 P.M., Sun. 11 A.M.–5 P.M.) here sells some of the best Día de los Muertos items in town.

PARK PLACE MALL

5870 E. Broadway Blvd., 520/747-7575,
www.parkplacemall.com
HOURS: Mon.-Sat. 10 A.M.-9 P.M., Sun. 11 A.M.-6 P.M.
`Map 3`

At the eastern edge of midtown and the core of the intensive east-central Broadway commercial sprawlscape, Park Place is probably the most popular mall in the city. It has big anchor department stores like Dillard's and Macy's, popular shops like Abercrombie & Fitch and Old Navy, and all the other usual mid-scale suspects along with a movie theater, a kids' play area, and a food court. The Borders bookstore here is among the top two busiest in Arizona, and always seems to be packed, as do the several square miles of parking lot around this retail temple.

PLAZA PALOMINO

2960 N. Swan Rd., 520/320-6344
HOURS: Mon.-Sat. 10 A.M.-6 P.M.
`Map 3`

There are nearly 20 shops and restaurants at this upscale midtown shopping center, including purveyors of Native American arts and crafts, Southwestern-style items and home decor, furniture, jewelry, fine art, and high-style women's clothing. The best time for a visit is during the weekly **Saturday Morning Market** (summer 10 A.M.–2 P.M., winter 9 A.M.–1 P.M.), when there's a farmers market, artisans selling their creations, and live music. There's a complimentary Shopping Shuttle (520/327-4674) that goes to most Tucson hotels.

SANTA FE SQUARE
7000 E. Tanque Verde Rd.
HOURS: Vary according to shop
Map 6

Several shops, galleries, and restaurants can be found at this charming east-side shopping center resembling the faux-adobe uniformity of its namesake. Visitors will find boutiques and shops selling everything from high-style clothes to bicycles, to gifts with a regional flavor.

❰ SPEEDWAY ANTIQUES DISTRICT
Speedway Blvd. between Country Club Dr. and Wilmot Rd.
HOURS: Vary according to shop
Map 3

Though not really recognized locally as such, there is an antiques and resale district along Speedway Boulevard just as there is along Grant Road just a block or so north. Along both sides of busy Speedway, roughly between Country Club and Wilmot, you'll find half a

Old Town Artisans is a must for those seeking unique Old Pueblo treasures.

dozen or more shops, both small and large, selling used furniture, antiques, and other used and historic treasures. The best of these is the sprawling **Copper Country Antiques** (5055 E. Speedway Blvd., 520/326-0167, Mon.–Sat. 10 A.M.–6 P.M., Sun. 11 A.M.–5 P.M.) at Speedway and Rosemont.

❰ TUBAC
Tubac exit off I-19
HOURS: Vary according to shop
Map 8

Tubac has more than 100 shops and galleries, many of them selling Mexican and South American imports. The village has a year-round Christmas gallery and several little shops whose wares simply must be seen. There are quite a few working art galleries, including the old adobe gallery of the late Hugh Cabot, a famous local artist. Pick up an illustrated map of the shopping district at any of the shops or at the visitors center.

TUCSON MALL
4500 N. Oracle Rd., 520/293-7330, www.tucsonmall.com
HOURS: Mon.–Sat. 10 A.M.–9 P.M., Sun. noon–6 P.M.
Map 4

On the north side of town near Oracle and River, Tucson Mall has several old-school department stores like Sears, JCPenney, and Dillard's, along with Eddie Bauer, The Disney Store, and all the others you'd expect. There's a vaguely Arizona-themed row of specialty shops, selling a mixture of tourist throwaways and leather, called Arizona Avenue. As in most malls in America, there are many roving packs of teens patrolling this one's generally clean and well-lit corridors.

VENTANA PLAZA
5425 N. Kolb Rd., 520/323-9576, www.ventanaplaza.com
HOURS: Vary according to shop
Map 4

This small, upscale strip mall near Kolb Road and Sunrise Drive features a few boutiques, restaurants, a dance and fitness studio, a day spa and hair salon, and a gallery. This is a perfect place to spend a few hours—shop for designer handbags and shoes and dip into **The Bag Company** (520/299-7775). Then it's time for a sushi lunch, a mani-pedi, and a massage.

Southwestern

CREATIVE VENTURES CRAFT MALL

522 N. 4th Ave., 800/543-2610,
www.tucson-creative-ventures.com
HOURS: Mon.-Thurs. 10 A.M.-7 P.M.,
Fri.-Sat. 10 A.M.-8 P.M., Sun. 11 A.M.-5 P.M.
Map 2

A more than 4,000-square-foot building on 4th Avenue has been converted into a series of small consignment booths from which local artists, artisans, and retailers sell their often-handmade wares. There are many one-of-a-kind items here, and most of them have some kind of Southwestern spirit about them. This is a good family-run place to purchase a fun and unique gift that just says "Southwest," as many of the items here seem to be geared specifically to tourists.

CRIZMAC TUCSON MARKETPLACE

1642 N. Alvernon Way, 520/323-8555,
www.crizmac.com
HOURS: Mon.-Fri. 10 A.M.-5 P.M., Sat. 10 A.M.-4 P.M., closed Sat. during summer
Map 3

A colorful, artistically decorated storefront on Alvernon Way near Pima Street, Crizmac offers an eclectic mix of folk art, art kits, arts and crafts books, jewelry, and kids' books and handicrafts at reasonable prices. They also hold lectures, classes, and workshops on various folk-art topics, and even organize trips for the truly dedicated crafter. Here you'll find handicrafts and artistic discoveries from all over the world, as well as items and advice that will undoubtedly inspire your own creativity.

Creative Ventures Craft Mall on 4th Avenue

© TIM HULL

© TIM HULL

Crizmac Tucson Marketplace

DEL SOL

435 N. 4th Ave., 520/628-8765, www.delsolstores.com
HOURS: Mon.-Sat. 10 A.M.-5 P.M., Sun. noon-4 P.M.

Map 2

For more than 30 years the folks at Del Sol, on 4th Avenue, have been scouring Central and South America for the finest in ceramic, wood, metal, glass, and textile handicrafts, clothing made from natural fibers—including hand-woven Guatemalan items—jewelry, and more; it's hard to beat their prices. The same folks own La Zia at Old Town Artisans downtown, selling excellent Native American jewelry and other handicrafts and art purchased directly from the artists themselves.

THE MEXICAN GARDEN

2854 E. Grant Rd., 520/795-4616,
www.mexicangardenaz.com
HOURS: Mon.-Sat. 9 A.M.-5:30 P.M., Sun. 10 A.M.-5 P.M.

Map 3

Reasonable prices and a huge inventory are the hallmarks of this friendly Mexican folk art, ceramic tile, Talavera, and *chimenea* (clay

outdoor fireplace) store along busy Grant Road in midtown. There are dozens of similar stores in town, and the village of Tubac, south of Tucson, is rotten with them, but I've found that the prices here are right in line with, if not cheaper than, everybody else. Go here instead of crossing the border and braving the hard-sell in Nogales, Sonora, for a *chimenea*, ceramic tiles with Day of the Dead characters on them, and much more.

◖ NATIVE SEEDS/SEARCH

3061 N. Campbell Ave., 520/622-5561,
www.nativeseeds.org
HOURS: Mon.-Sat. 10 A.M.-5 P.M., Sun. noon-4 P.M.

Map 3

You won't find any other store in town that has more uniquely Southwestern items than Native Seeds/SEARCH, from heirloom seeds for nearly lost regional crops to one-of-a-kind gifts and videos and handmade crafts and soaps (made of yucca root, for example)—all with a link to the region and its past. A perfect gift to take back home is one of the gift baskets sold

AUTHENTIC NATIVE AMERICAN ART

Despite being hundreds of miles from the Navajo and Hopi Reservations in northeastern Arizona, Tucson has long been known as a center for Native American arts. One of the finest, and now the oldest, dealers of Navajo, Hopi, and Pueblo arts in Tucson is Mark Bahti, owner of **Bahti Indian Arts** (4330 N. Campbell Ave., Ste. 72, 520/577-0290, www.bahti.com). In his small shop, Bahti sells several very useful books and guides on identifying and collecting Native American arts, including his own recent book *Silver + Stone: Profiles of American Indian Jewelers*. Bahti is currently in the process of researching a similar book on Native American pottery artists.

It's often difficult to know what is *authentic* Native American art and what isn't. This has been a problem from the very beginning, but if you learn a bit about the history of the art form, you'll likely conclude that words like authenticity are pretty slippery when it comes to this kind of art. According to Bahti's book, it was during the golden age of Southwestern tourism that the authenticity of Indian jewelry became an issue.

The artists were, of course, encouraged to create work specifically for tourists, who flocked to the reservations and pueblos on the Fred Harvey Indian Detours. Bahti writes that these pieces were often lightweight, with "horses, tipis, arrows, thunderbirds...designed to fit the tourist notion of what Indian jewelry was 'supposed' to look like." But, as Bahti points out, what was Indian jewelry actually "supposed to look like?" Nobody could really say, and they still can't.

By the 1920s, manufactured copies of Indian arts were being made outside the Southwest and then shipped in to be sold as authentic, spurring the native artists to join together in co-ops and guilds, many of which are still in operation and still training new artists. The 1970s brought about a boom in the market for Pueblo and Navajo jewelry, and today there is a really diffuse sense of what is traditional and what is innovative, and innovation—the artist responding not only to tradition but to the world around him or her—can be seen everywhere at Indian markets around the Southwest, including February's popular Indian Arts Fair at the University of Arizona's Arizona State Museum.

Because it's made by Native Americans, many people approach this art with a lot of preconceived notions; especially prevalent are notions about authenticity and tradition. Some people expect every Indian artist and artisan to be adhering to some ancient set of guidelines set down before real time began, a method that washes each squash-blossom necklace and kachina carving with some undeniable spiritual patina. Like most artistic movements, however, the provenance of the Southwestern Indian arts and crafts tradition is far more complex.

Think of these artists as working within similar confines as did painters and sculptors of the Western European tradition before and during the Renaissance. Such artists were bound more often than not to paint and sculpt imagery from the Bible or Greek and Roman mythology, and they could count on their public immediately recognizing the scenes and characters they depicted. However, within this rather narrow tradition, there existed astonishing variety.

Authenticity is a particular concern if you're looking to purchase a katsina doll. Only dolls made by the Hopi and other Pueblo Indians are real katsinas, while those made by the Navajo and other tribes are intended for the tourist trade and will not hold their value. The general rule, unfortunately, is that if a doll is inexpensive, it's probably a fake.

here, with all kinds of locally and regionally produced foods, soaps, and balms. This store also has an excellent selection of books about Tucson and the Southwest.

PHILABAUM GLASS STUDIO AND GALLERY

711 S. 6th Ave., 520/884-7404,
www.philabaumglass.com
HOURS: Tues.-Sat. 10 A.M.-5 P.M.
Map 1

The delicate, colorful glass creations built in this downtown studio are amazing, but more amazing still is watching the artists at work. Most days at this working studio and shop along 6th Avenue (look for the airplane rudder set up outside), you can sit and watch the strange process of glassblowing; be careful though, because you're going to want to buy something once you see how it's done. Glassblowing viewing is available most days, but it's a good idea to call ahead to be sure.

PICANTE

2932 E. Broadway Blvd., 520/320-5699,
www.picantetucson.com
HOURS: Mon.-Sat. 10 A.M.-6 P.M.
Map 3

This colorful store along Broadway Boulevard's busy commercial corridor offers a large selection of Mexican and South American folk arts and crafts, without the hassle of crossing the border. You'll find a wide and striking selection here of masks, *milagros* (religious folk charms), *nichos* (folk art), Day of the Dead items, Mexican silver jewelry, and depictions of the Virgin of Guadalupe, as well as clothing, furniture, mirrors, fabric, purses, and a large and playful population of ceramic figures.

POPCYCLE

422 N. 4th Ave., 520/622-3297,
www.popcycleshop.com
HOURS: Mon.-Thurs. 11 A.M.-6 P.M., Fri.-Sat. 11 A.M.-7 P.M.,
Sun. 11 A.M.-5 P.M.
Map 2

The concept of "upcycling" is a relatively new one, but it makes a lot of sense in our cluttered

world. The artists selling their wares at this charming 4th Avenue boutique take old pop-culture artifacts—record albums, found art, advertising, etc.—and create new and exciting items out of the detritus of the culture. You won't believe what a creative mind can come up with in just a bit of time spent in the attic or thrift store.

POTTERY BLOWOUT

3840 E. Grant Rd., 520/325-6683,
www.potteryblowout.com
HOURS: Daily 9 A.M.-6 P.M.
Map 3

Pottery has always been important in the Southwest, and as a contemporary art form, pottery still thrives in this region. To see Mexican, South American, and other styles of this essential human art form, head to Pottery Blowout, where there's always at least 1,000 different items in stock, and the prices are usually less than their competitors.

SACRED TIME MACHINE

245 E. Congress St., 520/977-7102,
www.sacredmachine.com
HOURS: Wed.-Thurs. 6-9 P.M., Fri. 5-9 P.M.,
Sat. 4-9 P.M., Sun. 3-6 P.M.
Map 1

This small "museum and curiosity shop" on Congress Street downtown showcases the mysterious, thrilling work and obsessions of world-famous Tucson artist Daniel Martin Diaz. They sell T-shirts, artwork, and strange, unique craft items—often with that mixture of the sacred and profane that so typifies Diaz's work. This place is part gallery, part retail shop, and part music performance space, and is definitely an essential stop for those looking for the cutting-edge in local culture.

SANTA THERESA TILE WORKS

440 N. 6th Ave., 520/623-8640 or 800/862-2198,
www.santatheresatileworks.com
HOURS: Tues.-Fri. 10 A.M.-6 P.M., Sat. 10 A.M.-4 P.M.
Map 2

Spend just a little time in the borderlands and you'll notice that everything here is tiled over.

Discover the artwork of Daniel Martin Diaz at The Sacred Time Machine.

© TIM HULL

Ceramic, Saltillo, Talavera, and other tile styles are ubiquitous in the homes of the Old Pueblo—nobody has carpet here. But tiles are also used as decoration, as knickknacks and gifts. At Santa Theresa Tile Works you'll find the state of the art, where each tile is handmade and hand painted, each one a mini work of art.

NATIVE AMERICAN ARTS AND CRAFTS

ARIZONA MERCANTILE: THE MUSEUM STORE AT THE ARIZONA HISTORICAL SOCIETY

949 E. 2nd St., 520/628-9774

HOURS: Tues.-Thurs. 11 A.M.-3 P.M., Fri.-Sat. 11 A.M.-4 P.M.
Map 2

Inside the Arizona Historical Society's main Tucson museum near the University of Arizona campus, this small gift shop has excellent desertland gifts, including some really outstanding Native American items like Tohono O'odham baskets, Navajo jewelry, and other Southwest-only treasures. There's also a fine selection of books about the state and other gifts for your friends back home, along with replicas of classic 19th- and 20th-century photographs of the romantic Old West, jewelry, and items by local artisans.

◖ BAHTI INDIAN ARTS

4330 N. Campbell Ave., 520/577-0290, www.bahti.com

HOURS: Mon.-Sat. 10 A.M.-6 P.M., Sun. 8:30 A.M.-3 P.M.
Map 4

First opened by current owner Mark Bahti's father, Tom Bahti, in 1952, Bahti Indian Arts, though no longer in its original location, is now the oldest shop of its kind in the Old Pueblo. The small shop at St. Philip's Plaza sells some of the finest examples of Navajo, Hopi, and Pueblo textiles, kachinas, jewelry, basketry, pottery, paintings, and sculptures in the state, as well as an assortment of art and artifacts from tribes outside the Southwest. Mark himself is a noted expert on Native American art, as his father was before him.

GREY DOG TRADING COMPANY

4320 N. Campbell Ave., Ste. 138, 520/881-6888 or
877/331-7367, www.greydogtrading.com

HOURS: Mon.-Sat. 10 A.M.-6 P.M., Sun. 10 A.M.-2 P.M.

`Map 4`

An excellent Native American arts boutique in
St. Philip's Plaza, Grey Dog sells top-notch basketry, pottery, and textiles (mostly by Hopis,
Navajos, Zunis, and other Southwestern native
artists), as well as a good assortment of books
about the Indian arts past and present. I particularly like their selection of contemporary
kachinas carved by some of today's greatest
Hopi artists, showing that even a largely conservative, religious-based art form can break
out of the mold to reveal something new and
meaningful.

MAC'S INDIAN JEWELRY

2400 E. Grant Rd., 520/327-3306,
www.macsindianjewelry.com

HOURS: Mon.-Fri. 9 A.M.-5 P.M., Sat. 10 A.M.-5 P.M.

`Map 3`

Longtime purveyors of Indian arts and crafts
in Tucson, the friendly, knowledgeable folks at
Mac's will help you find that playful kachina
doll, that delicately wrought basket, or that
substantial silver-and-turquoise heirloom
you've always wanted. The prices here are outstanding, and the selection is wide and eclectic, representing the best work of members of
the Navajo, Hopi, Zuni, Tohono O'odham,
and other tribes. Mac's also has a superior
selection of Day of the Dead tiles featuring

skeletons (calaveras) involved in activities
typically reserved for the living—the perfect
Southwestern-themed gift.

MORNING STAR TRADERS

2020 E. Speedway Blvd., 520/881-2112,
www.morningstartraders.com

HOURS: Mon.-Sat. 10 A.M.-6 P.M.

`Map 2`

This midtown store has a fabulous collection
of high-end Indian arts—kachinas, Navajo
textiles, pots and baskets, carvings, and historical artifacts—from the Southwestern traditions and others as well. Next door is **Morning
Star Antiques** (Mon.–Sat. 11 A.M.–5 P.M.),
which sells Spanish colonial furniture, antique
home decor, and other sought-after regional
home-arts.

NATIVE GOODS: THE ARIZONA
STATE MUSEUM STORE

1013 E. University Blvd., 520/626-5886,
www.statemuseum.arizona.edu

HOURS: Mon.-Sat. 10 A.M.-5 P.M.

`Map 2`

A visit to the Arizona State Museum is a must
for anyone interested in the native cultures of
Arizona and the Southwest, and a visit to the
museum is not complete without perusing its
excellent gift shop, which sells not only top-
shelf Native American arts and crafts but also
a great selection of Arizona-related posters, artwork, and books. The store is usually closed for
half an hour at noon.

HOTELS

If you're just looking for a place to store your gear while you're out exploring the desert, you'll find hundreds of mid-priced chain hotels in and around Tucson. But if you're the kind of person who likes a little style and atmosphere where you sleep and wake up—who takes pleasure in and inspiration from surprising architectural and artistic details, in stories and histories—you'll find a few unforgettable historic hotels, boutique inns, and bed-and-breakfast-style accommodations here as well.

Since the late 19th century, travelers have come to Tucson to find health, rest, and a new lease on life. Those who suffered from TB and other chest ailments came here in droves over the years, sent to the desert by their doctors for the supposed cure provided by the dry air. The first big hotels in Tucson, then, were tent cities thrown up in the streets to house the constant stream of hacking patients. Later, the business community got together and started marketing the sunshine and easy living in the Southwest, and Tucson became what it is today—a world-renowned spa destination and seasonless desert playground for those outrunning the snow and ice. And so the resorts and hotels and dude ranches and motor courts began to proliferate, as they still do today.

If you have pockets deeper than the vast majority of Americans, by all means book a week at Canyon Ranch, but try and get beyond the resort walls once in a while. If, like most of us, you fall somewhere in the middle—you want a bit of style and personality, but you don't want to leverage your future to have it—you will likely find what you've been looking for here in the Old Pueblo.

© TIM HULL

CHOOSING A HOTEL

There aren't a lot of inexpensive accommodations in Tucson worth taking a chance on. There is one hostel, in a clean and friendly house near downtown, and it's the best choice for budget travelers. On the I-10 frontage road just west of downtown is a long row of chain hotels, some of them inexpensive. This isn't the Old Pueblo's most charming district, however. Throughout midtown and on to the east side

HIGHLIGHTS

LOOK FOR ☾ TO FIND RECOMMENDED HOTELS.

© TIM HULL

Hacienda del Sol Guest Ranch Resort

☾ **Best B&B in the City:** With four tasteful rooms in a historic mansion built in the 1880s, **El Presidio Inn Bed and Breakfast** has a cool, lush, and peaceful courtyard garden with a babbling fountain, cobblestone walkways, and shady trees (page 166).

☾ **Most Affordable Historic Hotel:** Built in 1919 and remodeled only slightly since then, **Hotel Congress,** right in the heart of downtown's nightlife scene, offers charm and atmosphere for about $79–99 per night (page 166).

☾ **Best Hotel to Treat Like a Sight:** Stop by the secluded, elegant 1930s-era **Arizona Inn** and walk around the green, shady grounds,

taking in the style and history (page 169).

☾ **Best Resort:** Step into the glory days of Southwestern chic at the 1930s-era resort **Hacienda del Sol Guest Ranch Resort.** The history, architecture, and design of the high-style Southwest of yesteryear permeate the desert grounds (page 172).

☾ **Best Desert B&B:** A hiker's and birdwatcher's paradise east of town near Saguaro National Park East, **Hacienda del Desierto Bed and Breakfast** is a wonderland of hacienda-style details and quiet comfort for anyone looking to escape to the desert for a few days (page 176).

PRICE KEY

💲 Under $150 per night
💲💲 $150-250 per night
💲💲💲 Over $250 per night

there are dozens of big chain hotels to choose from, and of course there are dozens more around the south side near the airport.

For a truly memorable Tucson experience, consider staying in one of the small (though often relatively pricey) bed-and-breakfasts and inns in one of the city's many historic neighborhoods. These include the beautiful Arizona Inn in midtown, and the very affordable Hotel Congress right in the center of the action downtown. There are also inns in the Sam Hughes

historic neighborhood in midtown, and in the El Presidio district near downtown.

During the summer months, roughly from late May to late September, nearly all the hotels, resorts, and inns in Tucson slash their prices—some by as much as 50 percent, but most by around 20 percent. If you're planning on coming to town during those torpid, quiet months, you might just be able to afford to live like a robber baron for a few days. Also, it pays to explore the websites of the larger chains listed in this chapter; most of them offer all kinds of different packages, one of which will likely save you some money. If you're coming to town in February or March, book early and plan to pay a bit more; those two perfect-weather months feature several very popular festivals, events, and conventions in the Old Pueblo, and most places are booked solid.

Downtown   Map 1

Many of the inns and hotels in the Downtown and University District neighborhoods are popular with visiting parents of University of Arizona students, and as such they're often booked up in mid-May for graduation and in October for parents weekend. Staying downtown or around the university is a good idea for anybody visiting Tucson; the neighborhoods all meld together, and they represent the only pedestrian-friendly districts in town. Staying in any of the places listed here will put you right in the center of the action on all fronts.

◀ EL PRESIDIO INN BED AND BREAKFAST 💲💲

297 N. Main Ave., 520/623-6151,
www.elpresidiobbinn.com
The beautiful El Presidio Inn Bed and Breakfast in the Julius Kruttschnitt House, built in 1886 and remodeled over the years in various architectural styles, is one of the city's best small inns. It's located in "Snob Hollow" in the historic El Presidio neighborhood, on the same block where Tucson's wealthy pioneers

used to live in their big mansions. The inn has one of the finest garden courtyards I've ever seen; it's so cool and lush that you may not get out of the inn to see the rest of Tucson. The inn has four rooms ($129–169), two of which—the Carriage House and the Gate House—open onto the courtyard and have kitchenettes. The two small rooms inside the house have private baths. They only allow kids over 13 years old, and they don't allow pets or smoking. A two-night minimum stay is required October–May.

◀ HOTEL CONGRESS 💲

311 E. Congress St., 520/622-8848 or 800/722-8848,
www.hotelcongress.com
Hotel Congress ($89–149 d, about $10 less in summer beginning at the end of May), built in 1919, is listed on the National Register of Historic Places. Though the rooms are a bit creaky, the beds are comfortable and the historic atmosphere more than makes up for the lack of sumptuous amenities (plus, it's the best value in town if you seek personality in your sleeping quarters). There is noise some nights coming

from the Club Congress downstairs—although not too bad, there is a slight thumping that comes through the walls. The club is a venue for alternative bands and alt-country bands from across the nation, and the Tap Room bar will make you feel like a cowboy on his day off. The Cup Café off the beautiful old lobby has an eclectic mix of gourmet and Southwestern-style food for breakfast, lunch, and dinner.

ROADRUNNER HOSTEL AND INN ❸

346 E. 12th St., 520/628-4709 or 520/940-7280, www.roadrunnerhostelinn.com

The only hostel in Tucson, the Roadrunner (a block south of Broadway Blvd. downtown) is a clean and homey place to stay and offers the single best accommodations deal in town ($22 for dorm, $45 for private room). They provide free linens and blankets, showers, laundry ($1

THE NIGHT THEY CAUGHT THE DILLINGER GANG AT THE HOTEL CONGRESS

A hotel fire, a fireman with a good memory and a taste for lurid reading matter, and the hubris of a gang of outlaws all conspired over a few days in 1934 to bring down Public Enemy Number One, John Dillinger, right here in the Old Pueblo.

On January 21, 1934, two members of outlaw John Dillinger's gang pulled into Tucson with their molls at their sides, meaning to meet up over the next several days with their notorious leader and lay low for a while in the relative warmth of the Sonoran Desert winter.

According to writer and former Tucson police officer Stan Benjamin, the gang wanted to rent a small house downtown, but the landlady had just waxed the floors and wouldn't let them move in until the next day. So they booked a few rooms at the Hotel Congress, built in 1919 to serve passengers on the Southern Pacific Railroad—its depot was right across the street.

Dillinger and his moll, Evelyn "Billie" Frechette, wouldn't arrive in town until a few days later, but by then the small Tucson police force already had suspicions about the gang's advance party, and it was these suspicions that would lead to Dillinger's arrest.

As Benjamin writes in an article that is so far the definitive work on the locally famous incident, "Without A Shot Fired: The 1934 Capture of the Dillinger Gang in Tucson" (a reprint of which is available at the Hotel Congress for $5), early in the morning of January 22, a fire broke out in the Hotel Congress's basement, and the three-story hotel had to be evacuated. A few of Tucson's friendly firemen helped the members of Dillinger's gang and their girlfriends down

from a third-story room, and even returned to the smoky rooms to rescue the gang's luggage, which they later said was "very heavy" (eventually they found out that the bags contained several guns and over $20,000 in cash). At least the outlaws gave the firemen a $12 tip.

Unfortunately for the cocky bank robbers, however, those same firemen were, a few hours later, reading a copy of *True Detective Magazine*, in which they saw a "wanted" shot of the very men they'd hosed out of the hotel. Once the police got wind of this, and after a separate tip from some businessmen who the outlaws had tried to impress at a local bar the night before, the police began watching the gang's movements, which eventually led to Dillinger's capture at a rented house a few miles from the hotel.

If you want to learn more details about the capture beyond what Benjamin's fascinating article explains, check out the Arizona Historical Society Museum Downtown, which has an excellent display on the incident. Every year in January, the Hotel Congress and other venues host Dillinger Days, a celebration of 1930s popular culture and of Tucson's brief brush with national law-enforcement fame.

Dillinger wouldn't stay captured for long, but neither would he stay alive for long. After his capture in Tucson he was sent to jail in Indiana to await trial for murder. He had escaped from custody by March 1934, and continued robbing banks with the gang until a shootout with the FBI sent him deep underground. In July 1934, just about six months after his capture in Tucson, Dillinger was famously shot down by federal agents outside the Biograph Theater in Chicago.

per load), and a large kitchen for guests to use. The four private rooms are small and a bit spare, but for the money they are perfect; the three dorm rooms (one for just guys, one for women, and one that's co-ed) each sleep six on the usual bunk beds. They offer two computers hooked up to the Internet for guest use, plus free wireless throughout the place. There's a shady backyard patio for morning lounging with complimentary coffee or tea, and a living room with a big TV and lots of VHS and DVD movies to watch. They don't accept credit cards.

ROYAL ELIZABETH BED AND BREAKFAST INN ❸❸

204 S. Scott Ave., 877/670-9022, www.royalelizabeth.com

The Royal Elizabeth Bed and Breakfast Inn ($169–229 d) is in a beautiful home known as the Blenman House, built in 1878 in Tucson's El Presidio district. It's now on the National Register of Historic Places. There are six large rooms to choose from, all elegantly decorated in an Old World style, with big beds and footed stand-alone bathtubs. There's also a heated pool and spa and immaculate grounds. The inn has a two-night minimum on weekends.

University District   Map 2

ALOFT TUCSON UNIVERSITY ❸❸

1900 E. Speedway Blvd., 520/908-6800, www.starwoodhotels.com

Right across Campbell Avenue from the University of Arizona, this big, beautiful hotel opened in April 2013. Workers stripped the former Four Points Sheraton down to its husk and rebuilt it with stylish, modern rooms and inviting lounges. The hotel is part of the Aloft brand, which translates to accommodations that are upscale, comfortable, and really, really cool.

CATALINA PARK INN ❸❸

309 E. 1st St., 520/792-4541 or 800/792-4885, www.catalinaparkinn.com

The Catalina Park Inn ($139–169 d), in the West University historic district, was built in 1927 and has beautiful mixed gardens with many native plants in a private, peaceful walled courtyard. There are six rooms, two of which are detached from the main house and open onto the lush courtyard. This inn is close to the UA, downtown, and midtown. Breakfast here is always an elegant, gourmet affair, and wireless Internet throughout the property makes it a great place for combining business and pleasure. Each individually decorated room has a private bath, cable television, a stereo with an iPod dock, big thick bathrobes, and more. Since the inn is popular with parents visiting their kids at the nearby University of Arizona, in mid-May during graduation, and in early October for parents weekend, they require a three-night minimum stay and raise the rates on their rooms by about $120–130 (double occupancy) per night. This is true during Gem Show (first two weeks in Feb.) as well. The inn is closed June 15–September 25.

SAM HUGHES INN BED AND BREAKFAST ❸

2020 E. 7th St., 520/861-2191, www.samhughesinn.com

A charming Spanish-revival bed-and-breakfast in midtown's quiet, tree-lined San Hughes neighborhood, this inn is within walking distance of the University of Arizona and is close to downtown. The inn has four distinctively decorated rooms ($90–130 d) that offer free wireless Internet and private bathrooms; the large rooms have refrigerators and televisions. The enclosed courtyard out back is something to see—green and cool and perfect for relaxing and watching the sun dip behind the towering mountains.

TUCSON MARRIOTT UNIVERSITY PARK ❸❸

800 E. 2nd St., 520/792-4100, www.marriott.com

© TIM HULL

Tucson Marriott University Park

This high-rise chain hotel ($169–365 d) is situated within a few steps of the University of Arizona, close to the Main Gate district with its dozens of shops, bars, and restaurants, and with easy access to both downtown and midtown. There are nine floors, and anything above, say, floor three affords 360-degree views of the valley and the mountains. The 233 rooms are nice enough, each with a large television, desk, sitting area, wet bar, and a big comfy bed; there are 17 suites if you need more room. Free wireless Internet is offered throughout, and there's an outdoor heated pool, a fitness center, a whirlpool, and more. It will cost you at least $11 per day to park here.

Midtown   Map 3

Midtown is a sprawling, rather amorphous district, but pretty much wherever you stay here you'll be near some kind of big strip mall or shopping plaza with restaurants, chain stores, and supermarkets. Staying in midtown is a good idea if you're looking for mid-range and affordable options, and it's where families with small children should look first.

◖ ARIZONA INN ❸❸
2200 E. Elm St., 520/325-1541, www.arizonainn.com

This historic boutique hotel on a residential street in central midtown, founded in the 1930s by Arizona's first-ever congresswoman and still owned and operated by the same family, is the best place to stay in Tucson—as long as you have fairly deep pockets (from $259 d; from $169 d during the summer). They offer several different kinds of rooms, all of them decorated in the inimitable 1930s Southwestern-chic style. The standard room has wireless Internet, a king-size bed, and a television and DVD player, while the larger suites have patios, dry bars, and sitting areas. But you probably won't be spending a lot of time in the room, as the grounds and lobby have so much charm to offer—there's a 60-foot pool, old-school tennis court, and all kinds of quiet little corners in the verdant, retreat-like setting behind the high pink walls.

DOUBLETREE HOTEL AT REID PARK $

445 S. Alvernon Way, 520/881-4200,
www.doubletree3.hilton.com

This popular midtown chain (at Broadway and Alvernon just east of Reid Park) is centrally located and close to the golf courses, bike paths, and zoo at Reid Park. It has a huge enclosed courtyard with a very nice outdoor pool. Many of the 295 rooms ($119–139 d) have balconies that look out on the central courtyard, and they all have free high-speed wireless Internet and big plasma TVs. There are two restaurants on-site—the Southwestern bar and grill called the Javelina Cantina, with a nice courtyard for chilling out with a margarita, and a steak house. This 14-acre hotel also has a fitness room, a whirlpool, and tennis courts. Pets are allowed. Rates go as low as $79 per night in the summer.

EMBASSY SUITES $

5335 E. Broadway Blvd., 520/745-2700,
www.embassysuites3.hilton.com

This big chain-hotel compound at the Williams Center in east midtown (Broadway and Craycroft) is perfect for families. Each of the spacious suites ($139–159 d) has two rooms and two TVs, and has the option of having up to three beds. Every night the friendly staff passes out free drinks and popcorn during the Manager's Reception, and in the morning you can order up a complimentary big breakfast (no mere muffin and coffee here). They've got a great pool, and the lobby and lounge are decorated in an upscale, tasteful Southwestern style with big leather couches that you can just sink into. In summer the rates plummet, and you can get a suite for $109 or even lower. Check the website for all kinds of seasonal and themed deals.

LODGE ON THE DESERT $$

306 N. Alvernon Way, 520/320-2000,
www.lodgeonthedesert.com

The Lodge on the Desert ($75–180 d summer, $90–320 d during the rest of the year) recently changed hands and underwent a major $15 million expansion and renovation. The hotel's lobby and restaurant are beautiful, as are the hacienda-style rooms offering free wireless Internet, comfortable beds, and big cushy bathrobes. The grounds are green and private, and the patio lounge is one of the best in the city.

The Foothills

Map 4

You're not likely to find a cheap room in this neighborhood, but you will find some of the world's most exclusive resorts. Visitors and émigrés have sought healing in Southern Arizona since at least the early 19th century. Any tubercular patient lucky enough to flee the crowded, disease-ridden tenements of the Northeast or the malarial bottomlands of the South was invariably advised to seek the high and dry air of the Southwest. The medicine of the 19th-century being what it was, physicians had little else but this general, somewhat specious advice to offer the scores of Americans who suffered

from TB, fevers, dysentery, and other ailments of the chest and the blood.

Scholar Billy Jones, in his book *Health-Seekers in the Southwest 1817–1900*, estimates that some 20–25 percent of those who moved to the Southwest during the great migrations of the 19th and 20th centuries did so hoping to cure some ailment, creating a "Health Frontier" that, in Tucson, resulted in the haphazard construction of vast tent cities on the outskirts of town populated by consumptives and often destitute men and women not long for the world.

Medical science has since cured most of the diseases that once brought sickly travelers to the desert, but that hasn't stopped today's visitors from seeking health of a different breed. Tucson has long rivaled its ritzy northern neighbors Scottsdale and Sedona as a place where the afflicted, both physically and psychically, can find solace—usually very expensive solace.

RETREATS FOR THE SOUL

If you're looking for a few days of quiet, spiritual contemplation, there are several monasteries and retreat centers in Southern Arizona to choose from.

The **Redemptorist Renewal Center** (7101 W. Picture Rocks Rd., 520/744-3400, www.desertrenewal.org), about 12 miles west of downtown Tucson near Saguaro National Park West, offers personal retreats on their 120-acre campus in the foothills of the Tucson Mountains. For 40 years the Redemptorists, followers of St. Alphonsus Liguori, an 18th-century spiritualist who founded the Congregation of the Most Holy Redeemer, have offered personal retreats at this beautiful center. The center offers miles of hiking trails, a tranquil desert setting, and even petroglyphs left behind by the Hohokam Indians. According to the friendly, welcoming Redemptorists, "it is a place where a person may listen to the voice of God." Private retreats are offered here throughout the year. There are two seasons: In the low season, June–September and throughout December, a standard retreat home will cost you $100 per night for a single and $175 for a double; during the high season, January–May and October–November, prices go up just a bit, to $110 for a single and $185 for a double. They also offer many themed retreats and group activities. During both seasons there's a two-night minimum.

About 50 miles southeast of Tucson, in the lush San Pedro River Valley, the Benedictines at the **Holy Trinity Monastery** (520/720-4642, www.holytrinitymonastery.org) in St. David, a very green and shady historically Mormon village, welcome retreatants and even RVers. The monastery's 132 acres have sheep, chickens, cows, pecan trees, a 1.3-mile bird sanctuary trail along the San Pedro, and lots of peace and quiet. For $50–80 a night, a married couple can rent one of 11 rooms on the property; or singles can stay in the Hermitage, with a suggested donation of $70 for one day, $350 for a week, or $1,400 for a month—if you've really got some issues to work through or a lifetime's worth of stress to slough off. The rooms here are small and private with very few frills and no television or radio. Meals are also available: The main meal of the day is $9 per person, or you can get three a day for $20. Sunday meals cost $12 and feast-day meals cost $15. Prepare for a quiet, prayerful, contemplative time: "In keeping with the tradition of monastic hospitality, guest house facilities are offered for monastic retreats," the Benedictines say. "All retreatants, coming either singly or in a group, are expected to participate in the monastic exercises of silence, solitude, simple living, community, and personal prayer." Holy Trinity may be one of the few monasteries in the world with an RV park on-site, called the **Monte Cassino RV Park**—its regulars are referred to as the "Holy Hoboes." There are 16 sites with full hookups and 10 with water and electric offered for $20 per night, $120 for a week, and $350 for a month. If you're interested in joining the ranks of the Holy Hoboes, you might want to plan far ahead, as many people return year after year.

Finally, there's the Benedictine **Santa Rita Abbey** (14200 E. Fish Canyon Rd., Sonoita, 520/455-5595, www.santaritaabbey.org) near Sonoita, nestled in the foothills of the Santa Rita Mountains, about 48 miles from Tucson. You have to make a request to spend a retreat here, by either calling them or writing an email or a letter. The retreat house has a small kitchen and dining room where guests make and eat their own meals. The abbey requests a stipend of $35 per night.

HOTELS

CANYON RANCH ❸❸❸

8600 E. Rockcliff Rd., 520/749-9000 or
800/742-9000, www.canyonranch.com

Perhaps the valley's most famous resort, Canyon Ranch is representative of what the other top resorts offer. Here, of course, you can pamper yourself silly with spa treatments (an activity sure to lead to optimum, albeit temporary, good health), but then it's off to appointments with a staff nutritionist, chiropractor, acupuncturist, and internist. A personal trainer will work with you on keeping in shape long-term, while a meditation class will help you get in tune with your spirituality. After one of your three gourmet (but healthy) meals a day, you can attend lectures and classes on various topics in healthful living. For an experience so meaningful, it's not surprising that you're going to have to spend accordingly. A minimum three-night stay at Canyon Ranch is going to set you back $2,600–5,020 per person depending on accommodations. That's all-inclusive, however: For that price you get three gourmet meals a day, spa treatments galore, consultations with all the medical professionals on staff, and unlimited activities. The high season at Canyon Ranch is September 23–June 7, after which, as it is with all Tucson's resorts, prices drop rather dramatically.

🅲 HACIENDA DEL SOL GUEST RANCH RESORT ❸❸❸

5501 N. Hacienda del Sol Rd., 520/299-1501 or
800/728-6514, www.haciendadelsol.com

Founded in 1929 and displaying the elegant Spanish colonial architecture of a more civilized age, Hacienda del Sol gets my vote for the best foothills resort—not because it's the most inclusive or ritzy, but because it reflects more than any other local accommodations (save perhaps the Arizona Inn) the beauty and rustic-chic of the high-style Southwest of yesteryear. Each of the rooms ($109–515 d depending on the season) is distinctive, with custom-made furniture and a story all its own. The small, comparatively inexpensive Historic Rooms look out on the enchanting courtyard, with an inviting outdoor pool and hot tub. Like its younger foothills neighbors, this resort has a full-service spa, an excellent New American restaurant, a wonderful patio bar, riding stables, and more.

LOEWS VENTANA CANYON RESORT ❸❸❸

7000 N. Resort Dr., 520/299-2020 or 800/234-5117, www.loewshotels.com/hotels/tucson

One of the best things about this resort is its view—anywhere you stand on the grounds you get a long, clear look beyond the sweeping golf course to the valley below. With a fabulous restaurant, a top-notch spa, tennis courts, hiking trails, and one of the most scenic golf courses in the Southwest, it's no wonder this world-renowned hotel and spa ($345–495 d depending on the season) was rated number 31 of the top 100 golf resorts in the nation by *Condé Nast Traveler.* The resort also has a popular star-gazing program and a desert setting you won't soon forget.

THE WESTIN LA PALOMA RESORT & SPA ❸❸❸

3800 E. Sunrise Dr., 520/742-6000 or 800/937-8461, www.westinlapalomaresort.com

Guests of this resort and hotel along Sunrise Drive in the foothills are allowed to use the facilities of the nearby country club, which has a 27-hole Jack Nicklaus–designed golf course. The rooms here ($199–319 d, $109–159 d in summer) are spacious and have private patios looking out over the desert, huge sink-in beds, and wireless Internet; some have fireplaces and sunken spa tubs. The nearby Elizabeth Arden Red Door Spa will pamper you silly after you play a few sets on one of 10 championship tennis courts. There are also indoor racquetball courts, a huge pool area, pilates and yoga studios, and an exercise room.

WESTWARD LOOK RESORT ❸❸❸

245 E. Ina Rd., 520/297-1151 or 800/722-2500, www.westwardlook.com

First built as a private home in 1912, this hacienda-style resort has Southwestern charm to spare. Though it has been built up and remodeled over time (including a multimillion-dollar

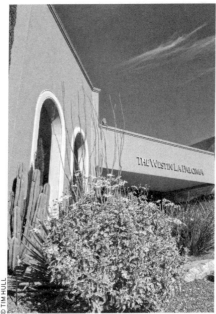

© TIM HULL

The Westin La Paloma Resort & Spa

facelift in 2008), the older, adobe portions still have the exposed vigas made from wood brought down from Mount Lemmon. The 241 guest rooms and suites ($139–339 d) have wireless Internet and plasma TVs and all the usual high-end luxuries, and the resort offers horseback riding, tennis, spa treatments, and 80 acres of desert foothills grounds with nature trails, stargazing programs, and exhibits about the desert's natural history and native peoples.

WINDMILL INN ❸❸

4250 N. Campbell Ave., 520/577-0007, www.windmillinns.com

This small chain hotel at St. Philip's Plaza, at Campbell and River, is one of the few non-resort places to stay in the foothills. The rooms ($111–239 d) are fantastic, with a mini-fridge, wet bar, cable TV, free wireless Internet, and continental breakfast. There's an exercise room, a heated outdoor pool and whirlpool, and bikes available for guests to use. The rooms are gathered around a poolside enclosed courtyard that feels private and serene even at this very busy intersection.

HOTELS

West Side and the Tucson Mountains   Map 5

The west side is dominated by the desert. Like the far east side, a stay out here will bring you close to nature, but keep you far from the madding crowd.

CASA TIERRA ADOBE BED AND BREAKFAST INN ❸❸

11155 W. Calle Pima, 520/578-3058, www.casatierratucson.com

Take a scenic 30-minute drive west of downtown into the Tucson Mountains and you'll find one of the best small inns around on five beautiful and secluded desert acres. This enchanting hacienda-style inn has three rooms and a two-bedroom suite ($135–325 d depending on the season) and is a perfect place to stay for those wanting the tranquility of the wild desert relatively close to town. The Spanish colonial home is open and airy, with

many patios and fountains and little nooks to discover; there's greenery everywhere and all kinds of astonishing little details that show the owners really wanted to create a special place. Each room has a private bath and a refrigerator, and every morning the hosts serve up a gourmet vegetarian breakfast. There's a two-night minimum here.

CAT MOUNTAIN LODGE ❸❸

2740 S. Kinney Rd., 520/578-6085, www.catmountainlodge.com

This charming bed-and-breakfast at Cat Mountain Station, a desert compound with shops, a restaurant, and even an observatory just outside Tucson Mountain Park's southern entrance, is the ideal place to stay if you want to spend more time in the desert than the city. The rooms are cozy and decorated, a tad overbearingly, in the Southwestern style; the grounds are beautiful, quiet, and peaceful; and the whole operation is geared to conservation. There are three standard rooms and two suites, all of them well-priced for their comfort, seclusion, and style ($129–199 Oct.–May 15, $99–179 May 16–Sept.). The lodge is quite near the Sonoran Desert Museum and the western portion of Saguaro National Park.

JW MARRIOTT TUCSON STARR PASS RESORT & SPA ⊛⊛⊛
3800 W. Starr Pass Blvd., 520/792-3500, www.marriott.com

A high-end resort and golf club about 15 minutes west of downtown in a beautiful desert setting, Starr Pass has 75 well-appointed guest rooms and 35 suites ($229–519 d depending on the season and amenities), each with wireless Internet, patio, flat-screen TV, and much more. There's a 27-hole Arnold Palmer golf course here, surrounded by the wild desert. Among the resort's amenities are a full-service spa, a gourmet restaurant, a fitness center, and personal trainers on staff.

East Side and the Rincon Valley   Map 6

You'll find several small, secluded bed-and-breakfast–style inns surrounded by wild desert on the far East Side, as well as one of the region's original dude ranches. These accommodations are for those who want to surround themselves with the rhythms and sounds of the desert.

HILTON TUCSON EAST ⊛⊛
7600 E. Broadway Blvd., 520/721-5600, www.hilton-Tucson-east.com

A large chain hotel with 233 rooms about seven miles east of downtown (Broadway and Prudence), Hilton East is a good choice for business travelers and families with kids. It has wireless Internet, a restaurant and bar with a nice terrace, an exercise room, a heated pool and hot tub, a beautiful atrium lobby, and free parking. They offer a host of different packages (including one that has a pizza delivered to your room), but expect to pay around $143–218 for double occupancy, less in the summer.

South Side   Map 7

The accommodations in South Side are rather bleak. Unless you want to call the casinos home, or you're here on a quick business trip, think about staying in a different part of the city.

DESERT DIAMOND HOTEL AND CASINO ⊛⊛
7350 S. Nogales Hwy., 520/294-7777, www.desertdiamondcasino.com
The rooms at this hotel and casino ($139–350 d) still have that new-room smell, as the whole complex was completely refurbished in late 2008. Each has a flat-screen TV, free wireless Internet, and a big pillow-top bed. The

neighborhood around Desert Diamond is a bit bleak, but there's so much going on inside this adult playground that it hardly matters what the outside looks like. The hotel features a fitness center, a pool, a hot tub, and a convivial fire pit, while guests have access to several restaurants, including an all-you-can-eat buffet, a coffee bar and a booze bar, a nightclub, and, of course, all the blackjack, poker, and slots you can afford to play.

HOLIDAY INN EXPRESS ⊛
2548 E. Medina Rd., 877/863-4780, www.ihg.com
There are few if any independent accommodations with character and style in this

neighborhood. There are of course half a dozen or more big, faceless chains here geared toward the business traveler; if you're looking to stay in this neighborhood, you'll have to choose one of these. I've found that the Holiday Inn Express chain offers a good value; they've all got comfortable clean beds, free wireless Internet, and a surprisingly well-stocked free breakfast come morning, all for around $75–100 (double occupancy) per night.

Greater Tucson   Map 8

The deserts, mountains, and river valleys surrounding Tucson offer several memorable places to stay. None of them are particularly inexpensive, and most are high-end. If you want to be away from the city, or if you are visiting friends, parents, or grandparents in Green Valley, Tubac, or Oro Valley, consider one of the listings below.

Madera Canyon used to be dotted with summer homes and getaway cabins, but beginning in the 1970s the U.S. Forest Service tore them down and converted the treasured ecosystem into a federal recreation area. Now only a scattered few homes remain on historic mining claims. Three of the lasting structures are lodges that welcome visitors year-round.

AMADO TERRITORY INN ⓢⓢ
3001 E. Frontage Rd., Amado, 520/398-8684, www.amado-territory-inn.com

A quaint little bed-and-breakfast inn ($130–250 d) along I-19 between Green Valley and Tubac (about 40 minutes south of Tucson), the Amado Territory Inn has rooms and suites with flat-screen TVs and refrigerators, as well as an art-filled lobby, tasteful decorating throughout, and fragrant, peaceful gardens. They offer some spa services and even have a few rooms with whirlpool tubs. There are several restaurants nearby, and it's close to the shopping and galleries in Tubac (plus there are a few galleries on-site) and the bird-watching and hiking of the Santa Ritas.

CHUPAROSA INN ⓢⓢ
1300 Madera Canyon Rd., Madera Canyon, 520/393-7370, www.chuparosainn.com

The Chuparosa has three excellent modern rooms ($150–200 d), each with a big comfy bed, a kitchenette, and a private entrance. The inn has a lush on-site bird-watching area where hummingbirds hang out, hovering together around the many feeders set up throughout the grounds. There's a barbecue that guests are allowed to use, and they serve a hearty continental breakfast, but you're on your own for lunch and dinner. This is probably the nicest place to stay in Madera Canyon, and the hosts are experts on the canyon and can direct you to all the best trails and bird-watching areas. Kids are not allowed.

DESERT DOVE BED AND BREAKFAST ⓢⓢ
11707 E. Old Spanish Trail, Tucson, 520/722-6879, www.desertdovebb.com

The Desert Dove is the perfect place to stay if you want to be surrounded by wild desert, within walking distance of Saguaro National Park East (there's a trail going from the inn to the park). The two-room adobe bed-and-breakfast ($145 Sept.–May, $130 June–Aug.) has the atmosphere of a hand-built desert sanctuary, with a tranquil and shady yard crowded with mature desert vegetation—great for wildlife-watching. The rooms are both decorated with antiques and interesting knickknacks and have private entrances and wireless Internet. There are no TVs, and neither kids, nor pets, nor smoking are allowed. Don't stay here unless you're looking for a bit of isolation and quiet—it's a half-hour or so drive to midtown from here. During the high season (Feb.–Mar.), you have to book more than one night.

HOTELS

HOTELS

ESPLENDOR RESORT 💲💲

1069 Camino Caralampi, Rio Rico, 520/281-1901,
www.esplendor-resort.com

About 50 miles south of Tucson along I-19, just north of Nogales and the border region, Esplendor sits on a hill overlooking the drylands below. It has a wonderful setting, a golf course, and basic rooms ($129–209 d) that are comfortable and clean. The pool area is magnificent, with comfy couches and lots of shade and friendly staff that will bring you rum and cokes poolside. The decor is all Spanish colonial—including the dresses worn by the waitresses in the dining room, which serves pretty good breakfasts. This is a fine resort, and it's a good option if you're going to be spending a lot of time along the border or in nearby Tubac or Green Valley.

🌑 HACIENDA DEL DESIERTO BED AND BREAKFAST 💲💲

11770 E. Rambling Trail, Tucson, 520/298-1764,
www.tucson-bed-breakfast.com

A hiker's and bird-watcher's paradise east of town near Saguaro National Park East, Hacienda del Desierto is a wonderland of hacienda-style details and quiet comfort for anyone looking to escape to the desert for a few days. The four rooms ($139–285 d) are tastefully decorated with Southwestern, Mexican, and Spanish colonial touches, all with private baths, private entrances, and kitchenettes. The courtyard patio here is overflowing with greenery, and there's a private nature trail on the inn's 16 acres where you might be able to see a desert creature or two. TVs, DVD players, and Internet access are available, as are neuromuscular and aromatherapy massages.

HILTON TUCSON EL CONQUISTADOR GOLF & TENNIS RESORT 💲💲💲

10000 N. Oracle Rd., Tucson, 520/544-5000,
www.hiltonelconquistador.com

About a half-hour drive north from Tucson, El Conquistador is a storied resort hotel nestled in the west-side foothills of the Santa Catalina Mountains (where they say bighorn sheep used to roam; don't miss seeing the huge life-like statue of a ram, an homage to what has been lost, out in front of this high-end resort). It's like its own city, and if you stay here ($129–400 d, many packages and deals offered year-round) you might not get into town proper for all the lazing around poolside you'll be doing. They offer amenities and services on par with the other top resorts in town, with 428 guest rooms and suites, a full-service spa, a 45-hole desertland golf course, a water park with a 143-foot waterslide that the kids will freak over, 31 lighted tennis courts, five restaurants, horseback riding, and pretty much whatever else your pampered heart desires.

THE INN AT SAN IGNACIO 💲💲

1861 W. Demetrie Loop, Green Valley, 520/393-5700,
www.innatsanignacio.com

Green Valley is a quiet, largely age-restricted retirement haven with about 20,000 year-round residents, half a dozen golf courses, and a commanding view of the mighty Santa Rita Mountains a few miles to the east, where bird-watchers from all over the world go to complete their life lists. There are several lodges in Madera Canyon, about a 15-minute drive from Green Valley and the most popular spot in the range, but you have to either bring your own food or drive down the mountain every night for dinner if you choose one of those places. An alternative is this quiet inn ($129–169 d) near a golf course in Green Valley, which offers suites with kitchenettes, TVs, Internet, and private patios with views of the mountains. If you're a couple with split priorities—one loves golf, the other loves bird-watching and hiking—you'll both be happy here.

MADERA KUBO 💲

1259 S. Madera Canyon Rd., Madera Canyon,
520/625-2908, www.maderakubo.com

The A-frame Madera Kubo has four cozy cabins ($95) and a gift shop, but no food. The cabins are decorated with handmade furniture and a country aesthetic, and the hosts are a friendly family that has lived in the canyon for decades. The place has a slightly junky look when you first drive up, but once you look a little closer it reveals itself to be charming and lived in. You'll likely be sharing your stay with a few bird-watchers, who flock to the canyon from around the world.

MIRAVAL RESORT & SPA ⓈⓈⓈ

5000 E. Via Estancia Miraval, Catalina, 520/825-4000 or 800/232-3969, www.miravalresorts.com

I know a young woman who spent three days and nights at Miraval—a favorite spot of no less an authority on living life to the fullest than Oprah Winfrey—and when she returned to the real world she said that henceforth her life would be divided into just two chapters: before Miraval and after Miraval. For what you pay ($798–1,300 d minimum, probably more with added activities and such), one should be able to expect some sort of life-changing experience. This world-famous resort, on 400 acres backed by the Santa Catalinas, has 118 rooms, a full-service (and then some) spa, a whirlpool, sauna, and Olympic-size lap pool, a full gym, an obstacle course and climbing wall, yoga and pilates centers, and much more. The rooms are very nice, but with all there is to do here you don't spend much time inside; still, most of the casita-style accommodations have TVs, DVD players, wireless Internet, and more.

SANTA RITA LODGE Ⓢ

1218 S. Madera Canyon Rd., Madera Canyon, 520/625-8746, www.santaritalodge.com

This quaint mountain lodge offers several casitas and freestanding cabins with private decks ($110–165 d). The lodge, the oldest in the canyon, has beautiful grounds along Madera Creek and attracts birds with feeders and provides benches for viewing. There's also a gift shop, but no food, so bring your own or plan to eat in Green Valley, about 12 miles away. March–May the lodge can fix you up with an experienced birding guide by appointment. Tours start early and last about four hours ($20 pp).

TANQUE VERDE RANCH ⓈⓈⓈ

14301 E. Speedway Blvd., Tucson, 520/296-6275, www.tanqueverderanch.com

The dude ranch has been a venerable Southwestern tradition since at least the turn of the 20th century, and few places carry that tradition on with more style and fun than the folks at Tanque Verde Ranch, a historic all-inclusive resort-ranch on the east side. A ranch since 1868, and a dude ranch since 1908, this huge desert property is about a 30-minute drive east from downtown, at the base of the Rincon Mountains, and offers all kinds of Old West–style activities, so many that you likely won't leave the grounds much. It's not cheap; the 76 ranch house–style rooms and suites, many with fireplaces and patios, go for about $275–350 per person, per night. However, that price is all-inclusive and comes with three meals a day, horseback riding, outdoor barbecues, guided mountain biking, and more. There are big indoor and outdoor pools, hiking trails, and children's activities galore, as well as tennis courts and evening entertainment.

TUBAC GOLF RESORT ⓈⓈⓈ

1 Otero Rd., Tubac, 520/398-2211, www.tubacgolfresort.com

This sprawling, historic, hacienda-style upscale resort ($140–265 d) has a popular lush golf course lined with casitas and rooms of various sizes and styles, two restaurants, a pool, hot tub, and other amenities. Over the last several years the resort has been going through a $40 million restoration. Check the website for great package deals; prices drop considerably in summer. It's a luxurious, elegant place to stay about 45 minutes from Tucson south on I-19 and within easy distance of the shops and galleries at Tubac and the trails of the Tumacácori Highlands and the Santa Rita Mountains.

TUBAC INN Ⓢ

12 Burruel St., Tubac, 520/398-3178, www.tubaccountryinn.com

The artist's village of Tubac—the first

settlement in what was to become Arizona—has all the shopping and art that enthusiasts of those activities could possibly want, and this tasteful, friendly bed-and-breakfast is right in the middle of it all. The small inn ($90–175 d depending on the season) is situated right in the heart of the village and offers suites with kitchenettes, TVs, and wireless Internet. Breakfast is served in a basket at your door every morning. Smoking is not allowed, nor are kids under 13 years old, nor pets of any age.

WHITE STALLION RANCH $$

9251 W. Twin Peaks Rd., Tucson, 520/977-2624, www.whitestallion.com

This historic 3,000-acre dude ranch about a 30-minute drive northwest of downtown Tucson is one of several places in Southern Arizona where you can discover your inner cowpoke. It's in a gorgeous location at the base of the jagged Tucson Mountains and close to Saguaro National Park West. There are 41 guest rooms, many of them multiroom suites that are perfect for big families or friends traveling together, all decorated in that familiar Mexico-influenced ranch-house style. As it is with other dude ranches, the prices here are high but all-inclusive. Expect to pay $127–905 per person, per day, depending on the season and which room you choose. That price includes three meals daily, horseback riding, various ranch activities, and even a ride to and from the airport.

EXCURSIONS FROM TUCSON

Just a few hours of scenic off-interstate driving east and south of Tucson, small historic mining towns, forested sky island mountain ranges, underground fantasy worlds still being formed by slowly dripping water, a secret landscape where rocks stand to attention, and a bustling, colorful, exotic borderland await discovery.

Even if you're only in town for a week or so, set aside one or two days to explore both Cochise County to the east and Santa Cruz County to the south. Both counties straddle the U.S.-Mexico border and are still willfully haunted by the violent past of the old territory, and both are rather sparsely populated, dotted with a few old-timer ranches still scraping along, and even more mass-produced pueblo-revival and hacienda-style high-dollar dream homes owned by baby-boomer runaways. The spirit and culture of Mexico pervades the towns of southeastern Arizona, but so does the crafty hippie ethos of the artists, artisans, and burnouts that have transformed once-moribund mining towns like Bisbee into tourist-friendly attractions. The legendary West of the imagination (along with a bit of real history as well) is on display in Tombstone; and the actual West, the one ruled by capitalists and their hard-rock-mining minions, is illuminated by headlamp-light on a tour deep underground. Also underground, Kartchner Caverns State Park, just an hour or so outside the city, beckons day-trippers to explore its otherworldly dripping-water innards, and its swirling colors and odd, thrilling mineral formations are nearly as memorable as the sweeping grassland deserts and high, isolated mountain ranges all around.

© TIM HULL

PLANNING YOUR TIME

Any of the excursions suggested here can be done as a leisurely day trip from Tucson, leaving after breakfast and returning in late afternoon. A major part of any of these day trips is the drive itself, and it's best to avoid the interstate and take the scenic two-lane backroads. If you want to spend a few days exploring southeastern Arizona, hiking along the San Pedro River or in the Huachuca Mountains, I'd suggest

HIGHLIGHTS

LOOK FOR ◖ TO FIND RECOMMENDED SIGHTS, ACTIVITIES, DINING, AND LODGING.

© TIM HULL

quaint and funky Bisbee

◖ **Best Time Spent Underground:** Enter the otherworldly caves at **Kartchner Caverns State Park,** which are still being formed by slowly dripping water and are home to bats and hanging multicolored formations (page 182).

◖ **Best Sweeping View of the Borderlands:** Along the U.S.-Mexico border at **Coronado National Memorial,** you can stand on a scenic overlook with expansive, windswept views of the San Pedro and San Rafael Valleys, all the way to Mexico (page 184).

◖ **Best Day Trip Turned Overnighter:** Explore **Bisbee,** a quaint old mining boom-

town that's now an enclave for artists, antiques shops, and several boutique hotels (page 186).

◖ **Best Native American Museum:** Discover Native American cultures from prehistory all the way to the Chiricahua Apache and beyond at the **Amerind Foundation Museum,** one of the finest private ethnological collections in the nation (page 197).

◖ **Best Photo Op in Southern Arizona:** Make sure to get a photo of the magnificent forest of hoodoos and twisted rock high in the evergreen mountains at **Chiricahua National Monument** (page 199).

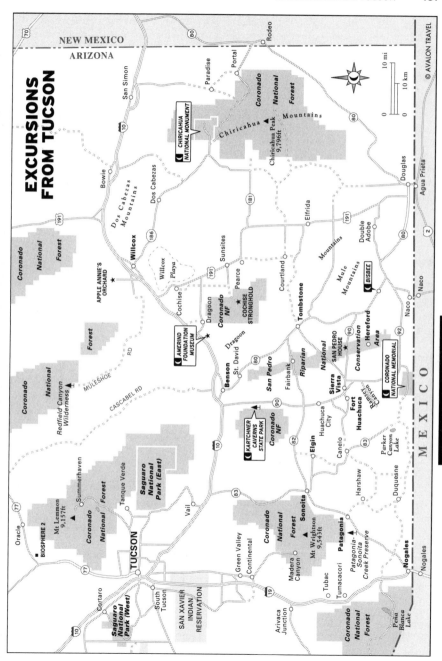

staying in Bisbee, where you'll find some of the best historic hotels and bed-and-breakfasts in the state, and making excursions from there. A trip to the Chiricahua Mountains from Tucson is definitely an all-day trip, and you really need to spend at least two days to truly enjoy this wonderful place. It's a long, empty drive to the Chiricahua National Monument, but at the end of it is one of the most spectacular sights this side of the Grand Canyon.

Let's say you only have one full day for excursions. In that case, head to Kartchner Caverns (1 hour from downtown Tucson) and Bisbee, taking the scenic route. It's a good idea to call ahead and reserve tickets to the caverns, though it's not as important to do so these days at it once was. Leave after breakfast, have lunch in Bisbee before heading to the caverns, and you'll be back in the Old Pueblo by dinner time, unless you fall in hopeless love with the off-kilter hillside town.

If you're headed down to Nogales and across the border, I'd recommend doing so around lunch or dinner time, as eating at one of the restaurants in the tourist district in Nogales, Mexico, is one of the joys to be had across the line. If you're across the line after dark, be careful. It's easy to get caught up in the scene—downing margaritas with lunch, then tequila shots, then some guy you don't know comes up from behind and in broken English offers to take you to a strip club...Remember that you've got an hour or so worth of driving north on I-19 to make it back to Tucson.

Kartchner Caverns and the Huachuca Mountains

The Kartchner Caverns are still alive, forming slow and steady over eons as water drips and falls into a secret world beneath the Whetstone Mountains, about 40 miles east of Tucson. The State of Arizona spent 11 years and more than $30 million developing Kartchner Caverns State Park, and it shows. It's really one of the must-sees of a visit to Southern Arizona. The Huachuca Mountains, rising high above the charmless military town of Sierra Vista, home to a U.S. Army intelligence center, offer sky island forests, cool mountain hiking trails, subtropical birds found few other places in the nation, and some of the longest, clearest views of the borderlands you'll find. Ranging in elevation from 3,934 feet at the base to 9,455 feet at the top of Miller Peak, the Huachucas are another of Southern Arizona's signature sky island ranges. You'll see the common transition from semidesert grasslands at the base, up into arid scrub, onto mixed oak forests, and all the way up to cool ponderosa pine forests in the higher reaches. There are dozens of trails in the range, and labyrinths of dirt roads that lead deep into the outback.

Both of these areas can be visited as day trips, or even half-day trips, from Tucson, but if you want to spend some time hiking and exploring the mountains, there are a few excellent bed-and-breakfast-style inns nearby. The restaurant scene here is rather bleak, with the usual interstate-side chains and sprawlville corporate eateries (especially in Sierra Vista). I'd recommend bringing along food with you in the car, especially if you're going to be driving around the dirt back roads in the Huachucas or hiking at the Ramsey Canyon Preserve (and even if you're just going to the caverns).

SIGHTS
◖ Kartchner Caverns State Park
Kartchner Caverns (Hwy. 90, Benson, 520/586-2283 for reservations, 520/586-4100 for information, www.azstateparks.com, summer daily 8 A.M.–5 P.M., winter daily 7 A.M.–6 P.M., parking free with tour reservation, $5 per vehicle up to 4 people) were discovered in the early 1970s by two cave-loving University of Arizona students. Gary Tenen and Randy Tufts knew right away that they had shimmied down a sinkhole in the Whetstone Mountains into caving immortality, as the small but "wet"

cave—meaning that it is still forming drip by drip, in a very real sense "alive"—is one of the most spectacular water-on-rock formations of its kind. And yet the explorers managed to keep their find a secret for several years in an effort to protect it from cavers less responsible than themselves. They called it Xanadu, after the great English poet Samuel Taylor Coleridge's famous unfinished poem *Kubla Khan,* a name given to the Throne Room's 58-foot main column—formed not so much by drips but by torrents of water flowing into the cave over millennia—the largest cave column in Arizona.

Eventually Tenen and Tufts told the property owners what they'd found, and the Kartchner family quickly joined those who wanted to see the cave preserved. A pre-tour film in the park's Discovery Center tells the whole story and explains what makes this cave so unique. There's also an interesting museum and a gift shop; just outside the Discovery Center a native-plant butterfly garden is worth a stroll.

There are two different tours you can take through the caverns. The **Big Room Tour** (1.5 hrs., $23 adult, $13 age 7–13, no children under 7) is offered only October 15–April 15—during the summer months a large colony of bats returns to the Big Room, as they have likely done for eons, to give birth to and rear their single pups. The **Rotunda/Throne Room Tour** (1.5 hrs., $23 adult, $13 age 7–13) is offered year-round and is more than enough to satisfy even the most discerning spelunker.

Because the cave is still "alive," much is made of its conservation. Visitors are warned repeatedly not to touch any of the formations, and guides are not shy about telling kids to stand back and keep their hands to themselves. The tour information is very repetitive if you've just watched the pre-tour movie.

If a tour of the cave isn't enough, the park offers campsites with electric hookups, water, a dump station, and restrooms with showers ($25).

Fort Huachuca and Sierra Vista

Much of the war against the Chiricahua Apaches was fought from Fort Huachuca, founded in 1877 in a canyon that had historically served as an escape route for one of the Southwest's final hold-out tribes. Currently the fort is a major center for military intelligence training; its stories, past and present, are told at two museums here. The main gate to get into the base of the fort is at Fry Boulevard and Highway 90 in Sierra Vista. Once you're let on the base, the guards will direct you to Building 41401, which houses the museums. The **Fort Huachuca Museum** (520/533-5736, huachuca-museum.com, Mon.–Fri. 9 A.M.–4 P.M., Sat.–Sun. 1–4 P.M., $2 suggested donation) has exhibits about army life on the Southwestern frontier, the famous battles with the Chiricahua Apaches, and the Buffalo Soldiers—African American cavalrymen whose story is one of the most fascinating of the West. The **U.S. Army Intelligence Museum** (520/533-1127, micastore.com, Mon.–Sat. 9 A.M.–4 P.M.) tells the 200-year story of the army's underrated intelligence corps. Since September 11, 2001, foreign nationals have not been allowed on the base, even if they are just there to see the museums.

Sitting at the base of the Huachuca Mountains, the military town of Sierra Vista is the largest town in the valley and the fort's host, but has little charm in and of itself. There are a lot of chain hotels and restaurants, and it's close to the southern end of the San Pedro River. It makes a good base if you're planning on spending some quality time in the mountains, but otherwise it's just a drive-through.

Ramsey Canyon

You'll pass the Coronado National Forest ranger station as you head up to the 300-acre Ramsey Canyon Preserve ($5 pp over 16), an easily accessible stream-influenced canyon protected by **The Nature Conservancy** (27 Ramsey Canyon Rd., 520/378-2785, www. nature.org, Mar.–Oct. daily 8 A.M.–5 P.M., Nov.–Feb. daily 9 A.M.–4 P.M.). This is a very popular area with bird-watchers, who come to see the more than 14 species of hummingbird and other avian species that stop over

a rufous hummingbird at The Nature Conservancy

© DERRICK NEILL/123RF.COM

in the cool riparian canyon, fed by babbling Ramsey Creek, protected by high canyon walls, and crowded with sycamores, maples, and columbines.

The upper part of the canyon is within the **Miller Peak Wilderness Area.** Make sure you stop at The Nature Conservancy's excellent visitors center, which has maps, trail guides, books, T-shirts, and helpful, friendly volunteers. It's a good idea to get there early; this area is very popular and the parking lot only has 23 spaces—first-come, first-served.

To reach the preserve, take Ramsey Canyon Road west from Highway 92 south of Sierra Vista (6 miles south of Fry Blvd.); the preserve is at the end of the road, four miles west of the highway.

Also along Ramsey Canyon Road, before you reach the preserve, you'll find the **Arizona Folklore Preserve,** a quaint little theater along the creek where Arizona State Balladeer and nationally known folky Dolan Ellis puts on acoustic folk concerts on Saturday and Sunday

at 2 P.M. The shows are popular, so call ahead (520/378-6165, www.arizonafolklore.com) for a reservation.

Coronado National Memorial

Named in honor of Spanish conquistador Francisco Vásquez de Coronado, who trudged north in 1540 searching for the Seven Cities of Cíbola—which turned out to be nothing more than a few hardscrabble pueblos—this beautiful landscape along the U.S.-Mexico border, on the southern end of the Huachuca Mountains, has a **visitors center** (Coronado Memorial Rd., 5 miles from Hwy. 92, 520/366-5515, www.nps.gov/coro, daily 8 A.M.–4 P.M.) with exhibits about its namesake, local history, and natural history. Three miles west of the visitors center is a scenic overlook at Montezuma Pass, with expansive views of the San Pedro and San Rafael Valleys and Mexico. You can have a picnic here and hike around on a number of trails leading to and from the lookout, but there's no camping allowed. To get there, go south on Highway 92 about 20 miles to South Coronado Memorial Drive, then it's five miles to the visitors center. (At the visitors center you can purchase a map of the Huachucas with all the trails on it for $5.)

San Pedro Riparian National Conservation Area

This 58,000-acre preserve protects some 40 miles of the upper San Pedro River between St. David and the border. There are about 400 species of birds here, 82 mammal species, and 45 reptile and amphibian species, some of which you're likely to see if you stay vigilant and quiet while exploring. Beavers, once plentiful in the now nearly extinct riparian habitats of Southern Arizona, have been reintroduced here. The Friends of the San Pedro River have converted a 1930s-era ranch house—in the shade of a beautiful 120-year-old Fremont cottonwood tree—into the **San Pedro House** gift shop and bookstore (9800 Hwy. 90, 520/459-2555, daily 9:30 A.M.–4:30 P.M.), where you can pick up information and pamphlets for a self-guided river walk and other trails and get advice from the volunteers. Here you'll also find the **Murray Springs Clovis Site and Trail,** a kind of stone-age butcher shop frequented by Clovis people 8,000–11,000 years ago. Scientists have dug up the fossils of several huge extinct mammals here, some of which are currently housed at the Museum of Natural History in New York.

RESTAURANTS

There is not an impressive restaurant selection near Kartchner Caverns and in Sierra Vista, but there is one little place that is worth recommending, and it has a bit of interesting history related to the nearby caverns. The **Horseshoe Café** (154 E. 4th St., Benson, 520/586-2872, Mon.–Sat. 6 A.M.–8 P.M., Sun. 6 A.M.–4 P.M., $5–15) serves pretty good steaks, burgers, and Mexican favorites—including big, sloppy, and tasty burritos. It's been around for something like 70 years and is right on Benson's main drag; it's decorated with all kinds of portraits of horses and a few antiques, but I can see how some people might consider it a borderline dive. At any rate, the food is filling and tastes good. Author Neil Miller, in his recent history of the caverns, reports that during the many years that Gary Tenen and Randy Tufts kept their discovery under wraps, every time they would visit their secret cave they'd invariably stop at the Horseshoe for a bite to eat before returning to Tucson. For some reason, nobody in the restaurant seemed to think it was strange that the two spelunkers always came in covered in mud.

HOTELS

The riverside **Casa de San Pedro** (8933 S. Yell Ln., Hereford, 520/366-1300 or 888/257-2050, www.bedandbirds.com, $169 d) is a territorial-style home with a central courtyard, a pool, hot tub, and all kinds of activities geared toward bird-watchers and nature lovers. **Ramsey Canyon Inn** (29 Ramsey Canyon Rd., Hereford, 520/378-3010, www.ramsey-canyoninn.com, $135–165 d), just outside the Ramsey Canyon Preserve, has six rooms named for hummingbird species, delicious breakfasts, and a setting that can't be beat.

PRACTICALITIES

If you're looking to put together a backpacking or camping adventure in the Huachuca range, talk to the staff at the **Coronado National Forest Sierra Vista Ranger District** (5990 S. Hwy. 92, Hereford, 520/378-0311). The **Benson Visitor Center at the Railway Depot** (249 E. 4th St., 520/586-4293, www.bensonvisitorcenter.com) has a lot of local information, including historical displays and guides to the area's lesser-known sights.

Getting There and Around

There are a few different routes you can take to Kartchner Caverns and the Huachuca Mountains, but there's really only one way to get there: by car. Every now and again you might see a skinny bearded man pedaling slowly along the highway, weighted down with packs and bags, but the vast majority of day-trippers take their own car—or their own motorcycle, typically a late-model, possibly rented Harley piloted by a gray-haired retiree who was born to be wild but didn't know it until just a few months ago.

The easiest way to get to the caverns is to take I-10 east of Tucson to the Highway 90 exit, then head south on Highway 90 until you see the entrance to the park. From the park to the mountains, take Highway 90 south into Sierra Vista, then head for the hills. For a longer, more scenic route, take I-10 east to the Highway 83 exit, then follow 83 south through the grasslands on the east side of the Santa Rita Mountains. Turn east on Highway 82, then north or south on Highway 90, depending on whether you're headed for the caves or the peaks.

A highly recommended trip stops first at Kartchner Caverns and then goes on to Bisbee for an overnight stay. Bisbee is about 55 miles from the caverns by way of Highway 90 south, a 45-minute drive. If you want to stop at Tombstone on the way, take Highway 82 east to Highway 80 east, a 57-mile drive that takes about an hour.

EXCURSIONS FROM TUCSON

Bisbee and Tombstone

Tombstone, the sight of the most famous 30-second gunfight in history, calls itself the "town too tough to die," but it is really Bisbee that deserves that distinction. Bisbee's huge open-pit copper mine flourished for a few generations, and after it closed the quaint little town found new life among artists, writers, and countercultural escapists, while still maintaining its role as a county seat and government center. Today Bisbee is actually growing, and there always seem to be new restaurants and stores opening in the quaint structures of Old Town.

Tombstone's mining boom—and it was mining, not cardsharps, gunfighters, and vigilantes, that put the town on the map—lasted only about seven years, from 1880 to 1887, give or take. These days Tombstone is a tourist trap, nothing more and nothing less.

Both former mining centers followed a similar economic cycle, however. Their impressive mineral wealth may have been found first by intrepid lone-wolf hard-rock miners, but the industry was very soon taken over by Eastern conglomerates owned by fat-cat "capitalists," as that species was called back then (by a group that included the territory's then governor), and the hills were denuded of their ore by broken-backed miners making about $4 a day. That was until the corporations couldn't make the mines pay anymore, owing mostly to flooding, so they packed up and went looking for another place to dig and blast, leaving the town and laid-off workers to fend for themselves. And fend for themselves they both have done, inviting tourists from all over the globe to discover their unique charms.

◖ BISBEE

The most charming town in Cochise County began life in the 1880s as a copper mining camp. Eventually several billion pounds of the useful ore would be taken out of the ground here, and by 1910 Bisbee was said to be the biggest city between the Midwest and West Coast.

Flooding in the 1,000-foot-deep tunnels and the boom and bust nature of the mining economy closed the mines by the 1970s, and the town, with its labyrinthine staircases and cozy little bungalows built precariously on the slopes of the Mule Mountains, was nearly moribund when it was discovered by hippies, artists, and artisans, a group that funkified the town into what it is today. Retired miners, retirees from elsewhere, county government workers, and sons and daughters of the pioneers also call Bisbee home. **Old Town** (where you'll likely spend most, if not all, your time) is stuffed full of shops, galleries, restaurants, historic landmarks, and some of the best old hotels in the state. Perhaps the most fun to be had in Bisbee comes from just walking around, climbing the scores of off-kilter steps and exploring its back alleys and narrow streets.

Sights

Driving in on Highway 80, just after the intersection with Highway 92, you can stop at a turnout along the side of the road and witness the **Lavender Pit Mine** and the huge tailings surrounding the largest open-pit mine in the state, now closed. Bisbee is still proud of its history as the queen of all mining towns, and you can learn all about it at the **Bisbee Mining and Historical Museum** (No. 5 Copper Queen Plaza, junction of Main St. and Brewery Gulch, 520/432-7071, www.bisbeemuseum.org, daily 10 A.M.–4 P.M., $7.50 adult, $6.50 senior, $3 child 4–16), housed in the building formerly occupied by the headquarters of the Copper Queen Consolidated Mining Company. Now an affiliate of the Smithsonian Institution, the museum has exhibits on local history and culture during territorial days, with an emphasis on the history and science of copper mining. You can see for yourself what it was like descending into the earth every day to coax the ore out of the mountain on the 75-minute **Queen Mine Tour** (478 N. Dart Rd., 520/432-2071 or 866/432-2071, www.queenminetour.

© TIM HULL

Bisbee Mining and Historical Museum

com, daily 9 A.M., 10:30 A.M., noon, 2 P.M., 3:30 P.M., $13 adult, $5.50 child 4–12). Retired miners lead these tours and will regale you with stories of what it was really like underground, as you ride deep beneath the earth on an old mine car, wearing a yellow slicker, a hard hat, and a headlamp. It's about 47°F in the shaft, so think about taking something warm to wear.

Restaurants

Café Roka (35 Main St., 520/432-5153, www.caferoka.com, Wed. and Thurs.–Sat. 5–9 P.M., $16.50–24) has some of the best Italian food around with a tasteful, elegant multilevel interior. **Angela's** (11 Howell Ave., 520/432-2116, daily 7–10:30 A.M., 11 A.M.–2:30 P.M., and 5–8 P.M., $9–23), at the Copper Queen Hotel, serves delicious American food and other dishes. The best breakfast in town can be found at the **Bisbee Breakfast Club** (75 Erie St., 520/432-5885, www.bisbeebreakfastclub.com, daily 7 A.M.–3 P.M., $10 and under), serving huge American-style breakfasts, along with a bit of Mexican spice, of course, in a

refurbished old building on the largely abandoned historic block next to the huge pit. You might have to wait to get a table, but the food is worth it.

Santiago's (1 Howell Ave., 520/432-1910, santiagosmexican.blogspot.com, Mon.–Thurs. 11 A.M.–9 P.M., Fri.–Sat. 11 A.M.–10 P.M., Sun. 11 A.M.–9 P.M., $10–20) is a small, often busy Mexican restaurant in Old Town Bisbee that serves impeccable dishes in a new traditionalist style. Everything here is familiar (ceviche, chiles rellenos, enchiladas, etc.), but it's so well made—the ingredients fresh and local, the sauces soothing and surprising all at once—that you'll swear you never had its like before. They also make a huge, mean margarita.

Be warned about **Old Bisbee Brewing Co.** (200 Review Alley, 520/432-2739, www.oldbisbeebrewingcompany.com, Mon.–Fri. noon–10:30 P.M., Sat.–Sun. 10 A.M.–10:30 P.M., $5–15): If you visit this brewery, so well situated in Bisbee's old "Brewery Gulch," and if it is pleasant out, which it so often is, and if you imbibe one or more of the several delicious and

© TIM HULL

Santiago's

nutritious beers brewed on-site, and if you are sitting there in the sun on the patio looking out over the quaint Old Town when you do so, you probably aren't going anywhere for a while.

Bisbee Table (2 Copper Queen Plaza, Bisbee Convention Center, 520/432-6788, daily 11 A.M.–9 P.M., $10–20) is a popular New American bistro in Old Town Bisbee that serves familiar (burgers, tacos, barbecued pork, fish and chips, mussels), well-made lunches, dinners, and desserts from locally sourced ingredients.

Festivals and Events

Like most of the old mining towns in Arizona and northern Mexico, much of Old Town Bisbee is perched rather precariously on the sides of the mountains, and the early residents installed steps all over town so folks could reach their homes. These days the steps are more at-mospheric than useful; they contribute much to Bisbee's quaint character. At the **Bisbee 1000 Stair Climb** (Bisbee, www.bisbee1000. org, $55–100), held every October, strange characters from all over the world gather in Old Town to run up and down these stairs. Don't ask me why. You too can join in, but the event fills up fast, so register early.

Shops

Old Town Bisbee has dozens of unique shops, and there always seem to be new ones open-ing. There are jewelry stores; shops selling local art and Mexican folk art; **Atalanta's Music & Books** (38 Main St., 520/432-9976, daily 10 A.M.–6 P.M.) with a huge selection of mostly used tomes and some new, including a large section of books by local authors; a shop that sells only things made out of copper; and several multilevel antiques and junk shops that you can get lost in for hours.

Hotels and RV Parks

There are all manner of accommodations in Bisbee, and bed-and-breakfasts prolif-erate along the narrow, twisty roads of Old Town. The **Bisbee Grand Hotel** (61 Main St., 520/432-5900 or 800/421-1909, www.

bisbeegrandhotel.com, $89–175 d) is in a Victorian building in Old Town. It offers small, well-decorated rooms with private baths, and a full breakfast is served on the veranda. It has wireless Internet and a saloon downstairs frequented by tourists and locals. The **Copper Queen Hotel** (11 Howell Ave., 520/432-2216, www.copperqueen.com, $89–197 d) is an institution in Bisbee, built in 1902 and still in beautiful shape—but almost certainly haunted, as anyone in Bisbee will tell you. It has a pool, a saloon, and a restaurant. The oldest brick building in Bisbee now houses the **Letson Loft Hotel** (26 Main St., 520/432-3210, www.letsonlofthotel.com, $115–175), an elegant, friendly, and truly memorable hotel. This small boutique hotel in the heart of Old Town offers romantic, high-end but affordable accommodations in a gorgeously remodeled and tastefully decorated space. All the rooms have modern amenities and are quiet and cozy, despite being located right in the thick of the action along Bisbee's narrow, shop-lined main drag, onto which some of the rooms look down

Letson Loft Hotel

from on high, giving the dweller a bit of a sense of what the old town was once like in its busy urban heyday.

For a truly unique experience, rent one of the 1950s vintage trailers at **Shady Dell RV Park** (1 Douglas Rd., 520/432-3567, www.theshadydell.com, $45–145 d), each beautifully refurbished and decorated. Many have polished chrome and wood interiors, and include black-and-white TVs and phonographs complete with 45-rpm singles from the era. Located on the premises is **Dot's Diner** (520/432-1112, daily 7 A.M.–2:30 P.M., $10 and under), a ready-made 10-stool diner from the 1950s that serves great food.

TOMBSTONE

Just outside the green and lush Mormon village of St. David, Highway 80 rises onto the dry scrubby plain where Ed Schieffelin struck silver in 1879, defying the soldiers who'd predicted he'd find only his own tombstone out there. The town of the same name became one of the largest, rowdiest, and deceptively sophisticated locales in the Southwest for a time, a place where legends were created daily by overheated newspapermen, and where a 30-second gunfight of dubious legality became a defining frontier myth. These days, about 1,600 residents still call Tombstone home, many of them retirees or people working in some capacity for the town's tourism industry, which attracts visitors, many of them from Europe, year-round.

Sights
BOOTHILL GRAVEYARD

Reportedly, many of Tombstone's gunfighters, along with their victims, lie alongside prostitutes, settlers, and obscure passers-through in this hilltop graveyard (daily 7:30 A.M.–6 P.M., donations welcome). You can walk among the more than 300 uniformly bland and refurbished graves and read the short messages on some of them that illuminate what death was like on the frontier. It doesn't feel authentic in the least, despite claims to the contrary, but it is free. Boothill is just off Highway 80 at the north end of town.

ALLEN STREET AND NATIONAL HISTORIC DISTRICT

Closed to cars and lined with wood-plank sidewalks, Western kitsch shops, and even a few genuine historical attractions, Allen Street *is* Tombstone to most. There are several saloons and restaurants here, and faux-gunfighters and saloon girls (some of them with somewhat anachronistic tattoos) mill about next to the working stagecoach replicas of **Old Tombstone Historical Tours** (520/457-3018, www.tombstonetours.com, $10 adult, $5 child). The National Historic District includes several streets off of Allen, including Toughnut Street to the west, Freemont Street to the north, and 6th Street to the south.

Within this historic district you'll find the *Tombstone Epitaph* **Museum** (5th St., daily 9:30 A.M.–5 P.M., www.tombstoneepitaph.com, free), where you can see the original press used to print the perfectly named *Epitaph* newspaper, first published in 1880 and still going, and other printing-related exhibits. The **OK Corral and Historama** (Allen St., 520/457-3456, www.ok-corral.com, daily 9 A.M.–5 P.M., $7.50 with gunfight, $5.50 without) has all the information you'll need on the famous, albeit short, gunfight between the Earps and Clantons. You can see a rather tired and dusty historical re-enactment of the fight, and watch a show narrated by Vincent Price on the major events in Tombstone history.

Among the saloons in the district, the **Crystal Palace Saloon** and **Big Nose Kate's Saloon** are worth a look, with Kate's being a fine place to kick back a few and look at all the pictures on the walls if you have the time. Both are on Allen Street. One of the best sights on Allen is the **Bird Cage Theatre** (Allen and 6th Sts., 520/457-3421, daily 8 A.M.–6 P.M., tombstonebirdcage.com, $6 adult, $5 child 8–18), an 1881 dance hall, brothel, saloon, theater, and casino that has been spectacularly preserved. A self-guided tour takes you through the building, which looks much as it did when it closed in 1889. On Freemont and 6th Streets, the **Tombstone Western Heritage Museum**

(520/457-3800, Mon.–Sat. 9 A.M.–5 P.M., Sun. 12:30–5 P.M., thetombstonemuseum.com, $5 adult, $3 child 8–18) has many relics of Tombstone's past, including a few personal items once owned by the Earps.

TOMBSTONE COURTHOUSE STATE HISTORIC PARK

A more sober treatment of Tombstone's history is presented inside this preserved 1882 courthouse (223 E. Toughnut St., 520/457-3311, daily 9 A.M.–5 P.M., $5 adult, $2 child 7–13). The museum features artifacts, pictures, and ephemera from the territorial days, and there's a rebuilt gallows in the building's courtyard. Particularly interesting are the two nearly forensic accounts of the gunfight, each with slightly differing details.

ROSE TREE INN MUSEUM

Planted way back in 1885, this Lady Banksia, sent all the way from Scotland to Tombstone as a gift, is believed to be the world's largest rose tree at 8,700 square feet—it is listed in *Guinness World Records* as such. The white blossoms are usually at their best in early April. The small museum (4th and Toughnut Sts., daily 9 A.M.–5 P.M., $3) exhibits photos and furniture owned by the tree's planter, who moved to the territory in 1880.

Restaurants

Nellie Cashman Restaurant (5th and Toughnut Sts., 520/457-2212, daily 11 A.M.–9 P.M., $3.50–8) has good American food, and the **Lamplight Room** (198 N. 4th St., 520/457-3716, daily 11:30 A.M.–9 P.M., $5–10) serves Mexican and American food for breakfast, lunch, and dinner daily. There are several eateries within the historic district, most of them serving cowboy- and Southwestern-style food.

Hotels

There are a few easy-to-locate chain hotels in Tombstone, and a variety of bed-and-breakfasts. The **Tombstone Boarding House B&B**

© TIM HULL

Tombstone's courthouse dates from 1882.

(108 N. 4th St., 520/457-3716 or 877/225-1319, $59–89 d) offers comfortable rooms in two adobe houses that date to the 1880s. The **Wild Rose Inn** (101 N. 3rd St., 520/457-3844 or 866/457-3844, $79–89 d, $109 with private bath) is in a Victorian home built in the early 1900s.

PRACTICALITIES

The **Bisbee Visitor Center** (478 Dart Rd., 520/432-3554, discoverbisbee.com, Mon.–Fri. 9 A.M.–5 P.M., Sat.–Sun. 10 A.M.–4 P.M.) is where you'll find brochures on self-guided walking tours and loads of information on what to do and see in town. Parking isn't easy, especially on weekends, so it's a good idea to find a space, stick with it, and explore the town on foot.

In Tombstone, stop by the **Visitor Information Center** (4th and Allen Sts., 520/457-3929, daily 10 A.M.–4 P.M.) for a nearly overwhelming amount of information about the town and its sights. In March, Tombstone celebrates its founder during **Ed Schieffelin Territorial Days.** In April the **Tombstone Rose Tree Festival** shines the light on the record-making rose tree, and in May, Tombstone's most famous citizen gets his own party during **Wyatt Earp Days.** The anniversary of that infamous gunfight warrants a celebration every year in October.

Getting There and Around

The quickest way to get to Bisbee and Tombstone is to take I-10 east from Tucson for about 40 minutes to the exit for Highway 80. Take Highway 80 south through Tombstone, then keep going south until Highway 80 meets Highway 90; take Highway 90 east to Bisbee. For a longer, even more scenic drive, take I-10 east from Tucson and turn south on Highway 83, then take Highway 82 east to Tombstone, go south on 80, pick up 90, and head on into Bisbee.

It's about 25 miles of easy driving from Bisbee to Tombstone along Highway 80; it takes about half an hour.

The Border Region

Anywhere you are in Cochise or Santa Cruz Counties, you're never more than a few miles from Mexico. Small towns like Bisbee and Douglas each have a Mexican twin right across the line (though they are fraternal twins—the Mexican counterparts are larger and more populous), and traffic between the two generally flows pretty easy. But the easiest, and in a sense the safest, way to visit our neighbors to the south for the day is to walk across the border at the Mariposa Port of Entry in Nogales, Arizona, about an hour south of Tucson on I-19. The Arizona side of what locals call Ambos Nogales ("both Nogales") is a somewhat sleepy government and produce-warehousing town with about 25,000 souls, while the sprawling industrial city just across the border teems with more than 500,000 residents. Most visitors stick to the tourist-friendly blocks just beyond the port of entry. A good portion of the nation's produce passes through the port of entry in Nogales, Arizona, as does a large amount of illegal drugs.

NOGALES, SONORA

Nogales, Mexico, in the state of Sonora, is a modern factory and produce-shipping center, but it's also a very popular tourist destination. It's easy to get there: Just walk across the international border in downtown Nogales, Arizona, after parking at one of the many pay lots (about $4 per day) near the port of entry. There's a tourist area of about a square mile just south of the border, with restaurants, curio shops, and, if you want, drugstores. You can drive into Mexico, but the lines of cars driving north into the United States are long and slow. If you need a ride, there are cabs everywhere and the drivers speak English; they, like everyone else who deals with tourists, take U.S. cash.

In recent years more and more merchants in Nogales's tourist district are competing for fewer and fewer tourist dollars due to the economy, gas prices, and much-publicized violence, making a slow, fun stroll along the narrow streets and souvenir-crowded shops an impossibility. Everybody puts on the hard sell these days, and the last time I was in Nogales to buy a bottle or two of Oaxacan mescal I was accosted at every step and begged repeatedly to have a look at this or that shop, all of which contain similar if not identical items. There's lots of leather and silver, Mexican handicrafts, Day of the Dead items, ceramics, Mexican vanilla, and cheap booze, but if you're not willing to deal with the incessant barking of the merchants, you may want to avoid shopping here.

If you've never been to Mexico, visiting Nogales is an easy and generally safe way to do so. There are *farmacias* on every block, and dentist and doctor offices everywhere, and their services are offered for a fraction of the price of their American counterparts. Most of them have barkers standing outside, calling you to come in and spend your dollars.

Restaurants

The main north–south street is Obregon, two blocks west of the border-crossing station. Popular restaurants include **La Roca,** east of the railroad tracks in downtown; **El Toro,** a steak house about two miles south of the border on Lopez Mateos; and **La Palapa,** a no-frills seafood place about a mile and a half south on Lopez Mateos. **The Oasis** has an outdoor balcony overlooking where two main thoroughfares, Lopez Mateos and Obregon, merge—reminiscent of Times Square, but much smaller. Sit there, enjoy shrimp in a warm cheese sauce, and watch the traffic. And yes, you can drink the water, but most restaurants will put a water bottle on your table to encourage you to buy it in a bottle.

NOGALES, ARIZONA

This small town is named, like its cross-border sister, for the walnut trees that once thrived in the area. It has long been Santa Cruz County's seat, and the beautiful old neoclassical,

THE BORDER SITUATION

There is some violence along Arizona's border with Mexico related to drug trafficking and human smuggling. Recent years have been particularly bloody in the larger border cities, including Nogales, Sonora, owing to the Mexican government's crackdown on the drug cartels and power plays among the cartels themselves. But it's not typical for tourists to get caught in the middle.

In the tourist blocks of Nogales, Sonora, just beyond the port of entry, the biggest annoyance you are likely to encounter is the constant barking of the hard-selling shopkeepers.

The lion's share of the illegal drugs that come into the United States do so over the U.S.-Mexico border in the Southwest. A rather large percentage of these drugs (mostly marijuana, cocaine, and methamphetamine)—not to mention undocumented migrants, though that flood has slowed along with the U.S.

economy—is transported via I-19 from Nogales to drop-houses in Tucson and Phoenix, from which they are distributed to the rest of the country. Borderland hikers and wilderness trekkers are likely to see evidence of the drug trade and human migration in the form of trash and blighted landscapes. But it is extremely unlikely that you'll get caught up in the illegal mix unless you willfully put yourself there.

Perhaps the mayor of Nogales, Sonora, said it best when he told the *Arizona Daily Star,* Tucson's daily newspaper, that "We can bet that if [tourists] come [to Nogales] 100 times, there won't be a single act of violence against them."

If you find yourself across the border in Nogales and in need of help, contact the **U.S. Consulate** (Calle San Jose, Nogales, Sonora, Mexico tel. 631/311-8150, http://nogales.usconsulate.gov).

shiny-domed **Santa Cruz County Courthouse** (2150 N. Congress Dr.), built in 1904 out of stone quarried locally, lends it a historic feel that belies the constant comings and goings of a border town. The **Old City Hall** building, built in 1914, now houses the **Pimería Alta Historical Society** (Grand Ave. and Crawford St., 520/287-4621, Wed.–Sun. 10 A.M.–4 P.M., free), with several interesting exhibits and artifacts on the history of the region. The town's historic downtown along **Morley Avenue** has a few stores that were established in the early 1900s and are still being run by descendants of pioneer merchants.

Restaurants

With dozens of authentic Mexican restaurants within an easy walk across the border, don't spend too much time eating on the Arizona side. If you insist on eating in Arizona, try the steaks and Sonoran-style food at **Las Vigas Steak Ranch** (180 W. Loma St. at Fiesta Market off Arroyo Blvd., 520/287-6641, Tues.–Sat., $8–20), or the excellent Mexican food at

Cocina La Ley (226 W. 3rd St., 520/287-4555, Wed.–Mon., $2–11).

PATAGONIA, SONOITA, AND ELGIN

With an average elevation between 4,000 and 5,000 feet, and average annual rainfall around 20 inches, the grasslands and creekbeds of the "Mountain Empire" on the eastern side of the Santa Rita range are much cooler than Tucson, and the landscape is unlike any other in Arizona. The towns here are tiny, but they serve an increasingly popular tourist spot, and little out-of-the-way inns are plentiful. In Patagonia, the largest town in the area with only about 800 people, there's a yellow train depot in the center of town, built in 1900, and a nearby butterfly garden. A few shops sell unique locally made items and other treasures.

There has been quite a proliferation of bed-and-breakfasts in this area over the last several years. You can find brochures for most of them at **Mariposa Books** (317 McKeown Ave., 520/394-9186, Mon.–Sat. 10:30 A.M.–4 P.M.,

HIKING IN THE TUMACÁCORI HIGHLANDS

The Tumacácori Highlands, northwest of Nogales, can best be accessed using exit 12 (Ruby Rd.) off I-19 just north of Nogales. West about 11 miles is **Peña Blanca Lake,** where bass and catfish can be lured in but not eaten because of high mercury content. There's a boat ramp and trail around the lake. Branch off on Forest Road 39 for the **White Rock Campground,** which has sites year-round, but no water ($5). Continue another five miles along Forest Road 39 to the trailhead for the **Atascosa Lookout Trail.** The popular steep trail to the 6,255-foot peak, a six-mile round-trip, takes you to a decommissioned fire lookout, which, for a few months in 1968, was manned by writer Edward Abbey.

There's a sign pointing to the trailhead for the **Sycamore Canyon Trail** on Forest Road 39 about 10 miles in from Peña Blanca Lake. This trail leads deep into a watered canyon, with steep walls dotted with saguaro, white sycamore trees, and jagged rocks jutting out from above. It's a five-mile hike one-way to the U.S.-Mexico border, marked by a barbed-wire fence. The trail isn't always well marked, as the creek often overtakes it, and you will certainly have to wade in parts. During the rainy season some sections may be impassable. The canyon is a major corridor for drug smuggling, and you are likely to see a lot of trash and other evidence of the trade.

Sun. 10:30 A.M.–3 P.M.), a great bookstore in Patagonia with a tourist information desk.

There are two ways to get to the grassland seas and cottonwood forests of the Mountain Empire, a historic ranching and mining district between the Santa Rita, Patagonia, Mustang, and Huachuca Mountains. If you're coming from the Santa Cruz Valley, take Highway 82 from Nogales 19 miles northeast to Patagonia and then on to Sonoita, where Highway 83 branches off north to I-10. If you're coming from Tucson, take I-10 east to Highway 83.

Patagonia Lake State Park

About seven miles south of Patagonia on Highway 82 is Southern Arizona's largest lake, 2.5-mile-long Patagonia Lake (400 Patagonia Lake Rd., 520/287-6965, daily 4 A.M.–10 P.M.), where you can fish for bass, bluegill, and catfish, and camp, rent a boat, swim and lie around Boulder Beach, water-ski (though not on weekends), and hike around the 5,000-acre Sonoita Creek State Natural Area. The campground has 72 campsites and 34 hookups ($17 no hookup, $25–28 with water and electric), and there are boat launches, restrooms, showers, a dump station, and a camp supply store. In March crowds head to the park to see the annual Mariachi Festival. From Nogales, head

12 miles northeast on Highway 82, then turn left at the sign and drive 4 miles to the park entrance.

Telles Grottos Shrine

Just southwest of Patagonia along Highway 82, near milepost 15.9, there's a shrine built into the rock face of the mountain. It's worth taking a few minutes to climb the steps and take a peek inside, where there will likely be candles burning and messages written to the dead. The shrine was built in the 1940s by the Telles family, whose matriarch vowed she would construct and keep up the shrine if her five boys returned safely from World War II. They did, and the shrine is still in use today.

Wine Country

With soil and growing conditions often likened to those in Burgundy, France, the Sonoita-Elgin grasslands are becoming a well-known and well-reviewed wine-making region. It's fun to drive through the open landscape and sample wines, but consider taking along a designated driver.

In Sonoita, just east of the crossroads on the east side of Highway 82, is the **Dos Cabezas Wineworks** (3248 Hwy. 82, 520/455-5141, doscabezaswineworks.com), open for tasting Friday–Sunday 10:30 A.M.–4:30 P.M. The tasting room and gift shop at **Sonoita Vineyards** (520/455-5893, www.sonoita-vineyards.com), located three miles south of Elgin on the Elgin-Canelo Road, is open daily 10 A.M.–4 P.M. Also along Elgin Road is **Callaghan Vineyards** (336 Elgin Rd., Elgin, 520/455-5322, www.callaghanvineyards.com), with a tasting room open Friday–Sunday 11 A.M.–3 P.M. The **Village of Elgin Winery** (520/455-9309, www.elginwines.com) has tastings Monday–Thursday 10 A.M.–4 P.M., and the **Rancho Rossa Vinyards** (201 Cattle Ranch Ln., Elgin, 520/455-0700, www.ranchorossa.com) is open Friday–Sunday 10:30 A.M.–3:30 P.M..

In April locals turn out in Elgin for the annual **Blessing of the Vine Festival** (www.elginwines.com).

Patagonia-Sonoita Creek Preserve

The Nature Conservancy protects a Freemont cottonwood/Gooding willow riparian forest—one of the best and last remaining examples of this lush landscape in Arizona—on about 750 acres along perennial Sonoita Creek (520/394-2400, www.nature.org/arizona, Oct. 1–Mar. 31 Wed.–Sun. 7:30 A.M.–4 P.M., Apr. 1–Sept. 30 Wed.–Sun. 6:30 A.M.–4 P.M., $5 pp). This small green paradise has six miles of easy trails leading through the forest, with its 100-foot-tall 130-year-old cottonwoods—the biggest and oldest in the country—and along the creek. The birding here is excellent, and it's not uncommon to see deer, bobcats, toads, and frogs in this verdant preserve. Friendly Conservancy volunteers lead nature walks every Saturday morning at 9 A.M. This is an extremely rare ecosystem, one that was once abundant in Southern Arizona but now has all but disappeared.

Restaurants

The Velvet Elvis Pizza Co. (292 Naugle Ave., Patagonia, 520/349-2102, velvetelvispizza. com, Thurs.–Sun. 11:30 A.M.–8:30 P.M., $6–25) serves delicious gourmet pizza and

has interesting pictures of the King and the Virgin. The **Steak Out Restaurant & Saloon** (3243 Hwy. 83, Sonoita, 520/455-5205, www.azsteakout.com, Mon.–Fri. 5 P.M.–close, Sat.–Sun. 11 A.M.–close, $10–25) is hard to miss since it is the biggest building in town. They serve delicious steaks and ribs.

Hotels

The Sonoita Inn (3243 Hwy. 82, Sonoita, 800/696-1006, www.sonoitainn.com), at the crossroads of Highway 82 and Highway 83, has 18 rooms with Western ambience, all with great views of the grasslands and mountains. The room rates are seasonal and vary depending on the time of year. There are several chain hotels in Nogales, Arizona, along Mariposa Road and Grand Avenue, both major thoroughfares. If you're looking for something special, there's the historic **Hacienda Corona de Guevavi** (348 S. River Rd., Nogales, 520/287-6503, www.haciendacorona.com, $199–239 d), a historic inn along the Santa Cruz that once hosted John Wayne and other stars. The inn features murals by Salvador Corona, a famous artist and bullfighter, and offers bed-and-breakfast-style rooms and stand-alone casitas. It has a swimming pool and offers horseback riding, stargazing, and many other activities.

PRACTICALITIES

For visitor information, go to the **Nogales-Santa Cruz Chamber of Commerce** (123 W. Kino Park Way, Nogales, 520/287-3685, www.nogaleschamber.com, Mon.–Fri. 9 A.M.–5 P.M.).

Although it's hassle-free to enter Mexico, coming back can present problems if you do not have a passport. American citizens now need a passport—no exceptions. There's a **U.S. Consulate** (Mexico tel. 631/311-8150 or 631/313-4797, from U.S. tel. 631/313-4820, Mon.–Fri. 8 A.M.–5 P.M.) in Nogales, Sonora, on Calle San Jose, about five miles south of the border. If you get in trouble on the weekend you'll be stuck until Monday, since a consulate officer checks the Nogales, Mexico, jail Monday through Friday only.

EXCURSIONS FROM TUCSON

Getting There and Around

You need a car to get to Nogales and the border region, but I wouldn't recommend driving into Mexico—it takes too long to get back across the border, and there's limited parking around the tourist district anyway. Take I-19 south to Nogales and follow the signs to the port of entry, then park at one of the safe and secure parking lots on the Arizona side (about $4 a day) and walk across. To get to the Mountain Empire, take I-19 to Nogales and then take Highway 82 northeast into the grasslands.

Willcox and the Chiricahua Mountains

These wondrous, storied mountains far east of Tucson, near the New Mexico border, comprise one of the most unique, diverse ranges in the state. Rugged and remote, this area is recommended primarily for its scenic qualities, unless you're a wilderness lover, a hiker, or a camper. The easiest way to see the mountains is to visit Chiricahua National Monument, where you can drive to the top of an overlook and behold an awesome view. On the way, stop off at the Amerind Foundation and learn about the Chiricahua Apache and other Native Americans, and in dusty, dilapidated Willcox you'll find a few quirky reminders of the old Southwest.

Though the former railroad and ranching town of Willcox has seen better days, the canyons, mountains, and grasslands around it are worth the 80-mile drive east on I-10 from Tucson. Willcox today has a few boarded-up buildings and abandoned motels along its main thoroughfare, but its **historic downtown** holds some interest and is worth a mosey. The famous singing cowboy Rex Allen grew up in the area, and a museum and an annual festival honor that fact. Willcox is also known as the place where Wyatt's brother Warren Earp met with a bullet in 1900; his body was later buried in the historic Willcox Cemetery.

SIGHTS
Historic Downtown and Railroad Avenue

This area used to be where life in Willcox happened, and even today it's the most interesting part of town. There's a shady, grassy park with

Rex Allen Arizona Cowboy Museum

a big bronze statue of native son Rex Allen, and across the street on Railroad Avenue the singing cowboy's life and career are celebrated at the **Rex Allen Arizona Cowboy Museum** (150 N. Railroad Ave., 520/384-4583, www. rexallenmuseum.org, daily 10 A.M.–4 P.M., $2 single, $3 couple, $5 family), which also displays a **Cowboy Hall of Fame** honoring area ranchers and cowboys. Just down the sidewalk a bit is the **Willcox Commercial Store,** which claims to be the oldest continually operating store in the state. The **Willcox Rex Allen Theater,** a 1935 art deco movie house, still runs new movies on weekends, and at the end of Railroad Avenue is the **Southern Pacific Depot,** built way back in 1880 and now used by the City of Willcox. The depot's lobby has exhibits on the history of the area and the railroad, and Rex Allen narrates a video played on a loop (Mon.–Fri. 8:30 A.M.–4:30 P.M.). The small town honors their most famous native with **Rex Allen Days** the first week of October every year.

Just around the corner from Railroad Avenue, the **Chiricahua Regional Museum** (127 E. Maley, 520/384-3971, daily 10 A.M.–4 P.M., $2) exhibits mining artifacts, weapons used by Native Americans and the cavalry, and rocks and minerals found in the region. There's also an excellent display on the history of the Apaches.

Apple Annie's Orchard

The Sulphur Springs Valley outside of Willcox has the perfect growing conditions for the apple, peach, pear, and Asian pear orchards at Apple Annie's (2081 N. Hardy Rd., Willcox, 520/384-2084, www.appleannies.com, July 3–Oct. 31 daily 8 A.M.–5:30 P.M.). From July to late October every year people flock to the "u-pick" farm to pick and purchase fruit by the bucketful. The farm also serves delicious hamburgers and cowboy beans for lunch, and you can buy all kinds of homemade preserves, sauces, condiments, and pies in the farm store. Take I-10 to exit 340, turn west on Fort Grant Road, and travel 5.5 miles to the Apple Annie's sign.

◖ Amerind Foundation Museum

On your way east on I-10, get off at the Dragoon exit (exit 318) to visit this excellent little museum (520/586-3666, www.amerind.org, Tues.–Sun. 10 A.M.–4 P.M., $8 adult, $5 child 12–18) in beautiful Texas Canyon. Established in 1937, the Amerind Foundation (Amerind is a

© TIM HULL

the Amerind Foundation Museum

THE WESTERN DESERT

Southwest of Tucson, the vast desert home-land of the Tohono O'odham Nation stretches out, a hot wasteland where few dare to venture. You can reach this 4,400-square-mile borderland reservation via Highway 86 west of Tucson, but there isn't much out there except gorgeous, mostly untouched desert. Straddling the border, the reservation is a popular, albeit deadly, corridor for illegal immigrants heading north, and dozens die crossing the reservation every year—only the O'odham know how to live out here.

About 90 minutes west of Tucson along Highways 86 and 386 (follow the signs), you'll find another of Southern Arizona's famous observatories. **Kitt Peak National Observatory** (520/318-8726, www.noao. edu, daily 9 A.M.-3:45 P.M., $2 suggested donation) operates 23 telescopes—the world's largest collection—atop the 6,875-foot peak in the reservation's Quinlan Mountains. Docent-led tours are available at 10 A.M., 11:30 A.M., and 1:30 P.M. and last about an hour ($4 adult, $2.50 child 6-12), or you can pick up a pamphlet and take a self-guided tour. The visitors center has exhibits on astronomy and a gift shop selling star- and planet-related items and O'odham baskets. Far off to the west, look for 7,700-foot Baboquivari Peak, the home of I'itoi, the tribe's sacred "elder brother" god.

The reservation capital, Sells, is a small outpost about 58 miles southwest of Tucson on Highway 86. There's a supermarket, a few businesses, offices, and a school. During the first weekend in February, O'odham cowboys join in the All Indian Rodeo and Fair, during which locals set up food booths, play music, march in a parade, dance, and show off and sell their crafts. Continue through the thick desert west on Highway 86 and you'll hit Ajo, a copper mining community with a few restaurants and a good place to see the scars that strip mining leaves open on the land.

South of Ajo on Highway 85, past the tiny town of Why, you'll find **Organ Pipe Cactus National Monument**. This rugged, beautiful monument along the border protects what amounts to pretty much all the organ pipe cacti in North America, along with many other species of cactus, and is a popular area for seeing spring wildflowers in bloom. It has in the past been named one of the most dangerous national monuments in the country, as the area is a major drug-smuggling corridor, but it is safe to visit. Just make sure to lock your car, and don't stray off the well-traveled park roads. The Kris Eggle Visitor Center (520/387-6849, daily 8 A.M.-5 P.M.) is named for a ranger who was killed during a shootout with drug smugglers. A campground with 208

contraction of American and Indian) preserves and studies Native American cultures from prehistory all the way to the Chiricahua Apache and beyond. It is commonly thought to hold one of the best private ethnological collections in the nation. The museum is fascinating, and the location, among the imposing boulders of Texas Canyon, makes it well worth the stop.

Cochise Stronghold

A bit farther east on I-10, exit 331 takes you to the former hideout of Cochise and his band in the Dragoon Mountains. (Head southeast on U.S. 191, then west nine miles on Ironwood

Road; the last four miles are on a dirt road.) The great Apache chief is said to be buried somewhere out here, but nobody knows where for sure. It seems an ideal place to hide, with plenty of bluffs from which to watch the plains for the oncoming army. There are a few easy trails at the Stronghold, including a short nature trail and a paved history trail with information about the Chiricahua Apache. A few campsites ($12) are sheltered by the same high boulders that once kept the Chiricahua hidden. If you want to hike deeper into the canyon, try the six-mile round-trip Cochise Stronghold Trail that veers off the nature trail.

sites has drinking water but no hookups or facilities ($12 per night). The 21-mile Ajo Mountain Drive, on a twisty dirt road that's usually passable, will take you into the monument's center, where you can see the goofy, many-armed cacti up close.

© FRANK BACH/123RF.COM

Organ Pipe Cactus National Monument

◀ Chiricahua National Monument

This place simply has to be seen to be believed. Precarious rock spires jut into the sky in this strange, wonderful landscape, called the "Land of Standing-Up Rocks" by the Apache. About 38 miles southeast of Willcox (120 miles from Tucson) on Highway 186, the national monument (520/824-3560, www.nps.gov/chir, daily 8 A.M.–4:30 P.M., $5 adult over 15) protects one of the most unique areas in Arizona. There's a visitors center two miles from the monument entrance on Bonita Canyon Road, a paved two-lane road that you can drive up six gorgeous miles to **Massai Point** and one of the most spectacular overlooks this side of the Grand Canyon. The visitors center has an excellent free guide with information on all the trails within the monument, their length, and how to find the trailheads, and there's a free hikers shuttle available. You can camp at the Bonita Campground 0.5 mile from the visitors center ($12 per night, no hookups). Bring your own food and water to this special place; there's none available for miles in any direction.

RESTAURANTS

The only town of any size in the area is Willcox, and the fare there is rather bleak. There are a

© TIM HULL

Chiricahua National Monument

few chains, but it's best to come prepared with your own food to take along in the car. The **Plaza Restaurant** (1190 W. Rex Allen Dr., Willcox, 520/384-3819, $5–15) serves pretty good family-style American food and other dishes, and **Salsa Fiesta** (1201 W. Rex Allen Dr., Willcox, 520/384-4233, $5–10) has decent Mexican food.

HOTELS

There aren't a lot of non-chain places to stay out here, unless you're camping or you have your own rig. Willcox has a few interstate chains that are easy to find, and there are a few bed-and-breakfasts tucked away in the mountains. The bucolic **George Walker House** (2225 W. George Walker Ln., Portal, 520/558-2287, www.thegeorgewalkerhouse.com) in Portal, a small historic settlement in the Chiricahuas, offers wood stoves, wireless Internet, kitchens, and even a stocked fridge. The small inn is open to only one party at a time ($75–189 depending on how many people, up to 7) and is popular with bird-watchers and hikers. They

recommend calling at least three months in advance for a reservation.

PRACTICALITIES

For information and advice on getting out into the less-accessible regions of the Chiricahua range, contact the **Douglas Ranger District** (1192 W. Saddleview Rd., 520/364-3468, Mon.–Fri. 8 A.M.–4:30 P.M.), 2.2 miles north of Highway 80 on U.S. 191 in Douglas.

Getting There and Around

A trip to this area takes you to some fairly remote places, so I'd recommend, just this once, shooting here as quick as you can along the 75-mile-per-hour I-10. It's an 82-mile drive to Willcox from Tucson, and from there it's another 38 miles to Chiricahua National Monument southeast along Highway 186. Gas up before you leave Willcox, and bring food and water and whatever else you think you might want. All the other sights in this section can be easily accessed off I-10 before you get to Willcox, and are well signed.

BACKGROUND

The Land

The Sonoran Desert is a deceptive landscape. The soft greens and yellows can appear monotonous, yet stop and look closely and they reveal staggering variety. It rains here only rarely, yet during the summer rainy season this arid land is positively lush. Once a year, in the spring, the land bursts with otherwise dormant wildflowers, like a one-night-only command performance. The region is dominated by desert, a flat land stretching out like a vast forgotten sea, yet increase your elevation into one of the region's sky islands and you will be hunting for tropical birds in a misty creekbed among oak and pine, or, if you go high enough, clamping on a pair of skis.

The Sonoran Desert is a much more varied desert than others in North America. Southern Arizona, of which Tucson is the largest city by far—really the only metro area of any size—is often referred to by those who study the region's biomes, as the sky islands. The region's "sky island" mountain ranges, some of which reach heights of 10,000 feet above sea level or more, are high, isolated mountains looking out over a sea of arid desert, and as such they support an astonishing variety of plants and animals. It's often said that driving from the desert floor in Tucson, at around 2,000 feet above sea level, to the top of nearby Mount Lemmon, at just above 9,000

© TIM HULL

feet—about an hour's drive—is akin, biologically speaking, to traveling from Mexico to Canada. The region's mountain ranges—the Santa Catalina Mountains north of Tucson, the Santa Rita Mountains to the south, the Rincon Mountains to the east, the Huachuca Mountains to the southeast, and other ranges farther east near the New Mexico border—represent a transitional zone from the colder Rocky Mountains to the more tropical and subtropical Sierra Madre Occidental in Mexico. The mid-ranges of the mountains are dominated by Madrean evergreen woodlands or Mexican oak-pine woodlands. Sometimes the whole region is referred to as the Madrean Archipelago. On the slopes of these mountains, called the "bajada," scrub oak turns into desert trees such as mesquite and palo verde, and at the base there are sometimes vast semi-desert grasslands sweeping across the land.

And in the middle of all this natural diversity and beauty sits Arizona's second-largest city, Tucson, the county seat of Pima County. It's not always necessary to delineate the Tucson metro area from Pima County as a whole; indeed, Tucson is really the primary metropolitan hub for four counties in the southern section of Arizona—Pima County, Cochise County to the southeast, Pinal County to the northwest, and Santa Cruz County to the south.

Created in 1864 around the same time as the Territory of Arizona, Pima County has about 9,184 square miles with elevations that range from 1,200 feet to 9,157 feet on top of Mount Lemmon in the Santa Catalina range, which looms over the northern portion of Tucson and adds significantly to the dramatic, exotic look of the city. Nearly half of the land in Pima County—about 42 percent—is set aside as reservations for the Tohono O'odham, formerly called the Papago, and the Pascua Yaqui, a small tribe of indigenous people that moved north from Mexico seeking refuge from persecution in the early 20th century. As is common in Arizona, a state created by the federal government out of a vast region gathered together under the indefinite rubric of New Mexico, only about 13 percent of the land in Pima County is privately owned. The rest, aside from the reservations, is either controlled by the state or the federal government. This, combined with the area's diverse natural wonders, is one of the main reasons Tucson has become a favorite spot for wilderness lovers and outdoorspeople.

Pima County has a population of about a million persons, about 530,000 of which live in the city of Tucson, making the Old Pueblo the nation's 32nd-largest city. Spread out and sprawling, Tucson comprises about 192 square miles and sits at an elevation of 2,389 feet above sea level. The city is connected to the rest of the nation via I-10, and is connected to Mexico, just 60 miles south, by I-19.

CLIMATE

One of the hottest deserts in the world, the Sonoran differs from other arid regions in North America in that it has mild winters.

Many Tucson residents harvest rainwater using collectors like this one.

IS IT GETTING EVEN HOTTER IN TUCSON?

According to at least one University of Arizona researcher, people have made it hotter in Tucson than it already was–and it was already the hottest desert in North America before we arrived en masse after World War II to begin changing the wilderness into car-centric, fossil fuel-dependent cities and suburbs. UA professor emeritus William Sellers, in a chapter on the state's climate in *Natural Environments of Arizona,* finds that the state's "minimum temperature averaged significantly higher during the 1953-2002 period than it did prior to the early 1940s." This is proof, Sellers writes, of the urban heat island effect, through which nighttime temperatures (which in other less-paved-over deserts tend to drop significantly, offering a cooling respite to the land while the sun is down) stay rather high because the heat is stored in buildings and asphalt. Indeed, Sellers finds that the average minimum temperature in the Phoenix area has increased by nearly seven degrees Fahrenheit since the early 1960s, while the average maximum temperature has gone up only about two degrees Fahrenheit in that time. Apparently we love the heat so much we never want it to cool down. Additionally, Sellers writes, average nighttime temperatures in the state's deserts were significantly lower prior to the 1940s than they are today. Temperatures as low as zero degrees Fahrenheit were recorded along washes in the Tucson area, and in 1937 Tucson's temperatures were below normal every day for a month. "The most likely cause for most of the increase in the average temperature in Arizona since the early 1940s is the rapid expansion in the population and the industrial development that occurred in the area during and following World War II," Sellers concludes.

There are only a few nights throughout the year when newscasters come on the air and breathlessly implore Tucsonans to bring their plants inside for fear of an overnight frost. According to the Center for Sonoran Desert Studies, nearly half the flora and fauna in the region are "tropical in origin." One of the defining climate characteristics of Tucson and the surrounding deserts and mountains is the unique bi-seasonal rain pattern. While Tucson typically receives less than 12 inches of rainfall annually—often much less; the region has been gripped by an ongoing drought for at least a decade—nearly all of the region's precipitation comes during just two brief rainy seasons. The most important of these is the summer rainy season, locally referred to as the monsoon, when, from July through (hopefully) about mid-September, surges of wet, tropical air move up from the south and build over the mountains, creating often violent, localized thunderstorms, mostly in the late afternoon and early evening after a long, hot summer day. The most violent monsoon storms, sometimes called "gully washers" or flash floods, can swell the region's usually dry riverbeds and washes in a matter of minutes. To say that these storms are "localized" is an understatement. It's a common joke in Tucson—though no less true for being a joke—that, during the monsoon, one can often observe rain falling in one's front yard but not in the back. One side of town can be awash in a flash flood, while a few miles away the sun is beating down clear and unbroken, without a cloud in the sky. The strength and, so to speak, success of the monsoon can vary greatly from year to year. For example, according to data collected by the National Weather Service in Tucson, in 1964 the monsoon season yielded an amazing 13.84 inches of rain in Tucson; in 2004, however, the area received just 2.42 inches of rain during the same season. The winter rainy season lasts from roughly October to March and is not as localized, nor as closely watched, as the monsoon. If winter brings a fair amount of precipitation to the desert, however, then the whole landscape explodes with dormant annual wildflowers, and the normally monotone landscape is transformed into a patchwork of colors.

ENVIRONMENTAL ISSUES

With its delicate and finely balanced biomes and some of the most dramatic and exotic scenery on earth, Arizona has over the generations been a haven, a laboratory, and a rallying point for environmentalists and ecologists. One of the biggest threats to the state's extremely varied ecosystems is growth; much of the desert has been paved over and crowded with homes, while the upland forests host droves of overbuilt homes just waiting for a wildfire to burn them to their foundations. There are no signs that this trend is going to let up any time soon, either. The constant influx of people has led over the years to environmental problems far beyond the mere pavement of desert and clearing of forests. Growth and the state's founding impetus to glean profit from the land have led to the overpumping of groundwater and the damming and taming of most of the state's rivers. This has altered the green riverways so completely that many species of native fish are now as good as gone, and nonnative plants line the mostly dry riverbeds, crowding out native riverine flora like cottonwoods and willows.

Climate change, scientists say, is likely to increase the state's environmental woes, and, coupled with an ongoing drought that has been more or less eating away at the state for over a decade, may lead to shortages on the Colorado River, water from which the vast majority of urban Arizonans, including Tucsonans, depend. Some scientists have recently predicted that Lake Mead may dry up by 2025, while others believe the current human culture in Arizona may, one day in the future, suffer the same collapse as did the Anasazi, the Hohokam, and other complex societies who have tried to make a go of it here, leaving behind the ruins of their rise and fall but not much else.

Flora and Fauna

FLORA
Wildflowers

In the early spring, especially after a rainy winter, the desert bajadas and valleys bloom with color as dormant wildflowers burst back to life. Various shades of photogenic whites, yellows, blues, reds, and purples contrast with the uniform rich green of the well-watered springtime desert to create a truly beautiful but ephemeral scene. Some of the most common bloomers are the light-purple **Arizona lupine,** the deep-yellow **Mexican goldpoppy,** the dark-pink **Parry pestemon,** and the virginal-white **desert lily.** In summer the northland meadows and grasslands bloom with wild color as well.

Trees, Cacti, and Bushes

Below 3,500 feet or so the Lower Sonoran Life Zone predominates, characterized by **creosote, palo verde,** and **mesquite** trees on the plains and thick stands of various cacti and other dry-adapted plants on the slopes and bajadas. Arizona is the only state where three major deserts converge: The Sonoran stretches across the southern portion of the state and includes the Phoenix and Tucson areas, while the Mojave dominates on the western reaches. The Chihuahuan Desert of Mexico stretches north into southeastern Arizona.

Between 4,500 and about 7,000 feet you're in the Upper Sonoran Life Zone, characterized by scrub oak, piñon pine, juniper, manzanita, and sagebrush grasslands; this zone is often called the chaparral. The midlands of the state, at around 6,000 feet and higher, are marked by the transition zone, and this is where you start to see the beginnings of the vast ponderosa pine forests. Above 8,500 feet or so thick

A DESERT AT RISK

In a June 12, 2008, review in the *New York Review of Books*, physicist Freeman Dyson wrote, "Environmentalism, as a religion of hope and respect for nature, is here to stay. This is a religion we can all share, whether or not we believe that global warming is harmful."

Yet it seems most of us need a local connection and ground-level evidence to spur a lifestyle change. Desert dwellers can turn to the research of Travis Huxman, director of the University of Arizona's Biosphere 2 lab and an associate professor of ecology and evolutionary biology, to understand why going green matters. Huxman and his colleagues are using that infamous bubble in the desert north of Tucson to find out how climate change and drought are changing the very desert under our feet.

"Deserts are very sensitive to change; you see big impacts in deserts before you might see them somewhere else," Huxman said during an interview at his campus office. He says that in the desert most of the effects of climate change are reflected in the way soil moisture changes, and that he's finding more boom-and-bust soil water characteristics, which means that sometimes there is a lot of moisture and other times there is no moisture at all. This is all leading to a change in the kind of plants we see in the desert.

That means more scrub is growing in the desert, leading to a movement toward a grassland-type system that is dominated by nonnative species. That in turn causes an accelerated fire cycle and changes in biodiversity—changes, Huxman explains, to "the very desert landscape that makes this area so attractive to tourists, and [that lead to] less resilient landscapes for ranching and other uses of the desert." And that includes potentially catastrophic changes to the watershed.

This means that big, representative species of the Sonoran Desert, most notably the mighty saguaro, are living under a very real threat. We could lose the saguaro and other large components of the desert because of fires sparked by invasive grasses, which are spreading as a direct result of global climate change. It's happening in North America's other deserts as well. In the Mojave Desert to the west, the great Joshua tree is similarly threatened, says Huxman.

"I don't have a projection for how long it would take [for the desert to fundamentally change as a result of drought and climate change], but you can hardly drive a freeway through the North American deserts and not see this change and the impact of fire on these landscapes," Huxman says. "It's fairly obvious."

Though a survey of the Sonoran is yet to be done, an assessment of the Great Basin Desert found that some 40 percent of the landscape has been affected by nonnative grasses, leading to a significant change in the character of the desert. In Arizona, such changes are most evident in the high deserts of the state's north-central pine belt. There the largest ponderosa pine forest in North America is on the verge of total collapse. The conifers are stressed due to drought, and that stress allows bark beetles and other killers to dig in, which in turn leaves this typically fire-resistant species ready to burn. And once they're gone, will they grow back, or has the ecosystem changed irrevocably? But that's not even the biggest problem, according to Huxman. What we don't know yet is how the water cycle will react if a single dominant species like the ponderosa pine is no longer part of the ecosystem. "That's the big research question," Huxman says. "How will all this affect water?...That's our problem on many different scales: How water and energy are related; so the most important thing we can do now is to remember that when we are thinking about energy efficiency, we are also thinking about water efficiency at the same time."

In other words, it's all related. When you turn off the lights, when you use a reusable tote instead of a throwaway bag, when you ride your bike to work, when you change to energy-saving lightbulbs—when you "go green" by making all those small, easy changes that are becoming so popular these days—you are also saving water. And water is one of the very few things that all of us will always need.

THE SAGUARO AND OTHER NATIVE CACTI

© TIM HULL

To the native inhabitants of the Sonoran Desert—be they cactus wrens, coyotes, screech owls, or Tohono O'odham tribespeople—the saguaro (pronounced sa-WAH-ro) is much more than a strange-looking plant. It is so supremely adapted to the arid environment, in which moisture from the sky comes but twice a year, that it anchors an entire busy community of living things, providing food and shelter to all sorts of desert creatures. The great cactus-tree grows slowly, and only during the summer rainy season. After living, shaded and protected by a mesquite tree, for 15 years, a saguaro is still only about a foot tall. But, then again, these green-ribbed giants can live to be 150 years old or more, so there's really no hurry. Not until it reaches 75 years old does a saguaro even begin to sprout its identifying arms; so when you see a tall, fat one with many arms, know that it is a venerable old guy, deserving of respect and awe.

The saguaro looks like it does because it is perfect: Every part has a function. Its green skin allows for photosynthesis, normally the job of leaves on less individualistic plants. Its spongy flesh and ribbed contours encourage water storage; from a single rainfall the saguaro can collect and store up to 200 gallons of water, which is enough to get it through the year. Its telltale needles protect it from the incessant gnawing of hungry desert creatures. Its splashy white blossoms (Arizona's official state flower, seen in April, May, and June) and juicy red fruits (eaten for eons by the desert's native inhabitants) ensure the rising of another generation. The best place to commune with these perfectly adapted desert plants is Saguaro National Park near Tucson.

You'll see various other species of cactus throughout the lower and into the upper Sonoran zones. Most cacti are easily recognizable if you know their names: Organ pipe, barrel, beaver tail, claret cup, and hedgehog cactus generally look like their sobriquets suggest, albeit spiky and standoffish versions. The famous prickly pear cactus can be identified by its red fruit-blooms, which are turned into jellies and even margarita mix.

stands of evergreen conifers and white aspen are common. Above 9,500 feet or so, a height reached in Arizona primarily by climbing up towering mountains, the Subalpine Zone has tough Engelmann spruce and bristlecone pine, and above that it's all barren rocks and tundra.

The official Arizona state tree is the palo verde, a green-skinned desert dweller that can grow up to 25 feet high. The tree proliferates throughout the Lower Sonoran Life Zone and is often a close neighbor to the saguaro, the baby buds of which use the palo verde's cover to hide and grow. Other common desert trees are the ubiquitous mesquite, which has often been used for firewood and building, and its beans have nourished people and animals alike. Both the mesquite and the palo verde bloom yellow in the spring. Ironwood trees and drought-resistant evergreens grow along slopes and washes in the desert. Bushy plants crowd the desert as well; creosote is everywhere, as is prickly **catclaw** and **rabbitbrush,** all of which bloom yellow. Adding a little red to the bloom time is the **ocotillo,** which is everywhere in the desert and resembles a sprouting group of pipe cleaners. Throughout the desert and into the chaparral of the transition zones you'll see several species of **agave,** an important plant to the human population in that it can be turned into mescal and tequila. The *Agave parryi,* or **century plant,** blooms only once, with a tall stalk of yellow flowers, before dying.

In the scrublands and chaparral and higher you'll see scrub oak, piñon pine, juniper, manzanita, and other brushy trees. In the high country, above 6,000 feet or so, you'll see ponderosa pine mainly. Higher still, in the montane forests at the highest elevations, fir, spruce, and aspen forests dominate. Along many waterways, called riparian areas, are big cottonwoods and willows and sycamores.

You are likely to see javelina in the desert.

FAUNA
Mammals

Arizona's official state mammal is the **ringtail,** a relative of the raccoon, often called a ringtail cat or a miner's cat because of its rodent-eating proclivities. Its huge, bushy, white-and-black-ringed tail is its identifying feature, but it's not likely you'll see one unless you're nocturnal. The **mountain lion,** or cougar, is found, and hunted, throughout the state; smaller **bobcats** are often seen lounging near water features in Sonoran Desert backyards, and scrawny **coyotes** can be spotted quickly crossing highways throughout the state. In the western deserts a few **bighorn sheep** still cling to the dry, rocky cliffs.

A few different species of **jackrabbit** can be found all over, and **white-tailed** and **mule deer** live from the bottom of the Grand Canyon to the mountain heights and most places in between. **Pronghorn** live on the high grasslands in herds. The **collared peccary,** or **javelina,** is everywhere in the desert and the transition zone, so much so that they are considered pests to some. The **black bear** lives in the mountains throughout the state, and various species of **bats** come out in the Arizona night, responsible for pollinating and continuing the state's signature cactus forests.

Reptiles

The desert is known as the home of the rattler, a snake seen more and more these days as the suburban attack on the desert continues. There are a few species of rattlesnake found in Arizona. The **western diamondback,** which has lent its name to the state's world-champion baseball team, lives in the desert and the mountains and has deadly venom. Its snakeskin is gray with brown, diamond-shaped splotches along the back and a series of black-and-white bands just above the rattle. As with nearly all

© HILMA ANDERSON123RF.COM

The gila monster is the only venomous lizard in the United States.

animals, the diamondback will leave you alone if you afford it the same courtesy. The light-brown **western rattlesnake** lives throughout the state, and the **Arizona ridge-nosed rattlesnake,** a reddish-brown or gray hunter of rodents and lizards, lives in the woodlands of southeastern Arizona.

Several different species of **lizard** can be seen all over the lowlands, doing push-ups on hot rocks. The desert's most recognizable residents, these tiny leftover dinosaurs come in many shapes and sizes. One of the biggest is the fat and venomous **gila monster,** with its beady skin and languid looks. The monster can sometimes be seen sunning itself in and around Tucson. The only venomous lizard in the United States, it should be given a wide berth if encountered.

The slow and wise **desert tortoise** hides out from the desert sun in its burrow, and if it makes it past its soft-shell youth, when it's a favorite of predatory birds, it can live up to a hundred years or more. Frogs and toads in Arizona include the **Arizona treefrog,** a lime-green forest resident, and the **western spadefoot toad,** which lives in the desert in a burrow and is a blotchy greenish brown with gray tints.

Insects

The **bark scorpion** is the crabby, pinching demon of the desert underworld; its venom is dangerous if it finds its way to the blood. The **grand western cicada** makes a racket in the woodlands on summer evenings. The hirsute **desert tarantula** looks much meaner than it is, cruising about in the early morning and early evening. You're bound to encounter gnats and mosquitoes and other tiny pests in desert riparian areas and around upland lakes.

THE BORDERLAND JAGUAR DETECTION PROJECT

Retired land surveyor and mountain-lion hunter Jack Childs and his wife, retired educator Anna Childs, founded the Borderland Jaguar Detection Project in 2001, several years after they'd become members of the very exclusive group of humans ever to see the roaring jungle cat in the wild. Researchers now believe, based on the work of the Childses and others, that the jaguar reaches the northernmost edge of its vast range in the misty, watered canyons of the neotropical Arizona borderlands.

As the Childses tell it in their book *Ambushed on the Jaguar Trail: Hidden Cameras on the Mexican Border*, the couple first encountered the jaguar while out riding mules in the Baboquivari Mountains, in late summer 1996, not really hunting so much as giving their lion hounds a chance to stretch their legs after being cooped up all summer. As hunting hounds will do, the dogs soon picked up a scent and followed it to its natural conclusion. But when the Childses arrived to see what beast the dogs had treed, expecting it to be a cougar, they found instead a spotted male jaguar resting calmly on a limb. Their lives were never the same.

The Childses cobbled together a few grants and donations to eventually begin their ambitious detection project, which is an ongoing and integral part of the efforts of the Arizona–New Mexico Jaguar Conservation Team. The couple, working with a few other researchers, place heat-and-motion-detecting "camera traps" in ideal jaguar habitat throughout the borderlands, and visit them regularly to change film and batteries. The project has been responsible for photographing, many times, two distinct male jaguars—called Macho A and Macho B—who stalk the canyons and mountains just north of the U.S.-Mexico border. The Childses have yet to photograph female jaguars, or to prove that Arizona's jaguars are anything but opportunistic wanderers, perhaps from a well-known resident population of male and female jaguars in the Sonoran wilds about 150 miles south of Douglas.

The Macho sightings have been enough to keep the project going, and that's as it should be. However, as the Childses' book makes clear, the longed-for jaguar is only one of more than 20 other large mammals that appear in the project's photographs—including *Homo sapiens*. Those photos show black bears playing and eating; cougars tussling around like house cats, marking their territory, and hunting; bobcats doing likewise; as well as various raccoons, coatis, skunks, foxes, ringtails, badgers, bovines, and many other borderland creatures doing what they do when we're not watching. These photographs show us a hidden, often nocturnal world of predator and prey, and a bustling dimension of the Arizona backcountry in which our own arbitrary borders have no meaning. The cameras have even photographed at least two species—the Gould's turkey and the Mexican brown-nosed opossum—that were thought to be all but gone from this region.

In a sad postscript to this story, in early 2009 Game and Fish officials out hunting for mountain lions and black bears to tag and collar as part of a large mammal research study came across Macho B and made a quick field decision to collar the jaguar in an effort to learn more about the elusive cats. A few weeks later the radio information sent from the collar suggested that Macho B was sick. Game and Fish veterinarians quickly moved in and discovered that Macho B was in the advance stages of kidney failure. The cat died a short time later while being treated at the Phoenix Zoo. I contacted the Childses shortly after the tragic event to express my sympathy, and this is what Jack had to say: "Macho B has left a great legacy. We will continue our quest for Macho C or maybe even Hema (female) A."

History

The Tucson region is one of the oldest continually inhabited areas in the United States; there's a record of human existence in the valleys and mountains of Southern Arizona going back some 12,000 years.

In the 1930s, University of Arizona archaeologists began an archaeological dig on the Tohono O'odham Reservation southwest of Tucson, in Ventana Cave, named for a nearby hole in a rock outcropping that resembles a window (*ventana* is Spanish for window). Over the course of the dig, the archaeologists found a record of more than 10,000 years of regular human use of the cave, including 39 bodies of "pottery-bearing" and even "preceramic" peoples. While such hunter-gatherers living light on the land likely dominated this area for thousands of years, the first relatively complex culture to settle in the river valleys around Tucson—including the Santa Cruz River Valley south of the city, and the San Pedro River Valley to the southeast, were the Hohokam people. They lived in the region, farming using irrigation canals, from about A.D. 200 to about 1450.

By the time the Spanish arrived in what is now Southern Arizona, and what at the time was the far northern edge of the New World, the Hohokam were gone and their likely ancestors, the Tohono O'odham ("the desert people," called the Papago for centuries) and the Akmiel O'odham (the "river people," called the Pima for centuries) had settled in the Tucson area at the base of Sentinel Peak west of downtown and along the area's rivers, which in those times were likely year-round streams that provided an abundance of food and other resources. It is widely believed that the name Tucson came from the Pima word *schookson,* which roughly translates to "spring at the foot of Black Mountain"—the black mountain in this case being the basalt Sentinel Peak. The Spanish also found another group of indigenous people living in Southern Arizona, the Apache. An Athabaskan tribe that moved into the area

a century or more before the Spanish arrived, the Apache were at that time a semi-nomadic, hunter-gatherer culture that had a habit of raiding their neighbors and drawing the unending ire of the Spanish, then the Mexicans, then the Americans, before finally being defeated by the U.S. Army after a long and bloody war. Their descendants now live on reservations in northeastern and central Arizona.

While the famed Coronado expedition to discover the mythical Seven Cities of Cíbola moved through southeastern Arizona in the 1540s, it wasn't until the 1690s, when the hardy Jesuit adventurer Father Eusebio Francisco Kino began his journeys into Southern Arizona and Sonora, that regular contact between the Spanish and the natives began. Kino brought cattle with him to the region for the first time and established several long-lasting missions including San Xavier del Bac near Tucson, to this day still celebrating Mass in its dark, cool interior. By the 1750s the Spanish crown had established a presidio, or fort, at Tubac, which was moved to the Tucson valley in 1775. Southern Arizona comprised the northern reaches of the Spanish New World empire, though it was sparsely populated and a violent, dangerous place to live. Spanish cattle ranchers and other hardy settlers fought Apaches and others for the right to live in the region, but for decades the north would remain too isolated and too dangerous to grow much. The Mexicans won their independence from Spain in 1821 and so took over administration of the vast northlands. The wilderness was exploited somewhat for its resources, used for cattle ranching and placer mining by tough Mexican explorers, but mostly it was too far from the center of power and had too many dangerous Indians to be of much worth to the new nation.

In the later 1820s trappers, hunters, and mountain men like James Ohio Pattie, Antoine Leroux, and Pauline Weaver became some of the first Anglo-Americans to venture through Arizona, in search of beaver pelts. Such men

THE TOHONO O'ODHAM TODAY

Here in the Southwest, where many native peoples and traditions are celebrated and studied, people are trying to survive in the post-modern world while holding on to some sense of their indigenous identity. The Tohono O'odham, who were already living in the Tucson valley when Capt. Hugh O'Conner rode north from Tubac in 1775 to establish El Presidio de San Agustín del Tucson, are one such native people.

According to **TOCA: Tohono O'odham Community Action** (520/383-4966, www.tocaonline.org), an O'odham-led nonprofit community development group, the "Desert People" have had mixed success in adapting to the modern world; it is a firm belief of such groups that going backward is the best way for the O'odham to move forward. For this, according to TOCA, they must return to the principles of *O'odham Himdag* ("The Desert People's Way").

They used to be called the Papago, a name given to them by the Spanish; there are about 28,000 members of the Tohono O'odham Nation, about 20,000 of which live on the sprawling desert reservation southwest of Tucson, a seemingly forbidding patch of Sonoran Desert the size of Connecticut that has been providing the Desert People with sustenance—though a hard-won sustenance to be sure—for eons.

These days, however, despite the fact that the O'odham operate two successful casinos near Tucson and are poised to build a huge casino-resort in the west of Phoenix, small-scale economic life on the reservation isn't exactly overflowing with plenty. TOCA says that the per-capita average income on the reservation is about $6,998 per year, far below the national average of about $22,000. Moreover, 50 percent or more of O'odham adults have Type II diabetes (the numbers for the United States as a whole are between 4 and 6 percent). TOCA goes on to say that fewer than half of reservation adults have even a high school education, putting them at the bottom of all Native American tribes in the United States in terms of education. And worse still, the group is worried that the Tohono O'odham language and their unique cultural traditions, ceremonies, and knowledge about the desert are in danger of dying out within a few generations.

In order to solve these seemingly insurmountable social realities, TOCA says it's committed to developing "indigenous solutions, rather than focus[ing] on the problems while importing the 'solutions' from the outside." But what does that mean in practice? Well, take for instance the diabetes problem, a health crisis of staggering proportions on the reservation today. In 1960 diabetes was completely absent from the reservation, TOCA says, adding that the cause of the epidemic over the last 50 years or so has been the "destruction of the traditional food systems and diet." Indeed, studies have shown that traditional O'odham foods like tepary beans, cholla cactus buds, wild spinach, corn, and squash served to regulate the O'odham's blood sugar, and that the sudden switch to a completely different diet over the last several decades has sent this age-old system out of whack. As a result of such studies, TOCA has begun to develop a food program that puts some of the old ways back into the O'odham diet. They've also instituted programs to revive the tribe's basket-weaving traditions, and to bring together youths and tribal elders in hopes that the Desert People's collective cultural memory survives for centuries to come.

If you're interested in learning more about the O'odham—their lifeways, their history, and their present—head west on Highway 86 across the reservation toward Sells and the **Tohono O'odham Nation Cultural Center and Museum** (520/383-0211, www.tonation-nsn.gov), in Topawa (seven miles south of Sells on Route 19). It's about a 70-mile drive that'll probably take about two hours.

PADRE KINO

More than 300 years after he first rode into this valley, the name Eusebio Francisco Kino still has meaning here.

The pious, intellectual, and exceedingly tough padre who, among many other accomplishments, established this region's world-renowned mission system and introduced cattle ranching to the Santa Cruz Valley, is a unifying figure in this culturally mixed locale.

"At a time when there is so much violence on both sides of the border, let this man of peace bring us together; let us remember a higher calling, and find it in Kino," said Gloria Alvillar, an organizer and member of the nonprofit group Patronato de Kino, who recently returned from a visit to the padre's hometown of Segno, Italy.

One of the stated goals of Patronato de Kino is to "promote Padre Kino to beatification," or sainthood.

Raul Ramirez, the secretary of Patronato de Kino, said, "We think about him as a symbol of hope. In the Catholic tradition you pray to saints for intercession with God, and we think that Kino would be a good symbol of unity; he tried to unite the tribes of Pimería Alta, and we are looking at him as a source of unity again."

The road to beatification, however, is a hard one. It may even be longer and more difficult than the thousands of arid and dangerous miles the padre traveled in the latter 1600s to arrive in what is now Southern Arizona and northern Sonora, where he not only attempted to convert the native people to his way of thinking but also introduced new lifeways.

would in turn guide the Army of the West and the Mormon Battalion through the state in 1846 and 1847 during the Mexican War.

After the war ended in 1848, much of what is now the Southwest became U.S. property, and in 1850 a huge area that included Arizona and New Mexico became the New Mexico Territory. In 1854 the land between the Gila River and the Mexican border—Southern Arizona, basically, some 29,644 acres—was added to the territory through the Gadsden Purchase at a price of about $10 million.

Beginning in 1849 and lasting for several years afterward, thousands of Americans passed through Arizona headed for gold and glory in California. Those hard-rock, hard-luck miners would return east to the state a few years later in search of the gold and silver most of them had failed to find on the coast. Several boundary, land, railroad, and scientific surveys of Arizona and the West during the 1850s brought this far corner of the continent greater attention and interest from the East.

It was the increasing mining activity in the state that, among other factors, led President Lincoln to establish the Arizona Territory in 1863, disconnecting it from the huge conglomerate of land called New Mexico. The capital was established at Prescott, in the state's mineral-laden midlands, and the East's economic exploitation of the land, albeit on a much smaller scale than it would eventually become, commenced. During the Civil War, Tucson was a Confederate hotbed for a time before being occupied by the U.S. Army. After the Civil War ended, immigration and exploration of the Southwest picked up considerably. Still, when John Wesley Powell completed the first river-run through the Grand Canyon in 1869, the population of the territory was less than 10,000 persons.

Indeed, for many years before and after the Gadsden Purchase and the Civil War, Tucson remained a sparsely populated outpost in a far, forgotten corner of the world. When journalist J. Ross Browne made a journey through Arizona and Sonora with Charles Poston, one of the first American pioneers to try his luck at mining and ranching in Southern Arizona, Browne had this to say about the far-flung outback (from a series of articles about the territory published in *Harper's Monthly* in 1864 and 1865):

> At the period of its purchase Arizona was practically a terra incognita. Hunters and trappers had explored it to some extent; but their accounts of its resources and peculiarities were of a vague and marvelous character, according well with their wild habits of life. Few people in the United States knew anything about it, save the curious bookworms who had penetrated into the old Spanish records. An impression prevailed that it was a worthless desert, without sufficient wood or water to sustain a population of civilized beings. Mr. Gadsden was ridiculed for his purchase, and it was very generally believed that Congress, in expending ten millions of dollars for such an arid waste, had in view some ulterior project of extension, based upon the balance of power between the Northern and Southern states. It was even hinted that this was to be a grand reservoir for disappointed office-seekers, who could be effectually disposed of by means of Territorial appointments.

But settlers trickled in over the coming years, spurred here to cure their tuberculosis, or there in search of treasure, adventure, science, or cheap land. Despite this, the territory remained a wild and dangerous place for most. The Apache, Navajo, and other tribes didn't feel they should have to give up the land they had conquered to white settlers, many of whom were looking to get rich quick by exploiting the land and then leave. From 1871 until the final surrender of Geronimo in 1886, the U.S. Army fought a brutal war with the Apache and other tribes. The Apache finally beaten, the territory moved one step closer to large-scale settlement and development.

From 1867 to 1877 Tucson was the capital of the Arizona Territory, until that distinction was handed over for good to the growing, largely American town of Phoenix, about 100 miles north in the Salt River Valley. On March 20, 1880, the Southern Pacific Railroad arrived in Tucson and completely transformed the city, bringing in more people and materials than ever before. By 1882, with a population of about 8,000 persons, the once-isolated adobe village could boast gas lights and even a few telephones.

STATEHOOD AND BEYOND

Arizona became a state on February 14, 1912. The first half of the 20th century in Southern Arizona and the rest of the state was dominated by the era of reclamation. The federal government used taxpayer money to develop the state's water resources—damming rivers for irrigation, water storage, and hydroelectric power—creating a huge agricultural industry in the process. Phelps-Dodge and other mining giants ripped huge holes in the lands to extract low-grade copper, while American owners and managers on the whole treated the Mexican and Native American miners and pickers poorly, even criminally on many occasions.

At the same time, increasing numbers of residents and visitors began to realize that there was more to the fantastic Arizona landscape than profit and loss, and this era also saw the rise of national parks and monuments, national forests, and state-level protection of important lands. Beginning around the 1920s, boosters in Phoenix and Tucson and elsewhere began to see the economic benefits of attracting tourists to the sunny state, and by 1950 or so tourism had replaced the extractive industries in importance. During the two world wars the federal government set up training bases and military installations in the state that led to a growth spurt, and the advent of swamp coolers and air-conditioners stimulated a population boom in Arizona that has yet to really let up. By 1960 Tucson's population had nearly doubled in a decade's time, as it would continue to do over and over. Today, there are about a million people living in the dry basin, and they just keep coming.

THE HISTORY AND FUTURE OF DOWNTOWN TUCSON

© TIM HULL

downtown Tucson

Downtown Tucson, where the Old Pueblo began its life as a far-flung outpost of the Spanish crown a year before the eastern colonies declared their independence from the English crown, is a rather contradictory place. While it is overstuffed with all manner of fascinating historical landmarks, plaques, and mini-attractions, not to mention dozens of restaurants, bars, and clubs, most weekdays it's typically as deserted as the farthest corner of the scrubby desert come 5 P.M.

For well over a decade there has been a sometimes robust, often half-hearted, but always vigorously publicized city and state effort to "revitalize" Tucson's downtown and nearby historic districts. The effort, branded Rio Nuevo, has moved along in fits and starts.

The truth of it is, there's really nothing wrong with downtown that needs fixing. It's already a pretty cool place, if you know where to look. Plus, Tucson doesn't have a good record with urban renewal. Back in the 1960s and 1970s, as Tucsonans were increasingly shopping at malls out in the sprawl instead of downtown, the city decided to demolish many blocks of the Barrio Libre in favor of a sprawling convention center. Today, Barrio Histórico, basically what's left of the once large and dynamic Barrio Libre, is among the city's most aesthetically interesting and representative—and certainly most photographed—neighborhoods. Revitalization, as many developers and bureaucrats imagine it, can often be at odds with a city's best interest, which usually can be found not in demolishing and replacing, but in fixing up, patching, building on, and most importantly, preserving history.

A new kind of developer seems to be recognizing this, and even during the dark days of the economic downturn over the last few years, downtown and the university district have seen quite a bit of new development, including a modern streetcar project. Best of all, several new restaurants have opened downtown, repurposing some of the sturdy old redbrick buildings into exciting new spaces. Check out the **Hub Restaurant, Reilly Craft Pizza,** and **47 Scott** for gorgeous examples of revitalization done right.

HOWARD HUGHES IN TUCSON

Everybody's heard about those weird few years that Howard Hughes spent hiding out on the top floor of a Las Vegas hotel, going mad.

Well, there are hints that the Old Pueblo could have been the site of Hughes's infamous hideout instead of Vegas. Bob Maheu, Hughes's right-hand man and official public face during the Vegas years, told Geoff Schumacher, author of the 2008 book *Howard Hughes: Power, Paranoia, and Palace Intrigue,* that in the mid-1960s, before moving to Vegas, Hughes first considered moving to Tucson, where he'd already set up a manufacturing plant in 1951.

Hughes loved the desert, considering it free of the germs that stalked him. There's a great scene in *The Aviator* in which the young Hughes, played by Leonardo DiCaprio, sees a stand of saguaros in a film he's watching and whispers something like, "So clean . . ." Ultimately, though, Hughes soured on the desert around Las Vegas due to his inability to stop nuclear testing at the Nevada Test Site, fallout from which he obsessively feared.

While he never moved to Tucson, Hughes did of course have a presence here. Hughes Aircraft, employing thousands of workers, built the Falcon, the world's first air-to-air guided missile, and many other missiles and weapons here. Hughes Missile Systems was eventually bought up by Raytheon, which is today Southern Arizona's largest private employer.

Government and Economy

GOVERNMENT

Arizona's government has had a contrarian relationship with the federal establishment since before statehood. The state's entrance into the union was delayed for some time because the legislature, backed by a majority of the public, refused to give up a section of its constitution that allowed for the popular recall of judges. Today the bickering between the two continues over public-land issues and border control. The truth is that the federal government made Arizona, and it controls a good portion of the land in the state still. With history as an example, it's easy to see that had the federal government not protected huge portions of the state as national forests, monuments, parks, and wilderness areas, outside economic interests, mostly from the East, would have used them for their own profit, as they have the lion's share of Arizona's natural resources since long before statehood.

Like nearly everybody else, the state's government has, for most of its history, been interested in developing and taking from the land, and the various land-hungry interests that at one time or another were in favor—whether mining, agricultural, ranching, or military—have dictated policy. This is not true as much today as it has been in the past, however.

While Arizona is known today as a staunchly red (Republican) state, there are a few blue (Democrat) enclaves, notably Tucson and the Navajo Nation.

ECONOMY

Southern Arizona's economy for much of the past was ruled by the boom-and-bust realities of the extractive and agricultural industries. Worldwide prices, the fickleness of the market, and the constant threat of a destructive act of nature made economic life here before World War II a wild ride. Booms in the cattle industry in the 1890s and cotton before and during World War I created large industries in the state virtually overnight. The overgrazing of an arid open range and agricultural monoculture took their individual tolls, however, and both cattle and cotton really only influenced life here on a major scale for a relatively short time. Of the state economy's well-known

"Five C's"—copper, cotton, cattle, citrus, and climate—the others have fared better than cotton and cattle, both of which are now very minor elements of the state's economy. Copper mining, the state's claim to fame in economic circles for several generations, was nearly moribund until 2005, when worldwide prices hit record levels (thanks, in large part, to a global building boom centered in China, and the ubiquity of copper in consumer electronic products and other modern necessities). Previously mothballed pits have opened again, and start-up firms from outside the state are searching the desert for new pit sites. This may be just a blip on the overall economic radar screen, however. The extractive and agricultural industries are no longer the primary economic engines of Arizona and the West, and haven't been for some time. According to a report by the Tucson-based Sonoran Institute released on September 29, 2006, fewer than 5 percent of the West's counties have more than 20 percent of employment in traditional extractive industries, and agriculture and ranching made up just 4 percent of total employment in the West as of 2000. In the Tucson area in 2008, just 1.9 percent of workers were employed in mining and ranching, according to figures compiled by the Pima Association of Governments.

A boom in single-family housing and urban and suburban development has enraptured the state for several decades, though as of this writing that boom has predictably gone bust. Still, despite its boom-and-bust ways the state has often been somewhat impervious to national economic slowdowns, primarily because of its always-steady growth. Growth fuels itself, and an economy that is growing is always perceived to be healthy. Between 2000 and 2006 Arizona's population grew by about 20 percent. The deep truth of the Arizona economy, and one that holds for the entire West, is that the service industry (much of it tourism-related), with its low wages and transient workers, is the hottest running economic engine here—and has been for many years. All over the West non-labor income like investments, disability, and retirement payments come in a close second to the service industry as a top economic driver. The median household income in Arizona is about $44,000 with 2.6 people per household. Some 15 percent of Arizonans live below the poverty line.

More locally, Tucson has a somewhat diverse economy, but much of it is based on the service industry. Something like 85 percent of the jobs here are service-related, according to the Pima Association of Governments. Top employers in town include the University of Arizona, the city and county governments, and Raytheon, a company that makes weapons systems. The tourism industry is also a particularly robust employer in the Old Pueblo. The average annual income in the Old Pueblo is around $30,690, and the median household income is around $52,000.

People and Culture

Tucson has a few different faces. Exploring the city and its environs, it's difficult to escape constant reminders that not too long ago this land was considered not the southern end of the United States but rather the northern end of Mexico. Before that it belonged to Spain, before that the Tohono O'odham and the Apache, before that the Hohokam. For more than 10,000 years varied, sometimes contradictory, cultures have developed and adapted in this desert basin encircled by ragged ranges, and somehow they've mixed themselves up into a distinctive culture that one might call Southwestern. This is how it is in Tucson, where mixture is celebrated and studied, pulled apart, dissected, and turned around itself.

Many Tucson residents are émigrés, but there's definitely a much higher percentage of born-and-bred locals here than in Phoenix, Arizona's only other urban region of any size. Indeed, the majority of the state's 6.1 million residents live in Pima and Maricopa Counties, in and around the two large urban areas of Phoenix and Tucson—about a million persons live in Pima County and some 3.7 million live in Maricopa. About 13 percent of Arizonans are over 65, but 26 percent are under 18. The former statistic is expected to rise significantly as more and more baby boomers retire and move to the Sunbelt, just as their parents did in the 1960s and 1970s. On par with nationwide averages, about 81 percent of Arizonans are high school graduates, and 24 percent have at least a bachelor's degree. A full 68 percent of Arizonans own their homes.

Tucson has a larger percentage of Mexican American and other Latino residents than most other places. According to the U.S. Census Bureau, in 2000, Tucson's Hispanic population was 35.7 percent, compared to about 20 percent nationwide. Those numbers are expected to rise after the 2010 census is complete. According to a City of Tucson report, Latinos could once again become the majority population in Tucson by 2015.

The Arts

Tucson is the arts capital of Arizona, though some might consider this a somewhat dubious distinction. There are scores of artists and artisans who call the desert home, and there are galleries throughout the Old Pueblo showing everything from your basic cowboy-and-Indian portraits to the cutting-edge avant-garde. World-famous Southwestern artists like Ted DeGrazia and Maynard Dixon have called the Old Pueblo home.

The city is awash in the arts and images of Mexico, and that nation's folk arts are particularly popular as both tourist souvenirs and local decor. Despite being hundreds of miles from the Navajo and Hopi Reservations in northeastern Arizona, Tucson is known throughout the Southwest as a center for Native American arts, and February's **Indian Arts Fair** on the grounds of the University of Arizona's Arizona State Museum is one of the largest and most popular events of its kind.

Tucson's most famous resident, though she doesn't live here full-time, is Linda Ronstadt, the beloved singer who hit her peak in popular music in the 1970s but continues to sing and tour and is a very popular figure in the Old Pueblo, as her family dates back here to territorial times.

LITERATURE

Tucson has a literary tradition going back to its early days, and in the early 20th century the nation's best-selling author, Harold Bell Wright, moved to the city because of sickness and later claimed that Tucson had saved his life. Perhaps the three best-known authors to have lived in the Old Pueblo are Edward Abbey, J. A. Jance, and Pulitzer-winning Barbara Kingsolver. Abbey, one of the West's most famous tricksters, polemicists, novelists, and nature writers, lived in Tucson off and on for many years and is buried somewhere out in the desert southwest of the city in a secret grave. Jance is a best-selling mystery novelist whose plots often play out in Bisbee and Cochise County. Kingsolver, author of a trilogy of novels that take place in Tucson, among many other works, lived in Tucson for many years and even freelanced for the *Tucson Weekly,* a popular alternative weekly here. Another Old Pueblo writer with a national reputation is the great Charles Bowden, who used to be on the staff of the dying afternoon daily the *Tucson Citizen* and has over the last 20 years or more written several nonfiction works revealing the darker sides of the Sunbelt and the borderlands. Friends of mine who work the few local big-box bookstores like Borders and Barnes & Noble have reported somewhat regular sightings of two great American writers: Cormac McCarthy, author of several novels about the Southwest, including one, *Blood Meridian,* in which Southern Arizona figures briefly; and Larry

McMurtry, author of *The Last Picture Show, Lonesome Dove,* and many others.

The First Work of Southwestern Literature

The impenetrable northern reaches of the Spanish Empire in Mexico were essentially unexplored by Europeans when Álvar Núñez Cabeza de Vaca found himself shipwrecked and lost in the grasslands and deserts of what is now the southwestern United States and northern Mexico in the 1520s. And though he and his companions—one of them, Esteban, was a Moorish slave or indentured servant—probably never made it to Arizona proper, the tales they told of their adventures when they finally returned to civilization inspired subsequent discoveries in the great north.

In 1539 Fray Marcos de Niza and Esteban trekked north to discover the Seven Cities of Cíbola, rumors of which Esteban and Cabeza de Vaca had heard during their ordeal. Esteban scouted ahead and was eventually killed by the Indians, who lived not in golden cities but in regular old mesa-top pueblos not too different from those that still exist on Hopi reservations in Arizona and in the Rio Grande Valley of New Mexico. Nevertheless, de Niza's report suggested that the golden cities may indeed be a reality, and that was enough to inspire an ambitious expedition in 1540 led by Francisco Vásquez de Coronado in search of the reported riches. Coronado found none, but his expedition moved through what is now eastern Arizona.

Later in his life, after his return, **Cabeza de Vaca** wrote an account of his travails and journeys called ***Adventures in the Unknown Interior of America,*** which many consider to be the first work of Southwestern literature.

FILM
Tucson's Homegrown Movie Industry

Over lunch several years ago, Bob Shelton, former owner of Old Tucson Studios, and the undisputed patriarch of Tucson's modern film industry, told me an apocryphal-sounding story. In 1914, legendary producer Adolph Zuker sent Cecil B. DeMille and Samuel Goldwyn to Flagstaff, Arizona. Zuker had bought the rights to *The Squawman,* a Broadway play with a Western theme. DeMille and Goldwyn stepped off the train into snow, finding themselves surrounded not by mesas and cacti but by white-capped mountains.

If they had traveled downstate to Tucson, they would have found exactly what they were looking for. Instead, they headed farther west. There they rented a barn and made the first full-length Western. Thus Hollywood was born and Arizona was passed over.

The film industry did (and does still) exist in Southern Arizona. There were a few films produced here, and a few studios set up offices. However, after Hollywood was established, not much happened here until Columbia Pictures came in 1939 and built Old Tucson, a replica of Tucson circa 1860. Columbia came to film an epic aptly titled *Arizona.* Other productions trickled in, bringing a host of stars to a region in its search for a national identity.

Old Tucson fell into disrepair and near obscurity; then, in 1959, Bob Shelton bought the land and opened for business in 1960. Today he is credited by many in the industry for single-handedly making Tucson a major film location. When Tucson's film industry was at its peak, between the 1960s and the early 1990s, it was third only to Hollywood and New York in film production, and made $20 million per year.

In 1995 the studio burned down. The fire ruined irreplaceable props and costumes, and eliminated jobs. But the business had been dying before the fire, as a phenomenon known as "runaway production" started to take a toll. The film production money had started flowing to Canada, where the government had created the Production Service Tax Credit, which offered foreign film and television production companies tax breaks. The PSTC created an employment boom, and left film-industry workers in California and smaller markets, like Tucson, out of work.

The city's most robust arts-related economy has since the 1940s centered on the film industry. This has largely been the result of the building of **Old Tucson Studios** and the popularity over much of the 20th century of the Western, for which Tucson and its environs often provided the iconic scenery.

TUCSON ON-SCREEN

Among the hundreds of films made in and around Tucson since 1914's *The Return* are arguably many of the best Westerns ever made, as well as a few classics and indie favorites. In this list, you are sure to find a few to check out.

- *Ridin' Wild* (1925)
- *In Old Arizona* (1928)
- *Arizona* (1940)
- *Bells of Saint Mary* (1945)
- *Duel in the Sun* (1946)
- *Red River* (1948)
- *Broken Arrow* (1950)
- *Winchester '73* (1950)
- *The Violent Men* (1955)
- *Oklahoma!* (1955)
- *A Kiss Before Dying* (1957)
- *3:10 to Yuma* (1957)
- *Gunfight at the O.K. Corral* (1957)
- *The Badlanders* (1958)
- *Rio Bravo* (1959)
- *Lilies of the Field* (1963)
- *McLintock!* (1963)
- *El Dorado* (1966)
- *Hombre* (1967)
- *Andy Warhol's Lonesome Cowboys* (1968)
- *Easy Rider* (1969)
- *Rio Lobo* (1970)

- *Life and Times of Judge Roy Bean* (1972)
- *Alice Doesn't Live Here Anymore* (1974)
- *The Outlaw Josey Wales* (1976)
- *A Star is Born* (1976)
- *Revenge of the Nerds* (1984)
- *Three Amigos* (1986)
- *Can't Buy Me Love* (1987)
- *Major League* (1989)
- *Gas, Food, Lodging* (1992)
- *Bodies, Rest & Motion* (1993)
- *Tombstone* (1993)
- *Boys on the Side* (1995)
- *The Quick and the Dead* (1995)
- *Tank Girl* (1995)
- *Tin Cup* (1996)
- *The Postman* (1997)
- *Three Kings* (1999)
- *Jesus' Son* (1999)
- *Traffic* (2000)
- *Confessions of a Dangerous Mind* (2002)
- *Pumpkin* (2008)

ESSENTIALS

Getting There

BY AIR

Tucson International Airport (TIA, 520/573-8000, www.tucsonairport.org) hosts 10 major airlines (including American, Delta, Frontier, Continental, Southwest and Northwest, and Alaska Airlines) making approximately 60 departures every day. It's a small but efficient airport, with free wireless Internet access and daily nonstop flights to Seattle, Chicago, Dallas, Atlanta, Salt Lake, Denver, Houston, Minneapolis, Albuquerque, L.A., Vegas, San Diego, and San Francisco. If you're coming in from or headed to a city not on this list, it's likely you'll stop first at the state's major airport, Sky Harbor International Airport, in Phoenix, and then desert-hop, as it were, about 45 minutes south (probably after waiting more than an hour or so at the terminal). If you find yourself at Sky Harbor and don't feel like boarding an absurdly short flight, you can rent a car there and make the easy 90-minute drive down I-10 across the desert—though the scenery along I-10 is certainly not representative of what you're in for once you get to Tucson. Or, you can call **Arizona Shuttle Service** (520/795-6771 or 520/795-6775, www.arizonashuttle.com), which offers 18 trips daily between Phoenix and Tucson.

If you're arriving or departing from TIA, remember that **Arizona Stagecoach**

(520/881-4111 or 520/889-1000, www.stage-coach.com) runs a 24-hour door-to-door shuttle to and from TIA. Life at TIA is not nearly as bad as it is at some of the nation's larger airports. Generally arrivals and departures at TIA are quick and easy, with relatively short lines; friendly, helpful people; and cheap, safe long-term parking. You can park at the airport's long-term lot for a mere $4 per day, and a free shuttle runs from the terminal to the parking area, or you can walk it if you're so inclined. There are always cabs waiting just outside the main entrance; expect to pay about $20 for a ride to midtown. To get to TIA from midtown, take Campbell; this turns into the Kino Parkway south of Broadway. Follow road signs to Benson Highway, which leads to Tucson Boulevard and the airport entrance.

BY CAR

Road-trippers, whether from the east or the west, will arrive in Tucson via I-10. If you're coming from Sonora, Mexico, you'll come in on I-19, which merges with I-10 near downtown Tucson.

BY BUS

For bus service from Tucson to all points on the map, there's the **Greyhound Bus Station** (471 W. Congress St., east side of I-10, 520/792-3475, www.greyhound.com).

BY TRAIN

The **Amtrak Station** (400 N. Toole Ave., 520/623-4442, www.amtrak.com) is downtown.

Getting Around

PUBLIC TRANSPORTATION

The City of Tucson operates the **Sun Tran** (4220 S. Park Ave., 520/623-4301, www.suntran.com) bus line. It has stops all over the Old Pueblo and operates Monday–Friday 6 A.M.–7 P.M. and Saturday–Sunday 8 A.M.–5 P.M. Full fare is $1, with kids under five riding free.

DRIVING

If you're flying into Tucson and you don't have friends or relatives to chauffeur you around the typically sprawling Southwestern city, you'll need to rent a car. The airport has several counters from which to choose. If you're booking ahead, try the locally owned **Adobe Car & Van Rental of Tucson** (3150 E. Grant Rd., 520/390-6708 or 888/471-7951), which has a free pick-up service.

As for getting around the city by car, it's fairly easy if you keep in mind a few landmarks and general rules. Tucson is in a valley surrounded by mountains, with the mighty Santa Catalinas to the north, the Rincon Mountains to the east, and the Tucson Mountains to the west. Far south in the Santa Cruz Valley along

I-19 are the Santa Rita Mountains. If you remember that the Santa Catalinas, the most imposing range around the valley, are to the north, it isn't too difficult to navigate Tucson. North of the city, on Oracle Road/Highway 77, are the small towns of Oracle, Oro Valley, and Catalina, all nestled in the backside foothills of the Santa Catalina Mountains. To the southeast is the old mining and ranching district of Vail and the Rincon Valley, now peppered with suburban housing developments, and beyond that the communities of Cochise County. South on I-19 are the big open-pit copper mines, the bedroom community of Sahuarita, the retirement haven of Green Valley, the artists colony and shops of Tubac, and then on to the U.S.-Mexico border.

Most of the major intersections around Tucson are blessed with left-hand turn signals, so don't panic if you're in the back of a long line of cars wanting to turn left—your turn will come soon.

TAXIS

Cab rides can get expensive in Tucson because everything is so spread out. Expect to spend about $15 for a ride from midtown to restaurants and bars downtown or on 4th Avenue. There are plenty of rides to choose from. Try

AAA Yellow Cab Co./Fiesta Taxi (520/624-6611 or 520/399-6062) or **All State Cab Company** (520/798-1111 or 520/887-9000).

Tips for Travelers

WHAT TO TAKE

Your Tucson-bound knapsack should include a few essential items, whether you're coming in spring, summer, or second spring. Definitely bring along a **swimsuit,** even if you're coming in January—most hotels have a heated pool and a hot tub. Bring **sunscreen** and a **hat** that casts a shadow over your face and your neck; even if it's not too hot out, that sun is always shining and its rays are dangerous. Bring **comfortable shoes** for walking, or even **hiking shoes**—you don't need big boots; a sporty low-top hiker will suffice for most hikes. Bring along a **small day pack** for carrying around snacks and drinks. You may want to invest in a good pair of **binoculars,** especially if you plan to do any bird-watching or other wildlife-viewing. If you are an avid biker—road or mountain—you should definitely consider bringing your wheels along with you. Otherwise, you can easily rent one. If you're going to be here in the summer, pack **light, comfortable clothes,** but don't forget a **windbreaker** or other **light jacket;** if you're in the mountains after dark, you may actually need it. Also bring along a pair of **flip-flops,** Tucson's official footwear, and wear them proudly with shorts or even jeans. A good map of the region is also helpful, though you can get one when you arrive. Make sure to bring your **camera.** You are definitely going to use it.

TIME ZONE

Arizona is in the Mountain Time Zone, and is one of the few places in the country that does not switch over to Daylight Saving Time from the second Sunday in March to the first Sunday in November.

ACCESS FOR TRAVELERS WITH DISABILITIES

Many of the best sights in Tucson are accessible in one way or another to travelers with disabilities. For advice and links to other helpful Internet resources, go to **www. disabledtravelers.com,** which is run out of Arizona and is full of accessible travel information, though it's not specific to the state. The **National Accessible Travelers Database** may also be helpful. For questions specific to Tucson and Arizona, you may want to contact the state Department of Administration's **Office for Americans with Disabilities** (100 N. 15th Ave., Ste. 361, Phoenix, 602/542-6276 or 800/358-3617, TTY: 602/542-6686, www. azada.gov).

GAY AND LESBIAN TRAVELERS

Tucson is no more or no less gay-friendly than most other cities its size, and the queer community is strong and diverse here. *The Tucson Observer* (520/622-7176, www.tucsonobserver.com) has news about the local gay community, politics, and national news. **Wingspan** (425 E. 7th St., 520/624-1779, www.wingspan. org) is the Old Pueblo's friendly and active GLBT community center. The **Tucson GLBT Chamber of Commerce** (520/615-6436, www. tucsonglbtchamber.org) publishes a free membership directory that's available at the visitors center at La Placita Village (110 S. Church Ave., 520/903-9900) downtown.

Health and Safety

West Nile and the hantavirus are the long-shot threats to your health in Tucson and Arizona, and both can be avoided by taking precautions. Use insect repellent to ward off the former (which is spread by mosquitoes) and simply stay away from rodents, which may transmit the latter. Similarly rare are those infamous rattlesnake attacks. Keep an eye on the ground while you're hiking—if a snake, rattler or otherwise, is in your general vicinity, leave the area; that's the best way to avoid most snakebites. Also cover your ankles and keep your hands and feet out of dark holes. To avoid heat stroke and dehydration, very real threats in the summertime desert, stay out of the sun during the hottest part of the day; restrict your activity to early mornings and after sunset. Drink lots of water, and never go out into the desert alone or unprepared. Don't underestimate the heat and its power to drain your resources. Threats from humans come in all the usual forms. Lock your vehicle wherever you go, even in the most remote locations. Don't pick up hitchhikers, anywhere. Drug- and people-smuggling, and the violence that usually goes along with such activities, is common in areas along the U.S.-Mexico border in Southern Arizona.

HOSPITALS AND EMERGENCIES

Dial 911 for emergencies anywhere in Southern Arizona. **University Medical Center** (1501 N. Campbell Ave., 520/694-0111) is the top hospital in Southern Arizona and has the region's only Level 1 trauma center, so if you are seriously hurt anywhere in the area, you are likely to be treated by the capable staff there. It's located on a sprawling campus across Speedway, at Campbell, from the University of Arizona, and the two are, obviously, connected. On the eastern edges of midtown, Southern Arizona's largest health-care facility, **Tucson Medical Center** (5301 E. Grant, 520/327-5461, www.tmcaz.com), began life as a tuberculosis sanitarium, welcoming TB sufferers from all over the world to the desert's dry climate. These days TMC is where patients from all over the region, including Sonora, Mexico, will find themselves if they're having a difficult pregnancy, heart problems, and other serious health issues. Primarily because of its state-of-the-art newborn intensive-care unit and extensive cardiac-care resources, TMC is a popular choice for middle- and upper-class Mexican nationals seeking a high level of care. A TMC nurse who works with newborns here told me recently that at least twice a month she'll work with a family from Mexico, usually well-to-do and fluent in English. On the city's west side, **St. Mary's Hospital** (1601 W. St. Mary's Rd., 520/872-3000, www.carondelet.org) is part of the large Carondelet Network, which also runs the east side's **St. Joseph's Hospital** (350 N. Wilmot Rd., 520/873-3000) and **Tucson Heart Hospital** (4888 N. Stone

WHY IS IT SO DARK HERE?

If it seems a little darker in and around Tucson than in other places, there's a good reason for that. Up on **Mount Hopkins** in the Santa Rita range, the Smithsonian Institution operates the **Fred Lawrence Whipple Observatory,** a state-of-the-art telescope array used by scientists to study the beginnings of our universe. To assist this important research, and to help out other observatories across Southern Arizona, Pima County, Tucson, and Sahuarita have all passed ordinances that require special outdoor lighting, keeping the sky dark so that scientists can see (or at least attempt to see) ever-so-faint objects millions of light years away in space.

If you have a history of poor eyesight at night, it might be a good idea to let someone else do the driving after dark.

Ave., 520/696-2328). St. Mary's has 402 beds and is more than a century old (it started with only 12 beds). It has a full-service emergency room and a long list of services; St. Joseph's has 309 beds, an emergency room, and state-of-the-art comprehensive care; and Tucson Heart Hospital is an award-wining facility dedicated exclusively to heart disease.

Information and Services

MAPS AND TOURIST INFORMATION

Make sure to stop by the **Tucson Visitor Center** (110 S. Church Ave., 520/624-1817, Mon.–Fri. 9 A.M.–5 P.M., Sat.–Sun. 9 A.M.–4 P.M.). The bureau produces a helpful guide to the city you can pick up at the office or out in front when they're closed. There are scores of tourist pamphlets for the perusing. Park in the metered parking on Church Avenue in front of the Technicolor La Placita Village, which houses the center and a few shops and cafés.

The **Arizona Office of Tourism** (1110 W. Washington St., Ste. 155, Phoenix, AZ 85007, 602/364-3700 or 866/275-5816, www.arizonaguide.com) will send you a free print or electronic version of the official state guide, and their website is full of information and lists of accommodations, events, and restaurants throughout the state. If you're planning to spend a lot of time in the state's national forests, you can get maps and information beforehand from the **National Forest Service, Southwestern Region** (333 Broadway SE, Albuquerque, NM 87102, 505/842-3292, www.fs.fed.us/r3), or by contacting the individual forests. The **Arizona BLM State Office** (1 N. Central Ave., Ste. 800, Phoenix, AZ 85004-4427, 602/417-9200, www.blm.gov/az/st/en.html) also has a lot of information on the state's wildlands, and the **Arizona State Parks Department** (1300 W. Washington, Phoenix, AZ 85007, 602/542-4174, www.pr.state.az.us) has information on all the parks managed by the state.

COMMUNICATIONS AND MEDIA
Internet Services
Please don't pay for wireless Internet access in Tucson. Even if your hotel doesn't provide free access to a wireless network (and nearly all the accommodations in this guide do), there's sure to be a coffeehouse or restaurant near you that does. Even Jack-in-the-Box has free Wi-Fi. Tucson has made pretty much the entire downtown area a wireless hot spot. You can access the network around 101 North Stone Avenue at **Jacome Plaza** outside the main library, and nearby on Alameda Street near the Pima County Courthouse. You can also access a free wireless network throughout the Pima County complex along Alameda. If that's not enough, the **main library** downtown, and all the myriad branch libraries around town, offer access to free wireless, as well as computers that can be used, with some restrictions, to access the Internet.

If you've brought your laptop with you to town and it's acting up, don't call one of those high-priced corporate "geeks" to fix it. Instead, call **Student Experts** (520/762-6687, www.studentexperts.com), a local company that employs UA students who know their way around computers. Day or night, they'll race to your home or hotel and get you back to work in as little time as possible. I have used them several times, and they have always been professional and competent. And, best of all, they charge about half as much as the big guys.

Magazines and Newspapers
The morning daily newspaper the *Arizona Daily Star* (azstarnet.com) has a local focus but isn't provincial by any means. The weekly alternative tabloid the *Tucson Weekly* (www.tucsonweekly.com) is the place to go for news on arts, entertainment, politics, and local news; you'll find it free on red racks throughout the city. *The Desert Leaf*, a free monthly distributed

TUCSON'S COMMUNITY RADIO: KXCI 91.3 FM

Hidden away in an old brick house in Tucson's Armory Park historic district is one of the best radio stations in the West.

Since the early 1980s, **KXCI Community Radio** (220 S. 4th Ave., 520/622-5924 request line, 520/623-1000 office line, www.kxci.org) has been broadcasting an outrageously eclectic mix of music, news, and cultural programming that has contributed greatly to making Tucson a place where people slightly left of center feel welcome and comfortable. This full-time job is done by a staff of mostly volunteer, nonprofessional DJs, many of whom learn the ropes in a DJ class offered annually by the station.

Most weekdays the majority of daytime air is taken up by the Music Mix, a brew of new and old alternative rock, roots, country, Latino, jazz, electronica, world music, and classic pop that's so unpredictable you shouldn't be surprised to hear Willie Nelson followed by the White Stripes followed by a new tune from your favorite Afghan hip-hop artist.

Because KXCI is supported by grants and donations from listeners, there are no commercials and nobody is beholden to an absentee corporation dictating playlists. This can make for near daily discoveries of music that you didn't know was out there. Tune in to KXCI at 91.3 on the FM dial, or at www.kxci.org.

throughout the city at coffeehouses, bookstores, and elsewhere, concentrates on the culture, lifestyles, and businesses of the foothills neighborhood, but really its editorial content is all over the map. Its articles will be helpful to anyone looking to learn about life in the high-end Southwest. *Tucson Lifestyles* magazine is a slick monthly with articles about local art and culture, real estate, restaurants, shops, and, of course, people. Every quarter a new edition of the slick *Tucson Guide* is released, stuffed full of interesting and informative articles on Tucson and the surrounding area, with an emphasis on all that is unique about this place. The weekly tabloid *Inside Tucson Business* covers the local business community and is sold from racks and at newsstands and some bookstores.

You'll find all of the above publications, plus hundreds more from around the world, along with national and international newspapers, political and literary journals, paperbacks, cigars, pipe tobacco, and cigarettes, at **Crescent Tobacco Shop & Newsstand** (downtown at 200 E. Congress St., 520/296-3102; and on the east side at 7037 E. Tanque Verde Rd., 520/296-3102).

Radio and TV

The local PBS affiliate is KUAT Channel 6,

operated on the campus of the University of Arizona. Every weeknight at 6:30 P.M. the smart news magazine *Arizona Illustrated* examines Tucson's life, politics, and culture in-depth, regularly presenting longish interviews and panel discussions with Southern Arizona politicians, movers-and-shakers, and journalists.

Venture onto the AM dial for several locally produced daily talk shows concentrating on politics and sports. The local NPR affiliate, KUAZ 89.1, also at the UA, broadcasts NPR from early in the morning with *Morning Edition,* and then continues throughout the day with *The Diane Rehm Show, Talk of the Nation, The World, Fresh Air,* and, at the end of the day, *All Things Considered.* After 7 P.M. on weekdays KUAZ plays a good mix of jazz programming. If you enjoy an eclectic music mix and news shows like *Democracy Now,* tune in to Tucson's community news station KXCI 91.3.

Public Libraries

The Pima County Public Library system has more than two dozen branches all over the county. The main branch in the vast system is downtown's **Joel D. Valdez Main Library** (101 N. Stone Ave., 520/594-5600, www.library.pima.gov, Mon.–Wed. 9 A.M.–8 P.M.,

Thurs. 9 A.M.–6 P.M., Fri. 9 A.M.–5 P.M., Sat. 10 A.M.–5 P.M., Sun. 1–5 P.M.), a center point of the Stone Avenue and Alameda Street business and government district with grassy knolls and public art around its central grounds. There's a parking garage directly under the library (look for the sign while heading either north or south on Stone); otherwise there are metered parking spots all around downtown that are free on the weekends. There are quite a few computers for public use at the main branch, and they have a large children's section and a program of kids' events that are very popular with local parents. Check out the library website for details and times. Of particular interest to visitors and tourists, the **Steinheimer Collection** at the main library is dedicated exclusively to books about Tucson, Arizona, and the Southwest. Additionally, every year a panel of Tucson librarians, writers, and book lovers presents a list of its favorite books about the Southwest published the previous year. For this year's list and those of past years, check out www.library.pima.gov/books/swboy/index.cfm.

No matter which neighborhood you're in, you'll find a clean, well-stocked, and well-lit branch, with mostly friendly librarians and assistants ready to help, and a bank of Internet-ready computers. In midtown, there's the **Himmel Park Branch Library** (1035 N. Treat Ave., 520/791-4397, Mon.–Thurs. 10 A.M.–8 P.M., Fri. 10 A.M.–5 P.M., Sat. 9 A.M.–5 P.M., Sun. 1–5 P.M.) at Himmel Park, and it's fun to combine a walk around the green shady park with a visit to the small branch. One of the newer branches, the

Martha Cooper Branch Library (1377 N. Catalina Ave., 520/594-5315, Mon.–Thurs. 10 A.M.–8 P.M., Fri. 10 A.M.–5 P.M., Sat. 9 A.M.–5 P.M., Sun. 1–5 P.M.), is in a residential area a few miles east of Alvernon off Speedway Boulevard. On the east side, the **Kirk-Bear Canyon Branch Library** (8959 E. Tanque Verde Rd., 520/791-5021, Mon.–Thurs. 10 A.M.–8 P.M., Fri. 10 A.M.–5 P.M., Sat. 9 A.M.–5 P.M., Sun. 1–5 P.M.) and the **Murphy-Wilmont Branch Library** (530 N. Wilmot Rd., 520/594-5420, Mon.–Thurs. 10 A.M.–8 P.M., Fri. 10 A.M.–5 P.M., Sat. 9 A.M.–5 P.M., Sun. 1–5 P.M.) are both very popular. On the south side, check out the **El Pueblo Branch Library** (W. Irvington Rd., 520/791-4733, Mon.–Tues. 9 A.M.–6 P.M., Wed.–Thurs. 10 A.M.–6 P.M., Fri. 10 A.M.–5 P.M., Sat. 9 A.M.–5 P.M.), and on the west side there's the **Mission Branch Library** (3770 S. Mission Rd., 520/594-5325, Mon.–Thurs. 10 A.M.–8 P.M., Fri. 10 A.M.–5 P.M., Sat. 9 A.M.–5 P.M., Sun. 1–5 P.M.). Foothills residents spend a lot of time at the **Dusenberry-River Branch Library** (5605 E. River Rd., 520/594-5345, Mon.–Thurs. 10 A.M.–8 P.M., Fri.–Sat. 10 A.M.–5 P.M., Sun. 1–5 P.M.).

The University of Arizona has an excellent academic research library system that includes a huge main library, a science and engineering library, a law library, and a music and architecture library. Students, faculty, and alumni (not to mention residents willing to shell out about $100 a year for a "community user card") have access to the millions of books and other media here. Check out www.library.arizona.edu for details.

RESOURCES

Suggested Reading

HISTORY AND GENERAL INFORMATION

Bandelier, Fanny, trans. *The Journey of Álvar Núñez Cabeza de Vaca*. Chicago: Rio Grande Press, 1964. This strange first-person account marks the true beginnings of American literature. The conquistador spent years of privation with various northern Mexico Indian tribes after being shipwrecked near Florida in the late 1520s. He became a slave, a shaman, and a trader before finally finding his way back to civilization and inspiring the later "discovery" of the Southwest by the Spanish.

Barnes, Will C. *Arizona Place Names*. Tucson: University of Arizona Press, 1988. The life's work of a famous Arizonan who first came to the territory in 1854, this classic mixture of history, geography, and anecdote is a must-have for any serious Arizona explorer. First published in 1935, just a year before Barnes's death, the book represents more than 30 years of work by the author.

Castañeda, Pedro de, et al. *The Journey of Coronado*. New York: Dover Publications, 1990. There are dozens of editions of this useful and fascinating collection of some of the original documents from the Coronado expedition, which moved through southeastern Arizona on the way north looking for the mythical Seven Cities of Cíbola. In this book, translated from the original Spanish version, you get the story as it happened, written by members of the expedition and others.

Griffith, James S. *Folk Saints of the Borderlands*. Tucson: Rio Nuevo Publishers, 2003; and *Beliefs and Holy Places*. Tucson: University of Arizona Press, 1992. Nobody explains the peculiar mixture of Catholicism and localized native beliefs that pervades the borderlands, creating new folk saints and holy places and infusing the land with meaning, better than "Big" Jim Griffith, a professor at the University of Arizona and the Old Pueblo's resident folklorist. Big Jim can often be seen on the local PBS affiliate, KUAT Channel 6, talking about the culture and legends of Pimería Alta.

Hart, John Bret. *Tucson: Portrait of a Desert Pueblo*. Woodland Hills, CA: Windsor Publications, Inc., 1980. This out-of-print coffee-table history of the Old Pueblo was sponsored by the Tucson Chamber of Commerce, but it's still a dependable, well-written account of the city's long history and has excellent historical photos throughout that really give one a sense of what the dusty old town was like not that long ago.

Miller, Neil. *Kartchner Caverns: How Two Cavers Discovered and Saved One of the Wonders of the Natural World*. Tucson: University of Arizona Press, 2008. Miller tells the complete, thrilling story—based on interviews with nearly all those involved who are still living—of the long, secretive years in between the discovery of Kartchner Caverns by two young cavers and the opening of the $30 million show-cave more than a decade later.

Along the way, he brings up some interesting questions about whether this cave should be open to the public at all.

Monahan, Sherry. *Tombstone's Treasures: Silver Mines and Golden Saloons.* Albuquerque: University of New Mexico Press, 2007. In a style that's more sedate and considered, though no less interesting, than what you'll find on Tombstone's dusty Allen Street, Monahan tells the real history of the world-famous mining camp.

Myal, Suzanne. *Tucson's Mexican Restaurants: Repasts, Recipes, and Remembrances.* Tucson: Fiesta Publishing, 1997. This book appears to be out of print, but it's still widely available online. It's an interesting and comprehensive guide to Tucson's Mexican restaurant scene, with several recipes from locally famous cooks. It's a bit out of date, but still a worthy guide to eating in Tucson.

Nequette, Anne M., and R. Brooks Jeffery. *A Guide to Tucson Architecture.* Tucson: University of Arizona Press, 2002. This is an easy-to-read and relatively comprehensive guide to all of Tucson's interesting and historic architecture. It also includes a good short general history of the region and its many architectural epochs.

Powell, Lawrence Clark. *Arizona: A History.* Albuquerque: University of New Mexico Press, 1990. A more recent edition of the book first published in 1976, Powell's history is not a definitive blow-by-blow, but rather a series of essays on various chapters in Arizona's history and culture. A much-admired Southwestern writer, librarian, and scholar, Powell lived in Tucson for many years. His *Southwest: Three Definitions* (Benson, AZ: Singing Wind Bookshop, 1990) is an excellent trilogy of essays on the landscape and culture of the Southwest.

Sheridan, Thomas. *Arizona: A History.* Tucson: University of Arizona Press, 1995. This is a very well-written and informative general history of the state, one of the better examples out there of New Western history. Also by Sheridan, an anthropologist and professor at the University of Arizona, *Los Tucsonenses: The Mexican Community in Tucson, 1854–1941* is a very readable and interesting account of the influence this community once held in Tucson, and what happened to it in the wake of the Anglo takeover after the Gadsden Purchase.

Smith, Dean. *The Great Arizona Almanac: Facts About Arizona.* Portland, OR: WestWinds Press, 2000. Former newspaperman Smith compiled this almanac, with entries on Arizona history, travel, current events, famous residents, mileage charts, zip codes, and area codes. It's in dire need of a new edition, but is still very useful and interesting.

Sonnichsen, C. L. *Tucson: The Life and Times of an American City.* Norman: University of Oklahoma Press, 1982. A thorough telling of the Old Pueblo's long history from its founding as a presidio in 1776 up to the early 1980s.

NATURAL HISTORY AND TRAIL GUIDES

Brown, David E., and Carlos A. Gonzalez Lopez. *Borderland Jaguars.* Salt Lake City: University of Utah Press, 2001. The only comprehensive and complete book on the natural history of the borderland jaguar, this book includes a complete listing of the time, place, and circumstances of pretty much every jaguar sighting in Arizona from the 19th century until the turn of the 20th. Nearly all of those sightings resulted in the jaguar's death by gunshot, by the way.

Carter, Jack L., et al. *Common Southwestern Native Plants: An Identification Guide.* Silver City, NM: Mimbres Press, 2003. A thorough but easy-to-use guide to plants you're likely to see in Arizona; includes common species of the deserts, the forested mountains, and the plateau country.

Ffolliott, Peter F., and Owen K. Davis, eds. *Natural Environments of Arizona: From the Deserts to the Mountains.* Tucson: University of Arizona Press, 2008. This recent collection of scholarly articles about the state's various biomes contains a lot of very up-to-date information about the sky islands and other natural wonders of Southern Arizona.

Grubbs, Bruce. *Desert Sense: Camping, Hiking & Biking in Hot, Dry Climates.* Seattle, WA: The Mountaineers Books, 2004. If you're going to be hiking or riding a bike in the desert, especially if you're doing it in the summer, consider picking up this or a similar book to familiarize yourself with desert survival beyond the basics of "bring water and wear a hat."

Hanson, Jonathan. *There's a Bobcat in My Backyard! Living With and Enjoying Urban Wildlife.* Tucson: University of Arizona Press and the Arizona-Sonora Desert Museum, 2004. More than most cities its size, Tucson is within easy and quick access to wilderness, and the more we encroach on that wilderness with our commercial and residential growth, the more contact we have with wild animals. This charming, informative book tells us how to avoid unwanted contact with the desert's wild creatures as well as how to live with them, and watch them, for our own pleasure and edification.

Leavengood, Betty. *Tucson Hiking Guide.* Boulder, CO: Pruett Publishing Company, 1997. Widely available online, this is the best hiking guide to the most popular trails around the Tucson valley. It includes hikes in all of the area's sky island ranges, and many desertland treks as well. Leavengood is something of a grand dame of Tucson hiking, and she prefers long, many-mile, all-day hikes. If this isn't really your bag, all her hikes can be personalized and shortened quite easily.

Logan, Michael F. *The Lessening Stream: An Environmental History of the Santa Cruz River.* Tucson: University of Arizona Press, 2002. A professor paints an attractive and elegiac portrait of what the river used to be like and explains why it isn't that way anymore.

Olin, George. *50 Common Mammals of the Southwest.* Tucson: Western National Parks Association, 2000. An introduction to Arizona's mammals, this slim book with attractive illustrations is part of a series available throughout the state.

Quinn, Meg. *Wildflowers of the Southwest.* Tucson: Rio Nuevo, 2000. If you're going to be hiking in the desert in spring, pick up this guide to the many wildflowers that bloom throughout the state.

Valenzuela-Zapata, Ana G., and Gary Paul Nabhan. *Tequila: A Natural and Cultural History.* Tucson: University of Arizona Press, 2003. This slim history of one of Tucson's favorite liquids will tell you all you need to know about tequila and mescal: what they are, how they're made, and how they have influenced different Southwestern and Mexican cultures over time.

NATIVE AMERICANS

Jacoby, Karl. *Shadows at Dawn: A Borderlands Massacre and the Violence of History.* New York: Penguin, 2008. This book is part of a recent mini-rush of scholarly works about the western Apache and the brutal Camp Grant Massacre of 1871, which saw more than 100 sleeping Apache women and children slaughtered by a coalition of Anglo, Mexican, and Tohono O'odham leaders who wanted the band wiped out. This is a fascinating, well-researched book about a violent, shameful period of history that most Tucsonans, let alone Americans, know little about.

Nabhan, Gary Paul. *The Desert Smells Like Rain: A Naturalist in Papago Country.* San

Francisco: North Point Press, 1982. Tucson-based ethnobiologist Nabhan writes with passion and verve about the Tohono O'odham and their desert homeland southwest of Tucson. This is a very readable, sometimes poetic account of this little-known people, from their ancient history to almost the present day, with a concentration on the unique adaptations they've made to the desert's harsh patterns.

Record, Ian. *Big Sycamore Stands Alone: The Western Apaches, Aravaipa, and the Struggle for Place.* Norman: University of Oklahoma Press, 2008. Record's is the best book I've ever read about the Apache. He includes a diversity of Apache voices from the past as well as the present, and native voices, until quite recently, have always been the one rather obvious element missing from most studies of Native Americans.

Spicer, Edward H. *Cycles of Conquest: The Impact of Spain, Mexico, and the United States on the History of the Indians of the Southwest, 1533–1960.* Tucson: University of Arizona Press, 1962. The long title of this monumental, classic study by a late professor of anthropology at the University of Arizona pretty much explains what it's about. It's a long, detailed book that chronicles the impact of the colonizers on all of Arizona's tribes, and the chapters on the O'odham and the Apache are excellent.

Stockel, Henrietta H. *Shame and Endurance: The Untold Story of the Chiricahua Apache Prisoners of War.* Tucson: University of Arizona Press, 2004. We've all heard of Geronimo, but few people know the story of how he and his people ended their days in captivity in Oklahoma, far from their beloved borderland home. This book is an eye-opening account of yet another shameful deed done to Arizona's indigenous peoples.

LITERATURE

Bowden, Charles. *Blue Desert.* Tucson: University of Arizona Press, 1986; and *Frog Mountain Blues.* Tucson: University of Arizona Press, 1987. Bowden's essays, reportage, and nature writing chronicle the darker side of the Sunbelt.

McCarthy, Cormac. *Blood Meridian, or the Evening Redness in the West.* New York: Vintage, 1985. McCarthy, the finest living American writer, chronicles the brutal and bloody days when the Mexican government put out a $100 bounty for Apache scalps in Southern Arizona. It's a beautiful, violent, and disturbing novel, but one that will never leave your consciousness. There's even a scene that takes place at the Mission Tumacácori in the Santa Cruz Valley south of Tucson.

Shelton, Richard. *Crossing the Yard: Thirty Years as a Prison Volunteer.* Tucson: University of Arizona Press, 2007; and *Going Back to Bisbee.* Tucson: University of Arizona Press, 1992. Shelton is a world-renowned, award-winning poet and creative nonfiction author and longtime University of Arizona professor. *Crossing the Yard* chronicles his decades-long efforts to teach creative writing classes in Arizona's notoriously hard-core prison system. *Going Back to Bisbee* is the story of a job he had teaching school in the small mining town in the 1950s, and includes the natural and human history of the region.

Silko, Leslie Marmon. *Almanac of the Dead.* New York: Simon and Schuster, 1991. Large sections of this Southwestern epic take place in Tucson, but it is a dark, rather dirty and underground Tucson that Silko conjures in this ambitious, rollicking novel about native peoples struggling with the past and the modern world. Born at the Laguna Pueblo in New Mexico, Silko received the MacArthur Foundation "Genius" grant and has lived in the Old Pueblo.

Wallace, David Foster. *Infinite Jest.* New York: Little Brown and Co., 1996. The author killed himself, at age 46, in 2008, but before that he wrote this epic story about addiction, America, tennis, and the funniest movie of all time. Portions of this huge novel take place in the Old Pueblo, and Wallace was enrolled in the University of Arizona's Creative Writing Program for a few semesters long ago.

Internet Resources

GENERAL INFORMATION

Arizona Office of Tourism
www.arizonaguide.com
If you're going to be traveling elsewhere in Arizona (and you should), check out the informative website of the state's tourism authority; there's a lot of information on Southern Arizona here as well.

Arizona-Sonora Desert Museum Center for Sonoran Desert Studies
www.desertmuseum.org/center
This website has a variety of interesting information on the desert's natural history and flora and fauna.

Bisbee Chamber of Commerce
www.bisbeearizona.com
This site has a lot of information about Bisbee, one of the top Southern Arizona attractions outside of Tucson, including a very comprehensive list of the town's many inns, restaurants, and shops.

City of Tucson
www.tucsonaz.gov
Tucson's city government Web hub has, one would hope, all the information you'll ever need on the goings-on of the town council, the mayor, parks and recreation, and the sewer department. There's also information that is likely more useful to the visitor, including a calendar of events, a bus schedule, and directions to every park in town.

Cochise County
www.cochise.az.gov
If you're doing any day-tripping southeast of Tucson in Cochise County, this official county website may help you get a feel for the area, and it has links to a plethora of information.

Metropolitan Tucson Convention and Visitors Bureau
www.visittucson.org
This is Tucson and Southern Arizona's official tourism site. It's got a lot of information on it, and some really beautiful images of the desert and the city.

Pima County
www.pima.gov
Similar in scope and subject matter to the City of Tucson site, Pima County's is even more comprehensive, including links to all kinds of information on living in and visiting the wider Tucson region, including a database through which you can check the food safety ratings of every restaurant in the county.

Santa Cruz County
www.co.santa-cruz.az.us
Tubac, Tumacácori, Patagonia, and Nogales are all great places to visit in tiny rural Santa Cruz County, about 45 minutes south of Tucson on I-19. This county website has information about everyday life along the border.

NEWS AND CULTURE

Arizona Daily Star
www.azstarnet.com
Tucson's morning daily is free on this site, with news and information on all of Southern Arizona.

Arizona Republic
www.azcentral.com
If you want to know what's happening in

Arizona outside of the Tucson region, check out the state's largest newspaper, free online every day; the site also has a robust Arizona travel guide and a useful dining and entertainment section.

Green Valley News
www.gvnews.com
A twice-weekly newspaper covering the Santa Cruz Valley; they regularly print stories about Tubac, Madera Canyon, and the Santa Rita Mountains.

Inside Tucson Business
www.azbiz.com
This weekly tabloid covers the business community in Tucson and Southern Arizona.

Nogales International
www.nogalesinternational.com
This twice-weekly paper covers the small border town of Nogales as well as the Mountain Empire communities.

Phoenix New Times
www.phoenixnewtimes.com
This site is the best place to go for entertainment and cultural listings and alternative news and commentary about life in the Valley of the Sun.

Sierra Vista Herald
www.svherald.com
Check out this site for information and news about Bisbee, the Huachuca Mountains, and all of Cochise County.

Tucson Weekly
www.tucsonweekly.com
Southern Arizona's best source of alternative news, political blogs, and cultural and entertainment news and listings.

Index

Restaurants Index

Nightlife Index

Shops Index

Hotels Index